The Social Effects of Free Market Policies

An International Text

Edited by

Ian Taylor
Professor of Sociology, University of Salford

HARVESTER WHEATSHEAF

New York London Toronto Sydney Tokyo Singapore

First published 1990 by
Harvester Wheatsheaf
66 Wood Lane End, Hemel Hempstead
Hertfordshire HP2 4RG
A division of
Simon & Schuster International Group

Typeset in 10/12 pt Times
by Keyset Composition, Colchester

Printed and bound in Great Britain by
BPCC Wheatons Ltd, Exeter

British Library Cataloguing in Publication Data

The social effects of free market policies: an
    international text.
    1. Capitalist societies – Sociological perspectives
    I. Taylor, Ian, *1944*–
    306.342

    ISBN 0-7450-0656-6

1 2 3 4 5   94 93 92 91 90

Among the delusions which at different periods have possessed themselves of the minds of large masses of the human race, perhaps the most curious – certainly the least creditable – is the modern *soi-disant* science of political economy, based on the idea that an advantageous code of social action may be determined irrespectively of the influence of social affection.

(John Ruskin, 'The Roots of Honour'
Essay I in *Unto this Last* (1862), in *Unto this Last, and Other Writings* (ed. Clive Wilmer),
London: Penguin, 1985, p. 167.)

Contents

Contributors

Ken Battle is Director of the National Council of Welfare, a semi-autonomous social policy advisory organization based in Ottawa, Canada. Educated at Queens University, Kingston, and at Nuffield College, Oxford, he has been with the National Council of Welfare since 1976, and has been responsible for a continuous series of critical analyses of Canadian government tax and welfare policies. The views expressed in this paper are those of the author and not of the National Council of Welfare.

David Brown is currently an Associate Professor in the Law School at the University of New South Wales, Sydney, Australia. He graduated in law at the University of Auckland, New Zealand, in 1971, and worked as a lawyer before doing the Diploma of Criminology course at Cambridge, United Kingdom, in 1973, where he then worked as a research assistant. He was appointed lecturer at the law school at the University of New South Wales in 1974. He has published widely in the criminal justice area and is the co-author of *The Prison Struggle* (Penguin, 1982); *Criminal Laws: Materials and Commentary on Criminal Law and Process in NSW* (Federation, 1990); and co-editor of *Critique of Law: A Marxist analysis* (1978); *'Policing: Practices, strategies, accountability* (Alternative Criminology Journal, 1984); *The Judgements of Lionel Murphy* (Primavera Press, 1986) and *Death in the Hands of the State* (Redfern Legal Centre, 1988). He is currently working with Russell Hogg on *The Politics of Law and Order* for Pluto Australia. Both he and Russell Hogg have been active in many criminal justice and penal groups and movements in Sydney.

Jeffrey Brown studied sociology at the London School of Economics and at the University of Michigan, Ann Arbor, United States, where he graduated in 1989. His undergraduate dissertation, 'Off the records: an investigation of underground economic activity at a British music club' is being revised for publication in the *Journal of Contemporary Ethnography*.

Philip Cohen is in the Institute of Education at the University of London, United Kingdom, where he is a key figure in the Cultural Studies Project, 'Tackling prejudice in the classroom'. He has been the co-author of *Knuckle Sandwich* (with David Robins, 1978) and *It Ain't Half Racist, Mum: Fighting racism in the British media* (with Carl Gardner, 1982), and also is the author of *Rethinking the Youth Questions* (1986). He is the joint editor of Macmillan's *Youth Questions* series.

Elliott Currie is the author of the much-discussed *Confronting Crime* (New York: Pantheon Books, 1986) and a well-known spokesperson for a social-democratic approach to issues of law and order in the United States. He is affiliated with the Center for the Study of Law and Society at the University of California, Berkeley, United States, but is currently mainly engaged in freelance writing on crime and social policy issues.

Miriam David is Professor and Head of the Department of Social Sciences at South Bank Polytechnic, London, United Kingdom, a post she has held for the last four years. Previously she taught social policy at the University of Bristol. She has also lectured in the United States and Canada – at Harvard University, the Universities of California and New York and the Ontario Institute for Studies in Education in Toronto. Her main scholarly and research interests are in family and social policy, especially women, child care and education. She has written widely in this area. Her book *The State, the Family and Education* (RKP, 1980) is widely used in North America and northern Europe as well as in Britain. She is also a co-author of the first textbook on women's studies known as *Half the Sky* (Virago, 1979; revised 1984). With Caroline New, she wrote a very important study of child care theory and practice entitled *For the Children's Sake: Making child care more than women's business* (Penguin, 1985). More recently she has turned her attention to issues of higher education and is directing a research study of mature women students, conducted by Rose Edwards. She herself has written an intriguing article on women in academic management entitled 'Prima Donna Inter Pares?' and published in an edited collection by Sandra Acker on *Teachers, Gender and Careers*.

Stuart Henry is Associate Professor in the Department of Sociology, Anthropology and Criminology, Eastern Michigan University, Ypsilanti, Michigan, United States. He is the author of *The Hidden Economy* (1978), editor of *Can I Have It In Cash?* (1981), author of *Private Justice* (1983), and co-editor of a special issue of the Annals of the American Academy of Political and Social Science on *The Informal Economy* (1987). He is currently co-authoring a book on post-disaster economics called *Making Market*.

Russell Hogg is currently a senior lecturer at the School of Social Justice Studies at Charles Stuart University, Bathurst, New South Wales, Australia. He completed a combined jurisprudence/law degree at the University of New South Wales in 1976 and gained an MA in Criminological Studies at the University of Sheffield, United Kingdom, in 1978, where he then worked as a Junior Research Fellow. On returning to Australia in 1981 he worked for the NSW Attorney-General's Department and the NSW Bureau of Crime Statistics and Research and lectured in the law schools of both the NSW University of Technology and Macquarie University. He was the principal researcher and author of *Robbery – An Analysis of Robbery in NSW* (NSW Bureau of Crime Statistics and Research, 1987) and a co-editor of *Policing: Practices, strategies, accountability* (Alternative Criminology Journal, 1984); *Understanding Crime and Criminal Justice* (Law Book, 1988); and *Death in the Hands of the State* (Redfern Legal Centre, 1988).

Mike Presdee has recently returned to the United Kingdom, after several years teaching and researching in the Youth Studies Programme of the South Australia College of Advanced Education in Adelaide. He is now Senior Lecturer in Youth Studies at Christchurch College, Canterbury, in the United Kingdom. He has written several important ethnographic and analytic studies on unemployment and youth, particularly in Australia.

Graham Riches is Director of the Social Administration Research Unit at the University of Regina, Saskatchewan, Canada. He is the author of *Food Banks and the Welfare Crisis* (Ottawa: Canadian Council on Social Development, 1986), as well as being the co-founder and joint editor of the *Canadian Review of Social Policy*.

Jennifer A. Roberts teaches Health Economics at the London School of Hygiene and Tropical Medicine and at the London School of Economics, United Kingdom. She has been involved in developing graduate programmes in the economics, planning and financing of health care. Current research includes economic studies of communicable diseases and the cost of waiting lists.

Ian Shirley is the Head of the Department of Social Policy and Social Work and Director of the Social Policy Research Center at Massey University, New Zealand. He has published extensively on social policy and social development in New Zealand and the Pacific. Professor Shirley was a member of the National Research Advisory Council's Working Party on Employment and Unemployment (1982), a consultant to INODEP Development Institute in Paris (1984), a participant in the UNESCO meeting of Experts on the Conceptual Range of Experiments in Development (1984) and a consultant to the New Zealand Government's Budget '85 Task Force on Taxation and Social Security. He is currently Chairman of the New Zealand Council for Education and Training in the Social Services, and an overseas Editorial Advisor for the *Journal of Social Policy*.

Ian Taylor is Professor of Sociology at the University of Salford in Greater Manchester, United Kingdom. He has taught at the University of Sheffield (1971–81) and at Carleton University, Ottawa, Canada (1981–9), and has also held visiting positions at LaTrobe University in Melbourne, Australia and the University of Cambridge, United Kingdom. He is the joint author (with Paul Walton and Jock Young) of *The New Criminology* (London: Routledge, 1973), and author of *Law and Order: Arguments for socialism* (London: Macmillan, 1981) and *Crime, Capitalism and Community* (Toronto, Butterworth, 1983).

Peter J. Usher is an independent consultant based in Ottawa, Canada, but spending much of his time in the Canadian North, in which he has been interested for over twenty-five years. He has worked for the Department of Indian Affairs and Northern Development and also for the Committee of Original People's Entitlement and Inuit Tapirisat (Eskimo Brotherhood) of Canada. He is the co-author, with David Ross, of *From the Roots Up: Economic development as if community mattered* (Toronto: James Lorimer, 1986), and he currently continues with his research into the political economy of northern and frontier development, the economics of northern Native communities, renewable resource management, social and economic impact assessment and aboriginal rights and claims. (He can be reached via Box 4815, Station E, Ottawa, Ontario K1S 5H9.)

Alan Walker is a professor of Social Policy and Head of Department of Sociological Studies at the University of Sheffield, United

Kingdom. He is author or editor of some ten books and numerous articles and chapters in edited volumes in the field of social policy. He has researched and written extensively on the subjects of poverty, the relationship between economic and social policy, the social impact of economic policies and the record of the Thatcher government. His books include *Public Expenditure and Social Policy* (ed., 1982); *Social Planning* (1984); *Ageing and Social Policy* (ed., with C. Phillipson, 1986) and *After Redundancy* (with J. Westergaard and I. Noble, 1989). His most recent book, *The Social Economy and the Democratic State* (edited with a group of social policy experts known collectively as The Sheffield Group, 1989), is part of an ongoing project aimed at developing a democratic socialist strategy combining economic and social policy.

Rob Watts is currently Dean, School of Community Services and Policy Studies at the Phillip Institute of Technology, Melbourne, Australia. He has written several books, including *The Foundations of the National Welfare State* (1987). He writes regularly for journals such as *Arena*, is active in developing alternative socio-economic policy agendas, including the Melbourne Economic Group's *New Economic Directions for Australia* (1989), and is working on stitching together alliances between various traditional and more recently arrived social movements. He is currently at work on a major text on the Australian Welfare State, to be published in 1991.

Acknowledgements

A collection of this kind takes several months, and even years, to assemble. I am very conscious, in this case, of the different work pressures under which the various contributors were labouring when they were first approached in November 1987. Some were able to respond fairly speedily to my original invitation to contribute to this volume. I am very grateful for the patience which these 'early' contributors have shown in waiting; I am equally grateful to those contributors who have found time in their over-worked and over-accelerated existence to produce a promised chapter just in time for this volume to be published in 1990, the first year of a new decade. I hope that the patience and the intense exertions of all the contributors are now rewarded.

I also want to express my gratitude to the Harvester Wheatsheaf editor who first expressed an interest in the idea of this collection, Peter Johns, and to his successor, the new sociology editor, Clare Grist, for the support and understanding which they have both expressed. I hope they too feel the result repays the interest they have shown.

Some of the research and discussion with social-democratically minded academics which gave rise to the idea of this book was made possible by my visits (from Canada, where I was then working) to Australia and New Zealand in the period August 1987 to February 1988. These trips were the result of a sabbatical leave and other assistance granted by the Faculty of Social Sciences at Carleton University and specifically by Dean Dennis Forcese. I am extremely grateful to him for this assistance and for the warm support he and other colleagues gave me at Carleton throughout the 1980s.

I am grateful too to my new secretary at Salford, Sheila Walker, for the speed and care brought to the typing of many materials associated with this collection.

Last but never, ever, least, I am, as always, grateful to Ruth Jamieson and to Jean and Anna Taylor for the political and intellectual stimulation, the inspiration and the personal support which they always provide. I just hope that this collection may be some kind of response to persistent enquiries from Anna, at the age of 9, on visits to London and Paris. She wanted to know, and she wanted me to tell her, why – 'in the modern world' – there are beggars. She also wanted to know whether there always have to be.

Ian Taylor
Salford, Greater Manchester
January 1990

1

Introduction
The concept of 'social cost' in free market theory and the social effects of free market policies

Ian Taylor
University of Salford, United Kingdom

> Three-fourths of the demands existing in the world are romantic;
> founded on visions, idealism, hopes and affections; and the
> regulation of the purse is, in essence, regulation of the imagination
> and heart. Hence, the right discussion of the nature of price is a very
> high metaphysical and psychical problem, something to be solved
> only in a passionate manner.
>
> (John Ruskin, 'Ad Valorem',
> Essay IV in *Unto this Last* (1862) in *Unto this Last, and Other Writings*
> (ed. Clive Wilmer), London: Penguin, 1985, pp. 214–15.)

Introduction: The end of the 1980s

This collection of essays was being submitted to the publishers just at the moment (November 1989) when politicians and the Press throughout the Western world were engaged in their first, celebratory reactions to the opening up of East Germany and the *de facto* destruction of the Berlin Wall. For the vast majority of these established commentators, the primary significance of the events in East Germany was not just that they were the death-knell of orthodox communism (Stalinism). It was also that they were evidence of the unquenchable desire of a people for something called 'freedom'. In the rhetoric of these commentators, this seemed to be a reference not only to the demand raised by the East Germans, and (by implication) the citizens of all other Soviet bloc societies, for free, democratic elections (which quite clearly *is* a fundamental aspect of this political struggle) but also the demand of Eastern European citizens for *economic* freedom. In particular, the suggestion was that there was a

1

widespread, popular demand in Eastern Europe for the rapid development of 'free market' economic practices in place of the existing
command economies dominated by the State. In Britain, in particular,
many of the accounts of the rapid changes taking place in Eastern Europe
offered out by spokespersons for the Government of Mrs Margaret
Thatcher were framed, very heavily, as further evidence of the growing
appeal and popularity of the free market ideas which the Thatcher
Government sees itself as having pioneered throughout the world.

This kind of account of events in Eastern Europe – as an expression,
above all else, of the growing influence of free market economic theories
– is far from persuasive. Some of the countries in Eastern Europe *have*
very clearly embarked on a project of free market 'liberalization'
(Hungary being the most widely discussed example), and other Eastern
bloc countries will no doubt follow suit. But it is also important to note
how most of the spokespersons for Eastern European opposition
movements (like the New Forum coalition in East Germany), as they
emerged into public prominence in the debates taking place in the freer
political environment, firmly described themselves as socialists or social
democrats. They also insisted that their project was *not* one of unpacking,
in some kind of total and irrevocable fashion, state intervention or a
government commitment to planning, social justice or social peace in the
economy or civil society. Rapidly developing events in Eastern Europe
may overturn these pioneering social democrats, but the evidence across
Eastern Europe as a whole does not suggest that the rebellion against
Stalinism and against the political unfreedom which it *has* imposed on the
citizenry *directly* translates into a popular movement in favour of the
central ideas and policy prescriptions of free market economic theory.

Nonetheless for many spokespersons for free market economic ideas in
the West, the events in Eastern Europe did provide a very welcome
opportunity, seized upon with great vigour, in order, once again, to insist
on the inseparability of the political idea of democratic freedom and the
idea of market liberalism. For the truth was, in 1989, that many western
governments committed to the theory of the free market economy were
beginning to encounter quite fundamental practical, strategic and
political difficulties of their own.[1] In the State of California, for example,
seen by many American commentators as the heartland of free market
economics, especially in the aftermath of the adoption in that state in a
referendum in 1978 of the famous Proposition 13 (putting a limit on tax
revenues), there was evidence of a very different kind of political
direction. Public opinion was apparently moving very strongly in favour
of state investment in public transport and health services, and also in an
enhanced role for the state in the strict regulation of private industry's
treatment of the environment. In many other parts of the world, at the

end of the 1980s, a widespread and growing interest in environmental or 'green' issues was threatening to unpack the kind of purely individualistic politics that were popularized during the 1970s and early 1980s.

I shall be returning to a discussion of these issues later in this chapter. My concern for the moment is simply to establish a sense that at the end of the 1980s we were witnessing *not only* a crisis in the authoritarian, coercive system of centralized state domination over the economy and civil society – especially in its Stalinist form – *but also and simultaneously* a significant rupturing of the progress and popularity of free market theory – especially in those societies, such as Britain, which have been host to its most thoroughgoing political application.

Not the least important problem that continues to confront the defenders of free market theory, particularly in its economic and social effects, is the recognition dawning amongst both opinion-forming interest groups and informed citizens in general that the most successful national economies in the world (Japan and West Germany) and also the fastest-growing economic trading area (the European Community) are conspicuous for their *disavowal* of pure free market theory, and remarkable for their pursuit of a pragmatic and modernizing version of economic and social corporatism. In all of these distances, the dynamism of economic activity seems clearly to be underwritten, not by the release of the individual entrepreneur from public responsibilities, but rather by a pronounced involvement of both state and private capital in the provision of health, housing and welfare for the work-force and also in the promotion of the education and training of the work-force in the kind of skills that are demanded by a complex, 'post-industrial' service economy. The significance of the current British Government's quite extraordinary attacks on the European Social Charter as Marxist scripture lies in the serious problem of credibility which is now posed for free marketeers by the palpable, demonstrable effectivity of a modernizing corporatism, organized across national boundaries, as an instrument for the provision of both private and public good.

One central purpose of this book is to contribute to the examination and critique of free market theory that is now more evident in western societies than at any time since the early 1970s – when these sets of ideas were first insistently offered as 'a solution' to the problems of post-Second World War 'Keynesian' economic and social policy.

The story of the rise of free market theory in different western societies has been recounted in a variety of scholarly and popular texts, and it is not the purpose of this chapter to go over these, by now very well-known, accounts.[2] My own purposes here are more prescriptive and transformative: the project of the 1990s is surely to think and to popularize the task of reform and reconstruction of free market economies in the name of social justice but also in the interest of the authentic, rather than merely ideological, attainment of efficiency in the production and distribution of goods in a modern international economy.

There is no question, however, that this project of reform and reconstruction *is* impeded by the continuing prevalence in many western societies – and in many other societies – of the political language and also the cultural assumptions of free market theory. In societies such as Britain, indeed, it could seriously be argued that *the* major achievement of the free market theorists working in support of the Thatcher Government has been cultural and ideological – giving sustenance to a political language articulated around the celebration *at the level of ideas* of the pleasures of the individual, private life, on the one hand, and the economic and social beneficence of the 'culture of enterprise', on the other. But, in the mean time, it is by no means clear that this essentially *cultural* or *ideological* revolution in Britain has in reality been accompanied by a radical improvement in the fundamental strength of the national economy or by a radical revision of the level of efficiency of, or the provision of service by, managers or workers in the British workforce.

Many of the central ideas of the kind of free market theory that has been influential at the level of national government policy in Britain, the United States and many other western societies were originally formulated in the key texts of 'organic intellectuals' of the New Right and most notably in the works of Hayek and Milton Friedman.[3] But important work was also carried out throughout the 1970s and 1980s – firstly, by economic advisors of the free market Right in reformulating these ideas into a new *policy-orientation* for government and, secondly, by a new breed of right-wing *apparatichnik* 'intellectuals' – writing in the serious and popular Press or being interviewed on radio or television – in relaying these ideas at the level of an accessible and popular *common sense*. The consequence of the political and cultural campaigns conducted in the name of the free market during the 1970s and 1980s is the inescapable domination of many western societies by a complex structure of free market ideas. These ideas consist of a powerful critique at the level of abstract philosophical principle of earlier post-war, centralized and statist forms of social democracy; a specific and detailed set of policy prescriptions directed, in particular, at the privatization of many erstwhile functions of government; and an accompanying set of popular cultural ideas, disseminated throughout the media of mass communication, in celebration of the idea that the pursuit of private economic interest is the most useful measure of efficiency and good work performance, as well as forming the basis of the good and worthwhile life.

It is by no means my intention, in this introductory chapter, to deny the continuing power and influence or the genuine popularity of many of the apparently 'commonsensical' ideas through which free market policies have been advanced and, in many instances, legitimized amongst citizens of western societies. [4] I do, however, want to insist that the presence of this set of cultural assumptions (around the legitimate, 'well-earnt' and deserved pleasures of *private* consumption and the *private* life in general) has had the important effect of distracting popular attention from the accelerating inequalities and injustices that have characterized the freeing of the free market during the 1980s.

Seen in another light, it is by no means clear that the development of these new 'forms of social life' – organized around the private consumption of goods and pleasure – *are* an expression in themselves of the popular embrace of *free market theory* as such: seen across a European and international terrain, they seem rather to be an effect of the rapid acceleration of a rationalized and transnational competitive economy, emerging out of the ruins of the era of mass manufacturing industry, generating its own profit out of the fulfilment, in consumerism, of personal dreams and desires. It may be the international growth of *consumerism* as such which has achieved 'popularity' rather than the fact that such consumerism is presently being fed, in many western societies, by 'deregulated' free market institutions.

Distinctions of this order – between 'consumerism' and the free market idea itself – do not attract much attention in the language of free market theorists themselves, and they do not excite much commentary in current public, political debate as a whole. That they do not is some measure of the extraordinary success of free market theorists and politicians in western societies in mobilizing a grossly generalized and popular political language, focused around the ideas of 'freedom' and of 'choice'.

The political language developed by free market theorists over the last twenty years has had at least two important functional features. In the first instance, it has been developed as a form of publicly accessible and publicly usable common-sense language, with which to challenge and/or subvert the common-sense language of Keynesian and welfarist social democracies. So the populist intellectuals of free market theory have been involved in the creation and elaboration of a language constructed around notions of 'choice', and the 'freedom' of *the market* and 'the rights of the individual' over and above notions of social justice, the 'community' and, indeed, of 'welfare' as such. This language has been actively and insistently offered as the framework of reasonable, acceptable discussion of political possibilities, and as the prism through which to glimpse the direction that should be undertaken by 'free', democratic societies. [5] Interestingly enough, however, surveys conducted in the United Kingdom and the United States suggest that the continuing mobilization of this kind of political language by intellectuals and spokespersons of the free market Right have not undermined the level of public support for specific instances of welfare state provision (and, in particular, for universal access to free public health provision). But that does not in itself deny the enormous influence which the mobilization of a free market 'common sense' seems to have had in inflecting the character of orthodox political debate – the parameters of 'the consensus' – in western societies in the late 1980s: there really is no alternative social democratic language on offer which actually gives voice to notions of welfare, care and social justice as a matter of popular *common sense*.

The absence of any such alternative language no doubt helps to lend support and confirmation to free market theorists' own preferred free market common sense. For there is no doubt that a second important 'function' of the language of free market theory has been to construct a powerful form of theology which, like the language of Marxism–Leninism it frequently subjects to violent attack, operates in a kind of self-confirming fashion. It is impervious to epistemological enquiries regarding the 'truth value' of its claims, and inattentive in its language and the over-all theoretical posture which such language encourages, to the challenge of empirical developments in 'the real world'. Simply put, the adoption of a language which speaks only to some aspects of contemporary social reality serves also to blind the user of that language to other aspects of that reality or, perhaps, to the 'complex totality' of that reality as a whole.

One absolutely core belief in the theology of the free marketeers is the belief in the superiority of free market forms of social organization over the forms of social organization of Keynesian welfare state society. The free market economy is seen as an unambiguous advance on welfare state social democracy – as a provider of economic efficiency and as a guarantor of a sense of individual freedom and responsibility (the obverse of the 'state dependency' encouraged by the welfare state). The free market economy is therefore seen more or less inevitably as having 'buried' the welfare state by virtue of being more economically rational, more liberating to individuals and, therefore, by extension, more *popular* than the welfare state which preceded it. This is a form of *theological* political language which – like the Marxism–Leninism it seems, in these respects, to resemble very closely – is in principle *open to challenge* by reference to developments or individual events in the 'real world' that is the free market society. One of the most important areas in which there should have been more prolonged and persistent debate and discussion in the 1980s was precisely around the question of the social effects or social consequences of free market policies – or around the issue which classical economists refer to as the question of social cost.

One of the central features of the advance of free market policies in many western societies in the 1980s was the advance of unemployment and of the set of social and personal deprivations and harms which many would associate, using a form of social democratic common sense, as an 'effect' or a consequence of that unemployment. A considerable literature did, indeed, develop in the United States and in Britain in the early 1980s with the object of detailing the particular sets of consequences or effects of such unemployment. Professor Harvey Brenner was the most well known of such scholars in the United States, pioneering the use of 'time-lag analysis' in a demonstration of the causal relationships which he thought to exist and to be demonstrable in quantifiable terms between the fact of unemployment in an individual's biography and the facts of early mortality, morbidity and ill-health and a series of other personal harms or pathologies (Brenner, 1971a, 1971b, 1977, 1978, 1979a, 1979b). Similar, but generally less rigidly positivistically formulated, relationships between 'unemployment' and its social effects were explored in respect of Britain by Adrian Sinfield (1980, 1981), Jeremy Seabrook (1982) and many others (Smith, 1988).

Social democratic studies of this kind were, however, subjected to powerful critique by the economist Jon Stern on the issue of the causal ordering of the relationship between unemployment and personal or social pathology (Stern, 1981, 1982a, 1982b). In Stern's view, it is just as valid, on the basis of a time-lag analysis, to speak of ill-health or personal disability being a *cause* of unemployment and redundancy as it is to speak of such ill-health and disability being the result of the unemployment experience. Those who have failed to take responsibility for their own health could be seen to have visited their own redundancy upon themselves, by virtue of being less useful to potential employers and, therefore, 'the first to be fired' in a situation of economic rationalization. Arguments of the kind developed by Stern have fed into the common sense from which many thinkers on the free market Right routinely proceed. The truth is that no conclusive challenge to such a common sense *can* be mounted purely and simply on the basis of the kind of correlational analysis offered out by Brenner, Sinfield and others.

It is true that arguments of this kind have not been very widely taken up and mobilized in the *public* rhetorics of free market politicians: any such attempt at 'blaming the victim' of unemployment for his or her own fate has been understood to have a doubtful purchase on the sympathies of electorates which, at various times during the 1980s, were quite anxious with respect to their *own* continuing employability in rapidly changing free market economies.

What has been mobilized, instead, however, is a political language which does not seem to recognize the idea of a *social* effect or *social* cost at all, but which is concerned to offer an alternative and differently focused account.

This particular kind of language has surfaced on several occasions in the public speech of free market politicians – not least in the famous interview given by Margaret Thatcher to the *Woman's Own* magazine in October 1987, wherein she actually denied outright the idea of 'the social' altogether.[6] Our argument here is that the sentiments which Mrs Thatcher was expressing in this interview – so far from being a casual or unreflective aside – were an expression of an argument which has been very heavily worked over in the 'think-tanks' which have prepared the ground for the Thatcher Government's experiment in free market economics.

In the year before Mrs Thatcher's election victory of 1989, a 'Hobart Paper' was published by the Institute for Economic Affairs (IEA, a 'research and educational trust' that undertook much of the theoretical and empirical work on which free market politicians relied when mounting their successful attack on the failing of post-war social democracy).[7] This paper took the form of a critique of welfare economics, by Steven Cheung, an American professor of economics, and was triumphantly released under the title *The Myth of Social Cost* (Cheung, 1978). One must assume that Cheung's paper, like all such IEA papers, has had an important influence – in this case refining the specific languages of free market politicians and directing their gaze very specifically towards certain impacts of free market policies and not others.

Like many of the other IEA papers, Cheung's paper is couched in the technical and private language of specialist economics: the target of Cheung's critique is the tradition of economic analysis initiated, in 1897, by the Italian Vilfredo Pareto (1980)[8] and subsequently developed and popularized by the Cambridge-based economist, A. C. Pigou (1920).

Pareto's original argument arises out of the recognition – which, one assumes, would be surprising only to the most blinkered of apologists for the development of bourgeois economic order during the nineteenth century – that there might be some discrepancy or contradiction between the unfettered pursuit of economic self-interest by 'individuals' and 'welfare *between* individuals'. The specific concern of Paretian analysis is with the problem of the *effect* which the pursuit of economic self-interest by one individual (or firm) may have on another individual that is not party to it: this effect being referred to as an 'externality' or a 'transactional cost'. The substantive focus of the 'welfare economics' which is then constructed out of the analysis of such externalities and their cost is on the use of taxation by the state. The objective of this use of tax policy is that of limiting the costs of such 'externalities' by deterrence or by the use of the state revenue so earnt to compensate individuals who have been harmed by the pursuit of self-interest by others.

It is important to understand how the Paretian concept of 'welfare' in use here is focused, very narrowly, on the welfare of relatively wealthy and propertied individuals competing in the market-place. That is, the *problem* being addressed in Paretian analysis is the mitigation of the effects on some of these individual entrepreneurs that are consequent upon the pursuit of self-interest by other individuals (or firms): there really is no interest in Paretian welfare economics in the kind of critical analysis of nineteenth-century industrial society – whether in terms of its institutionalization of unequal class, authority and power relations or in its development of a formal division of labour – developed by sociological commentators of that time (like Max Weber or Emile Durkheim). The concept of 'the externality' is a reference not to the *character* of the social relations (the type of 'community' or 'moral economy' which is so created) produced by an industrial capitalist economy, but rather to the management of the *purely economic costs* that might be implicated in transactions between individual actors who are active in a capitalist market. It is not just the restrictiveness of these kinds of concepts which is extraordinary and unwarranted to the non-economist. It is also the ways in which these restrictive concepts (of transactional costs on the individual entrepreneur) are imposed upon the broader social reality, as if they could exhaust all that needs to be said about elaborate and unequal social structures.

One of the most influential subsequent applications of Paretian welfare economics was Professor Pigou's analysis of factory smoke, and its cost on people living in the immediate neighbourhood of factories, originally published in 1920. Pigou's analysis at least had the consequence of recognizing the interests of 'people' (and, in this case, their health) over and above the interest of individual firms or capitalists, and it constituted the basis for at least fifty years of government policy in respect of this kind of industrial pollution. Since the publication of Pigou's analysis, governments have generally held factory owners responsible for the costs of smoke pollution more or less in relation to the amounts of smoke that have been emitted, and, at least in theory, factories have been excluded from areas where they would be particularly or excessively harmful to individuals.

It does have to be said, however, that Pigou's revision of the original formulation of Paretian welfare economics is itself a very restrictive project. The concern is to arrive at a balanced assessment of the benefits to *individual firms* from industrial production and the identifiable, measurable costs *to individual neighbourhood residents* of such production; and then to initiate, through government, a system for the compensation of *individuals* who have been measurably harmed. There is certainly no hint here of any kind of critical analysis of 'industrialism' *per se* in its effects on 'environment', of the kind that has been offered by ecological thinkers over the last century and a half or, indeed, of any other impact of industrialism on 'society as a whole'. Perhaps even more importantly, given the realist preoccupations proclaimed by many practising economists, there is little serious attempt to apply an economic and welfarist analysis to a broad understanding of the *patterns* and *quality* of social existence (its real possibilities and constraints) over and above the impact of 'externalities' such as the extent of industrial pollution. What are the measurable costs, for 'individuals', for example, of years of employment in a low-wage job or of years of unemployment, in terms of the quality of life for individuals who are so positioned in a market economy? From the perspective of most non-economists, what is absolutely remarkable is that even this narrowly restrictive idea of a social cost developed by Pigou should now be under attack in the name of 'pure' free market theory.

The basis of this attack lies in a paper by Professor Coase, originally published in 1960, but then reformulated by Professor Cheung in his IEA paper of 1978. Briefly stated, the argument advanced by Professors Coase and Cheung, as an attack on welfare economics as such, is predicated on the need to *reinstate* the individual property rights of owners and producers quite unambiguously at the centre of economic policy. The argument is that the advance of an idea of welfare as an externality, consequent on the development of Paretian analysis by Pigou, has created ambiguity over questions of the right to property. The consequence of this ambiguity is that there has been no 'final determination' in law or in the culture of who has the right to pollute, and the consequence of this, in turn, has been a lack of clear-cut control of pollution on the part of owners of industry and/or on the part of consumers or users. According to Professors Coase and Cheung, all this hangs on the originating ambiguity with respect to the question of 'property rights'. If individuals do not know whether an activity is directly costly to their own interests (because they do not have a clear concept of their own property interest or right), then they will not be able to place a value, for example, on pollution. The answer to such problems (and therefore to pollution) must be a reassertion in law of a clear concept of the right to property, so providing an *incentive* to owners to minimize the direct costs to themselves of such pollution and the indirect, transactional costs to others.

One can only understand the construction in free market theory of this kind of policy-thinking by looking at the vital *domain assumptions* on which such market theory is originally premised, and, in particular, the insistence of such market theory on the sovereign role of *propertied individuals* in civil society. What is being targeted by Professors Coase and Cheung is the idea that the state itself, acting in the name of some other idea of the public or social interest, should intervene coercively, or in a regulatory fashion, *vis-à-vis* the 'private' – capital-accumulating – activities of individuals in the economic market-place. In the prologue to Professor Cheung's 1978 IEA pamphlet, Professor Charles Rowley teased out the implications of Cheung's technical argument against welfare economics quite unambiguously. Referring, still, to the question of the control of pollution, Rowley averred (1978):

> the implications for *individual freedom* should not be ignored when assessing the argument for government intervention. Freedom implies the right of any individual not to be coerced by another individual. The supposed existence of 'social cost' has been one of the foremost pretexts for which such freedom has been transgressed and by which the authority of government has been extended.

The fundamental problem which is being addressed by these free market economists is that of the intervention by government in the activities of propertied individuals amassing wealth in the market-place: there is no attempt, here, to privilege any kind of concept of the over-all *public good*.

The 1990s: the idea of a public good and public services in free market societies

In the early 1990s, there are many reasons for believing that the free market policies adopted by many western governments may be encountering a key contradictory moment, most notably in respect of popular perception of free market policies' effects in the sphere of public provision and public services. It may be *precisely* at this level – namely, in respect of the claims advanced by its advocates as to the power of the free market to deliver public services and a benign sense of a secure and safe social order – that the free market idea is most vulnerable. It may be at this level that a clear sense of the *social cost* of free market economic policies – namely, the virtual collapse of the idea of public provision, may be most widely understood. In Britain, in 1990, this sense of the social cost of the coerced withdrawal of the state from social provision and public service, in the name of free market objectives, is most palpable and urgently debated in respect of the virtual collapse of a public transport system, in respect of the amisseration of urban space by vandalism, litter and general dilapidation consequent on the withdrawal of the state from imaginative municipal responsibility, and in respect of the heightened stresses and strains being experienced by workers in the public education system and in the National Health Service. Similar but distinctive developments are being reported for all other societies where free market theory has been embraced at the level of national policy.

It is not the primary purpose of this book to develop the argument over the crisis of public provisions in free market societies in the extended and detailed form it deserves. The concern here *is*, however, to bring together a number of informed analytical pieces on the ways in which the provision of education, health, law and order and other social services in different societies were affected by the withdrawal of state provision and the move towards 'free market' organization during the 1980s. In so doing, our concern is, in part, to recognize that the 'effects' of this ground-change in the relations of the state to the economy were being felt at very many different levels within the social formation, and that also they were and are experienced in different measures and combinations in different societies. It *is* part of the purpose of this text to show that the 'effects' of free market policies *are* uneven and complex, but nonetheless important and 'real'. In absolutely no simple sense are these effects reducible to the narrow notion of 'social cost' identified and targeted by Professors Coase and Cheung and neither are they straightforwardly equivalent to the social cost of 'unemployment' alone.

This complexity and unevenness of effects may be one reason why the publicity which has been given by the 'poverty lobby', concerned academics and social democratic politicians to one of the most well-understood effects of free market policies (namely, unemployment) has had little effect on the general population's attitudes to free market policies. We need to investigate this issue further.

Free market societies and the social effects of unemployment

In the early 1980s, as most western economies seemed to be moving ineluctably into what economists were describing as the condition of 'stagflation' (a combination of ever higher levels of unemployment and continuing increases in the level of inflation), there was a widespread tendency among social commentators of all persuasions to compare the social and economic conditions of the 1980s with those of the early 1930s. The concern was to suggest that the kinds of dislocation and personal deprivation which had been made familiar (for example, in film and television documentaries) were about to be repeated in the early to mid-1980s. Such a comparison was most readily justified by reference to the sharp increases in unemployment that were being experienced, particularly in areas of the advanced capitalist societies which were dominated by heavy manufacturing. There *were* real similarities, in these areas, between the catastrophic personal effects that the closure of large manufacturing industries had on their workers in the 1930s and the effects which had been experienced, very often by workers employed in precisely the same industries (coal, steel, shipbuilding, etc.), some fifty years before. For many social commentators on the Left, another key comparison between the 1980s and the 1930s was the offensive which was mounted, in both periods, on the organizations of industrial labour based in the work-place (the trade unions) and their political representatives (the organized labour movement), by organized capital and the political representatives of the middle class and ruling class alike. Not least of these attacks was the return of mass unemployment itself. Nearly all European societies throughout the 1980s and until 1986 (excluding West Germany) experienced increases in unemployment that were unprecedented in the post-Second World War period.

In the United Kingdom, the statistics (adjusted to OECD concepts) demonstrated an increase from 5 per cent in 1979 to 12.5 per cent in 1983 (with a reduction down to 8.8 per cent by 1988, albeit produced to a significant extent by redefinitions of the official status of 'unemployment'). In Spain, in the meantime, unemployment remained in 1988 at 19.5 per cent of the labour force looking for work, and in France and Belgium the rate continued at over 10 per cent. In three of the countries discussed in this volume, the official rates of unemployment in 1983 reached 11.8 per cent (in Canada), 9.9 per cent in Australia and 9.5 per cent in the United States. (By 1988, these rates, as then officially redefined, had fallen back to 7.9 per cent in Canada, 7.0 per cent in Australia and 5.5 per cent in the United States.)[9]

It *is* important to recognize the parallels between the social, economic and political processes that have occurred during the 1980s and similar processes obtaining in the 1930s. But it is also important to recognize, to register and to explain *fundamental differences* between the circumstances of the 1980s and the crisis of 1929–33, provoked as this was by speculative activity and by the absence of any national or international instruments for the regulation of deep cycles of boom and slump. It is not only that the crisis of the early 1930s was *pre*-Keynesian, and that it occurred in advance of the development of the vast range of interventionist measures which have been developed nationally and internationally throughout the period subsequent to the Great Crash and the Second World War. It is also that the crisis of the 1930s occurred in the context of a period which was in all other ways characterized by a certain stability of social and class relations.

In Britain, in particular – by contrast with earlier periods during the twentieth century, such as the years before the First World War and the middle 1920s (which *were* periods of significant labour unrest) – the period from 1927 to 1939 was a period of considerable social cohesion and class compromise and very little political rebellion or opposition. The unemployment experienced by an (overwhelmingly male) 'breadwinner' working class did not result in any marked over-all radicalization of that class. Nor did it result in any perceptible increase in other forms of social disruption, such as interpersonal or property crime. What it undeniably did produce, continuing well into the 1930s, was a widespread sense of despair amongst the population of particular manufacturing regions (as was vividly expressed, for example, in Wal Hannington's *The Problem of the Distressed Areas* (1937)), and a sense of anger, most marked amongst a small number of politicized individuals, as to the unchecked and continuing effects that the economic crisis had had on particular communities. This anger was clearly evident, for example, in Ellen Wilkinson's classic account (1939) of the condition of Gateshead in the mid-1930s, subsequent to the closure of its shipyards.

The 1980s *have* exhibited some of these processes of national and regional disruption, and there have, in particular, been seriously destructive effects visited on individuals and on particular communities as a result of the process which is now, rather benignly, refeired to as the process of *de-industrialization*.[10]

But it is clear that the dislocations resulting from such unemployment have not been understood, at the level of public discussion and popular common sense, in the manner of the effects of unemployment in the 1930s. In the public–political discussion of unemployment in the 1930s, for instance, there was very little suggestion that such unemployment might have resulted from the personal failings (the work habits or levels of skill, etc.) of those who had been made redundant, and no subsequent reinterpretation of 1930s unemployment has attempted to construct such an account or explanation. Neither was there a strong sense, in the public–political discussion of unemployment in the 1930s, that the levels of unemployment then emerging had in some sense been *created* by the failure of governments, in an earlier (Keynesian) period, to innovate economic policy with a view to ensuring future prosperity and dynamism. In the 1980s there seems to have been a sense in public and political discussion that 'societies' have visited much of the new unemployment upon themselves, precisely because of becoming dependent on increasingly inefficient and bureaucratic state-run industries for their livelihood, or because of the development of inappropriate attitudes to work.

To note these sets of ideas that were circulating about the new unemployment, as one possible reason for the relative lack of obvious public anxiety over such unemployment in the 1980s, is to recognize, once again, the important influence that the ideological work of the free market right has had on dominant and popular forms of common-sense talk. But it is clearly not the only operative influence. It seems likely, for example, that the anxieties of parents and young people over unemployment in the 'youth labour market' may have been assuaged, to some degree, by the creation of a range of government initiatives in the area of job-training and job-creation, targeted in particular at constructing some kind of work opportunity and some kind of income for youth.[11] It also seems likely that the kind of anxiety and despair that was apparently created in the 1930s – given that the unemployment of that period affected the solitary 'breadwinner' for most working-class families with no alternative source of income – may actually not have emerged in so intensive, unconditional and unambiguous a form in the 1980s, in circumstances where some alternative jobs were available, particularly in the service industry and for women. In North America, in particular, but increasingly in Britain, another important factor distinguishing the 1980s from the 1930s (especially in respect of public debate about unemployment) may be the quite extraordinary acceleration of the working day – and, indeed, the working week – on the part of those who are actually in work. Recent statistics speak to the emergence not of a more leisured society but, instead, of an ever more extended working career, with *more* hours spent at work and fewer hours spent in leisure or on vacation. Critical commentators on the United States allude to a vastly 'over-accelerated' work culture, with a population increasingly unable to see or to think beyond the parameters of their own work-place or career, and unable, therefore, *to think* the problems of the unemployed or the long-term implications for 'society' of unemployment or of *any* other public, apparently impersonal, problem.[12]

These remarks, however, are only speculations, and they are *not* intended to suggest that the unemployment of the 1980s has not had powerful and destructive effects, both at the community and the individual levels. The concern is, instead, to suggest that the various consequences of the adoption by governments of free market policies during the 1980s cannot be understood on some kind of analogy with the 1930s, but that they must be grasped in terms of their specific contemporary form. It may be, for example, that the contemporary effects of these free market policies are more significantly articulated around the social division of region, gender and ethnicity than they are an expression of the brute inequality of social class.

So we are arguing, in effect, for greater curiosity with respect to the effects of unemployment and the other social changes that have been wrought by the 'liberalization' of economic markets of the 1980s. And in arguing for a greater curiosity with respect to the massive social changes of the 1980s, we are also actually arguing for the application, quite specifically, of the *sociological imagination* to the careful analysis of these changes. For one of the other quite bizarre features of the period of rapid social change through which most western societies have recently passed is the relative absence of any well-grounded and empirically focused analysis of the effects of the emergence of free market economic policies on the character of what I would call 'lived social relations'.

There have, on the one hand, been some important studies of the transformations of global political economy[13] and the impact of these transformations on the bargaining position and economic prospects of organized labour, and, in particular, the associated fragmentation of the working class into identifiable, differentially well-placed interest groups or 'fractions'.[14] And there have also been descriptive accounts, at the other extreme, of the transformation of the overall *culture* of late capitalist societies in the era of free market economics, focusing on the impact and influence, in particular, of the individualistic consciousness[15] and, in one account, the self-oriented 'narcissism',[16] which is encouraged amongst the 'successful' and the propertied by the incessant marketing of consumer products. In some quarters, there has also been an interest in that most abstracted and unfocused body of ideas known as 'post-modernism', wherein the puzzle of how social relations are now lived and experienced, at all levels of the social formation, seems to be resolved in terms of a cynical ennui of small numbers of liberal intellectuals. Many such intellectuals have apparently decided that History is at an End (and 'there is nothing left to do but go to the shops'): holding such a view, there is, of course, no *need* to investigate how other people conduct their lives.[17]

At the end of the 1980s, it is worth while recalling and reasserting one of the central preoccupations and objectives of classical social theory: specifically, that of elucidating the connection between the 'grand logic' of *economic change and development*, the *forms of social organization* (for example, the division of labour) characteristic of an individual society and the *lived experience* of that society. The work of Emile Durkheim was, of course, particularly influential in establishing this version of sociology and its 'project', and it has been specifically influential in its mobilization of the concept of 'anomie' or 'normlessness' as an account of the personal discontent which is liable to be experienced by social actors who are inappropriately placed in society with a 'forced' division of labour, and who therefore do not feel the force of the dominant values – the *collective conscience* – of the broad society. The notion of anomie has been very influential in American sociology, particularly as revised by Robert Merton and elaborated into the famous 'typology of individual adaptation'. This is an account of the strains that are present at different levels of a society in which the prescribed and dominant social goals (of 'material success') are not equally attainable by all the citizens of that society – in which there exists a 'disjunction' between 'dominant goals' and the 'institutionalized means' (the opportunity) for their achievement. Mertonian anomie theorists have tried 'to read' the character of social relations in the United States (as being prey to a certain lack of moral regulation, particularly for those segments of the society experiencing a blockage of opportunity) in terms of the absence of national economic policies directed at unpacking such blockages and at the achievement of a real, rather than ideological, condition of social equality.

Mertonian anomie theory was applied by American sociologists to the study of American society, even in the relatively affluent 1950s and 1960s, as an account of the sources of a variety of 'social problems', ranging from school failure and delinquency to the character of the spiritual life of the society. In such accounts, the source of the normless character of life at some levels of American society continued to be identified in terms of the continuing *blockage of opportunity* experienced by some segments of the American population. Only a very few American sociologists had the courage or the insight to scrutinize more closely the unchallenged existence of the 'cultural dominant' – the pursuit of unlimited material success – as being in itself a source of social division and social disorder and normlessness.[18] But, in so doing, these sociologists were surely asserting one of the most important tasks of sociology as such: namely, the project of making the connection, at the level of explanation, between the particular forms or objectives of economic organization developing within particular societies and the moral character of social life obtaining within such societies. This project of 'making the connection' – between economic organization and the moral character of social relations – may be more *difficult* and *problematic* given the increasingly complex sets of social divisions that have been thrown up and accentuated by the advent of free market economic policy (and also by the apparent diminution of the nation-state as the primary site of economic policy and decision making), but that is precisely the challenge that confronts any worthwhile *sociological* approach to the realities of 'free market societies'.

The objectives which have informed the production of this book on the social effects of free market policies now become more straightforward to identify.

The contributors to this collection share the following with the editor:

1. A commitment to the view that the adoption during the 1980s by many western governments of free market policies has, indeed, involved significant social effects and also that it is important to understand these effects as a part of the *social cost* of such policies. In this respect, the collection here can be seen as a challenge, especially as an empirical challenge, to that version of classical economic theory which would restrict the analysis of 'social costs' to the transactional financial costs of certain economic activity to individual capitalists or corporations, and certainly to that version of free market economics which would deny the utility of social cost altogether. In this respect, the collection is intended to underwrite that kind of critical post-Keynesian economic and social analysis that remains committed to a notion of a 'universal interest' rather than being organized exclusively round the 'interest' of the entrepreneur or the propertied – a version of economic analysis that was once again, in the late 1980s, being advanced with real confidence and concern. Professor J. K. Galbraith's (1989) post-mortem in the 1980s (a decade which, he observes, had seen the break-up in both the United States and the United Kingdom of the social contract between the rich and the poor struck in the first half of this century) concludes that:

    > our poor in the U.S. have remained poor, and the number so classified has substantially increased, as has, more markedly, the share of income going to the very rich. The conditions of life in the centres of our large cities is – the word is carefully chosen – appalling. Housing is bad and getting worse. Many of our citizens are without even the barest element of shelter, their income at near starvation levels. Schools are also bad, and young and old, sustained often by crime, contrive a temporary escape from despair with drugs. (*Weekend Guardian*, 1989)

    To the extent that this book offers any evidence of the costs which have been paid by particular populations for the pursuit of free market policies in particular societies, it can be seen as a resource for use by political and social commentators in those societies, who are now recognizing the need to examine the consequences of the defeat of post-Second World War Keynesian social and economic thinking by 'free market' thinkers and true believers.

2. In displaying the costs to particular social groups (for example, to women or to residents of particular regions) of free market policies, the chapters of this book can be read as preparing the way for a grounded *sociological* analysis of the complexity of social relations as they are now lived and experienced in particular free market

societies. In this respect, the book is intended as a preamble to the development of the (hitherto rather thin) sociological literature on the effects of free market policies on lived social experience – an advance on the Mertonian sociologies of 'post-war affluence', on the one hand, and the abstractions of post-modern theory, on the other.

3. The concerns of the contributors necessarily have a more immediate purpose, particularly in respect of ongoing and continuing debates over social policy, in the key areas of health, education and personal and social support. Most of the reforms and revisions that have occurred in the area of social policy in western societies during the 1980s have been driven by the objectives of free market individualism, and, in cases where they have not actually been publicly presented in a strategically deceptive or secretive manner, they have actually been presented, in a celebratory and triumphalist fashion, in terms of the victory of 'choice', 'freedom' and, indeed, of 'efficiency' and 'modernism'.[19] There is absolutely no need to deny that these *are* all desirable qualities of a dynamic contemporary society, but it is also important to see how this kind of political language has encouraged a highly restrictive vision, particularly with respect to the *evaluation* of the broad effects of government policy during the 1980s.

The insistence is clear, throughout these chapters, that there *is* an inescapable connection between the economic policy decisions of government and the kinds of issues thrown up in the realm of social policy. We are fully aware that the realm of social policy is a sphere of activity which many free marketeers would prefer not to recognize ('true' free marketeers would prefer the state to withdraw altogether from the exercise of any such responsibilities), but it is also a sphere in which 'public opinion' continues to exhibit many expectations.[20] In recent years, we have suggested, these popular expectations have been most apparent, internationally, in respect of a demand for *government* action in respect of the shared environment. These demands are also increasingly apparent in respect of demands for effective government policies in the sphere of public transport and the protection or restoration of a sense of order, and a sense of personal safety, in the public territory of the streets. One important concern of this book is to investigate other areas of tension and contradiction in the development of free market policies in western societies, and to begin to address the implied 'demand' that is posed in different areas for an alternative *social* policy of government.

In this last respect, we are interested in prising open the contradiction between free market economic policy and the notion of a social policy articulated in the interests of a public good. In contrast with many recent sceptical analyses, we are indeed suggesting that the increased emphasis on the role of the market in economic life is in no sense an argument for the reduction of the responsibilities of government, particularly in respect of the provision of public services and in respect of the protection of the social and individual rights of all citizens (particularly, the rights to shelter, education and health) through the imaginative and committed articulation of policy.

The chapters gathered here focus on the impact of free market policies in five English-language-speaking societies (the United Kingdom, the United States, Canada – which is, of course, officially a bilingual society – Australia and New Zealand). This collation is a product of my own recent travels in these societies as well as the personal connections I have developed as a largely unilingual academic based throughout the 1980s in Canada and the United Kingdom (with a three-month stay in Australia). The selection of countries discussed here should in no sense be interpreted to suggest that the development of free market economic ideas or policies is less significant elsewhere: quite dramatic developments have obviously occurred during the 1970s and 1980s in South-East Asia, and a sweeping 'liberalization' of economic activity is a key feature of the blueprints now emerging for the future of the European Community.[21] At the time of the compilation of this collection, however, my experience of these societies was minimal and my personal connections were concentrated elsewhere.

The societies discussed in these papers are often thought of, in general terms, as sharing a common heritage – not least in their use of the language which is the common language-in-use of the international economic and financial communities. But what this book makes clear, even in its discussion of societies with such a common heritage, is how the generalized movement towards the free market economy that has occurred on the part of most western governments during the 1980s takes different forms in different societies. So the advent of a 'free market solution' in Britain has involved a headlong assault, at the ideological level and also in terms of individual policy innovation, on the institutions of organized labour and the welfare state, whereas in Australia and New Zealand the development of such free market solutions seems to have worked through the political parties and institutions representing organized labour.

In the United States, where there is no pronounced or institutionalized tradition of labourism or social democracy influential at the level of government, the project of the free marketeers has perhaps been rather more straightforward: an attack has been mounted on the notion of Big Government in the name of a very familiar American folk-hero, the individual businessman-capitalist, and, in the course of a very few years (beginning with the election of Ronald Reagan in 1980), the main achievements of President Roosevelt's 'New Deal' policies, underwriting the survival of the American underclass in a highly competitive, individualistic capitalism, have been put into rapid reverse.

In Canada, a society which above all eschews most kinds of public ideological debate and dissension, the development of 'free market solutions' occurred almost invisibly in the early 1980s (most characteristically, through a large-scale national Commission of Enquiry, initiated by the Government) and was then released on a largely unprepared Canadian public in the form of the Free Trade Agreement entered into with the Government of the United States in January 1988.[22]

What seems clear, in any examination of developments in these five societies, is the extent to which the mobilization of preferred free market economic policies in each society has had to take account of the particular and specific cultural and political 'history' of that society. In Rob Watts's contribution to this book, for example, we may recognize the importance in Australia of the populist and egalitarian emphasis, in everyday 'folk' culture and tradition, on the idea of the 'fair go', and the ways in which this has restricted and constrained radical reform by free marketeers in the area of welfare. In the chapters on Canada (especially those by Ken Battle and Peter Usher), we may see evidence of the continuing importance in this particular pioneer and immigrant society of the idea of a *universalistic* system of state welfare provision (described even by Prime Minister Mulroney as 'a sacred trust'), and the problems that this has created for the Conservative Government's project of radically reducing state expenditure in Canada. In New Zealand, the unfolding of Finance Minister Roger Douglas's 'consumer-pay' policies in respect of health, education and welfare, has always had to pay strategic attention to certain fundamental defining features, widely understood in that society, of New Zealand's cultural identity. Not least of these understandings is the recognition on the part of the white settler population (the Pakeha) that the islands of New Zealand are shared, in a full partnership, with the Maori peoples (who were themselves never finally defeated in the military struggles occurring at the time of settlement): a recognition which is celebrated on the main national holiday in New Zealand (Waitangi Day). Even in Britain – where arguably the most intense ideological assault of all has been mounted on the central ideas of welfare social democracy – important fields of state activity (like the National Health Service) still remain largely intact even if, as Jenny Roberts's chapter in this collection describes, it too has been subjected to the 'discipline' of 'market forces' in a series of significant respects. There would seem to be important cultural, historical and political reasons why health provision itself is thought to be inappropriate, strategically, for the project of total privatization which the Thatcher Government has mobilized in a wide variety of other areas.

To point to unevenness and difference in the development of free market policies in different societies is not in itself to argue that the adoption of 'free market solution' is fundamentally obstructed by such cultural 'specificities'. But it certainly *is* to suggest that the mobilization of free market policies in particular societies has always had to proceed *in recognition* of these specificities. Seeing how governments have had to recognize the necessary role of the state in certain areas of public provision may constitute some grounds for optimism on the part of commentators and analysts who want to reject wholesale the idea of a 'market solution'. But a more subtle response, of greater long-term importance, might be to see these problematic areas of government and market activity (like the Canadian North so authoritatively discussed in this volume by Peter Usher) as being precisely those areas in which the 'limits to markets' *and also* the limits to orthodox Keynesian solutions are most powerfully displayed or encountered. One thinks, by analogy, of problematic areas in the other societies discussed in this volume (such as the inner cities of the North of England, the ghettoes of the Northern United States and also of a de-industrialized Los Angeles, the peripheral Canadian 'regions' of Nova Scotia and Newfoundland, the de-industrializing towns of south-western Ontario and the public housing areas of urban Australia and New Zealand). One also thinks, however – as we have suggested throughout this introductory chapter – of the overarching importance in all these societies of the position of *public services*, in respect of transport, of environmental protection and of a sense of public order and well-being, in the shared spaces, the public territories, of the free market city. There seems little doubt that this mix of issues, oriented around the question of who will provide for the public interest in these different but connected respects in free market societies, will become one of the pressing set of questions on the agendas of deregulated free market societies in the 1990s, whether expressed at the level of national politics or, ever more significantly in Europe, at the level of the *international governmental institutions* of an economic community.

The chapters have not been organized according to a rigid or exhaustive theoretical or empirical logic. I have tried to cover as many key topics as possible, although I am conscious of not having covered all (there is no chapter, for example, on the impact of free market policies on the situation of ethnic minorities in any of the five metropolitan and colonializing societies) and I am also conscious that a topic covered in one country has not necessarily been covered for another (the impact of free market policies on women has only been examined in relationship to

Britain). But I have always been aware that any attempt to cover all areas in each of these five societies would have made for an impossibly heavy, expensive and therefore completely inaccessible monograph. I am hopeful that the collection presented here will at least have the merit of addressing the bulk of the pressing areas of 'strain' and 'effect' in contemporary free market societies.

This collection is offered as a contribution to the evaluation and critique of the 'free market' experiment of the 1980s, and also to the careful sociological examination of its 'real' social and personal effects. I hope it will be of value to all those observers, in these and other free market societies, who recognize that these *are* important questions: but I hope that the contributions gathered together in this volume will persuade others who have not as yet looked at the 'social effects' of the market solution that this is indeed an important way to understand the transformations of the 1980s. The 1990s, we could then hope, might be different.

Notes

1. Cf. the article by William Keegan in *The Observer* (1989).
2. Cf., for example, on the United States, Steinfels (1979); on Britain, Hall and Jacques (1983).
3. Cf., *inter alia*, F. A. Hayek (1944, 1948, 1960) and Friedman (1962, 1970).
4. It is important to note how the advocacy of free market ideas by economists and other spokespeople for the free market in Australia and New Zealand has been most effectively popularized in and through the previously 'statist' and 'social democratic' Labor Party, in the course of its tenure of government. (See, for example, Chapter 6 by Rob Watts and Chapter 14 by Ian Shirley.)
5. Chapter 4 by Jenny Roberts explores how the political language of the free market Right is given a specific focus and purchase, and then mobilized in public, political debate, in respect of the future of the National Health Service in the United Kingdom.
6. Margaret Thatcher, interviewed in *Woman's Own* (October 1987). It was in this interview that Mrs Thatcher made her infamous comment that 'there is no such thing as the social; there are only individuals and families . . .'. Enquiries for copies of this speech to Conservative Central Office in London encounter the response that copies of the speech 'may be available from the magazine'; but also the insistence that the Prime Minister's remarks should be read 'in context'.
7. The Institute for Economic Affairs has since taken on the role of strategic advisor for the British Government's policy of privatization of key public amenities.
8. For discussion see Cirillo (1978).
9. All data from Central Statistical Office (1989).
10. For a powerful discussion of the effects of de-industrialization in one

'region' in the United States, the State of Michigan, see Chapter 13 by Stuart Henry and Jeffrey Brown. For a general discussion of the ongoing effects of the 'new' 1980s unemployment in accelerating already existing inequalities (of life chances, etc.) between regions in the United Kingdom, and in creating what they call 'sinks' of unemployment, see Massey and Meegan (1982).

11. For a powerful analysis of the ideological and discursive effects of the Manpower Training Scheme, and other related job-training programmes, in the United Kingdom, see Chapter 3 by Phil Cohen.

12. The notion of an 'over-accelerated' work culture originates from a piece originally published in *Vanity Fair* by Tony Schwartz (1989).

13. See the pioneering study of *The End of Organised Capitalism* Lash and Urry (1987).

14. I have in mind, in particular, the work on the fragmentation of the working class in Britain by the freelance economic analyst, Charles Leadbeater. Cf., for example, Leadbeater (1987).

15. Cf., for example, the discussion of the 'cultural effects' of recent transformations in political economy by Dick Hebdige (1988) as well as the important journalistic commentaries of Zygmunt Bauman (1987, 1988).

16. Cf. the critique of the spiritual impact of consumer culture on everyday life in North America during the 1970s by Christopher Lasch (1979).

17. One example of this trajectory – from progressive politics into a highly generalized, remorselessly pessimistic and politically abstentionist form of post-modern theory – is the work of the Canadian social philosopher, Arthur Kroker, especially in his recent monographs on the condition of North American culture and personal relationships (Kroker and Cook, 1986, 1989; Kroker and Kroker, 1987). Kroker's embrace of nihilism is by no means an isolated example amongst frustrated 'progressive' intellectuals, whether in North America or Europe.

18. Cf., for example, Simon and Gagnon (1986).

19. The charge that the social effects of free market policies have been suppressed from public view by revisions of the ways in which official statistics are collected and presented is well known, especially with respect to the control over information exercised by the Thatcher Government in the United Kingdom. Cf., for example, the report of the 1989 meeting of the Royal Statistical Society by Nick Cohen in *The Independent* (1989). The chapter included in this collection from the Director of the Canadian National Council of Welfare, Ken Battle, is significant for its detailed, and knowledgeable, exposé of the way in which a Conservative government in another country was able to manage not only the presentation of statistics but also its *actual public presentation of policy* – specifically, a policy of cut-back – by the strategic adoption of the language of 'reform' and modernization.

20. For an examination of the uneven, but unmistakeable, impact of free market ideology on public opinion and 'popular expectations of Government' see Duke and Edgell (1991), Chapter 4.

21. For a critique of the free market logics now emerging from the previously corporatist consensus of the European Community, see Patrick Camiller (1989).

22. See Royal Commission (1986). For a useful critique of the process by which the MacDonald Commission went about gathering its evidence from across

Canada, see Daniel Drache and Duncan Cameron (1985). But for a cautious defence of the Commission, see Richard Simeon (1987).

References

Bauman, Z. (1987) 'Fighting the wrong shadow', *New Statesman* 25 September, 20–3.

Bauman, Z. (1988) 'Britain's exit from politics', *New Statesman* 29 July, 34–8.

Brenner, M. H. (1971a) *Time-series Analysis of Relationships between Selected Economic and Social Indicators*, Volume 1, text and appendices, Washington, DC: US Government Printing Office.

Brenner, M. H. (1971b) 'Economic changes and heart disease mortality', *American Journal of Public Health* **61**, 606–11.

Brenner, M. H. (1977) 'Health costs and benefits of economic policy', *International Journal of Health Services* **7**, 581–623.

Brenner, M. H. (1978) 'Impact of economic indicators on crime indices' in *Unemployment and Crime* (Hearing before Subcommittee on the Judiciary, House of Representatives) (59th Congress, first and second sessions), serial no. 47, pp. 20–54.

Brenner, M. H. (1979a) 'Mortality and the national economy: commentary and several principles' in L. A. Ferman and J. P. Gordus (eds.) *Mental Health and the Economy*, Kalamazoo, MI: W. E. Upjohn Institute for Employment Research.

Brenner, M. H. (1979b) 'Mortality and the national economy: a review of the experience of England and Wales 1936–1976', *The Lancet* **ii**, 568–73.

Camiller, P. (1989) 'Towards a continental politics', *New Left Review* **175** (May/June), 5–18.

Central Statistical Office (1989) *Social Trends 19*, Table 4.22, London: Central Statistical Office.

Cheung, S. N. S. (1978) *The Myth of Social Cost: A critique of welfare economics and its implications for public policy*, London: Institute of Economic Affairs. (Prologue by Charles K. Rowley and Epilogue by John Burton.)

Cirillo, R. (1978) *Economics of Vilfredo Pareto*, London: Cass.

Coase, R. H. (1960) 'The problem of social cost', *Journal of Law and Economics* **III** (October) 1–45.

Drache, D. and D. Cameron (eds.) (1985) *The Other MacDonald Report*, Toronto: James Lorimer.

Duke, V. and Edgell, S. (1991) *A Measure of Thatcherism*, London: Unwin Hyman.

Friedman, M. (1962) *Capitalism and Freedom*, Chicago: University of Chicago Press.

Friedman, M. (1970) *Counter Revolution in Monetary Theory* (Wincott Memorial Lecture), London: Institute of Economic Affairs.

Hall, S. and M. Jacques (eds.) (1983) *The Politics of Thatcherism*, London: Lawrence & Wishart.

Hannington, W. (1937) *The Problem of the Distressed Areas*, London: Gollancz (Left Book Club).

Hayek, F. A. (1944) *The Road to Freedom*, London: Routledge.

Hayek, F. A. (1948) *Individualism and Economic Order*, Chicago: University of Chicago Press.

Hayek, F. A. (1960) *The Constitution of Liberty*, London: Routledge & Kegan Paul.

Hebdige, D. (1988) *Hiding in the Light*, London: Comedia.

Kroker, A. and D. Cook (1986) *The Post-modern Scene: Excremental culture and hyperaesthetics*, Montreal: New World Perspectives.

Kroker, A. and D. Cook (1989) *The Panic Encyclopedia*, Montreal: New World Perspectives.

Kroker, A. and M. Kroker (eds.) (1987) *Body Invaders: Panic sex in America*, Montreal: New World Perspectives.

Lasch, C. (1979) *The Culture of Narcissism: American life in an age of diminishing expectations*, New York: W. W. Norton.

Lash, S. and J. Urry (1987) *The End of Organised Capitalism*, Cambridge: Polity Press.

Leadbeater, C. (1987) *The Politics of Prosperity*, Fabian Society Tract No. 523, London: Fabian Society.

Massey, D. and R. Meegan (1982) *The Anatomy of Job Loss*, London: Methuen.

Pareto, V. (1980) *Manual of Political Economy* (ed. by A. S. Schweir and A. N. Page), New York: Kelley.

Pigou, A. C. (1920) *The Economics of Welfare*, London: Macmillan.

Rowley, C. K. (1978) 'The "problem" of social cost', in S. N. S. Cheung, *The Myth of Social Cost*, p. 18, London: Institute of Economic Affairs.

Royal Commission (1986) *Royal Commission of the Economic Union and Development Prospects for Canada* (The MacDonald Report), Ottawa: Supply and Services.

Schwartz, T. (1989) 'Acceleration syndrome: does everyone live in the fast lane nowadays?', *Utne Reader* (The Best of the Alternative Press) **31**, 36–41. (Originally published in *Vanity Fair*.)

Seabrook, J. (1982) *Unemployment*, London: Quartet.

Simeon, R. (1987) 'Inside the MacDonald Commission', *Studies in Political Economy* **22**, 167–79.

Simon, W. and J. H. Gagnon (1986) 'The anomie of affluence: a post-Mertonian conception', *American Journal of Sociology* **92** (2), 356–78.

Sinfield, A. (1980) 'Unemployment in an unequal society' in B. Showler and A. Sinfield (eds.) *The Workless State*, Oxford: Martin Robertson.

Sinfield, A. (1981) *What Unemployment Means*, Oxford: Martin Robertson.

Smith, R. (1988) *Unemployment and Health*, Oxford: Oxford University Press.

Steinfels, P. (1979) *The Neo-Conservatives*, New York: Simon & Schuster.

Stern, J. (1981) *Unemployment and Its Impact on Morbidity and Mortality*, London School of Economics, Centre for Labour Economics, Discussion Paper No. 93.

Stern, J. (1982a) *The Relationship between Unemployment, Morbidity and Mortality*, London School of Economics, Centre for Labour Economics, Discussion Paper No. 427.

Stern, J. (1982b) 'Does unemployment really kill?', *New Society*, 10 June, 421–2.

The Independent (1989) 'Statisticians demand an end to "manipulation" of figures', 7 December.

The Observer (1989) 'Capitalism: opiate of the masses', 10 September.

Weekend Guardian (1989) 'The death of ideology and the dawn of new thought in both East and West', 16–17 December, p. 17.

Wilkinson, E. (1939) *The Town that was Murdered*, London: Gollancz (Left Book Club).

PART 1
United Kingdom

2

The strategy of inequality
Poverty and income distribution in Britain 1979–89

Alan Walker
Department of Sociological Studies, University of Sheffield, United Kingdom

Introduction

The free market ideology of the New Right has been firmly entrenched in government in Britain for the last decade. The Conservative administration headed by Mrs Thatcher, elected first in 1979 and subsequently re-elected in 1983 and 1987, has been the most ideologically committed government since the 1945–50 Labour Government. Indeed Mrs Thatcher has, rather flatteringly, been awarded an 'ism' to append to her name to denote the British brand of New Right ideology and practice and she has gained notoriety at home and abroad for her resolute pursuit of them. This Government, particularly in its first two periods of office, projected its neo-liberal ideas primarily in economic terms, such as free enterprise and monetarism. But Thatcherism, like all other variations on the New Right theme, has been as much a social strategy as an economic one. In fact Britain may be said to have undergone a unique social experiment over the last decade – in acting as a test-bed for the trial of a series of neo-liberal-style policies in the context of an established welfare state – with some of its hapless citizens, particularly the poorest and most vulnerable, as the guinea pigs.

One of the chief targets for the Government's hostility has been the welfare state, because it represents the embodiment of the extended state created and legitimized by social democracy. As a result the welfare state has undergone a mixture of restructuring, marketization, privatization and straightforward cuts over the last decade, with some of the most radical measures being introduced in the Thatcher administration's third term. It is important to assess the social impact of these policies – not least to determine whether or not the experiment has been a success – and the main purpose of this chapter is to do so with regard to the distribution of income and life chances. In particular there is the social impact of monetarism and the Government's pursuit of inequality as a conscious act of social policy. This analysis reveals a growing divide between rich and poor, and the return of inequalities not witnessed in Britain on such a large scale for a hundred years.

This ideological and practical assault on the welfare assumptions, values and structures established in the Keynes–Beveridge settlement and sustained over thirty years of political consensus has been accompanied by its own neo-liberal justification. In particular there is the Government's assertion that its strategy of increasing the incomes of the better-off will improve the life chances of the worse-off. The main elements of this case are reviewed as a prelude to the examination of their impact. The final section of the chapter addresses why these New Right policies, which are at odds with some of the values underlying one of the world's most long-established welfare states, were introduced with so little resistance, and what alternative policies might be assembled to reverse the strategy of inequality and its social impact.

The New Right's social and economic strategy

The New Right is not a unified social movement with a monolithic doctrine. It is a combination of distinct liberal and neo-conservative discourses. The market liberal dimension is concerned with the conditions necessary for a free economy, while the neo-conservative dimension gives priority to the maintenance of authority particularly in civil society. In combination there is a coincidence of interest in the promotion of a 'free economy and a strong state' (Gamble, 1988). But, equally, there is an inherent tension between the enhancement of state power, necessary to ensure that the market order is maintained and policed, and the danger that state authority will inhibit a free economy. These part-complementary and part-conflicting interests are characteristic of the New Right and the Thatcherite variation in Britain is no exception.

Like most right-wing ideologies a clear distinction is made by the New Right between two spheres of state intervention (Dunleavy and O'Leary, 1987). On the one hand there is the state's role in providing a legal framework for the market and civil society, protecting national security as well as upholding traditional moral values and, on the other hand, there is the role of the state in the management of the economy (including the promotion of employment) and the redistribution of income. The New Right favours intervention of the first sort and disapproves of the second sort, whereas left-wing ideologies usually reverse this order. The first is said to require a small, but strong, state while the second implies an extensive state apparatus.

Thatcherism is most closely identified with the supply-side macro-economic prescriptions of monetarism and, since 1985, neo-monetarism. At a technical level monetarism is concerned with the control of the money supply to generate non-inflationary growth. It is the duty of a responsible government to ensure that the rate of growth of the money supply does not exceed the growth of output, otherwise inflationary pressures will occur. During the 1980s this supply-side thesis increasingly dominated the macro-economic policies of other western (and some eastern) societies. But as well as being a doctrine of economic management, monetarism is the macro-economic element of a much broader economic and social philosophy. The policies of the Thatcher Governments of the 1980s cannot be understood unless the other key elements of this philosophy are taken into account.

At the heart of the New Right's economic and social strategy is the commitment to individualism. In the economic sphere there is the conviction that if the economy is free it has an inherent capacity to expand and prosper. In other spheres a similarly negative concept of freedom – freedom from coercion – also reflects the sanctity of the individual. Economic and social order spring from the unplanned and unintended consequences of cooperation between self-interested individuals. In these conditions free enterprise will operate to full effect, spearheaded by a minority of entrepreneurs and risk-takers and will foster economic growth (Friedman and Friedman, 1980). Thus economic growth forms a primary integrative force in society through the commitment it commands from individuals ('economic men') operating in a free market to maximize their welfare. The market is idealized to the point that it is regarded as the most efficient mechanism for distributing virtually all goods and services.

The strategy of the New Right is not based solely on a belief in the effectiveness of the free market: there is also a strong conviction that state intervention in the market is damaging. Not all forms of state intervention are opposed, indeed as indicated above such measures may be necessary to uphold the free market system, but any attempt to plan or 'politicize' the market itself is certainly quite stringently opposed (Bosanquet, 1982, p. 7). Thus the Thatcher Governments have concentrated on the removal of direct state intervention in the market, including the labour market, by deregulation, but have increased the regulations governing trade unions. There are also severe dangers said to be associated with the growth of public expenditure in both crowding out private investment and in the deleterious impact of high tax levels on entrepreneurship and financial incentives. Hence the numerous measures taken to limit the growth of public spending over the last ten years (Walker, 1982; Robinson, 1986; Hills, 1987).

As a result of the commitment to individualism and the primacy of an unfettered market, inequality is a fundamental assumption of the New Right model. This belief in inequality is based on the negative view that intervention in the economic sphere to create greater equality would entail unacceptable levels of coercion and limitations to individual freedom as well as economically damaging consequences. But, in addition, there is the positive view of inequality as both the proper outcome of the operation of the market – reflecting differences in rewards based on individual talent and initiative – and as a source of incentives in society. As Sir Keith Joseph (Joseph and Sumption, 1979, p. 78) put it: 'Since inequality arises from the operation of innumerable individual preferences it cannot be evil unless those preferences are themselves evil'. Although the various components of the New Right-inspired Thatcher Governments can be analyzed separately, the strategy under-lying them consists of a coherent fusion of the economic and the social. This much was clear from the very early days of the first Thatcher administration (see, for example, Walker *et al.*, 1979). For example, the Government's first Budget speech stressed four 'principles' which extended far beyond conventionally defined economic management:

> First, the strengthening of incentives, particularly through tax cuts, allowing people to keep more of their earnings in their own hands, so that hard work, ability and success are rewarded; second, greater freedom of choice by reducing the state's role and enlarging that of the individual; third, the reduction of the borrowing requirement of the public sector which leaves room for the rest of the economy to prosper; and fourth, through firm monetary and fiscal discipline bringing inflation under control and ensuring that those taking part in collective bargaining are obliged to live with the consequences of their actions. (House of Commons, 1979, col. 240)

Thus 'monetarism' was the leading edge of the Thatcher Government's economic and social strategy aimed at promoting inequality, reducing the role of the state in a wide range of long-accepted areas, encouraging free enterprise and individual initiative and breaking the power of trade unions. Moreover this was obviously conceived of as a strategy to transform economic and social relations permanently, and not one for the lifetime of a single Parliament that might be overturned by the whim of the electorate. The establishment of a free economy and low tax regime would reduce the scope for future government intervention to alter the distribution of income in favour of greater equality. A smaller and tightly controlled public sector coupled with strong and poorly regulated financial markets would ensure that any politicians tempted to argue for increased public expenditure would be kept in check. With a small state, closed to corporatist influences, and in the face of a dual labour market, it was expected that trade unions would be exposed to the discipline of the market.

Policies towards the welfare state

As the embodiment of the interventionist and egalitarian sentiments of social democracy, as represented in the post-Second World War settlement, the welfare state has attracted much of the New Right's philosophical disapproval and, therefore, the Thatcher Government's practical attention. The Government's neo-liberal-inspired strategy towards the welfare state, in essence a strategy of inequality, consists of five main interwoven strands. First, cutting social expenditure. Second, state-subsidized privatization or the extension of market principles (e.g. charges) within the welfare state. Third, replacing universal benefits and services, such as unemployment benefit, with selective or 'targeted' ones. Fourth, reducing taxation to provide incentives and encourage the growth of alternative forms of private and voluntary welfare. Fifth, centralization of resource control and decentralization of responsibility for operations, thereby neutralizing any potential power of welfare state users to increase the share of public expenditure devoted to them.

The Government came to power in 1979 committed to rolling back the frontiers of the welfare state. It insisted in its first public expenditure white papers that 'Higher public expenditure cannot any longer be allowed to precede, and thus prevent, growth in the private sector' (HM Treasury, 1979, p. 2). The specific objective has been to limit the growth of public spending below the rate of economic growth and thereby 'reduce public spending as a proportion of national income' (HM Treasury, 1988, p. 4). In view of the fact that expenditure on welfare state services makes up nearly two-thirds of total expenditure (social security alone makes up one-third of the total) a policy of constraint could not avoid these programmes even if ideology had not placed them in the firing line. Moreover, because the Government has increased expenditure to promote its own authority (e.g. defence) and that of the market (e.g. subsidies to the private sector), public welfare has had to yield a much larger than average proportion of spending cuts.

During the Thatcher Government's first two terms of office, measures affecting the traditional realm of the welfare state were largely confined to the over-all policy of constraint on spending, piecemeal privatization and limiting the scope of social security by targeting benefits towards the poorest. Some programmes were cut directly, particularly housing which has been reduced by nearly two-thirds since 1978–9 (HM Treasury, 1988, p. 149), while the growth of others has been held back relative to inflation and the rise in need resulting, for example, from demographic changes. The health service, particularly the hospital sector, has been systematically underfunded in this way (Social Services Committee, 1986).

The most significant single cut occurred within the social security system when, soon after coming to office, the Government altered the uprating rule for pensions and related benefits so that they were no longer linked to rises in earnings, only prices. This has cut a cumulative sum of £10,000 million from the social security budget and reduced the pension for an elderly couple by more than £17.50 per week (or 25 per cent) compared to what it would have been had the earnings link been retained. However, most of the big distributional changes were implemented outside the traditional welfare state by fiscal and employment policy. This consisted of a strategy of reducing income tax particularly at the higher rates, to encourage enterprise through financial incentives, and the shift from an active demand-side programme of job creation to a more passive supply-side one focused on training and reductions in unit-labour costs.

With the advent of Mrs Thatcher's third term in office, following the 1987 General Election, the attack on the welfare state was stepped up considerably. Thus a barrage of major policies were introduced in the late 1980s in all sectors of the welfare state which, without the benefit of hindsight, seemed to represent a concerted move against what was seen as the last important challenge to the spread of neo-liberal values in civil society. Certainly the Government's rhetoric against the welfare state became more strident in this period, as exemplified in a series of speeches by the then Secretary of State for Social Services, John Moore.

In a widely quoted speech, in September 1987, Mr Moore set out the Government's case against the welfare state and revealed that 'the next step forward in the long evolutionary march of the welfare state in Britain is away from dependency towards independence' (Moore, 1987, p. 2). In the first place it was asserted that state welfare creates dependency and, by implication, that dependency on the state is the most morally debilitating form of dependency:

> this kind of climate can in time corrupt the human spirit. Everyone knows the sullen apathy of dependence and can compare it with the sheer delight of personal achievement. To deliberately set up a system that creates the former instead of the latter is the act directly against. . . the welfare of individuals and society. (Moore, 1987, p. 7)

Secondly there was the classic *laissez-faire* aversion to the public sector – that it stifles individual initiative and responsibility – and the belief that the market offers consumers greater choice. The assumption underlying this aversion to the welfare state is that it took over functions once performed by self-help, by the family and by charities. Therefore, it is argued, if the frontiers of the state can be rolled back, these forms of provision will reassert themselves. The belief that the market offers the prospect of greater choice and consumer power is based on the theory of consumer sovereignty.

Thirdly it was argued that the goal of welfare should be subservient to the goals of economic growth and the creation of an enterprise culture. The assumption behind this argument is that the fruits of economic growth, spearheaded by entrepreneurs, 'trickle down' to benefit the rest of society, including the poor. In the words of another former Secretary of State, Lord Young (1985, p. 2):

> Successful enterprise does bring material reward in society. General standards of living rose steadily and substantially through most of the Victoria era. . . So in looking at the generation of Victorian entrepreneurs and the results of their achievements, we need not feel guilty that their success was at the expense of the poor.

Herein lies both the rationale (at least the public rationale) and the moral justification for the strategy of inequality pursued by the Thatcher Government. How far the policy achieved the wider effects claimed for it is discussed in the following section.

The social impact of the Government's strategy

Over the last ten years the Thatcher Government has consistently tried to distance itself from the social effects of its economic policies. Blame is laid elsewhere: individual workers who have 'priced themselves out of jobs', trade unions for bargaining up the unit price of labour and, in the early 1980s, the world recession. However responsibility for economic management cannot be separated so easily from responsibility for its social consequences. This is because macro-economic policies themselves are based on assumptions about the sort of society and structure of social relationships that a government is attempting to create. Choice between economic policies as well as the method of their implementation is not a politically neutral scientific matter of which will function best, but of which policies will achieve the broader social and political aims that the government has set itself. This, as we have seen, monetarism was part of a comprehensive social and economic strategy pursued throughout the period under review.

Economic policies imply a set of distinct social values and distributional goals – which group's living standards will advance and which will decline

– and are therefore also, in part, social policies (Walker, 1984, p. 66). Writing in 1925, when monetarism was also the adopted economic orthodoxy of the British Government, Keynes (1972, p. 207) described the policy as 'simply a campaign against the standard of life of the working classes [operating through] the deliberate intensification of unemployment'. Similarly in the early 1980s it was the Government's excessive overvaluation of sterling that accounted for the much greater rise in unemployment in Britain than other comparable countries (Treasury and Civil Service Committee, 1983). In the first quarter of 1979, the official rate of unemployment in the United Kingdom was 5.9 per cent; by the third quarter of 1982, it had risen to 12.9 per cent. Yet over the same period of world recession the rise in unemployment in the fifteen major OECD countries was less than half that of Britain's: 5.1 per cent to 8.3 per cent.

The social consequences of this Government-created unemployment are discussed in Chapter 3. Here our primary concern is with income distribution. What effect did the Government's social and economic strategy have on the distribution of income in the 1980s? Did trickle-down occur and thereby, to some extent, legitimate the Government's strategy of inequality? Evidence on three interrelated distributional effects of the Government's strategy – poverty, inequalities in income and inequalities in wealth – is reviewed in order to shed light on these questions.

The growth of poverty

The most widely accepted measure of poverty, in Britain and other advanced industrial societies, is with reference to the prevailing levels of social assistance (the 'safety net' state income scheme for those not in employment called, in Britain, supplementary benefit until 1988 and then income support). Although there are obvious difficulties involved in using this social standard of poverty, not least that it may be manipulated by the state, it does have the advantage of being approved annually by Parliament (Townsend, 1979).

A commonly stated objective of the Thatcher Government is to reduce dependency on state benefits. However since the Government took office, the numbers receiving income support (IS) have increased by 45 per cent, from 3 million to 4.35 million. Moreover the total reached nearly 5 million in 1987. When other members of the recipient's families are included, some 7.39 million people were dependent on IS in May 1988, an increase of 75 per cent since 1979 (DSS, 1989, p. 362). Most of this increase was due to the rise in unemployment in the early 1980s referred to earlier. Between 1979 and 1983 the number of people in unemployed families receiving IS (then supplementary benefit) tripled to 2.6 million, overtaking old age as the major characteristic of poverty (Piachaud, 1987, p. 23). Comparative figures for the previous Labour Government show that the numbers of families in receipt of supplementary benefit increased by only 6.6 per cent between 1975 and 1979 and 7.5 per cent when all dependants are included.

While poverty measured by receipt of social assistance increased markedly there is also evidence that the numbers living *below* the state poverty line have risen sharply in the 1980s. Here, however, data are less up to date. Although later information from the annual Family Expenditure Survey is available to the Government (see below) the latest published results (in December 1989) related to 1985. By then the number of families and persons with incomes below the IS level had increased by 14 per cent and 16 per cent respectively. The numbers living below the poverty line peaked in 1983, at 2.78 million, again following the pattern of unemployment. In addition the numbers of families headed by someone earning a wage below the poverty line showed a marked increase, of nearly one-fifth, between 1979 and 1985 (DHSS, 1988).

The numbers of people living on the margins of poverty (with relative net resources below 40 per cent of the relevant IS level) have also followed the upward trend of the 1980s. In 1985 some 8.5 million people were living on the margins of poverty compared with 7.6 million in 1979. Table 2.1 summarizes the data on poverty. As these data suggest, the 1980s was a period of increased economic insecurity for a significant minority of the British people, involving some three in ten of the population in the early 1980s. While the macro social and economic

Table 2.1   The increase in poverty

Persons below IS level	1979	2,090,000
	1983	2,780,000
	1985	2,420,000
Number receiving IS	1978–9	3,020,000
(not including dependants)	1987–8	4,930,000
	1988–9	4,352,000
Persons on IS or below	1979	6,070,000
IS level	1983	8,910,000
	1985	9,380,000
Persons on IS or within	1979	11,570,000
40% of IS level	1983	16,380,000
	1985	15,420,000

Note: IS was supplementary benefit until 1988.

Sources: Piachaud (1987, p. 25), DHSS (1988).

strategy was determined centrally by the Government, the social costs associated with this massive increase in economic insecurity are, of course, borne by the individuals affected. What this increase in the incidence of poverty meant for the individuals and families involved has been documented by a wide range of both official and independent research studies. All portray a similar picture of the social imprisonment that poverty entails, constant restriction in virtually every aspect of their lives, poor amenities, poor diets, poor health and premature death.

For example, in 1983 a representative quota sample of the British population was surveyed for London Weekend Television: the findings catalogue the deprivation associated with poverty. This study concentrated on *enforced* lack of basic necessities resulting from low incomes and found just under one in five of those in the bottom 10 per cent of the income range were without necessities such as heating, a warm waterproof coat, sufficient bedrooms for children, and had to buy second-hand clothes and live in damp accommodation (Mack and Lansley, 1985, p. 101). Of those in the bottom decile over half could not afford at least two basic necessities and over one-third could not afford four or more necessities. A smaller-scale study of the living standard of unemployed people and their families living on IS in Tyne and Wear in 1988 concluded that 'The lives of these families, and perhaps most seriously the lives of the children in them, are marked by the unrelieved struggle to manage, with dreary diets and drab clothing' (Bradshaw and Holmes, 1989, p. 138). An earlier study using budget standards techniques to examine how families with children on supplementary benefit spent their money came to a similar conclusion: 'by the standards of living of most families today, the evidence reveals that families on supplementary benefit can only afford an extremely restricted and drab lifestyle' (Bradshaw and Morgan, 1987, p. 13).

Research among the aristocracy of skilled labour in the Sheffield steel industry who had enjoyed rising affluence over the post-Second World War period, but who were among the first victims of the shake-out following the election of the Thatcher Government, found a substantial reduction in income following redundancy and, as a result of both, high levels of distress and anxiety (Westergaard *et al.*, 1989, pp. 95–6). A recent official study of the impact of unemployment found that after three months the average disposable incomes of unemployed families was 59 per cent of previous income levels (Heady and Smyth, 1989).

Recent research has also confirmed the link between poverty and other forms of deprivation. For example a study of health inequalities in the northern region found a close association between indicators of poverty and low incomes and poor health. Furthermore a similar pattern of variation, according to deprivation, class and other social factors, was revealed in premature mortality (Townsend *et al.*, 1988, pp. 75, 84). The national study of poverty and deprivation conducted at the height of the 1980s' recession showed that the poor have the worst housing conditions: three-fifths of households lacking seven or more basic necessities lived in bad housing (Mack and Lansley, 1985, p. 142).

Some ever-present consequences of poverty are that people have to borrow money, go without meals and not buy food. These applied to two in every three of people lacking seven or more necessities in the Breadline Britain study (Mack and Lansley, 1985, p. 158). Not surprisingly, high levels of debt, relative to income, are a common feature of the lives of poor people and one that has grown sharply over the last decade. Emphasizing the individualized and private nature of the social costs of macro-economic policies is the fact that depression and feelings of despair are concentrated on the poor. Thus nine out of ten of those lacking seven or more basic necessities in the Breadline Britain study reported at least one regular worry. Over half reported depression and three-fifths lacked hope for the future (Mack and Lansley, 1985, p. 163).

It has already been shown that much of the poverty and deprivation documented above was the direct result of the Government's monetarist economic strategy. But, at the same time, the Government purposely failed to mitigate some of the social impact of its policies. Indeed, in pursuit of its over-all strategy it actually exacerbated their impact. For example, at the same time as drastically reducing the demand for labour, the Government restricted both the level of social security benefits and the groups entitled to them. Housing benefit, which has risen steeply, and the real growth of pensions and child benefit were restricted. For example in November 1979 the married person's retirement pension was 43.3 per cent of male average earnings; by April 1989 it had been reduced to 32.7 per cent. The figures for child benefit were 4.6 per cent and 3.4 per cent respectively. But it was the series of changes to national insurance unemployment benefit – including changes in the rules for eligibility, and the abolition of child additions and the earnings-related supplement culminating in the benefit being turned into a means-tested one in late 1989 – that demonstrated the intention of the Government to allow the social costs of its policies to lie where they fell.

Young people were particularly harshly exposed by the Government to the effects of its own policies, and especially so in its third term of office. Thus, in April 1988 the eligibility of 16- and 17-year-olds for IS was abolished – one of fourteen cuts in benefits available to young people since 1980 (Randall, 1989, p. 5). The stated objective of the Government was to provide YTS places for all young people but these never materialized (due to delays in the young person getting a place or places not being available). Also there was undoubtedly a determination on the part of the Government to encourage young people to remain at home or to return home. One result of this policy was the surge in homelessness and destitution among young people in the late 1980s (Randall, 1989). In the words of a recent report from the National Association of Citizens Advice Bureaux (NACAB, 1989, pp. 7–8): 'Throughout the country CABX have been seeing young people who are sleeping rough, penniless, and who are unable, for a variety of reasons, to return home. . . The distress experienced by young people in this situation is very acute.' The same report highlights the stark choice faced by some families between getting into debt or evicting their son or daughter.

Another example of the way in which the social policy component of the Government's strategy has worsened the impact of its economic policies is the scrapping of additions to IS to meet special needs, in April 1988, and the introduction of a cash-limited social fund to provide loans to claimants. This has meant that high-priority needs have been refused because there is insufficient money available. A recent national survey of CABX users found that four-fifths of unemployed people, one-fifth of lone parents and four-fifths of single young people were refused loans (NACAB, 1990, p. 3).

The growing divide

As well as increasing poverty and deprivation over the 1980s, the neo-liberal-inspired social and economic policies of the Thatcher Government have thrown into sharp reverse the slow post-Second World War trend towards a narrowing of differentials in income and wealth. The strategy of inequality has been pursued by policies directed at both ends of the income distribution. Despite the expansion in need created by its own policies, as we have seen, the Government cut social security spending. In addition it reduced the incomes of the lowest-paid workers by, for example, removing protective legislation. At the same time it embarked on the most radical tax strategy attempted in the post-war period.

In 1979 4.64 million adult full-time workers in Britain (over 28 per cent) earned less than the Council of Europe's decency threshold, according to official statistics. By 1989 this had increased to nearly 6 million – 37 per cent of all full-time adult employees (Bryson, 1989, p. 11). Moreover the gap between the highest and lowest paid has widened markedly. Since 1979 average gross weekly earnings of the highest paid fifth of men have increased by 190.6 per cent, while those of the lowest paid fifth have risen by 131 per cent. In fact the poorest paid are now worse off in relation to the highest paid than they were in 1986 when such statistics were first collected, with the difference reaching its widest point, so far, in 1989 (Byrne, 1987; Bryson, 1989). The main factors behind this widening pay divide in the 1980s were the growth of unemployment in the early part of the decade and the rise in the number of poorly paid service sector jobs in the latter half of the decade. Again government policies were influential, including the rescinding of the Fair Wages Resolution, repeal of part of the Employment Protection Act 1975, weakening of the wages councils (that set the minimum wages for many of the lowest paid) and the introduction of employment subsidy schemes designed to depress low wages still further. Young people were specifically targeted by some of these and other measures and, as a result, their earnings have fallen relative to older age groups (in 1989 the earnings of 18–20-year-olds were 53.8 per cent of the earnings of those aged 21 and over, compared with 60.8 per cent in 1979). The only small ray of light in the gloom of these low-pay statistics is the slight narrowing of the differential in women's earnings as a percentage of men's, from 73 per cent in 1979 to 76.4 per cent in 1989 (Bryson, 1989, p. 13).

This side of the two-pronged strategy of inequality was matched by a new tax policy aimed at a massive reverse redistribution of incomes from poor to rich:

> Capital taxes on rentier incomes were virtually abolished, although taxation of the corporate sector was allowed to increase, perhaps reflecting the Government's preference for finance rather than industrial capital. Wage taxation also increased, within the context of a sharp redistribution of the tax burden from the rich towards the poor. The once progressive system of income tax was converted into virtually a single rate structure, with 95 per cent of tax payers subject to the same basic rate of tax. (Pond, 1989a, pp. 35–6)

The regressivity of the tax system has been enhanced by a sharp increase in national insurance (NI) contributions (in part a knock-on effect of increased unemployment). For every £1 raised in income tax in 1988–9 NI contributions raised 76p whereas in 1978–9 it was only 53p (Pond, 1989b, p. 111). NI contributions are extremely regressive in their effect because of the 'poverty trap' they help to create for low wage-earners by their low exemption threshold and, at the opposite end of the income distribution, the upper ceiling on contributions.

The fact that these tax changes have been targeted on the better-off and particularly on the very wealthy can be demonstrated by looking at their distribution. Between 1979 and 1989 a cumulative total of some £91,000 million was cut from income tax. Of this total just under three-tenths (29 per cent) went to the top 1 per cent of taxpayers, over half went to the top 10 per cent, and the bottom half of taxpayers received only 12 per cent of the tax cuts, with the bottom tenth getting just 1 per cent (House of Commons, 1988, col. 30). Not surprisingly, therefore, the tax burden shifted dramatically during the 1980s: single people earning half the average wage saw their income tax burden (including NI contributions) increase by 7 per cent between 1978–9 and 1987–8, while those earning ten times the average received a cut of 21 per cent. The comparable figures for a married couple with two children were 163 per cent and 21 per cent (Byrne, 1987, p. 32).

The main effect of this dual strategy to promote both high and low pay has been to halt the slow post-Second World War trend in Britain towards a reduction of inequality in the distribution of pre-tax incomes. Using the Gini coefficient as an over-all measure of the degree of inequality, Stark (1987, p. 6) has shown both the long-term decline in pre-tax income inequality, from a Gini coefficient of 41.1 in 1949 to 37.5 in 1978–9, and the sharp reversal of this trend in the early 1980s when, by 1981–2, the coefficient had reached 40.0. (The Gini coefficient ranges from 0 to 100, i.e. from complete equality to a situation where all the income is received by one person.) Later information reveals that this is a continuing trend, even when the impact of taxes and benefits is taken into account. By 1985–6 the richest fifth of the population were receiving 42 per cent of final (post-tax and benefits) income compared with 38 per cent in 1979. In contrast the poorest fifth of households saw their already small share of income cut from 7.1 per cent to 6.3 per cent (CSO, 1989).

The data show that the Government's strategy of inequality has imposed, on an already unequal structure of income and wealth, a more extreme social polarization than has been seen previously in post-war Britain. This 'growing divide' (Walker and Walker, 1987) is reflected in regional disparities in income and life chances but also within regions. Thus an extreme North–South divide has been created in the 1980s by increasingly sharp differences in incomes, unemployment and government spending. For example, in 1979 the average earnings of full-time male workers in the northern region were 91.9 per cent of those in the South-east; by 1986 they had declined to 82.8 per cent (Winyard, 1987, p. 45).

There is evidence too of widening inequalities in health, with, for example, a more rapid decline in death rates among higher than lower social classes and increasing differences in chronic sickness rates between manual and non-manual groups (Whitehead, 1988, p. 266). Within regions there is an increasing social polarization between rich and poor as their incomes, forms of consumption and life chances become more widely differentiated. A recent study in London found that between 1981 and 1985 the disposable income of the poorest fifth of households in

London fell by 14 per cent while that of the richest increased by 7 per cent (Townsend, 1987a). In 1986 the Archbishop of Canterbury's Commission (1986) on urban priority areas highlighted this new phenomenon:

> rich and poor, suburban and inner city, privileged and deprived, have been becoming more sharply separated from each other for many years. . . the impoverished minority has become increasingly cut off from the mainstream of our national life. . . These trends add up to a pattern warranting the label of polarisation in a new, comprehensive and intractable form.

This extreme form of social polarization that has been created by government policies in the 1980s has led some commentators to conclude that a significant underclass exists and is growing rapidly (Dahrendorf, 1987; Murray, 1989). However such analyses are largely speculative and offer little objective evidence of a detached minority with different values and aspirations from the rest of society, as distinct from being simply a social expression of the strategy of inequality as outlined above (Walker, 1990). Scientific investigations among those who have been so fundamentally affected by these neo-liberal-inspired policies conclude that far from being a culturally detached group they share the values of wider society but lack the resources necessary to participate fully in that society:

> They are just the same people as the rest of our population, with the same culture and aspirations but with simply too little money to be able to share in the activities and possessions of everyday life with the rest of the population. (Bradshaw and Holmes, 1989, p. 138)

In sum then, as a conscious act of public policy, the Thatcher administration implemented and sustained throughout the 1980s a radical strategy aimed at widening already substantial inequalities in income and wealth. Cuts in social security benefits and protective machinery for low wage-earners have been coupled with massive reductions in income and wealth taxation for those at the top end of the income distribution. Moreover these changes have been exacerbated by reductions in welfare state services in relation to growing needs created in part by government policies (Hills, 1987, p. 96). Since there was a sustained period of economic growth in the 1980s it is possible to test the Government's thesis that the fruits of this growth would trickle down to the poor. In fact what the evidence shows, as we have seen, is that the share of total income and wealth commanded by the poor has actually been reduced. This indicates that the economic prosperity of the better-off has been built, in large measure, on the reduced incomes of the poor. Therefore the attempt to justify the strategy of inequality in terms of the benefits it would supposedly yield for the worse-off was, at best, misguided and was more likely a deliberate attempt by the Government to mislead the people about its true intentions.

Support for the more cynical of these conclusions concerning the Thatcher Government's motivation for its strategy of inequality is reinforced by the various attempts that it made to obscure the real social effects of its policies. The changes in the presentation of official unemployment statistics, more than twenty since 1979, have been well documented (Taylor, 1987) as have the attempts to cover up information on inequalities in health (Townsend, 1987b). In addition, the House of Commons Social Services Committee issued a report in 1988 that was critical of both the Government's failure to release data on poverty and low incomes promptly and its decision to change the basis for the calculation of these statistics which resulted in a significant reduction in the recording of those living on low incomes (Social Services Committee, 1988).

Conclusion: towards an alternative strategy?

The preceding analysis begs this question: why was the Government able, with electoral impunity, to pursue its strategy of inequality? First, the Government's arguments have been convincing, not simply because they were well presented but because they provided solutions to widely perceived problems such as inflation, high rates of taxation and trade union power. In particular, the Government was regarded as competent at economic management and, at elections, this issue has outweighed concerns about social justice. Second, there was the lack of an alternative: the Labour Party was in disarray for much of the 1980s. Third, the strategy of inequality itself has only severely disadvantaged a substantial minority of society while ensuring rising living standards for the majority. This two-thirds/one-third strategy is designed to minimize electoral risk. Fourth, the Government has recognized and exploited the faults in the traditional welfare state, particularly the intrusive control it exerted over the lives of its users.

In addition to these negative lessons there are positive ones which suggest that there is a basis for an alternative democratic socialist strategy to be developed in the 1990s. In the first place, the main lesson for the Left from 1980s neo-liberal-style policies is their demonstration of the interconnectedness of economic and social policy (Walker, 1984). This provides the opening for the reorientation of both economic and social policies away from market individualism towards social justice: for example, in the form of policies to promote a more equal distribution of employment and greater equality of incomes between different socio-economic groups in employment as well as between the employed and non-employed (Walker, 1985). Secondly, while the New Right articulated the deficiencies of the welfare state it failed to recognize the wide consensus underlying the redistributory functions of state welfare. Thus the Government's success at altering the goals and institutions of the welfare state has not been matched by any shift, so far, in the fundamental values in British society that gave birth to the welfare state. These include a belief in 'fair shares' in income, wealth and taxation and support for free universal access to certain (if not all) welfare services (Taylor-Gooby, 1985). This important role for collective responsibility is likely to be reinforced, in the 1990s, by both the rise of the welfare state, that existed even before 1979, and particularly the welfare state's inability to abolish poverty, its unresponsiveness to need and its lack of democratic accountability. Thus, as the New Right has demonstrated, the welfare apparatus of the state requires radical overhaul.

One attempt by democratic socialists to rearticulate the values underlying the post-war settlement, but in the light of the lessons learnt about the welfare state during the 1980s and in earlier decades, has been called the social economy and the democratic state (The Sheffield Group, 1989). This would mean, on the one hand, a refusal of social and economic policy geared towards meeting needs and, on the other, a more open, participative and democratic state reflecting the rights and duties of citizenship. This strategy is based on a new conception of welfare consisting of an assessment of common human needs. It implies the transformation of social welfare from a *residual* economic category depending on surplus economic growth into a rationale for economic management in the general interest. The division between social security for the poor and fiscal and private welfare for the rich would be replaced by universal provision based on the assessment of need and rights associated with citizenship. The State and the individual would operate in partnership, with the former providing or enabling economic security while the latter's first duty would be employment (including domestic labour, education and training).

The prospects for this sort of alternative strategy look distinctly rosier at the end of the 1980s than they did at the beginning of the decade. Indeed the failure of the Thatcher Government to mitigate even the worst social effects of its own policies may have contributed to the chances of alternative policies favouring social justice. The main question for the 1990s is, therefore, has the strategy of inequality been successful in changing the post-Second World War consensus on welfare or does it contain the seeds of its own destruction?

References

Archbishop of Canterbury's Commission (1986) *Faith in the City*, London: Church House.

Bosanquet, N. (1982) *After the New Right*, London: Heinemann.

Bradshaw, J. and H. Holmes (1989) *Living on the Edge*, Tyneside: CPAG.

Bradshaw, J. and J. Morgan (1987) *Budgeting in Benefit*, London: Family Policy Studies Centre.

Bryson, A. (1989) 'The 80s: decade of poverty', *Low Pay Unit Review*, No. 1, 11–14.

Byrne, D. (1987) 'Rich and poor: the growing divide' in A. Walker and C. Walker (eds.) *The Growing Divide: A social audit 1979–1987*, pp. 27–8, London: CPAG.

CSO (1989) *Economic Trends*, London: HMSO.

Dahrendorf, R. (1987) 'The underclass and the future of Britain', Tenth Annual Lecture, St George's House, Windsor Castle.

DHSS (1988) *Low Income Families – 1985*, London: HMSO.

DSS (1989) *Social Security Statistics 1989*, London: HMSO.

Dunleavy, P. and B. O'Leary (1987) *Theories of the State*, London: Macmillan.

Friedman, M. and R. Friedman (1980) *Free to Choose*, Harmondsworth: Penguin.

Gamble, A. (1988) *The Free Economy and the Strong State*, London: Macmillan.

Heady, P. and M. Smyth (1989) *Living Standards During Unemployment*, London: HMSO.

Hills, J. (1987) 'What happened to spending on the welfare state?' in A. Walker and C. Walker (eds.) *The Growing Divide: A social audit 1979–1987*, pp. 88–100, London: CPAG.

HM Treasury (1979) *The Government's Expenditure Plans 1979/80 to 1982/83*, Cmnd 7439, London: HMSO.

HM Treasury (1988) *The Government's Expenditure Plans 1987/88 to 1990/91*, Cmnd 288, London: HMSO.

House of Commons (1979) *Hansard*, 12 June.

House of Commons (1988) *Hansard*, 9 May.

Joseph, K. and J. Sumption (1979) *Equality*, London: John Murray.

Keynes, J. M. (1972) *The Economic Consequences of Mr Churchill*, Hogarth Press, 1925; republished in the *Collected Writings of John Maynard Keynes*, Vol. 9, London: Macmillan.

Mack, J. and S. Lansley (1985) *Poor Britain*, London: Allen & Unwin.

Moore, J. (1987) *Speech to Conservative Constituency Parties*, 26 September.

Murray, C. (1989) 'Underclass', *The Sunday Times Magazine*, 26 November.

NACAB (1989) *Income Support and 16–17 Year Olds*, London: NACAB.

NACAB (1990) *Hard Times for Social Fund Applicants*, London: NACAB.

Piachaud, D. (1987) 'The growth of poverty' in A. Walker and C. Walker (eds.) *The Growing Divide: A Social Audit 1979–1987*, pp. 20–25, London: CPAG.

Pond, C. (1989a) 'The changing distribution of income, wealth and poverty' in Open University, *Restructuring Britain*, D314, Milton Keynes: Open University.

Pond, C. (1989b) 'Socialism and the politics of taxation' in The Sheffield Group, *The Social Economy and the Democratic State*, pp. 110–31, London: Lawrence & Wishart.

Randall, G. (1989) *Homeless and Hungry*, London: Centrepoint Soho.

Robinson, R. (1986) 'Restructuring the welfare state: an analysis of public expenditure, 1979/80 – 1984/5', *Journal of Social Policy* **15**, 1–22.

Social Services Committee (1986) *Public Expenditure on the Social Services*, 26 July, London: HMSO.

Social Services Committee (1988) *Families on Low Income: Low income statistics*, HC 565, 29 June, London: HMSO.

Stark, T. (1987) *Income and Wealth in the 1980s*, London: Fabian Society.

Taylor, D. (1987) 'Living with unemployment' in A. Walker and C. Walker (eds.) *The Growing Divide: A social audit 1979–1987*, pp. 70–81, London: CPAG.

Taylor-Gooby, P. (1985) *Public Opinion, Ideology and State Welfare*, London: Routledge & Kegan Paul.

The Sheffield Group (1989) *The Social Economy and the Democratic State*, London: Lawrence & Wishart.

Townsend, P. (1979) *Poverty in the United Kingdom*, Harmondsworth: Penguin.

Townsend, P. (1987a) *Poverty and Labour in London*, London: Low Pay Unit.

Townsend, P. (1987b) 'Poor Health' in A. Walker and C. Walker (eds.) *The Growing Divide: A social audit 1979–1987*, pp. 82–7, London: CPAG.

Townsend, P., P. Phillimore and A. Beattie (1988) *Health and Deprivation*, London: Croom Helm.

Treasury and Civil Service Committee (1983) *International Monetary Arrangements*, House of Commons, Session 1982–83, London: HMSO.

Walker, A. (1982) (ed.) *Public Expenditure and Social Policy*, London: Heinemann.

Walker, A. (1984) *Social Planning*, Oxford: Basil Blackwell.

Walker, A. (1985) 'Policies for sharing the job shortage: reducing or redistributing unemployment?' in R. Klein and M. O'Higgins (eds.) *The Future of Welfare*, pp. 166–85, Oxford: Basil Blackwell.

Walker, A. (1990) *Blaming the Victims*, London: Institute of Economic Affairs.

Walker, A. and C. Walker (1987) (eds.) *The Growing Divide: A social audit 1979–1987*, London: CPAG.

Walker, A., P. Ormerod and L. Whitty (1979) *Abandoning Social Priorities*, London: CPAG.

Westergaard, J., I. Noble and A. Walker (1989) *After Redundancy*, Oxford: Polity Press.

Whitehead, M. (1988) *The Health Divide*, Harmondsworth: Penguin.

Winyard, S. (1987) 'Divided Britain' in A. Walker and C. Walker (eds.) *The Growing Divide: A social audit 1979–1987*, pp. 39–49, London: CPAG.

Young, Lord D. (1985) Speech at St Lawrence Jewry, 6 November.

3

Teaching enterprise culture
Individualism, vocationalism and the New Right

Philip Cohen
Institute of Education, University of London, United Kingdom

Thatcherism as a fairy story

Fairy stories, unlike myths, are woven out of the materials of everyday life, and, unlike daydreams or fantasies, show us how we can symbolically overcome the frustrations engendered by our encounters with the social structures we inhabit, in order to 'live happily ever after'. Adults tell them to children in order that they may learn to grow up without illusions as to the difficulties in store for them, but with some sense of hope that they may win out in the end.[1] Political ideologies, if they are to work, in the sense of carrying the persuasive force of common sense, must also construct narratives which convince us that the promises they make not only articulate our real wishes, but also possess the means to ensure that they will come true, so that we too will live happily ever after – at least until the next election. According to this view the success of Thatcherism does not lie in the coherence of its policies or even in its strategies of 'impression management' centred on the public persona of the Iron Lady herself, but in the way a certain kind of fairy story has been told to convince us that we can indeed overcome our problems and reach a happy ending, provided we realize that there is no alternative to the plot which is being unfolded before us.

The central theme in the Thatcherite fairy story is that of a nation enslaved by the illusions of socialism being set free and converted into an enterprise culture, thus regaining the greatness which belongs to it by tradition and historical destiny. It is a story made to be told to children because they have a special role to play within it, and it goes something like this:

Once upon a time, Britain was a nation of shopkeepers which became the workshop of the world. Industry and trade prospered, while from an early age fair Albion's sons and daughters prepared themselves diligently for a life of service and toil. But then along came some nasty people with a lot of foreign ideas about poetry and politics, none of which was any good for helping them earn a living or learning the skills which Britain needed to compete in the market-place and stay Great. And so industry declined and trade ceased to prosper, and even some of the shopkeepers went bankrupt. Things got so bad it was decided to have a Great Debate, so that everybody could blame somebody else for the state of affairs. Trade unionists blamed the employers, industrialists blamed the teachers, teachers blamed the government, politicians blamed the world economy, moralists pointed the finger at the permissive society, while ecologists put it down to the impact of new technologies and almost everyone blamed young people and the working class for failing to adapt to the new realities. But help was at hand. In England's darkest hour a second Britannia appeared to lead the nation's children into a new and promised land – a land where sunrise industries flourished, trade unions were kept in check, everyone knew their place and lived within their means, and young people priced themselves back into jobs, or set up new businesses. The messiah had a simple message 'God helps those who train themselves – and God help those who don't'. Many were converted to the new vocationalist faith, and those who continued to voice doubts were told to keep quiet and make way for those made of sterner stuff. Schools were rapidly converted into training centres, youth unemployment was declared illegal and the British economy was once more set on the road to recovery. For like all fairy stories there is only one possible happy ending.

There are a number of reasons why education should have provided the privileged terrain for this exercise in wish fulfilment. It was here that the State of the Nation Debate with its historical links to 'Victorian' values was most easily and directly connected to strategies for 'modernizing' British capitalism. The so-called Black Papers produced by a group of New Right educationalists in the 1970s succeeded in yoking an archaic vision of the body politic to a futuristic image of a 'post-industrial' society.[2] Secondly, educational issues in Britain have always tended to condense and displace other wider relations of conflict in society, and given them a particular inflection. Mrs Thatcher grasped the fact that the 'battle for hearts and minds' could be more easily won over in education than in other areas of social policy. It was relatively easy to caricature the policies of left-wing labour administrations – or the practices of anti-racist teachers – as vicious forms of political indoctrination aiming to 'brainwash' innocent children, to the detriment of 'standards' and 'discipline'. By appearing to side with parents against both teachers and educational experts she was able to exploit a deep vein of popular resentment against state schools.[3] The spectacle of Mrs T teaching the teachers a lesson and giving them a good ticking off must have struck a responsive chord in the hearts and minds of many working-class parents who had been made to suffer in the classrooms of the 1950s and 1960s; the rhetoric of parental choice was even sweeter music to the ears of their classmates who had been the official success stories and who now wanted to ensure that their own children followed in their footsteps into the new middle class. Not for nothing has the Great Educational Reform Bill (GERBIL) been called a 'Yuppies' Charter'.

However, it is only the most sentimental fairy story which relies on an actual fairy to wave her wand and make everything come true. Whatever her personal delusions of grandeur Mrs Thatcher has no special magical powers to turn her policies into practice. The Thatcherite project would not have got off the ground if certain elements in its programme had not won the active support of mainstream educationalists. In fact there has been a convergence of opinion over the last decade on what constitutes 'good education' and 'effective schooling'. And central to this new settlement is the idea that school should equip children from all social backgrounds with a greater understanding and experience of the world of work, and in the process equip them with social and technical skills required by employers. The test of the relevance of any subject, its place in the hierarchy of classroom knowledge, depends not on the insight it gives into the fundamental workings of nature or culture, nor the extent to which it develops particular creative or critical sensibilities, but how far it contributes to the formation of general dispositions for manual or mental labour in capitalist or bureaucratic organizations.[4]

The ideology of the new vocationalism is appropriately summed up in a recent advertisement for a 'progressive' system of vocational qualifications. The poster shows a young woman 'flying high' against the background of a modernist office (or polytechnic) block, over a caption which reads 'If you want more than a job, get more than an education'. This poster juxtaposes the meritocratic vision of technical training with the élitism of liberal education, and privileges the former over the latter. The implicit message is that if you want to fly high, to have a career, rather than just a job, then it's no good burying your head in a lot of useless academic books. Mental labour must become thoroughly rationalized and trained up for its occupational functions in much the same way as manual labour has been. The poster cleverly plays upon popular prejudices against 'academics' and 'intellectuals', whilst at the same time appealing to working-class aspirations to join the ranks of the new petty bourgeoisie. And there is a set of apparently progressive arguments to back it all up. For example it is often claimed that to vocationalize all levels of education thoroughly in this way is to remove the privileges of the traditional aristocracy of learning, as well as to sweep away the last bastions of the apprenticeship system associated with the old aristocracy of labour.

Vocationalism is a modernizing strategy which finally removes the structures of inheritance from the transmission of cultural capital. Of course it does nothing of the kind, given the way mechanisms of parental choice will harden the tripartite structure of public education – to say nothing of the growth of private, fee-paying schools, and the persistence of patriarchal structures in the skilled manual trades. A liberal education is indeed still the preferred formation of the professional and managerial élite, and a skilled trade is still the preferred route for boys from the manual working class. If the Thatcherite project was to carry through a bourgeois revolution in education it has won something of a pyrrhic victory. For the more these 'aristocratic' codes have been marginalized within the educational apparatus, the greater their pulling power as referential models seems to have become.

It is, however, amongst people of working-class origins, who have been denied access to the traditional kinds of intellectual or technical apprenticeship, that the anti-élitist rhetoric of the new vocationalism has gained hold, articulating their aspirations for betterment in a way that the language of 'equal opportunities' and 'comprehensivization' no longer does. This bit of the fairy story works partly because so many people, for different reasons, want it to come true. The education of popular desires by the mass media of the enterprise culture has, at least for the time being, taken the place of the desire for popular education as a means of social emancipation. Really useful knowledge has come to mean skills which help you get on and make it, not insights that help you combine with others to build a better world. But it also convinces because it corresponds to real changes in labour processes, both mental and manual, which have been brought about by the introduction of new information technologies within a 'post-Fordist' framework for acquiring and transmitting knowledge.[5]

The essential shift is from a long apprenticeship with an inherited body of general or fundamental knowledge (whether belonging to a manual trade or profession) towards the learning of functional skills and specialized routines related to the manipulation of operationally defined 'information environments'. A modular curriculum which allows maximum scope for selecting and combining given 'bits' of knowledge in an opportunistic way, plus an active pedagogy based on hands-on experience is the essential format for this vocational model and it is one which is increasingly institutionalized within Higher and Further Education. Applied to the professional training of various kinds of public servants and industrial managers it produces skilled mental technicians who can be flexibly deployed to supervise various systems of work but who are unable to innovate at a deeper level or respond imaginatively to emergent change outside their own immediate field. In other words their dynamism is superficial and this can sometimes cause more problems than it solves, as witness the disarray which is currently being produced in many corporate manpower planning strategies by the advent of the integrated European Community (EC) market in 1992.

Ironically it is the more élitist and conservative forms of intellectual apprenticeship which retain the ability to generate really new knowledge (i.e. thought which anticipates and creates, rather than passively adapts to, change), by equipping people with the means firstly to grasp and then to question inherited structures of understanding in their totality. This is why many large corporations still prefer to recruit graduates with firsts in such 'useless' and 'unvocational' subjects as classics and philosophy; but by the same token the use value of this knowledge to society is often radically curtailed, or else is forced into the mould of a new orthodoxy. This outcome might seem to be the worst of all possible worlds; nevertheless a techno-meritocracy for the masses supervised by a new modernizing élite, whose dynamism is still contained within essentially conservative structures of thought and action, would seem to be a winning formula for Thatcherism. In fact the prolonged series of cuts in university funding, the abolition of academic tenure, and populist onslaughts on 'experts' have ensured that Mrs Thatcher has effectively united and mobilized most of the intelligentsia against the effects of her policies, if not always against the vision of education and society they represent.

Further down the line, in secondary schools and youth training schemes, government policies designed to promote the new voca-tionalism have met with much greater success.[6] Here the idioms and practices of liberal education, with its emphasis on child-centredness and individual self-enhancement, have been subsumed and re-articulated within a more competitive and utilitarian framework to produce a whole series of new pedagogic and disciplinary regimes. In the process, radical critiques of working-class schooling, made by parents and children as well as by educationalists, have often been appropriated and turned against the teaching profession itself. Two discourses have been critical in negotiating this shift.

The first belongs to what Foucault has called bio-politics – the science of surveillance and control over subject populations.[7] One branch of this has been particularly focused on policing the youthful body, whether by subordinating adolescent desires to the disciplines of work, protecting juveniles from undesirable forms of popular pleasure, promoting 'impro-ving' or 'rational' forms of recreation amongst the poor, or rescuing delinquents from their deprived environments. These concerns helped to organize the moral panic over youth unemployment which rose to a peak in the wake of the 1981 riots in many inner city areas. The spectacle of black and white youths confronting police on the street, creating no-go areas, burning and looting shops, played on all the traditional fears of the hooligan mob, and invoked the usual authoritarian response, a call for a tightening of discipline in the family and school, more effective policing, a closing of ranks against 'these barbarians encamped in our midst'.[8]

Racism undoubtedly fanned the flames not only in enumerating the grievances of the 'silent' white majority, but by defining the whole problem of youth unemployment in terms of the numbers game. Blacks, like youth, are always and only seen as a problem when there are too many of them, never when there are too few. The problem then was to find new ways of warehousing this surplus population, of disciplining the reserve army of youth labour, perhaps by bringing in some form of conscription and/or removing them from the labour market altogether. This was the solution favoured by the neo-conservative wing of the New Right. They succeeded in getting unemployment benefit withdrawn from 16- and 17-year-olds, and prevented young people from moving to seaside towns in search of casual work while continuing to claim the dole; school-leavers were thus both immobilized in areas of high unemployment, made absolutely dependent on family support and forced to sign on to Youth Training Schemes (hereafter YTS) – which many of them regarded, rightly or wrongly, as slave labour.[9] The neo-conservative rationale for all this was simply that the intervention of a strong state was needed to hold the line against these new 'dangerous classes', until, with a declining birth-rate, and possibly a little assisted emigration, their numbers dropped. These are the people who now proclaim that the youth question is officially solved, because the demographic 'bulge' of the 1960s cohort is past.

In contrast, neo-liberal tendencies on the New Right saw the problem of balancing the supply and demand for youth labour in terms of quality, not quantity. The problem was that schools were not equipping young people with the right skills and personal dispositions to make themselves sufficiently attractive to employers. Here was a chance to reform secondary schooling, and restructure the transition to work in a way which conformed to the requirements of the 'post-Fordist' economy. At the same time, the fact that the traditional system of apprenticeship had become obsolescent, creating unnecessary bottlenecks in the production process, also provided an opportunity to dismantle the cultural forms which supported working-class solidarities and powers of resistance. For the neo-liberals, it was not a question of holding the mob at bay until their numbers fell by natural attrition, but of developing a positive strategy for remaking the working class in its own image, by endowing a new generation of young workers with the individualistic values and practices associated with enterprise culture.

This is where the second major discourse comes into play, aiming not to confine or repress youthful energies but to empower them as agents of capital rather than labour. We might call this an orthopaedic strategy in that it aims at the correct formation of children's attitudes by controlling the conditions under which they acquire basic skills. Given that this strategy is so important to the hidden curriculum of the new vocationalism it is perhaps worth looking at it in more detail.

A short history of skill

One of the constant refrains of employers over the last ten years has been about the chronic shortage of properly skilled workers. The poor performance of the British economy compared with West Germany or Japan has frequently been attributed to this factor, which in turn is put down to poor quality of training. In all these debates the issue of what constitutes a skill is rarely discussed. The skilled worker is trained and the unskilled worker is not. It's as simple as that! The notion that skill might itself be an ideological construct, rather than a simple material factor in the labour process, that the same practice might be regarded as skilled, semi-skilled or unskilled according to the particular occupational culture within which it was transmitted, or the gender of the worker performing it, such ideas have been discussed only on the academic fringes of public debate. Nevertheless it is not possible to understand the true import of recent innovations in vocational training without looking at the historical discourses of skill in and against which they are located.

The dominant construct of skill is the outcome of a historical compromise between two leading reproduction codes – the code of the aristocracy, with its paradigm of the amateur and the gentleman, and the code of the bourgeoisie predicated on the position of the professional and the self-made man.[10] Under the former, skill is constructed as a natural aptitude, an *inheritance* of cultural capital, a birthright and a legacy of effortless mastery. The latter code, in contrast, defines skill in terms of personal initiative and drive, measured through an incremental grid of status or *career*. The rise of the 'career code' can be traced in the history of its meaning. From its eighteenth-century usage as a largely derogatory term applied to the rake's progress of younger sons of the aristocracy ('careering about'), the word gradually took on the sense of orderly progress up an occupational ladder associated with competitive success in examinations. By the end of the nineteenth century careerists have made their appearance, and by the 1960s we not only have a careers service for young people whose school 'careers' have disqualified them from pursuing one, but even criminals and delinquents are said to have 'careers', albeit ones closer to the original meaning of the word! The extent to which it is a male construct can be judged from the derogatory connotations of 'career woman'.

However, the code of inheritance is far from having been eclipsed. It continues to dominate common-sense constructs of skill, such as the 'natural athlete', the 'born teacher', etc. In combination, the two codes thus relay a contradictory message: skill is both an inherent property and a socially achieved practice, both the cause and the effect of mastery.

There is, though, another major construct of skill, which increasingly mediates between the terms of this contradiction. It has its own distinctive history, and moreover has come to lend its name, if not its substance, to the preparation of young people for work.

From the time of the seventeenth-century Puritan revolution, the code of vocation has offered an image of skill as a special gift or calling, acquired through a purely interior process, governed by the voice of conscience or the presence of an 'inner light'. Skill here becomes a sign of grace, which may be spiritual, aesthetic or purely physical in mode. In any case it remains the prerogative of the self-elected few.

This code was open to multiple articulations. In one such, the notion of natural aptitude is reworked; it is divorced from its rendering as a congenital mark of birth or breeding, and constructed instead as an 'inner bent', a decidedly more mystical reading of 'innate dispositions'! A quite different set of relays enabled careerists to claim that personal drive had nothing to do with a material quest for fame and fortune, but was simply the realization of a 'God-given' gift. But in its most powerful and popular articulation the code invested the 'congenital destiny' to labour for capital, with a special sense of inner-directed purpose or mission. For according to the protestant work ethic, skill, like virtue, was to be its own reward, measured as an index of an inner, moral worth, rather than in terms of wage differentials.

Yet the vocation code also retained an independent existence albeit one confined to feminine, or Bohemian, pursuits, both, of course, being regarded as equally 'unproductive'. If these activities continued to be valued as skills, it was precisely in so far as they remained economically marginal or unpaid – as generations of housewives, artists, nurses and others have found to their cost! The code thus instructed middle- and upper-class girls that their true calling was caring for men, rather than the 'selfish' pursuit of career. Motherhood was constructed as an exercise in creative self-fulfilment, on the same plane as the male pursuit of the Muse. Whereas the code of inheritance reproduced the patriarchal order as a quasi-biological grid of origins and destinies, under the vocation code this was inscribed in the subject as a project of desire – a far more insidious mechanism.

Working-class ideologies of skill, though no less patriarchal, operate according to quite different principles. Here skill is constructed under the sign of an *apprenticeship*, as the progressive mastery of techniques of dexterity associated with the performance of manual labour, both in the home and for wages. However, these skills could only be legitimately mastered from a position of subordination *vis-à-vis* elders – who always 'know better'. Apprenticeship, in other words, has customarily been to an inheritance of sorts, a patrimony of concrete skills, transmitted through the family, the shop-floor or the wider institutions of the class-culture and community. This entailed a whole process of socialization into the customary practices of the work-place, including special rituals of initiation and the mastery of skills associated with practices of informal bargaining and a resistance to line management. Learning a trade under the tutelage of 'old hands' meant informally absorbing the folklore of the trade, and often an oral history of shop-floor struggle. This was not something confined to the indentured few; it characterized the 'on-the-job training' of young people in a whole range of officially unskilled occupations, from textile factories to street markets, and involved girls as well as boys. Moreover, similar modes of learning informed practices of popular pleasure, for example in the structures of sexual apprenticeship to be found in many working-class communities. Political apprenticeships were often modelled on the occupational form, and in the autobiographies of many working-class leaders we can read just how closely technical training and political education went hand in glove.[11]

There are several consequences of this kind of code. It is strongly patriarchal, the power of male elders, as guardians of both the class patrimony and the family wage, over both women and children being almost absolute. Secondly, resistance to technical innovation and social change is intense. Where jobs are regarded as being held in trust by one generation for the next, they will not so easily be sold for productivity deals or redundancy payments. The code has thus been a major stumbling block to attempts to impose a properly capitalist rationality on both the immediate labour process and the labour market.

However, in the post-war period there has occurred a pervasive weakening and fragmentation of these grids. Cultural apprenticeships are no longer so easily or frequently connected to occupational inheritances. The practice of dexterity is no longer anchored to the sign of manual labour; it takes place increasingly in leisure contexts, in the mastery of popular dance forms or video games, for example. As a result positions of 'skill' and 'unskill' are no longer tied so rigidly to divisions of labour or their relations of generational transmission, but are negotiated primarily through the peer group. The body is no longer engendered solely as a bearer of labour power, specialized according to productive (male) or reproductive (female) functions. One effect of this is to make the forms of adolescent sexuality more dependent on what Freud called 'the narcissism' of minor differences, i.e. differences of taste, clothes and personal life-style. Whether the escape routes this opens up are more imaginary than real, and just how far they undermine working-class sexism, may be open to debate. But the desire to escape a universe of fixed reference, whether of gender or class, could potentially be connected to the kind of mobile individualism currently being promoted through the new regimes of skilling.

The systematic preparation of school-leavers for their future occupational roles, by state agencies, is a relatively recent development. It is designed to gear the transition from school to the requirements of the economy in a way which, it is argued, neither individual employers, nor market forces, alone can do. It is no coincidence that these initiatives came to be defined as *vocational* guidance and preparation, or that a *careers* service should initially have been put in charge of implementing them – since the aim is precisely to establish the hegemony of these codes over working-class constructs of skill.

It is in this context that attempts to introduce new regimes and strategies of vocational training must be understood. Their hidden agenda is to complete the disintegration of the apprenticeship–inheritance model and to strengthen all those forms of working-class individualism which can be articulated within the enterprise culture. This manoeuvre pivots on a redefinition of the functions and meaning of skill. First, skills are dissociated from specific practices of manual labour, or from general forms of mental coordination exercised by workers over the immediate labour process. Secondly, skills are divorced from their historical association with particular trades or occupational cultures, and their acquisition is no longer entailed in a power of social combination tied to a process of cultural apprenticeship. Instead work practices are reclassified into 'occupational training families' defined according to a set of purely functional properties of coordination between atomized operations of mind–body–machine interfacing within the same 'information environment'. In this discourse skills have become abstract universal properties of the labour process. This indeed is what is supposed to make them transferable between one industry and another. In fact training in transferable skills is essentially training for what Marx called abstract labour – that is labour considered in its generic commodity form as an interchangeable unit/factor of production. What transferable skilling corresponds to in reality is the process of deskilling set in motion by

Table 3.1   New voxspeak

Learning outcomes	The student should: 1. communicate effectively with the client to determine requirements; 2. analyze the hair, devise a cutting strategy, and select appropriate tools and equipment; 3. perform the cut safely and effectively.
Content/ context	*Corresponding to learning outcomes 1–3:* 1. Good questioning technique; interpretation of client's wishes; communication of possible difficulties with tact and reaching of agreement over any necessary compromise. 2. Consideration of client's personal characteristics and beard/moustache idiosyncracies; selection of method taking account of possible hair growth limitations. 3. Methodical pattern of work; avoidance or correction of scissor marks; check cutting; the achievement of a balanced result to the client's satisfaction.

information technologies – a process which is here represented as its opposite: an occasion for perpetual reskilling. The main function of this redescription is in fact to undermine the residual forms of control exercised by conventionally skilled workers by increasing elasticities of substitution between different occupational categories. This ploy is usually code-named 'flexibility'.

One of the most notable features of the obsessive inventories and check-lists which are generated by this discourse is the way in which a language of abstraction is deployed to describe labour processes as if they were models of impersonal or bureaucratic rationality. This produces a managerialist perspective which bears little or no real relation to actual working conditions. In so far as this model is applied to concrete forms of manual labour, the resulting descriptions can be positively surreal – as for example in Table 3.1, from a document prepared by the Scottish Education Department, which modestly describes itself as a 'Specialist Module to enable the student to enhance his/her haircutting skills in the specialist area of beards and moustaches'.

However, when it comes down to 'suggested learning and teaching approaches' it becomes quite clear that these involve quite traditional forms of apprenticeship: the technique is demonstrated, the apprentice watches; the apprentice then copies, while being watched and given advice on how to improve. Moreover since the module is 'salon-based' we might well suspect that other traditional aspects of hairdressing apprenticeship are also likely to be reproduced. Having learnt how to 'put together two metal blades unpowered' (use a pair of scissors) students may find themselves 'operating an unpowered cleaning device suitable for removing superfluous material' (sweeping up) and 'operating electrical equipment to produce steam pressure' (boiling a kettle to make the staff tea).

These elements of 'proto-domestic' labour have been an integral part of the cultural apprenticeships of most young workers; being made to fetch and carry, run errands, sweep up, etc., is something which marks their subordinate quasi-feminine status *vis-à-vis* others, i.e. male/elders, and constitutes the first stage of their initiation into adult shop-floor culture. Yet there is a more positive side to this process. As well as being treated as a dogsbody, the hairdressing apprentice may pick up lots of 'really useful knowledge' about how to deal with awkward customers, or salon managers, how to maximize earnings from tips, even how (not) to run your own business. But because the vocationalist approach is committed to an ideal hyper-rationalized model of the labour process, it cannot admit many of these real techniques which young workers actually need to learn if they are both to humanize their work and combine effectively – and hence productively – with others. It could be argued that it is these skills of resistance and accommodation to work discipline which are the truly transferable ones.

Along with the abstraction of the labour form goes an individualization of the pedagogic regimes through which labour is skilled and disciplined. The trainee is inducted into methods of learning which focus not on the social relations of production, but on the formation of 'correct' personal attitudes and interpersonal competences. Here also the new vocationalism has introduced a decisive innovation. For the aim is to teach youth trainees how to sell themselves to customers, clients or employers, by learning specific techniques of self-presentation. These techniques are designed to enable the individual to manipulate or project a 'positive image', or at least to conform with occupational norms whilst successfully controlling any anger or resentment this may produce. Training in these so-called social and life skills is essentially training in behavioural etiquettes which concretize in a subject form the general commodity form of abstract labour. What is in reality a position of class subjection (the selling of labour power) is thus represented as its opposite – a position of individual mastery (the marketing of a self-image).

There is also a gendered dimension to this inversion. The aim here is to replace the old masculinist disciplines of apprenticeship, including the arcane rituals of humiliation designed to 'toughen' the young worker, with a code based on the positive acquisition of 'feminine' techniques of tension and impression management. Not that this change necessarily undermines the sexual division of labour. Indeed, given that these skills are so clearly tailored to work in personal service industries, their impact is likely to confine girls even more tightly to occupational roles in this sector. As for boys, learning these skills may help to shift them into non-traditional gender roles, whilst also serving to wean them away from their more 'boisterous' forms of resistance to the exploitative 'proto-domestic' features of youth labour. In either case what is often represented as a progressive move to liberate young people from repressive patriarchal structures, turns out on closer inspection to be a device for subjecting them secretly and individually, and hence all the more effectively, to the 'discipline' of market forces.

This shift in methods of work discipline, from a system of external controls and negative sanctions tightly policed by line management, to a more invisible process of self-regulation on the part of individual employees is an essential part of the strategy for remaking the working class for its functions in a post-Fordist economy. But the ideology of the enterprise culture has a much wider remit than that. Its hegemonic project is to reshape the aspirations of all social classes according to a new model of individualism, and it is to this we must now turn.

The enterprise culture as a morality tale: from Samuel Smiles to Richard Branson

When I was growing up in the early 1950s it was still possible to get given 'improving books' for one's birthday, consisting of biographies of self-made men, engineers, inventors, industrialists, entrepreneurs, phil-anthropists and the like. These men, and they were all men, had usually lived in the 'heroic' age of nineteenth-century capitalism and the books themselves were clearly prepared for the edification of the young. I soon learnt to ignore these 'worthy lives' along with the earnest enjoinders written on the flyleaf to 'go forth and do likewise'; instead like many of my friends I turned to more modern and exciting figures; Dan Dare followed by Dick Barton, Special Agent, and then, in turn, Elvis, Camus, Dylan, Sartre and the Rolling Stones.

Whereas the old heroes triumphed over adversity through hard work and persistent effort, our new role models celebrated their transcendence of all the more mundane concerns of life and labour in favour of Bohemian adventures, philosophizing about the adsurdity of human existence or playing in a rock'n'roll band, preferably all three at once!

It is tempting, then, to characterize the cultural politics of Thatcherism as a kind of counter-revolution – the reinstatement of Victorian values swept aside by the 'swinging sixties'; what sweeter revenge for all those lower-middle-class youths at grammar school and university who stayed in to study while everyone else was out having a good time? That subtext seems to be the one which Mrs Thatcher prefers, which is as good a reason as any for questioning its salience. Perhaps, after all, Thatcherism is more complicated than she herself supposes?[12]

For example, one of the most genuinely remarkable figures thrown up by Thatcherism is Richard Branson. A 'hippy entrepreneur' made even better than good, who turned Virgin Records from a small 'alternative' label into a multinational company with interests in every section of the leisure industry, including tourism and airlines, Branson cultivates a careful public image which combines swashbuckling adventures out of the pages of *Boy's Own Paper* with all the classical capitalist virtues and just a touch of bohemianism thrown in for good measure. Here is a romantic individualism in which the protestant work ethic and a libertarian life-style have been effortlessly reconciled. Branson may indeed be the Yuppies' great folk hero; there is certainly no parallel to be found amongst the eminent Victorians, or even the more eccentric Edwardian entrepreneurs. The contemporary forms of self-improvement have a quite different *raison d'être* from the original Victorian version. The figure of Richard Branson has a complex and contradictory provenance which takes some unravelling. In tracing a line of descent from Samuel Smiles, through the Dale Carnegie era between the two World Wars, personal growth movements of the 1960s up to the social and life skill pedagogies of today, the tensions and breaks between those successive forms are as significant as their continuities.[13]

For example, the nineteenth-century version did not always relay an individualistic message about 'pulling oneself up by one's own boot-straps'. It did not necessarily involve the deferential imitation of the manners and morals of 'elders and betters'. It also informed the movement for independent working-class education, supported popular demands for better cultural amenities and living conditions and it has been an element in both the religious and secular visions of socialism. In other words it can take on cooperative forms which stand against the ethic of possessive individualism. In sharp contrast the dominant model gave an aggressive competitive edge to the notion of betterment. Here self-improvement is an exercise in contest mobility, not forelock-touching. The typical mortality tale which features in this literature concerns the hero (almost always male and usually the author) setting out on life's journey, beset by the temptations of pleasure and 'vice' at every turn. The road to fame and fortune follows a very straight and narrow path dictated by conscience and ambition marching hand in hand. Along the way tempters and failures would be met, individuals whose early promise had been confounded by the evils of drink or sex, their role as much to introduce an element of suspense – would the hero fall, be led astray? – as to underline the terrible consequences of ignoring the prescriptive code laid down as the key to success. A very ancient theme, but what is original about this code is the way it legitimizes competition, makes rivalry respectable; the message often seems to be 'stand on your own feet, even if it means treading on other people's toes'.

In the last thirty years, the cooperative vision of self-improvement has virtually disintegrated, while the competitive model has undergone a series of rapid transformations. Many of the old links between material and moral betterment have snapped, but new ones have taken their place. State education promised to provide an institutionalized route to social mobility, in a way that made the lonely struggles of the autodidact or the self-made man stand out as 'heroic' exceptions to the rule. Consumer life-styles emerged in which new and improved self-images could be bought, fully-fashioned, and changed as easily as clothes. These developments are exemplified in post-Second World War forms of rational recreation, always the mainstay of self-improvers. These forms have either become privatized and embedded in costly technologies of leisure consumption; or taken in under state provision. In the first case they constitute symbols of success, rather than a means of achieving it; in the second, they have become a means of providing 'safe activities' for 'dangerous' groups (such as the young, black, unemployed, etc.) rather than a leg up the social ladder. But perhaps the most significant shift has been the way a whole range of bodily pleasures and expressive forms which had hitherto been ruled out of bounds have been legitimized as 'rational recreation' and incorporated within strategies of self-improvement adapted to the codes of the new middle class. At last the old moral economy of fixed and sublimated drives gave way to a liberal therapeutics of 'personal growth' whose slogan might be 'incremental insight equals interpersonal effectiveness equals success in work and play!' Creative individualism has here become a recipe for social success, rather than a symbol of Bohemian excess. In contrast to Smiles, the subject to be improved is a private or inner self rather than a public one, yet the object is still 'promotion'. In effect, the inner-directed features of the vocation code, and the other-directed features of the career code have become inextricably fused, or rather confused!

In the diverse elements which compose social and life-skill (SLS) training, both the Smiles and the liberal therapeutic models have their place. The former has been operationalized in so-called 'assertion training' and given a radical, though no less individualistic, edge; the latter can be found in various kinds of counselling of adolescents in schools and youth projects. Yet at present both approaches remain marginal to the core curriculum of SLS. The reason is not hard to find. The translation of a self-improvement programme into the formal pedagogic context of the state school or training scheme imposes its own selective constraints. What had essentially been a method of self-help, learned through the personal example of mentors who had themselves successfully mastered it, hardly provided a model for institutional provision on a large scale, nor did it fit in with the prevailing relations of educational transmission. It is nevertheless highly significant that it was at the point where the notion of *skill* was made central to self-improvement that the apprenticeship model was dropped in favour of the behaviouristic model of learning applied to the whole field of vocational preparation.[14]

Initially SLS emerged out of an apparently radical critique of state schooling, designed to expose the irrelevance of academic curricula to working-class pupils, and concerned to develop an alternative approach to learning related to their real lives outside the school gates. How did it come to be, so quickly and easily, incorporated within youth training schemes?

Of course the notion that schools or training schemes should be preparing young people for 'life' as well as labour does help give a nice liberal gloss to an otherwise all too crude utilitarian philosophy, and it also provides a convenient safety clause when trainees reach the end of the job-training programmes and find there are still no jobs for them. But the promotion of SLS is not the story of the corruption of an ideal. From the beginning it was conceived as a form of compensatory education suitable for 'non-academic' children; and what had to be compensated for was not only the inadequacy of existing forms of classroom knowledge, but the deficiencies of the pupils' cultures as well. It was a *double* deficit model in which the school's failure to connect with the 'real world of work' was mirrored in a failure of the working-class family to transmit the kinds of communication skills and interpersonal competencies which employers were now demanding for white collar jobs. But, never mind, those skills and competencies could be taught in the *same way* as woodwork or metalwork.

From the outset, then, a new micro-technology of self-improvement is proposed; the social is dissolved into the interpersonal as a condition of the expressive becoming fully instrumentalized. Behaviourist theories of learning were thus the most appropriate pedagogic model for social- and life-skilling. Amongst the pioneers in the field was the Industrial Training Research Unit with its programme entitled CRAMP (Comprehension, Reflex learning, Attitude development, Memorization, Procedural learning).

Even more significant was the work carried out by a group of social psychologists under the direction of Michael Argyle at Oxford. Inspired by ethological studies of animal and human communication, this team set out to devise a rehabilitation programme for long-term inmates of prisons and mental hospitals. This started from the somewhat circular proposition that 'social deviants' had failed to learn 'normal' techniques of social interaction. In the case of mental patients and prisoners we might suspect that their long periods of incarceration might have had something to do with it but, never mind, they could at least now be taught how to behave themselves in public once they were released! The programme consisted of a crash course in verbal and non-verbal communication techniques (rules for eye contact and body posture in various social settings, how to pick up and respond to social cues, how and when to smile appropriately, conversational rituals, etc.). It was assumed that once the subject had learnt to release these signals 'correctly', social relations would become unproblematic.

In many ways Michael Argyle is the Frederick Winslow Taylor of the human relations industry. Just as Taylor attempted to establish a science of production-line management based on time and motion studies, so Argyle is aiming at a science of impression management also based on breaking down social practices into standardized, quantified and controllable units of 'interaction'. But where Taylorism was concerned to maximize the physical efficiency and output of the factory worker, Argyle's programme is somewhat more ambitious. For the norms of interpersonal efficiency he uses make the notion of 'social skill' highly transferable between a whole range of contexts. They are not only designed to increase the productivity of the white-collar worker, but also that of the housewife (tension management!). These are techniques for selling yourself to a prospective lover as well as to a personnel manager. The very transferability of these 'skills' is an index of their real disciplinary function and scope. For their effect is to anatomize the speaking body into a set of 'proper' features silently regulated by law – the law of 'free and equal exchange' (Argyle's 'interaction') – which systematically conceals the structural inequalities in power governing the production of the discourse. Despite the claims that this legal body has an 'instinctual foundation', it turns out to be the bearer of a behavioural ideology combining the calculating rationality of the boardroom with the social niceties of the bourgeois drawing-room. As for the real behind the ideal, it is perhaps worth noting that the result of the proposed 'reskilling' of the mental patient or prisoner seems a lot closer to the fragmented routines of the deskilled labourer than to the 'whole personality of the informed citizen' that is claimed.

Given this, it might seem at first sight rather odd that social and life skills should have been taken up so enthusiastically by educationalists; but the paradigm was all too easily recast in terms of demands for a 'relevant' curriculum for early leavers. For here was a method which would teach them 'how to communicate effectively, how to make, keep and end relationships, how to make effective transitions, how to be positive about oneself, how to manage negative emotions, how to cope with unemployment, how to cope with stress, and how to be an effective member of a group' and much else besides.[15] A veritable panacea for those concerned to free working-class pupils from the 'double tyranny' of mechanical solidarity and abstract thought.

Yet the essential appeal, to teachers as well as pupils, was the promise to forge new and more substantive links between self-improvement and self-employment. To be your own boss was still supposed to mean not simply being in control of your own self-image, but to own and control a small business. In many ways the career of Richard Branson dramatizes that articulation between new and old versions of petty bourgeois individualism. But this merger of enterprise culture with youth culture, like Branson's own preferred strategy for success, is in reality a take-over bid. And as Thatcherism strengthened its hold, it was private philanthropy rather than public education which took the initiative in promoting the view that the answer to youth unemployment was to 'create yourself a job'. From 1982 onwards the argument was increasingly heard that self-employment, whether in the hidden economy or in small enterprises based on the new cultural industries, was the most fruitful way in which young people could turn skills and interests generated by their life-styles into a means of livelihood. Dance, music and other elements of do-it-yourself culture could all be turned to good account. What is practised for pleasure can be practised with profit!

In this way the initial threat posed by the emergence of (especially black) counter-cultures was significantly neutralized. The Prince Charles Trust, for example, sponsored training schemes which aimed to turn unemployed youth into cultural capitalists of one sort or another. One of its advertising posters shows a scowling skinhead with the caption 'Help him to create wealth, not aggro'; another shows a black youth and reads 'Help him keep the right company – his own'. These are rhetorical images designed to construct a certain kind of Thatcherite common sense to the effect that anyone (even blacks!) can make it if they try, provided they have a little help from their elders and betters (like Prince Charles). A poster advertising 'Youth Action 89' – a display of youthful endeavour promoted by the Government's enterprise allowance scheme – is even more explicit in its message; a picture of Norman Tebbit (then Mrs Thatcher's right-hand man – Chairman of the Conservative Party) dressed in a preparatory school uniform with the caption 'if he hadn't realized his potential he might have ended up on a park bench, not the Front Bench'. The rags-to-riches story is here given a subtle twist to convey a hidden threat to all those who do not subscribe to dreams of ambition and career success.

Many of the small self-help enterprises set up and run by young people with starter finance from public funds are initially inspired by an alternative and altogether more cooperative vision. However, they often involve the kind of work already performed by young people in domestic or leisure contexts – so many variations on the 'odd job' collective, doing window cleaning, baby-sitting, gardening, decorating, household and bike repairs. Traditionally this kind of work was included in the category of blind alley occupations, but now it is redescribed as a stepping-stone to a better future. Often these set-ups only survive by drastically under-cutting rates for the job charged by unionized firms or qualified workers. So although they may start with good intentions about creating socially useful jobs and organizing themselves according to principles of demo-cratic self-management, all too many of them are forced by the economic logic of their situation to subscribe tacitly or openly to the values of the enterprise culture. The names they choose for themselves – 'Bootstraps', 'Ladders', etc. – give the game away.

The combination of romantic individualism and penny capitalism exemplified in many of these schemes has a potentially wide appeal to young people whose traditional routes into wage labour have been blocked. The 'greening' of Mrs Thatcher in the late 1980s – however superficial – may give added impetus to this kind of solution. The slogan 'small is beautiful' thus reaches its final apotheosis in giving a slightly more hedonistic or human face to popular capitalism. But once again this is a morality tale with a complex genealogy. It originated in a historical compromise between the bourgeois work ethic and aristocratic pleasure principles in mid-Victorian Britain, a compromise cemented in the rational recreation movement and the civilizing mission to the working classes. Mr Gradgrind was forced to admit that 'all work and no play made Jack a dull boy' (though it made Jill a good wife!), while the Marquess of Queensbery wrote 'Leisure Earned is the Devil Spurned' into his rule book. The construction of the Great Outdoors as a playground for the urban masses was designed both to spur them on to greater industry and channel their interests away from politics and crime. But, more than that, it symbolized a peculiar alliance between different sections of the governing class, which in turn made it easier to neutralize popular anti-industrial sentiment and even convert it to a programme for modernizing both capital and state. In this unique coalition of forces, the dissenting voice of English socialism, as represented by Morris and Ruskin, was squeezed to the margins of public debate, where it was tolerated as an eccentric or merely Utopian presence.

In the 1980s socialists who wish to reclaim self-improvement or other elements of petty bourgeois radicalism have to start from this weak point. They also have to compete with the New Right's own vision of a return to England's 'green and pleasant land' based on 'organic', family-centred and home-owning communities, small-scale hi-tech production units, and freedom from state control. The training of young people in practices which militate against their identification with organized labour, the displacement of job creation to the un- or deregulated margins of the economy, the construction of 'leisure' as a cottage industry for the unemployed, all help to ensure that the vision of the 'New Jerusalem' remains captive to the enterprise culture.

However, it is also important to realize some of the limitations of this 'strategy' as a means of incorporating the underclass as a whole. Historically, self-improvement, of whatever kind, has appealed only to those sections of the lower middle and upper working classes whose social aspirations have, for one reason or another, been structurally blocked. It has never caught on amongst the poor, the unskilled and the unemployed. But is this changing? Will the present generation of school-leavers, living, as they say, 'on the rock and roll', find more survival value in techniques of self-improvement than their predecessors did? Certainly the handbooks, teaching kits, visual aids and other SLS materials that are currently pouring off the production lines take great pains to dress up their improving message in fashionable clothes. A closer look at some of this literature may therefore be useful, both to give us a clearer idea of the kind of discoursive strategies being employed by these latter-day Samuel Smileses, and to help us assess what is likely to be their impact on their young readerships.

Janet and John in Thatcherland

All the texts I looked at[16] were designed to appeal to young people whom the publicity handouts variously described as 'non-academic', 'under-achievers' or 'poor readers with short attention spans' – in other words, the working class. It was clear from the handouts (and the materials themselves) that a common set of assumptions was being made about 'the kids': they are ignorant of their rights and weakly motivated to defend them. They lack any kind of work experience. They have no access to useful information and advice other than that provided by official agencies and professional experts. They have difficulty in organizing their lives in a rational or satisfactory way.

Now this does not remotely add up to an accurate account of the way school-leavers deal with their real situation. It is simply a deficit model of working-class culture used to provide a rationale for SLS as a form of compensatory education. As to their actual content, all the texts offered very similar information and advice about looking for a job, going for an interview, fitting in at work, claiming state benefits and getting on training or further education courses. A section on safe sex was usually included in the package, along with advice on 'personal relations'. Youth politics, whether to do with unemployment, housing or cultural questions, is conspicuous by its absence. What were, in effect, pills of information and advice were offered in an easily digestible form; the objective seemed to be to give the reader quick-acting, if not permanent, relief from a range of social ills (poverty, boredom, discrimination, etc.). 'If you take this advice regularly (before and after interviews?), you'll be OK' was the basic comforting message.

But perhaps the messages are not quite so straightforwardly reassuring as the authors intended. The explicit prescriptions – the texts are full of check-lists of do's and don'ts – also have to stake their claim to credibility or 'realism' by acknowledging unpleasant facts, such as unemployment, homelessness or racism. Yet the anxieties these situations may arouse in young people are in no way assuaged by the way the issues are actually dealt with. For instead of explaining the origins and causes of these phenomena, or documenting the struggles which are being waged against them, they are presented as social calamities which can neither be understood nor prevented, but whose effects may be avoided by purely individual measures of precaution. Yet the guarantees of 'personal safety' which this offers are not likely to stand up against the lived experience of school-leavers, especially in areas of high unemployment. Nor is the attempt to sugar the pill by wrapping the exhortatory messages in photo-stories or cartoons likely to take away the bitter taste which is left.

It is in their claim to be purely factual or practical that these materials reveal themselves as ideological through and through. School-leavers are indeed being invited to enter into an imaginary relation to their predicaments; not because the ways suggested for dealing with them are in themselves impracticable, or inexact, but because they are premised on a *subject position* which turns real relations to capital or the state upside down and inside out. For the reader who is addressed, whether directly, or indirectly, is always a *legal* subject, i.e. an individual centre of contractual rights and obligations, free and equal before the law. It is from this position that we are urged to join a trade union, resist racism and sexism, start our own business, be polite to policemen and dress sensibly for interviews. It is also, as a legal subject, that the reader is supposed to recognize the situations shown, identify with the 'exemplary' figures of youth portrayed in them, and clutching a check-list of prescriptions in hand, go and do likewise.

But this is not just an exercise in conforming to external rules and regulations. These texts counsel young people to police their own behaviour, not by appealing to the wisdom or authority of 'elders and betters', but by referencing the experience of peers. The testimonies of young people who have apparently followed the advice and succeeded is a recurring device used to lend credibility, or realism, to the text. In the process, the legal subject is subtly converted into a *judicious self*, a super-ego, based not on the father (whose word is no longer law) but on an imaginary peer, a double representing the reader's 'better self'.

Through this beguiling figure, the voice of self-improvement speaks, and constructs its special effects of meaning. But of course everything now depends on whether readers do indeed recognize themselves in the mirror images projected by these 'judicious selves'. I showed a sample of this literature to a group of twenty unemployed school-leavers in north London; I asked them whether they thought the situations that were portrayed in the photo-stories or cartoons were realistic, and whether the information and advice amounted to really useful knowledge. The response was almost entirely negative. They found the story-lines artificial, the language used patronizing, and the information and advice completely abstracted from the real social context of their lives.

To illustrate this, let us look in more detail at one fairly typical example of the genre. *The School Leaver's Guide* (Symonds, 1981) sticks very closely to the core curriculum of SLS. A separate topic is dealt with on each double-page spread, and the format consists of a photo or cartoon story accompanied by a checklist of do's and don'ts. In the stories, all the young people are shown dressed sensibly, as if for interviews. They spend most of their time posed in empty space, occasionally framed by the odd corner of a table, or brick wall, saying things like 'Hi Sheila, I've been told to leave my job because I'm pregnant' or 'Magic, it's my cheque from the *DSS* [Department of Social Security]. I'll cash it and have some money to spend at last.'[16] The characters are continually hailing each other, and the reader, with lines like 'Hi. Last week I went for my seventh interview and I think I've finally got it right. I thought I'd pass on a few ideas to you.' Sometimes we get what passes for a dialogue:

Girl A   Hi! I haven't seen you for a few months, did you get a job after all?

Girl B   No, but I took your advice and applied for a place at college.

Girl C   Colleges have typing, nursing, mechanics, electrical work, dressmaking, engineering, photography, art, catering, maths, hairdressing and loads of other courses and you don't always need exams to get in.

Girl A   I started last week. It's OK.

As you can see, these youngsters are not arresting conversationalists despite all the hailing that goes on. They would, however, provide great material for a Monty Python sketch! Even when relaxing at the youth club, they are likely to have earnest discussions about the role of industrial tribunals, or social security appeal procedures. They are surrounded by kindly officials, including the police who are presented as a more or less benevolent agency of the welfare state. The section entitled 'Arrest' begins:

> Most people only contact the police when they have some sort of a problem. They go to the police station voluntarily to register a complaint or seek information. However there are occasions when the police may seek your help. You may wish to help them, but you should also know your rights.

An even more strenuous exercise in wish fulfilment is to be found in the section dealing with trade unions. A West Indian boy and girl are shown having an argument about the pros and cons of joining one. The girl is initially hostile, but is finally won over by the lad's assertion that unions are in the vanguard of the fight against sex and race discrimination!

The script throughout is written in a bizarre mixture of childish language and 'bureaucratese'. There is no real dialogue or debate between the characters because whatever their role, everyone speaks either in the name of the law or in the language of the judicious self. The Everyboys and Girls who people the stories are persons without personalities, ventriloquists' dummies manipulated by the hidden hand of an ideology not their own. The device of putting official information and advice into the mouths of a multi-ethnic cast of working-class teenagers may strike you as a rather pathetic piece of sleight-of-hand, one which tells us a lot about the authors' patronizing attitudes. But the point is, it is *structurally* necessary to maintain the coherence of this particular universe of discourse. The problem the authors had to solve, whether they recognized it or not, was this: if the text is to work, in the sense of getting the message across, then readers have to identify with its 'senders' (the characters) as speaking on their behalf, or in some way representing the real world. But if the text is to work as an enunciation of official codes of practice, then everything which would enable working-class school-leavers to identify with the characters in terms of language, culture or ideology has to be cut out. In trying to get round this problem – which the use of familiar graphic forms highlights, but does not solve – the authors are impelled to construct a story-line which is both mystifying and obtuse. Let us look at a typical case in point.

Really cool knowledge?

Two pages of the book deal with applying for a job by phone (see Figure 3.1). A white boy and black girl are shown ringing up a garage in reply to an advertisement for a salesperson. The boy does it all wrong, while the girl follows all the correct procedures as laid down in the accompanying check-list. However *both* applicants are turned down. The manager thanks them for ringing but says 'there are a lot of people we have to interview'. No other explanation is given. On the face of it, then, the implication seems to be that there is no pay-off for learning 'good' interview techniques, since they make absolutely no difference to the outcome. That, indeed, is the conclusion which the young people reading this sequence reached. Why should a book which is devoted to life and social skills put across such a self-defeating message? Why was not the black girl, shown as such an adept at 'impression management', rewarded by being offered an interview, while the lad who is made to break all the rules, has to suffer the consequences?

One reason is that if the book is to maintain any credibility with the reader, it has to maintain a semblance of economic realism. It has to take into account the fact that in a situation of structural unemployment *and* credential inflation, the links between educability and employability on which so much of the teachers' authority rests, can no longer be made with any degree of conviction. School-leavers are coming to realize that no matter how impressive their interview manners, how good their personal or academic credentials, irrespective of how many dozens of immaculately written letters they send out or how diligently they follow the instructions in their job-hunter kits, the cards have already been dealt and theirs read 'sorry, no vacancies'.

How then to motivate them, to cool out their immediate demands for real work at a living wage, and persuade them to go on a training scheme instead, without simultaneously practising a cruel deception? This is the problem which teachers face, and which this sequence (and the whole book) tries to solve. It does so not by suppressing the contradiction, but by displacing its terms into a magical resolution: the salvage of individual victories out of collective defeats.

How is this effect achieved here? Consider for a moment the position of the garage manager. Despite the marked differences between the two applicants, in terms of race, gender and class 'attributes', he is shown addressing them identically throughout. Obviously an equal opportunities employer, he rejects them both!

In other words the manager is constructed as an exemplary legal subject. He conforms to employment legislation (the Race Relations and Sex Discrimination Acts) and this in turn legitimates his freedom to hire and fire according to the laws of the market (lots of others to interview, sorry). What in fact is being guaranteed is his freedom *not* to hire and *not* to give any substantive reason why. The applicants are left with their 'freedom' to remain unemployed. The interview is presented as an equal exchange between free subjects, rather than what it is, an unequal power relation between capital and labour mediated by patterns of social discrimination institutionalized by the state. The symmetry of the manager's responses is necessary to maintain the legal fiction and suppress the social facts.

If he had been shown differentiating between the boy and girl, following a policy of either negative or positive discrimination, then the real relations in play would have had to be depicted simply to maintain the congruity of the story-line. His silences are equally functional. Because this is an exercise in public propriety we are not told what he might be thinking or feeling in contradistinction to what he says. No advantage can thus be taken, here or elsewhere, of the cartoon's capacity to demystify, e.g. by using 'think-bubbles' to articulate a sub-text of what is truly going on but is censored, distorted or covered over in official discourse. In the process, the power of the interviewer to remain silent, to withhold information or to lie, and the interviewee's powerlessness to challenge these prerogatives without offending against the code, all this is massively endorsed – and this in a book which ostensibly upholds young people's rights!

There is, however, a further twist to the tale, which concerns the type of qualities associated with the occupation chosen for the exercise. 'Salesperson in a garage' can refer equally to men's work (car salesman) or women's work (behind the counter) *without* putting in question the fundamental rule governing the sexual division of labour (the closer the job is to operating the machine, the more likely it is to be a masculine preserve).

Moreover no school-leaver would be taken on as a car salesman – it is indeed regarded as a 'man's' job, not a boy's. Salesperson therefore in this context has the connotation of shop girl. The qualities which are normally demanded for shop work – selling one's self to sell the product, looking good to make the customer feel good – are of course constructed as 'essentially feminine'. Now none of this is problematized in the text. Instead the girl is shown as having effortlessly mastered the art of selling herself whereas the boy apparently sees no reason even to try. Her 'success', his 'failure', does not therefore represent some role reversal. It reinforces gender stereotypes in the crudest possible way.

At the same time a far more subtle and insidious displacement is effected in the story-line. As I have said, the even-handedness of the garage manager is mystifying, in that it works to conceal the real

Figure 3.1   The telephone interview (Source: Symonds, 1981)

asymmetry between his class position and that of the young people, but the asymmetry that *is* shown operating between the two job applicants is no less mystifying. For the distinction between right and wrong interview manners not only cancels the real differences between them but also conceals the fact that they are being positioned *symmetrically* within *the same system of double binds*. How does this occur?

The lad is allowed to drop his aitches, confess he doesn't really want the job, run out of money for the telephone and forget the name of the 'bloke in charge'. The nearest anyone in this book is ever permitted to come to a position with which the reader could identify! This character can be a 'speaking subject' within a certain code of working-class masculinity, affirm something like a cultural identity, but only as an index of *social disqualification*, a transgressor of 'the law'.

The black girl, in contrast, is made to give a flawless performance of deference to white middle-class etiquette. Even when she gets the brush-off, she politely thanks the manager for his help! But she is allowed to exist only as a subject spoken for by the dominant culture, one who suppresses anything that would affirm her real identity. The line that is drawn between the two characters is not one of gender, ethnicity or class; that would destroy the whole fragile grid of legal subjectivity on which the story rests. In contrast, the distinction that *is* made reinforces the grid, for it rests on the opposition between judicious and injudicious selves.

Injudicious selves 'show themselves up', 'give themselves away', 'lose control'. Judicious selves remain *self-possessed*, on condition that they first *disown* everything that would invest them with the properties of speaking subjects. Which is better? To remain calm, cool and collected by taking the role of 'The Other' or show yourself up as being incompetent or worse, 'uncool', by 'being yourself'. That is the double bind into which *both* these characters are implicitly locked.

Self-possession has been turned into a highly convertible currency – both a selling-point for prospective employers and an insurance policy against feelings of indignation or disappointment triggered by rejection; a 'therapeutic' for dealing with anxieties of the first interview or the traumas of a first date. It is by these means that young people are supposed to conjure individual victories out of collective defeats, or, as here, black girls do better than white boys. Instead of being helped to confront their shared predicaments within a wider framework of knowledge and action, they are offered a purely personal tactic of disavowal.

What this means in classroom practice, as I found, is that even when a political issue, such as job discrimination, is implicitly posed, it cannot be clarified or made explicit within the terms of reference set out. I asked my group why they thought the garage manager had turned the applicants down. Was it because the girl was black and he was a racist? 'Well, no, because he couldn't see her, and she talked posh, so he couldn't tell by what she said.' Was it because she was a girl? 'No, because it wasn't a particularly male job anyway.' Why did the boy get rejected? 'He messed up the interview . . . no it couldn't be that 'cos the girl did everything right and she got the brush off too.' Did the manager then turn them down on different grounds? 'No.' Why? 'Because he said the same to both, treated them the same way.' But he might have been thinking different things about them? 'Well, you couldn't know, could you?' So what was the point of the story? 'We don't know. It's pointless, stupid. The people who wrote it must be mad!'

They are not mad, but they are certainly unconscious of the way their ideological grammar serves to close off any space for critical engagement by the reader, subverting their own undoubtedly progressive intentions.

I have tried to show how here the ideal of 'self-possession' plays a key role in shifting the ideology of self-improvement onto a new terrain. In the classic Samuel Smiles version, it was at least recognized that legal subjects were free to negotiate or bargain with real competitors in the market-place, to find the highest price for their labour and so on. I think it is very significant that no one in this book is shown doing so. The competition between the boy and girl is not set up in these terms at all. Rather it is invisibly structured by a purely symbolic exchange, a system of trade-offs between a public and a private self. The public self is made to adjust to undesirable realities (viz., the Youth Training Scheme or unemployment) by suppressing its real features (as in the case of the black girl). By the same token, the private self is made the focus of unrealizable desires (the dream job, or the job you really want, as with the boy). Subtly, the right of collective bargaining is transmuted into the obligation to conduct a purely interior negotiation between two halves of a divided self. Impression management makes its cultural capital out of just that split, even as it promises to resolve it. The full formula for its 'therapeutic' double bind should be written: 'privatize what you publicly are – publicize what you privately are not', and *enjoy* the duplicity for the sense of power it gives you over the means of self-representation.

Clearly we have come a long way from old-style bourgeois individualism. There is no place for the strong inner-directed ego, voice of conscience and morality in this scenario. Nor are young people being trained to measure themselves competitively against their peers, to run and win in the rat race. Yet elements of both the vocation and career codes are still in play; they have been transposed into the figures of a new individualism, more flexible and 'desirable' than the old, capable of adapting itself continually to the changing demands of market forces, while sustaining the illusion of its autonomy from them. It all adds up to a subject form ideally suited to a 'Hi-tech' version of consumer capitalism and one that is increasingly being mobilized against the residual forms of resistance which this is throwing up.[17]

The 'cooling out' of school-leavers' aspirations is no longer being left to the cumulative effect of educational failure, or the sudden pressures of the labour market. A new set of pedagogic and counselling devices is being developed, of which existing forms of careers guidance and SLS are but the crude prototypes. So let us take a brief look at some possible trends for the future.

I think it is possible to envisage a scenario in which the whole process of disqualification was turned to rather different account; instead of being coerced into conformity or bribed into better ways, classroom resisters would be encouraged to follow the example of those of their peers who have learned to win against the system by pretending to play its game. In other words they could be officially counselled how to 'play it cool'.

There are probably as many styles of playing it cool as there are terms to describe the practice. It is part of the survival tactics of every subordinate group, a way of neutralizing the consequences of powerlessness without challenging the prerogatives of power. Playing it cool avoids the risks of open defiance and the humiliation of abject surrender to the dominant norm. Indeed the very success of this game depends on how skilfully the ambiguous status of the practice is played upon. Its basic elements involve the following:

1.   The construction of a position of inner detachment or mental reserve which enables people to dissociate themselves from acts of compliance imposed upon them by a superior authority.
2.   The systematic inhibition of spontaneous feelings, whether positive or negative, in contexts where this would be interpreted as a sign of weakness.[18]

The central paradox of this whole manoeuvre is that it preserves the integrity of an oppositional identity only by practising a calculated duplicity: you pretend to be playing according to the official rules, whilst secretly bending them to the advantage of your own, rather different, game – that of 'loser wins'. Thus, for example, a 'cool' way for young soldiers to get a free discharge from the army may be to pretend that they are gay. But if you are really gay, and happen to like army life, then the 'cool' thing to do is to pretend that you are as heterosexual as the other lads, while in secret, in the company of your gay friends, continuing to 'be yourself'.

As this example shows, 'playing it cool' is a very double-edged weapon. In some contexts it may be a rational survival tactic; in others it may be profoundly self-destructive, and it is often very difficult to tell which is which – who is playing whose power game, who is losing and who winning – first because the game involves the suppression of true feelings (which is why it is a predominantly masculine technique) and second because this form of one-upmanship is simply a mirror image of real power relations, a way, precisely, of conjuring imaginary victories out of positions of real defeat.

'Playing it cool' is thus a rather more 'hip' version of the techniques of impression management already being taught to school-leavers in SLS. The cultural contexts may be different but the mechanisms (of splitting, etc.) are essentially the same, and this is what some of the new vocationalists are beginning to realize.

In our telephone interview story, if the black girl is represented as someone whose conformity to the dominant code involves the abject surrender of her identity, few readers will support her position – especially not black girls. The boy, in contrast, becomes a popular hero. But what if the story-line is contextualized in a slightly different way? What if the black girl is represented as *pretending* to play 'whitey's' game, while secretly laughing up her sleeve at him? Why, then she is 'playing it cool' and it is the boy who is being stupidly 'uncool'. I offered just such a reading to a control group of school-leavers and that indeed was their response.

The question this leaves us with is a disturbing one. For we seem to be looking at a mode of resistance which systematically fractures and undermines the inner strengths required to sustain a collective sense of predicament and struggle. But is this the only possible outcome? Or is the enterprise culture truly digging its own grave by releasing ambitions which cannot possibly be realized within the political and economic frameworks at its disposal? Is there a new and specifically post-modernist form of individualism which subverts the kinds of identifications which Thatcherism seeks to promote? Meanwhile, on the other side of the equation, are there alternative forms of vocational education or youth training which can promote a more cooperative vision of self-improvement and really useful knowledge?

Negative capabilities: taking after Thatcherism?

The creation of an enterprise culture is central to the Thatcher 'revolution'; it is here that the political, economic and ideological dimensions of the programme are most clearly and decisively integrated. The privatization of the public realm, the permeation of market values into the most intimate reaches of social life, the modernization of traditional forms of individualism, these aims required the creation of an

institutional framework, cutting across and linking industry and education, civil society and the state in a radically new way. Other elements of
the New Right philosophy, for example, its espousal of monetarism and
'Little Englander' nationalism, are important, but they remained essentially tactical interventions, to be jettisoned as soon as they had outlived
their usefulness. The question still to be decided is whether the
construction of an enterprise culture does indeed represent a genuine
process of socio-economic transformation or whether it too is yet another
heraldic device, lacking real substance. Will it survive as a permanent
monument to Thatcherism, or is its fate too intimately bound up with that
of the Iron Lady herself? Will the spell of the fairy story be finally broken
now that the economic miracle it forecast has so evidently failed to come
to pass?[19]

When Harold Macmillan was asked this question he answered by
quoting the Victorian adage 'children often run to Nurse, for fear of
finding something worse'. The image of Mrs Thatcher as a nanny figure, a
stern governess who keeps our noses to the grindstone while holding
socialism and the permissive society at bay, may indeed speak to infantile
fears and fantasies, especially on the part of men who had an upbringing
in which such authoritarian figures played a central role. But by the same
token it can hardly have the same appeal to all those who have lost out
under her regime – and that includes large sections of the professional
middle class, women, organized labour and the black underclass.

It could be argued that the enterprise culture never depended solely on
material indicators of prosperity. It was much more a moral crusade,
whose fervour was not dented by the high failure rate of small businesses.
After all, even the appeal to monetarism turned out to have more to do
with the moral economy of family budgeting and the iconography of
'sound money' than with actual fiscal policy.

A slightly more realistic argument is that the spell worked only as long
as there were just enough people visibly better-off to make even those
who were not think that it might one day happen to them. In other words
as long as the economy (and especially the housing market) was
sufficiently buoyant to transform the neurotic envies of relative deprivation into a soothing daydream of affluence just around the corner. But the
impact of the Poll Tax, coupled with high interest rates and the return of
'stagflation', was enough to dispel this hope. For an increasing number
the Thatcherite dream has begun to turn into a waking nightmare.

However useful such an argument is against the tendency to overestimate the 'special effects' of Thatcherism, it still cannot explain the fact
that however socially polarized Britain has become, however manifestly
unjust or inequitable some of the policies, there has been no corresponding movement to the Left; indeed the political opposition is now largely

fighting on the ground staked out by the New Right. For example the strategic importance of consumer choice, the new stress on individual as opposed to collective solutions, the development of more flexible work practices, the property- and share-owning democracy, all these themes pioneered by the New Right have been taken up in the Labour Party's recent policy review. This exercise clearly succeeded in convincing many floating voters that Labour would continue to support the central values and structures of the enterprise culture, merely ensuring that hitherto disadvantaged groups would have greater opportunity to participate in them. *En route* any alternative or more generous vision of social justice (let alone socialist policies) has been made unthinkable as well as unworkable.[20]

The continual reiteration of 'There is no alternative' seems to have worked as a self-fulfilling prophecy! But if so much of the New Right's thinking has come to be accepted as common sense, then this is only because it articulates basic changes in the structure of economy and society which in turn have created the ideological conditions for its hegemony. This is not just a passive process, or a matter of 'values'. Everyone who sets up their own business as a result of the Enterprise Allowance Scheme, or who buys their own council house, has a material stake in a particular kind of vision of society. Of course Mrs Thatcher is famous for her belief that 'society' is an abstraction dreamed up by Marxist sociologists, to make life awkward. But perhaps, after all, a little sociology might help us to understand the changing terrain on which the battle for hearts and minds has now to be fought?

Clearly we are living through a period in which the mechanical solidarities of kith and kin, neighbourhood and community, work-place and trade union are fast disintegrating; where they remain they take on increasingly overt – and violent – racist and sexist overtones. At the same time the political ideologies and institutions predicated on this type of solidarity have undergone a similar decay. Both state socialism and the collectivist ethic associated with classical parties of the Left are withering away.

Marx and Durkheim in their different ways foresaw this process, if not always the consequences, as the division of labour became increasingly specialized, and as new technologies replaced 'living labour' in the production process.[21] Durkheim thought it would usher in a new era of pluralistic socialism, based upon 'organic' solidarities, i.e. loose-knit associations between functionally differentiated but interdependent groups of producers and citizens. Marx argued that in principle the increased productivity of labour could liberate workers from the tyranny of the immediate labour process and help create the conditions for an eventual erosion of the basic divisions between manual and mental work.

Obviously we are a long way from this state of affairs, though the emergence of a new kind of cultural worker, and new forms of organization in the 'alternative' movements (black, gay and feminist) based on networking and affinity groups seems to point, partially, in this direction.

The actual situation is most hopefully characterized as a long-drawn-out and painful process of transition between Durkheim's two types of solidarity. There are no grounds for thinking that we have reached the end of history, let alone ideology, as the philosophers of the New Right have claimed. In any case, I have argued that it is more useful to consider the present conjuncture as the advent of a new technology of individualism which is better adapted to the formation of the 'collective worker' in a Hi-tech system of production as well as to the organization of popular consumption. I have tried to show how this has occurred within the shell of 'old' occupational and pedagogic forms and how, in the process, the desire to be different is both fuelled by a sense of powerlessness and social atomization, but also works to invest positions of subjection with an aura of false mastery. The 'modern religion' of individualism is so powerful precisely because it offers a source of integration which can never be attained under the existing divisions of labour, and which for that very reason stimulates an insatiable quest for its possession.

Here I believe lies the key to understanding why the fairy story of self-improvement continues to be believed even and especially when the economic indicators of success are so evidently absent. For if others fail then that is all the more reason to redouble one's own efforts, pushing oneself to the limits of self-exploitation and beyond, in order to grasp the holy grail of 'being your own boss', or 'being your own person'. In this context the actual splitting of social identity does not so much liberate people from 'totalizing' ideologies and 'fixed positions' as the post-modernists claim, as furnish them with strategies of dissociation, based on magical positions of omnipotence, reinforcing their real conditions of oppression.[22]

Yet to stop the analysis at this point is to ignore the energies which the enterprise culture has so clearly released. We have to recognize that the majority of people do feel empowered by owning their own home or small business in a way they do not by participating in more collective forms of undertaking. It is useless to argue that they are simply suffering from 'false consciousness'; equally the desire to be recognized in the first person singular is an existential imperative, not just the product of the machinations of 'Thatcherism'. For example, children in school do not want to be recognized as 'Green Class' or 'working-class under-achievers' or 'ethnic minority pupils' or even as 'black' if it means that they stop being treated as human subjects with unique personal histories. Teachers are valued precisely in so far as they are able to relate in a distinctively appropriate way to particular children, rather than simply pigeon-holing them. Moreover the way in which children negotiate and make sense of the social structures they inhabit does indeed vary dramatically from one to another, even where common patterns can be discerned. The kind of sociology which recognizes people as only the bearers of structures or functions has proved conspicuously unable to grasp these more intimate and subtle dialectics.

One attempt to do just that is to be found in the work of Roberto Unger.[23] For Unger, the motor for social change lies in what he calls (after Keats rather than Hermann Khan) negative capability – the permanent ability of human beings to transcend the given conditions of their social existence either through elementary acts of refusal, or through the active imagination of alternatives. In the absence of institutional structures which allow this sociological imagination to flourish at the level of policy making as well as everyday life, negative capabilities will necessarily take on individualistic, nihilistic or regressive forms, and this is precisely what the enterprise culture has so successfully engineered. There are many signs of this: the rampant careerism which has penetrated into large sections of the oppositional intelligentsia; the business ethics practised by many organizations supposedly committed to alternative codes of conduct; the cultural politics of narcissism based on making capital out of one's own specific oppression rather than making links with other, different, struggles. The rhetorics of hate and envy turn the demand for social justice into a drive for revenge.

But Unger argues that this is not the end of the story. He appeals to the tradition of artisan and petty bourgeois radicalism as an indication of the small-scale, decentralized and cooperative forms which negative capabilities might yet take, within the framework of a pluralistic socialism; it is not always clear from his account how these forms might be renewed under late capitalism or how they might overcome the sectarianism and fragmentation of current opposition, but perhaps this is less important than the purchase his model gives us on the contradictory tendencies of the present. A lot of contemporary cultural practice begins to make sense as the site of a continuing struggle between these two, reactionary and progressive, versions of negative capability, or rather as forms of compromise solution between them.

For example, to be 'young, gifted and black' is to experience the tensions between the drive to individual success and the adherence to a communal sense of roots. Recently those tensions have been explored in the humour of Lenny Henry, which pokes fun at black Yuppies and white racists with equal glee. Sharp dressing, cynical, street-wise, above all self-possessed, Henry's humour comes precisely from situations in which he 'blows his cool' *and* succeeds in disarming his adversaries, with a wisecrack or a bit of fancy footwork. He has the best of both worlds: this is the key to his success.

The Lenny Henry persona may be used to advertise the virtues of health foods to the new black middle class, but his style is still recognizably part of the experience of the black underclass. His symbolic importance lies in the way he straddles these two worlds, worlds which increasingly exist side by side in inner city neighbourhoods which have been gentrified. The relations of mutual exploitation which obtain between these two groups indeed provide the source of much of his best jokes. But if the tensions are resolved through his humour, the Lenny Henry laugh remains just nervous enough to signal that the contradictions remain and it might just be 'the fire next time' (James Baldwin).

Perhaps the best case study in the contradictory articulation of enterprise culture and youth culture, showing how the two sides of negative capability are actually being lived out, is to be found in Manfred Karge's play *The Conquest of the South Pole*. The play tells the story of four unemployed young men who make a last-ditch attempt to stave off total depression by beginning to act out the story of Amundsen's successful expedition to the Antarctic. The fantasy takes over their lives to varying degrees. For one of them it comes to represent an absolute, self-enclosed universe of meaning in which everything which is no longer available to him in the real world (a heroic sense of masculinity, comradeship, a purpose and direction to life, the triumph over adverse conditions) is magically retrieved and celebrated. For one of his friends, with a wife and child to support, the game is merely an interesting interlude, a brief moment of escape before returning to the painful realities of the dole queue and the search for work. The other two members of the game use the situation in yet another way, to work out their attitudes to life and death. At one point, one of them proposes changing the script, to base it on Shackleton's expedition because as he says:

> It's not triumph we need to act out. We do failures better. They're our staple diet. Every trip to the Job Centre, every phone call about a job is a failure. Even work is a failure, a paid failure, a badly paid failure. And so the failure must go on until we're all sick to death. It's only when you're up to your eyes in shit, desperately gasping for air, when you're really on your last legs, that the vomit might rise so high in your throat that you lash out in all directions. . . We are Shackleton and his crew, poor buggers who can see their goal ahead of them however hazily, somewhere there in the distance. (Karge, 1988)

This is an extreme version of the power of negative capability to conjure victories out of defeats. The question posed by the play is what is lost and gained in these 'victories'. The family man eventually settles down and is able to afford a package holiday in which he actually gets to visit the South Pole, though only as a tourist in the comfort of a Boeing 707! Meanwhile his friend remains at home, unemployed and immobilized by his imaginary conquests. The play seems to be saying that neither the actual fruits of consumerism nor the fairy tale successes of the enterprise culture offer sustainable identities to these youths, but neither are they entirely able to subvert their struggles towards an alternative sense of their lives, even if these are only immediately representable through the medium of fantasy or myth.

But do more material and overt practices of resistance offer a more hopeful resolution? Certainly a good deal of Unger's analysis is borne out by recent responses to the Government's education policies. There has been no shortage of 'negative capability' on the part of both teachers and pupils! Both have developed quite sophisticated strategies for reworking what is imposed upon them in the name of education or training, subverting or neutralizing the more extreme effects, while adapting other elements to their own, often conflicting purposes. For example, personal and social education (PSE), which was officially supposed to instil social and life skills, has in many cases provided a haven for critical pedagogies ousted from the core curriculum. The Tories' call for schools to educate 'active citizens' has similarly given a boost to forms of political literacy which put in question the processes which disenfranchise particular social groups. Within pre-vocational education, media studies work has been extended from teaching 'communication skills' to undertaking various kinds of cultural studies, in which that kind of instrumental attitude towards language is 'deconstructed' by the students themselves. Young people on YTS have not been cowed or dragooned into becoming model workers, but have sometimes used the opportunity, with or without official encouragement, to exercise their own kind of sociological imagination via '*samizdat* publications' and graffiti art attacking the more repressive aspects of the regime.

Meanwhile, further up the line, public and private service workers who have undergone assertiveness training may find that it helps them stand up to their bosses as well as their customers. Finally, recent research has shown that a significant number of working-class girls are putting their own personal ambitions first, and boyfriends and marriage later or last. This not only brings them up against the entrenched sexisms of male working-class culture, but may also push them towards non-traditional occupations. This may not turn them into ideological feminists, but it is likely to orient them towards forms of collective action which undermine the competitive logic of market relations.[24]

In many cases, these are *ad hoc* initiatives, improvised and uncoordinated responses. There are at present no structures which could transform

negative capabilities into positive ones, acts of refusal into the envisaging
of a different kind of education and society. Nevertheless the range and
diversity of these examples may give us some realistic grounds for hope. It
is to these practices that we should be looking for the elements of a new
kind of really useful knowledge, one which may resist incorporation into
particular curricula or pedagogic forms, but which nevertheless does
point us beyond the narrow pragmatics of vocationalism and towards a
different sense of enterprise.[25]

Notes

1. For an analysis of fairy tales see Bettelheim (1978). A classic psychoanalytic
    view of political ideology as wish fulfilment is to be found in the work of
    Lasswell (1948). However the position taken here is that political ideologies
    are necessarily programmatic, and propose strategies premised on a rational
    framework of implementation. However the relationship which is asserted
    between means and ends may be purely magical, and involve various kinds
    of primary process thinking. This follows the line of thinking developed by
    Murray Edelman (1977 and 1988), who argues that both the realism and the
    rationality of political ideologies is constructed through particular kinds of
    narrative devices, employed as part of their persuasive rhetoric.
2. The first Black Paper appeared in 1969, as a set of dissenting right-wing
    essays. By 1975 the fourth such paper laid out the terms of what
    subsequently became known as the Great Debate inaugurated by the then
    Labour Prime Minister James Callaghan. In her first government Mrs
    Thatcher appointed one of the Black Paper editors as Minister for Higher
    Education and subsequently many of the ideas first put forward by this
    group have been taken up and elaborated by right-wing think-tanks and
    influential journals such as the *Salisbury Review*. The original 'state of the
    nation' debate took place in the 1890s and centred on the lack of mental and
    physical fitness of working-class youth to meet the demands of a modern
    industrial economy. On this first 'Great Debate' see M. Weiner (1982) and
    the rather different interpretation of J. Ahier (1989).
3. For a good account of the way Thatcherism exploited the weakness of
    Labour's education policy see CCCS (1981). For an analysis of the different
    tendencies within New Right Educationalism see Johnson (1989). For a
    more general discussion of New Right ideology see the contributions to
    Levitas (1986).
4. It has been the major argument of sociologists of education that schools
    reproduce the division between manual and mental labour precisely through
    the forms of knowledge and subjectivity to which they give priority. In this
    perspective, the new vocationalism simply makes explicit the principles of
    power and division hitherto 'buried' in the hidden curriculum. See the
    contributions to Dale (ed.) (1985).
5. For a discussion of this complex of changes see Hall and Jacques (1983) and
    Hall (1988); also Lash and Urry (1987). An analytic framework which
    makes these changes central to the problematics of education can be found
    in Apple (1982). The concept of 'post Fordism' has been used to describe a

structural shift away from the material culture of mass production associated with an industrial working class, as originally described by Gramsci (1971), towards a service economy segmented into particular consumer markets and powered by capital intensive information technologies. This thesis is developed in Murray (1989).

6. The basic programme of the new vocationalism was first spelt out in a series of policy documents produced by the Manpower Services Commission (MSC) concerning the introduction of youth training schemes to deal with the high levels of youth unemployment experienced in the 1970s and early '80s. See Rees and Atkinson (1982). The role of the MSC was then extended backwards into secondary education with the creation of the Technical and Vocational Education Initiative (TVEI) and the Certificate in Pre-Vocational Education (CPVE). This latter was designed to provide otherwise unqualified school-leavers with sufficient training in work discipline to make them attractive to employers. For the development of the MSC see Finn (1987) and also the contributions to Benn and Fairley (1986). Most recently an attempt has been made to rationalize the whole structure by abolishing the MSC and putting in its place a network of Training and Enterprise Councils. These are supposed to provide local bases of cooperation between employers, education authorities and training agencies. This is not however a partnership between equals, but rather a framework within which the hegemony of the enterprise culture can be established over education as well as training.

7. Foucault (1977) has argued that discipline is not a purely repressive force but actively empowers the subject through its regulation of bodies. Conversely it could be argued that skill regulates the subject through the mastery of techniques. Both these aspects of socialization are present in the 'bio-political' strategies discussed below. Foucault's concept of a 'technology of the self' is also useful in pinpointing some of the discursive strategies which are deployed in and through youth training regimes.

8. The phrase is that of John Biggs-Davidson, a member of the extreme 'Old Right' within the Tory Party. For a history of the moral panics focused on youth see Pearson (1983).

9. The best recent studies of YTS, combining ethnography with structural analysis, are Cockburn (1988) and Hollands (1990).

10. For an account of how this historical compromise functioned to construct an 'anti-industrial spirit' at the time when Britain was supposedly the 'work-shop of the world' see Weiner (1982). Much of what follows draws on the theory of reproduction codes outlined in Cohen (1986). An application of this theory to the understanding of changing forms of working-class transitions from school can be found in Cohen (1984a). For an account of the role which codes of inheritance, vocation and careers have played in the formations of educational and class ideologies see the work of Bisseret (1978). For their role in constructing notions of skill see More (1980).

11. For a historical analysis of changing forms of political socialization within working-class culture see Cohen (1984b).

12. See the contributions to Hall and Jacques (1983), and the critique of this position in Jessop *et al.* (1987).

13. Historical accounts of youth policy and provision have tended to over-emphasize these continuities. See, for example, the otherwise interesting study by Horne (1984). Historical studies of rational recreation and

self-improvement movements such as Bailey (1978) and Morris (1970) are useful but do not focus on the kinds of discourse which were mobilized by them. In contrast, the work of Ahier (1989) provides a much more sophisticated reading of these kinds of ideological text. Samuel Smiles's works (1859, 1894) would repay similar close analysis. Lasch (1980) puts forward a trenchant critique of the post-war personal growth movement and this is developed further in Richards (1989). Both studies, however, remain at the level of 'histories of ideas'; a discourse analysis of popular ideologies of self-help in contemporary psychology is to be found in Treacher (1989).

14.   In tracing the provenance of the disparate elements which make up SLS ideology I have followed Griffith (1983) in concentrating on its core elements and forms of implantation. For this reason I have taken the work of Argyle (1978, 1980) as paradigmatic because it maps out the main framework within which this set of practices has developed. This is not to deny the specificity of purely educational variants such as Priestley and Maguire (1978) or Hopson and Scally (1981a, 1981b) and the extent to which these adaptations may modify some aspects of Argyle's own behaviourism.

15.   Quotation from Hopson and Scally (1981a).

16.   The materials reviewed here were all published between 1979 and 1984. Many of them were produced in association with the National Extension College and linked to a 'new wave' of Teen TV programmes which combined pop music, 'life-style' issues and practical advice on training and work. They include 'Roadshow', 'JobMate', '16 Up', 'Help', 'Just the Job' and 'The Job Hunter Kit'. *The School Leaver's Guide*, which is quoted in this and the following section, was published by Longman's as part of a pre-vocational educational package. More recently Life Skills Associates have produced some rather more sophisticated and interactive texts for use in personal and social education (PSE). See also the materials published by the Careers Research Advisory Centre (CRAC) which belong to the more traditional genre of careers guide.

17.   The classic study of individualism by Macpherson (1962) deals only with its *strong* bourgeois form and its conditions of reproduction as a *political* ideology. The approach which has been adopted here draws largely on the pioneering work of Maurice Edelman (1979). Edelman outlines the constitution of legal subjectivity in civil society and then looks at how this is transformed by the advent of new consciousness industries. Unlike the theories of 'post-modernism', developed by Jameson (1984), Lyotard (1984) or Baudrillard (1988), Edelman does not relate changing modes of individualism to some generalized 'cultural logic' or 'structural tendency' of advanced capitalism, but to specific transformations of property relations and to the way these relations are represented, articulated or lived in particular contexts. See Abercrombie *et al.* (1986) for an attempt to develop an equally grounded and differential model of individualism. Williams (1983) also makes some characteristically insightful comments on what he calls 'mobile privatization' as a point of transmutation between competitive and self-possessive modes of individualism. The weakness in all these accounts lies in the failure to grasp the power of individualism as an *existential* ideology; this is being remedied in recent studies influenced by the psychoanalytic theories; see for example the contributions to Henriques *et al.* (1984) and Rustin (1989).

18. Winnicott (1965) from a Kleinian perspective argues that the splitting mechanisms described here are attributable to specific developmental difficulties which prevent a normal process of integration taking place. Post-modernists, influenced by Lacan, tend to celebrate this fragmentation and argue that integration is an illusory quest on the part of a decentred or split subject. The view taken here is that if, indeed, splitting is a necessary defence mechanism, it appears to be one which is especially characteristic of the subcultures produced by oppressed groups. However, most strategies of consciousness-raising involving such groups attempt to challenge splitting at the level of individual consciousness by setting in motion a process of collective self-affirmation. Nevertheless this often involves conserving splitting at a higher level of abstraction, i.e. by dividing the world into good and bad reference groups. On this point see the contributions by Hoggett and Richards in Richards (1989).
19. A good summary of debates on the enterprise culture is to be found in the journal *Theory, Culture and Society* (1985).
20. The Labour Party's Policy Review (1987–9) was an attempt to outflank the fundamentalist Left and to distance the party apparatus from its trade union base. To defeat both labourism and ultra-leftism it was necessary to mobilize some of the more libertarian elements of New Left thinking against the central tenets of 'command socialism', whilst at the same time moving the party to the right to capture the political centre ground from the then emergent Alliance parties. This in turn meant abandoning unpopular aspects of Labour Party policy, most notably its commitment to unilateralism. The policy review was thus essentially a strategic device for strengthening Kinnock's base of support inside the party and signalling to the mass media the rout of its favourite 'loony lefties', such as Tony Benn and 'Red Ken' Livingstone. Not surprisingly it did not produce any substantively new policies in the field of education and youth training, but it has proved an exceptionally effective electoral device.
21. For a discussion of some points of correspondence between Marx and Durkheim see Schnorrer (1984). For the political implications of these changes for the labour movement see Gorz (1982).
22. The recent play by Catherine Johnson (shown at the 1989 Edinburgh Festival), 'Boys Mean Business', provided a brilliant exploration of forms of self-exploitation current within youth-enterprise culture. See also the discussion in Hebdige (1987).
23. The concept of negative capability as outlined in Unger (1983 and 1987) is very close to Sartre's theory of *depassment* and Sartre's work is indeed a central influence on his thought. A useful overview of Unger's work is given by Anderson (1989).
24. For strategies of resistance to YTS, see Hollands (1990), and with particular reference to girls' transitions, Cockburn (1988). For a general discussion of girls' cultures see the contributions to McRobbie and Nava (1984).
25. The 'No Kidding' project, directed by the author of this chapter, 1984–7, set out to develop such an alternative approach to pre-vocational education based on the critical pedagogy of cultural studies. For a detailed account see Cohen (1990).

Bibliography and references

Abercrombie, N., S. Hill and B. Turner (1986) *The Sovereign Individuals of Capitalism*, London: Allen & Unwin.

Ahier, J. (1989) *Industry, Children and the Nation*, London: Falmer.

Anderson, P. (1989) 'Politics, passion, plasticity', *New Left Review* **173**.

Apple, M. (1982) *Education and Power*, London: Routledge & Kegan Paul.

Argyle, M. (1978) *Social Skills and Mental Health*, London: Methuen.

Argyle, M. (1980) *Social Skills and Work*, London: Methuen.

Bailey, P. (1978) *Leisure and Class in Victorian Britain*, London: Routledge & Kegan Paul.

Bates, I. *et al.* (1984) *Schooling for the Dole*, London: Macmillan.

Baudrillard, J. (1988) *Selected Writings*, Cambridge: Polity Press.

Benn, C. and J. Fairley (eds.) (1986) *Challenging the MSC*, London: Pluto.

Bettelheim, B. (1978) *The Uses of Enchantment*, Harmondsworth: Penguin.

Bisseret, N. (1978) *Education, Class Language and Ideology*, London: Routledge & Kegan Paul.

CCCS (1981) *Unpopular Education*, London: Hutchinson.

Cockburn, C. (1988) *Two Track Training*, London: Macmillan.

Cohen, P. (1984a) 'Losing the generation game' in J. Curran (ed.) *The Future of the Left*, Cambridge: Polity Press.

Cohen, P. (1984b) 'Against the new vocationalism' in I. Bates *et al. Schooling for the Dole*, London: Macmillan.

Cohen, P. (1986) *Rethinking the Youth Question*, London: University of London, Institute of Education.

Cohen, P. (1990) *Really Useful Knowledge*, Stoke-on-Trent, Trentham.

Curran, J. (ed.) (1984) *The Future of the Left*, Cambridge: Polity Press.

Dale, R. (ed.) (1985) *Education, Training and Employment*, Oxford: Pergamon.

Edelman, B. (1979) *Ownership of the Image*, London: Routledge & Kegan Paul.

Edelman, M. (1977) *Political Language*, London: Academic Press.

Edelman, M. (1988) *Constructing the Political Spectacle*, Chicago: University of Chicago Press.

Finn, D. (1987) *Training without Jobs*, London: Macmillan.

Foucault, M. (1977) *Discipline and Punish*, London: Allen Lane.

Gleeson, D. (1984) *Youth Training and the Search for Work*, London: Routledge & Kegan Paul.

Gorz, A. (1982) *Farewell to the Working Class*, London: Pluto.

Gramsci, C. (1971) *Prison Notebooks*, London: Lawrence & Wishart.

Griffith, T. (1983) *Skilling for Life*, Toronto: OISE.

Hall, S. (1988) 'The Toad in the Garden: Thatcherism among the theorists' in C. and L. Grossberg (eds.) (1988).

Hall, S. and M. Jacques (eds.) (1983) *The Politics of Thatcherism*, London: Lawrence & Wishart.

Hebdige, D. (1987) *Hiding in the Light*, London: Comedia.

Henriques, J. *et al.* (1984) *Changing the Subject*, London: Methuen.

Hoggett, P. (1989) 'The culture of uncertainty' in B. Richards (1989).

Hollands, R. (1990) *The Long Transition*, London: Macmillan.

Hopson, B. and M. Scally (1981a) *Life Skills Training*, London: Tavistock.

Hopson, B. and M. Scally (1981b) 'Life skills teaching in schools and colleges', *Liberal Education* **44**.

Horne, J. (1984) 'Youth unemployment programmes – A historical perspective' in D. Gleeson *Youth Training and the Search for Work*, London: Routledge & Kegan Paul.

Jameson, F. (1984) 'Postmodernism or the cultural logic of capital', *New Left Review* **146**

Jessop, R. *et al.* (1987) 'Thatcher and the Left', *New Left Review* **165**

Johnson, R. (1989) 'Thatcherism and English education', *History of Education* **18** (2)

Karge, M. (1988) *The Conquest of the South Pole*, Edinburgh: Traverse.

Lasch, C. (1980) *The Culture of Narcissism*, London: Abacus.

Lash, S. and J. Urry (1987) *The End of Organised Capitalism*, Cambridge: Polity Press.

Lasswell, H. (1948) *Power and Personality*, New York: Norton.

Levitas, R. (ed.) (1986) *The Ideology of the New Right*, Cambridge: Polity Press.

Lyotard, J.-F. (1984) *The Post Modern Condition*, Manchester: Manchester University Press.

Macpherson, P. (1962) *The Political Theory of Possessive Individualism*, Oxford: Oxford University Press.

McRobbie, A. and M. Nava (eds.) (1984) *Gender and Generation*, London: Macmillan.

More, C. (1980) *Skill and the Working Class*, London: Croom Helm.

Morris, R. J. (1970) 'The history of self help', *New Society* **167**

Murray, R. (1989) *Life After Ford*, Cambridge: Polity Press.

Nelson, C. and L. Grossberg (eds.) (1988) *Marxism and the Interpretation of Culture*, London: Macmillan.

Pearson, G. (1983) *Hooligans – A History of Respectable Fears*, London: Macmillan.

Priestley, J. and H. Maguire (1978) *Social Skills and Personal Problem Solving*, London: Tavistock.

Rees, T. and P. Atkinson (1982) *Youth Unemployment and State Intervention*, London: Routledge & Kegan Paul.

Richards, B. (ed.) (1989) *Crises of the Self*, London: FAB.

Rustin, M. (1989) 'Post Kleinian psychoanalysis and the post-modern', *New Left Review* **173**

Schnorrer, P. (1984) *Marx, Durkheim and the Post Modern World*, Calcutta: New Perspective Books.

Smiles, S. (1859) *Self Help*, London: Murray.

Smiles, S. (1894) *Character*, London: Murray.

Symonds, G. D. R. (1981) *The School Leaver's Guide*, Harlow: Longman.

Theory, Culture and Society (1985) *The Fate of Modernity* **2** (3), special issue.

Treacher, A. (1989) 'Be your own person' in K. Richards (ed.) *Crises of the self*, London: FAB.

Unger, R. (1983) *Passion – An Essay on Personality*, New York: New York Free Press.

Unger, R. (1987) *Plasticity into Power*, Cambridge: Cambridge University Press.

Weiner, M. (1982) *English Culture and the Decline of the Industrial Spirit*, Cambridge: Cambridge University Press.

Williams, R. (1983) 'The end of an era', *New Left Review* **181**

Winnicott, D. W. (1965) *The Maturational Process and the Facilitating Environment*, London: Tavistock.

Young, M. F. D. (ed.) (1971) *Knowledge and Control*, London: Macmillan.

4

The marketeers and the National Health Service

Jennifer A. Roberts
*London School of Hygiene and Tropical Medicine,
United Kingdom*

> The mystique of the market – the supposition that the market does
> no wrong, that markets do not malfunction (only governments do) –
> is more the work of propagandists than economic scientists of any
> era.
>
> (Edmund S. Phelps, *Political Economy*, New York: W. W. North)

The general surge towards extending the domain of the market in the
United Kingdom has now reached health care. It is, thus, necessary to
assess whether health care is marketable and consider how the proposed
changes in the National Health Service will affect the efficiency and
equity of health care provision.

Weber (1968) defined marketability in relation to the regularity with
which an object was exchanged in the market. Health care has not
historically been regularly or generally freely exchanged in the market-
place. Instead, in most societies, formal and informal conventions have
constrained the exchange of health care. In fact, general wariness about
allowing health care to be exposed to market forces goes back at least
2,000 years. The Greeks were concerned lest physicians should allow
self-interest to affect their treatment of patients. Physicians were
cautioned 'not to be anxious about fixing a fee', 'sometimes give your
services for nothing, to those who are strangers in financial straits'.
Aristotle considered the function of medicine to be the 'production of
health not wealth' (Sohl, 1988). In 1676, William Petty in his 'Anatomy
Lecture' considered that medicine was too important to 'leave Phisitians
and Patients to their own shifts', (Petty, 1676, p. 176; discussed in Fein,
1971).

The principles of the National Health Service set out in 1948 also sought to distance economic man from medicine (Roberts, 1989a). The principles behind the scheme are most clearly stated by Aneurin Bevan (1952, p. 75), the minister responsible for the establishment of the National Health Service:

> The collective principle asserts that the resources of medical skill and the apparatus of healing shall be placed at the disposal of the patient, without charge, when he or she needs them; that medical treatment and care should be a communal responsibility, that they should be made available to rich and poor alike in accordance with medical need and by no other criteria. It claims that financial anxiety in time of sickness is a serious hindrance to recovery, apart from its unnecessary cruelty. It insists that no society can legitimately call itself civilized if a sick person is denied medical aid because of lack of means.

The service was designed to provide comprehensive medical care free at point of use to all who needed it. Within the budget constraints set by the Government and the administrative framework of the service, doctors were able to provide care for patients according to need and no other criteria.[1] As it was assumed there was an identifiable need and an agreed method of meeting it, there was no economic problem: there was no reason to choose what to produce or how or for whom to produce it. Economic incentives were purposefully excluded. In contrast, the White Paper produced by the British Government in 1989 on the future of the same National Health Service, 'Working for Patients' (HMSO, 1989a), sets out specifically to harness economic incentives to medical practice. How did the NHS, that 'most unsordid act of social policy' (Abel-Smith, 1978), become embroiled in the current extension of market ideology?

The New Right's belief in the market-place propels them to seek solutions to 'market failure' by removing 'obstructions' to the market rather than in state intervention in the finance and provision of health care. Commentators have noted that there are two strands to the New Right's thinking about markets: the libertarian and authoritarian strands (Bosanquet, 1983; Levitas, 1986; Gamble, 1986). The libertarians see markets as a liberating force encouraging entrepreneurship and as a protection against collectivism. The authoritarians see markets as a disciplinary force propelling organizations to ever greater efficiency to ensure survival. The libertarian and authoritarian strands of New Right policies came together (sometimes, as we shall see, unwittingly aided by defenders of the NHS) to bring health care within the ambit of the Government's programme for radical reform of the 'public sector'.

The most fundamental reason for the proposed changes in the NHS is to be found in the philosophy of the minimalist state. This includes the belief that individuals have the right to all lawfully acquired property: tax is theft. This belief leaves unresolved problems relating to the justice of the initial distribution of property, but these difficulties have not impeded the implementation of government policy which has moved away from universal comprehensive provision towards a 'safety-net' approach to welfare.

The policy shift proceeded very slowly in health care. It took the form, in the early 1980s, of a gradual erosion of services by underfunding – a response which was in line with government policy to reduce its involvement in the public sector. Previous budgetary policies had aimed to maintain the 'real' level of services by increasing the budget to take into account changes in the prices of resources used in the health sector and adjusting, to some extent, for demographic and technological changes. This approach was replaced by a budgetary system which was 'cash limited', and no longer adequately compensated for inflation in the health sector (HMSO, 1988). Reasons for the change were given in February 1988, by the Chief Secretary to the Treasury, 'We feel that not indexing effectively the relative price effect is a good counter-inflationary measure and an incentive to economy'. These budgetary changes took place during a period of structural adjustment in health care, which resulted from the application of the Resource Allocation Working Party (DHSS, 1976)[2] formula and from developments in community mental health services. The costs of rationalization, tight budgetary constraints and staffing shortages stretched health services to breaking point in the autumn of 1987 and the winter of 1988. This crisis was then seized upon by the British Government as an opportunity for a major review. The proposals laid out in 1989 in the document *Working for Patients* are the result (HMSO, 1989a). This document is the most revolutionary to have been issued since the formation of the NHS. The proposals are in tune with government policy and provide a framework for subsequent privatization.

This review took the form of a secret investigation undertaken by a selected group of government ministers and their policy advisers. But it stimulated a more public debate, orchestrated by the parliamentary inquiry undertaken by the Social Services Select Committee (HMSO, 1988) in the spring and summer of 1988. A torrent of work was produced and most of it was referred to or presented as evidence to the Committee. The main thrust of the evidence was to support the opening up of the provision of health care to the market, whilst advocating that funding should remain predominantly from general taxation.

Advocating the use of markets in health care is not an easy task. Health care is not unique in posing problems for the operation of markets. But health care stands out as posing more problems for markets than most other 'goods'. It has problems associated with markets structure, as well as having characteristics which markets, of whatever structure, have difficulty in accommodating. The traditional neo-classical reservations about the use of markets have been swept aside by those who see the market as a defence against collectivism – interpreted to include state provision for all, financed by general taxation – and as a force which squeezes inefficiency from the system. These alternative perspectives are explored and then used to assess the changes proposed.

Markets and health care

Social and cultural problems

The discussion about the use of markets in health care has to be seen in the context of social and cultural constraints which limit the use of certain resources and also determine whether they can be bought and sold in the market-place. There are strong feelings and social taboos about the marketability of certain goods which become apparent when conventions are contravened. The activities of an entrepreneurial German Count, Count Adelman, during the late 1980s are an example. The Count has been busily employed in taboo areas such as buying babies for adoption from Brazil, recruiting mercenaries for African states; and he has now moved into kidneys *(British Medical Journal,* 1988, p. 1292). These activities evoke very different responses (from the BBC programme 'That's Life' broadcast in January 1988): 'Buying and selling organs is repugnant to our conscience and dangerous to the moral fibre of our society. It represents the exploitation of the poor by the rich.' Alternatively, it can be seen as an acceptable gain from trade, 'I'm not worried, he has the money and is satisfied, someone who was dying is saved and happy'.

Advertisements for kidneys appealed to those with 'merciful hearts', but those buying kidneys have sought out those in 'financial straits' – Count Adelman wrote to those recently bankrupt. In West Germany legislation was proposed in 1988, to prevent the use of kidneys from living patients, in line with the agreement of European Health Ministers *(Hansard,* 1989b). In Norway those not able to obtain treatment for kidney failure are precluded from buying it (Mooney and McGuire, 1988).

The problems of people with kidney disease were discussed at a conference in October 1988, on Occupational Health and Fitness for Work (Edwards *et al.,* 1988). A personnel manager told a story of an employee whose life was being threatened by kidney disease. He needed a transplant. He was a valued colleague and employee. 'What', asked the personnel manager, 'could the company do to help? What did the clinician suggest?' An uncomfortable silence preceded the clinician's reply, 'Do all you can to ensure that the public donate kidneys', he said. He, thus, gave a collectivist answer to an individual problem. There was audible relief from the audience. Kidneys were not for sale in Britain. Unfortunately, even as he spoke this principle may well have been breached, for it was later discovered that Turkish donors had been used by a private clinic in London to provide kidneys for transplantation (*Hansard*, 1989a). Now legislation is to be introduced, in the United Kingdom, to preclude the buying and selling of organs (*Hansard*, 1989b). This, and the recent prohibition on the sale of ova for extra-uterine fertilization, sets limits to the use of markets in Thatcher's Britain. But even where markets are used, markets for health care present problems.

Competition and health care

The idea of a market system is that it brings together buyers and sellers who exchange goods at a mutually acceptable rate. The notion of efficiency within the market system focuses upon a particular type of firm: the 'perfectly competitive firm'. If perfect competition existed in all sectors of the economy, and if distribution was socially acceptable, it can be argued that the use of society's resources would be optimized. But perfectly competitive markets have very special attributes. In a perfectly competitive market there are a large number of firms compared to the size of the market, the products are homogeneous, entry and exit are free and all parties to transactions are fully informed. Few of these attributes are likely to be found in the real market-place: 'The theory of competition is at once the pride and the shame of economics, a logical structure of the greatest elegance which has only the most tenuous connection with the reality it is supposed to interpret' (Downie, 1958).

In the health care 'market', the connection is even more tenuous. In health care it is unlikely that there will be many firms compared to the size of the market. Because of the technical characteristics of medical care there will often be only a limited number of doctors and perhaps only one hospital near to those who use the services. Thus, there will be a tendency towards monopolistic markets. This tendency is increased by restrictions of entry into medicine imposed by the profession, by government regulations, controls on training and licensing and by possibilities of economies of scale in health care.

Monopolies tend to produce insufficient goods relative to society's demands and are unlikely to produce them at least cost. Monopolies are viewed with suspicion by economists on both sides of the political spectrum, though some on the New Right find greater sympathy with the Schumpeterian belief in the potential of monopolies to encourage initiative and invention, at least initially. They have, however, different policies to contain monopolies. Whereas those on the Left advocate government intervention to control undesirable monopolistic character-istics of health care markets, those on the Right consider that government and professional intervention in health care create more divisive forms of monopoly. They would control monopoly tendencies differently, e.g. by time-limited franchises allocated by competitive bidding – a method commonly used to allocate television channels or the 'right' to 'set up shop' at airports or on motorways.

The medical profession has traditionally asserted that each profession-al provides the same service, i.e. provides a homogeneous service. This has been disputed and is seen, by New Right critics, as an attempt by the profession to avoid competition (Green, 1986). Evidence that differences exist has been available for a long time (Ashley *et al.*, 1972), but it has become the focus of increased attention in recent years and is mentioned in the White Paper (HMSO, 1989a). Even if each professional produced homogeneous services, however, homogeneity in health care differs from that of many ordinary goods as health care is often unique to and embodied in the patient. Thus, unlike most other products, it cannot be stored or retraded. This ability to retrade is an important element in making competition effective. In the absence of retrading possibilities, clinicians can discriminate amongst clients and patients, thus becoming, in effect, 'discriminating monopolists', able to squeeze the maximum from each buyer. In the past, they have sometimes been given licence to operate in this way, provided they used the proceeds gained from the rich to subsidize the poor.

Another requirement of a perfectly competitive market is easy access to information by all parties. This too is unlikely to be met. A large information gap exists between doctors and patients which imbalances the power relationships between the parties giving advantage to the doctor. The New Right see regulations limiting advertising as adding to these imbalances.

This approach, however, assumes that there exists a pool of informa-tion which can be distributed amongst the parties. A more serious issue, however, is the lack of information about many health care activities (Cochran, 1972; Bunker, 1982). There is a very limited pool of information available for distribution amongst doctors and patients. Many treatments are unevaluated and often difficult to evaluate. This is the 'black box' of medicine which needs to be opened up to the scrutiny of medical audit and evaluation in order to expand our understanding of health care and so improve the quality of care and the efficiency of services.

This lack of information is related to another facet of health care: uncertainty. Uncertainty about the likelihood and possible costs of treatment is a feature of health care (Arrow, 1963). Insurance is the usual solution to uncertainty, but in health care markets there are a number of problems. Insurance is based on the premise that although an individual's risk may be unknown, risks for society as a whole can be foreseen with greater confidence. Thus, by pooling resources, the unfortunate can be reimbursed out of a common fund.

However, because the likelihood of the need for health care is unpredictable for any one individual, those who are risk-avoiders will insure against future illness, but those who are more optimistic will not. This has serious implications for any society which does not wish to exclude anyone in need from care. Thus, an insurance-based system faces a 'free-rider' problem: those who do not insure will get treatment at the expense of those who do. To avoid the problem, many societies have adopted compulsory insurance which is contributed to by all except those who are very old, very young, too sick or too poor to pay. The payment is usually shared amongst individuals, governments and employers. It can become a tax upon employment with adverse effects upon those industries which are not able to pass on the charge in the form of lower wages to workers or higher prices to consumers. For these reasons, it is unpopular with employers and it is often supplemented by income or sales taxes.

Free-riders are not the only problem facing insurance-based systems. Insurance operates on the principle that there is a known risk *for society*, but for any *one individual* the probability of an event happening is less than 1. For many individuals, however, health care will certainly be required: the probability will equal 1. Chronically ill, physically and mentally handicapped people and those with certain degenerative diseases will, thus, be uninsurable without government support. In addition, the old and the young, high users of health care, are likely to be amongst the poorer sections of society and unable to pay the premiums. In 1985–6, 63.8 per cent of health care expenditure in England was spent on those under 15 or over 64 who made up 35.9 per cent of the population (HMSO, 1988). Government intervention in funding appears inescapable. Even in the United States, which has a low public involvement in health care, some 40 per cent of the health budget is spent by government on the uninsurable: the elderly, the chronically sick, the poor and those with high-cost diseases such as renal failure. But, in the United States, in spite of this 'safety-net' some 37 million remain uninsured.

'Adverse selection' is another difficulty facing insurance-based systems. This occurs because those with high risks are likely to opt in and those with low risks are likely to opt out. The high-risk groups are likely to incur higher costs causing premiums to rise, thus forcing out more low-risk groups and the poor. The adverse selection amongst those seeking insurance is countered by adverse selection by insurance companies who exclude certain groups, raise premiums or restrict coverage. It is also extended to those who provide the services, who, under certain reimbursement schemes, may seek to 'select out' patients likely to be costly (Scheffler, 1989).

Moral hazard is another problem. This is a term used to refer to the tendency of some of the insured population to take more risks or use services more than they would have done had they not obtained insurance. In health care, concern about moral hazard has also been extended to the action of agents of patients; the doctors, who, it is argued, may be extravagant in the use of resources if their patients are insured or paid for by third parties. Moral hazard will also be introduced if providers of health care treat patients in ways which allow them to take advantage of loopholes in contractual arrangements, e.g. if emergency treatment is covered by insurance but other care is not, there may well be a shift in the definition of an emergency. As well as facing these considerable problems, insurance schemes for health care are costly to manage.

Health care on every criterion fits rather badly into the neo-classical ideal of a perfectly competitive market. Yet it is argued by neo-classical economists that once outside this ideal, the main advantages of the market-place will not accrue. Society's welfare will not be maximized. Firms will tend to fight for market shares, collude against the consumer, not produce at the lowest cost, differentiate their products and be sluggish in responding to market signals. The main neo-classical advantages of markets will not apply to health care.

Many of the arguments for and against the market for health care outlined in this chapter are concerned with markets as 'static' entities. Economists of the New Right find this static presentation of markets rather boring and lacking in predictive power (Hayek, 1949). And it is in respect of the dynamics of markets that we find the core arguments of the New Right's attack.

Much has been said in the past about the dynamics of markets. As Ignatieff (1984, pp. 122, 124) reminds us 'For [Adam] Smith a market society could remain free and virtuous only if all its citizens were capable of stoic self-command. Without this self-command, capitalism would become a "deluded scramble".' Alfred Marshall in 1904 referred to the brutal aspects of markets which, he argued, emerged when 'Free competition was set loose to run like a huge untamed monster its wayward course' (p. 8). These tendencies could, according to Marshall, be brought under control, not by virtue, but by the State. But constant vigilance would be required to curb the tendency of firms to collude and operate against the best interests of society as a whole. For the contemporary New Right, however, markets are seen as the key to freedom from encroachment by the State. They are considered to foster initiative, encourage growth and react quickly to market signals in the endless search for better products and better ways of getting things done. Monopolistic periods will be accepted as nodal growth points in the system; a necessary stage in the adjustment to new products and new technology. The New Right sees no problem with this as long as the markets are potentially 'contestable' – open to competition from others. These views of markets mostly derived from arguments developed by Hayek (1949) are very important elements in the current debate.

Limits to markets

Health care has characteristics, however, which most economists have considered to be beyond the scope of markets. These are externalities and distributional issues. Externalities refer to the effects which occur when those who are not directly involved in a transaction are affected by it. There are many examples of this in health care. We benefit from knowing others are cared for; we benefit from protection from infection – immunization, by reducing the risks of infection, benefits not only those being immunized but also those who are not. We suffer from the side-effects of industry; its waste products pollute the air and water and alter the environment. Yet these social costs are not included in the cost of the product to the producer or in the price which the consumer pays.

In addition to externalities some health-related goods have characteristics of public goods. Consumers are not rivals for public goods – there is enough for all and it is difficult to exclude anyone from benefits or costs. Such goods require cooperation if they are to be produced at all. Many traditional public health activities, such as control of pollution and infectious diseases, fall into this category. By endeavouring to include everyone in the provision of health care (even visitors to the country were eligible initially) and by stating that one person's care should not be affected by the needs of another, Bevan, the architect of the NHS, appears to have endowed the NHS, as far as he was able, with the characteristics of a public good (Bevan, 1952, p. 80).

The New Right often denies the existence of external benefits and public goods, or at least claim they are not extensive (Cheung, 1978).[2] Present concern about public and environmental health problems however – e.g. the scare in the United Kingdom about the *Salmonella enteritidis* bacteria in eggs and poultry in December 1988 – keeps these issues on the health agenda (Communicable Disease Reports, 1988–9). They are not readily amenable to the New Right's policies of dealing with externalities by bringing together those who benefit or suffer, thus enabling them to bargain. In the *Salmonella* case in Britain, those who provided the affected eggs could not be identified. Similarly, those responsible for polluting the air are numerous and those who suffer as a consequence are widely dispersed: individual bargaining is not possible; collective international action is required.

Markets cannot resolve issues of distribution and equity which are central to the debate about the marketability of health care. In practice there is little congruence between the need for health care and the ability to pay for it. Markets operate not to meet needs but to meet demand which is accompanied by the ability to pay. And whilst we appear to be willing to put up with wide differences in wealth, most people are less willing to allow wide differences in health care. So some form of intervention on behalf of the indigent sick is required.

This equity argument is central to the principles of the National Health Service. Yet the New Right found the demolition of the equity argument supporting the NHS easy. Both the Department of Health and Social Security Report on *Inequalities in Health Care* (the Black Report) (DHSS, 1980) and Margaret Whitehead's *The Health Divide* (1987) have demonstrated that health inequalities or differences in life chances in Britain have not diminished since 1945. These studies were intended to show that much still needed to be done both within the National Health Service and in other sectors of the economy, such as housing, to improve health. These intentions were largely ignored; instead the evidence they produced was used to demonstrate that the National Health Service had failed to remove inequalities. No use was made of counter evidence showing the greater inequalities which exist in more market-oriented health systems, such as those in the United States as described by Currie in Chapter 12. A further demonstration which served to undermine the equity argument for the service was the evidence provided by Julian Le Grand (1982) that the middle classes had reaped more from the National Health Service than the poorer working-class groups. Instead of being used to improve the care given to the poorer groups, this evidence has been used to undermine the arguments for universal coverage, and to replace it where possible with selective provision, which has become known as 'targeting'.

Whilst both neo-classical welfare economists and economists of the New Right agree that externalities and distributional issues present problems for markets, they differ in the importance they place upon them. They have different levels of tolerance with respect to market failure and very different policies to deal with it.

Neo-classical welfare economists in the earlier post-war period and even today regarded market failure as a reason for government intervention. This intervention often took the form of governments replacing markets by raising finance and providing services. But the interventionists spent more effort in incanting the reasons and justifications for government intervention than in ensuring that such interventions were organized and managed efficiently. This left them in a weak position from which to defend public-sector activities when they came under attack from the New Right. It has been said that the interventionists regarded governments as 'economic eunuchs', whose task was merely to steer the economy to a social optimum (Burton, 1978). The orthodox interventionists, however, offered few tools which could be used to guide the system towards such a position.

The theoretical underpinnings of the attack on the efficiency of public-sector organization lay in studies of the professions and bureaucracies. This work appeared to show that professional groups and those working in organizations 'not for profit' tended to protect their own interests rather than those of the organization. It was considered that managers in such organizations were less than vigilant about the achievement of the goals of the organization and significantly more concerned to achieve a satisfactory working environment for themselves. Only 'for the sake of profit' could managerial energies be unleashed. These Smithian sentiments are basic to the arguments of those seeking to reduce state involvement in providing services in health care (Smith, 1776).

Compared to the benefits of markets, the bureaucratic organizations developed by the State are portrayed by the marketeers as sluggish, inefficient and lacking in innovative drive. These arguments have proved crucial for those who wish to advance provision of health care through 'the market', giving them a basis from which to attack public-sector provision. The evidence upon which such attacks are based is not substantial and is fraught with methodological difficulties. It was, however, deemed sufficient to undermine the public-sector approach to providing services.

Many of the arguments about the usefulness of markets suggest that – unlike bureaucracies – they are good mechanisms for transmitting information. They are seen to convey information effortlessly and freely throughout the economy, enabling rapid decision making. This is the frictionless market mechanism, 'the invisible hand', which, like so many other components of neo-classical markets analysis, offers only a partial explanation of activity in the market-place. Major modification to market theory has been made by the development of the branch of economics concerned with transaction costs (Williamson, 1975, 1985). This branch of economics shows that markets are seldom frictionless; information rarely flows freely and transactions take time and effort and can affect the quality of the product:

> In the mechanical system we look for frictions: do gears mesh, are the parts lubricated, is there needless slippage or other loss of energy? The economic counterpart of friction is transaction cost. Do the parties to the exchange operate harmoniously, are there frequent misunderstandings, conflicts, delays, breakdowns and other transactions? (Williamson, 1985)

Organizations and firms, if they seek to be efficient, must operate so as to minimize these transaction costs as well as all other production costs. The application of this approach to the whole process of setting up the NHS might indeed interpret its creation not only as an egalitarian gesture, but as a way of reducing transaction costs by facilitating the free flow and coordination of activity as frictionlessly as possible. Market systems require negotiation and bargaining at each stage and this can be costly and time-consuming. The more stages at which negotiations take place, the greater the chance that time will be wasted and resources absorbed in the process. In health care such time may be vital for the care of patients. The fewer negotiating boundaries across which patients pass whilst getting treatment, the better the quality of care is likely to be. It could be argued that this was the original idea underlying the generic notion of the National Health Service: doctors and their patients should face as few administrative contractual obstacles as possible to providing care. Bevan, when discussing the reasons for not choosing an insurance-based health service, clearly recognizes these issues. He says,

> In the case of health treatment this would give rise to anomalies, quite apart from the administrative jungle which would be created . . . They create a chaos of little or big projects, all aiming at the same end, assisting the individual in time of sickness . . . Why should all have contribution cards if all are assumed to be insured? This merely leads to a colossal Records Office, employing thousands of clerks solemnly restating in the most expensive manner what the law will already have said; namely, that all citizens are in the scheme. (Bevan, 1952, pp. 76–9)

In contrast to the National Health Service, the system in the United States (Enthoven and Kronich, 1989) seems to be an unwieldy, incomprehensible range of contracts, provisos and loopholes which can deprive those in need of care.

Whatever the administrative arrangements, however, the 'agency relationship' between patients and doctors means that decisions about health care are rarely made by patients in any health care system. The relationship is very uneven as doctors have more information than patients; and their decisions tend to dominate. Doctors are, thus, the major source of demand for health care resources. This is one of the foremost reasons for government and professional regulation of the activities of doctors. The financing arrangements for health care usually involve the doctor in a dual relationship acting as agent for third-party payers – insurance companies or governments – as well as for patients. This can lead to a conflict of interests with doctors defending their rights to clinical freedom and asserting that their primary responsibility is to patients whilst working within the constraints of the third-party payers (Mooney and McGuire, 1988). Increasingly, as we shall see below, third-party payers are seeking ways of monitoring the activities of doctors and making them accountable for the resources used. Another characteristic of this agency relationship, which we discussed earlier, uncertainty, is likely to confound such attempts. These uncertainties allow the agent scope to take credit for and to allocate blame to outside factors.

From this pastiche of post-modernist economics of markets in health care, we can explore the policy proposals now being advanced by the Thatcher Government for the National Health Service and their potential effect upon health care in the United Kingdom.

Proposals to change the National Health Service

The changes proposed by the British Government are advanced in the name of greater efficiency, accountability and choice: 'We aim to extend patients' choice; to delegate responsibilities to where the services are provided to secure the best value for money' (HMSO, 1989a). The proposals sweep away the power of pressure groups, bureaucratic structures and monopoly interests. They create markets within the National Health Service and encourage links with markets in the private sector. They provide a framework, as indicated earlier, from which subsequent privatization to a 'for profit' or 'not for profit' health sector will be extremely easy. The focus is on the 'supply side': on the provision of health care.

Quite early in the Thatcher administration enthusiasm for radical changes in the financing of the National Health Service – from general taxation to insurance – was dampened by the considerable problems facing insurance-based systems, discussed earlier in the critical work of Brian Abel-Smith (1981); and by the political sensitivities to changes in the National Health Service (Young, 1989). The difficulties with insurance-based schemes were confirmed in 1988 by the deliberations of the

Social Services Select Committee (HMSO, 1988). So radical changes in funding were shelved to be replaced by radical changes in provision. The basic idea in this new approach was the idea of providing a set of 'competitive providers' in the market for health care.

Many British health analysts have supported this approach – but within the over-all structure of the National Health Service (HMSO, 1988). By May 1988, these reform-minded defenders of state health care had offered the Government radical solutions largely adapted from schemes used in the United States – such as Health Maintenance Organizations – some of which were already facing difficulties (Gardner and Scheffler, 1988). These suggestions were readily grasped and shaped into policy proposals by the Government's review body. Those anxious to liberate the 'supply side' of health care failed to appreciate that many problems which had caused difficulties in funding health care by insurance schemes, such as 'adverse selection', would re-emerge as problems of provision.

The proposals segment the provision of health care into a large number of units – these include National Health Service hospitals (some with self-governing status) and private hospitals – each competitively seeking to provide cheap services and choice, supposedly for patients but mainly for their buying agents – either health authorities or doctors.

Health authorities will be responsible for buying services rather than providing them. Instead of paying for services from National Health Service hospitals by allocating funds annually, health authorities will be required to buy the best services they can from National Health Service hospitals, from self-governing units or from private hospitals. District authorities have to provide accident and emergency services locally, but for services which do not require immediate access they must 'shop around'. This is their new 'freedom'. It is this searching out, the ability to grant or withhold contracts, that is seen as the tool to ensure that health authorities are able to force from the system the most efficient use of resources. The opening up of the market to competitive providers does not, however, remove the monopoly buyer, i.e. the health authority. The Government's other suggestion – which involves 'liberating' general practices which have more than 11,000 patients from health authorities by allowing them to manage a budget for non-emergency care of their patients – reduces this monopoly power.[3] General practices which opt to manage their own budget will, like health authorities, be able to shop around for the best buy.

These competing units will not be perfectly competitive: this cannot be achieved given the geographical and structural characteristics of the health care market. The aim, following the Hayekian approach to monopolies, is, however, to make them contestable. Contracts granted to hospitals will be 'time-limited' and, when the contract expires, new bids will be sought from all the contesting parties. In many areas of the country there will not be much of a contest: there will be very few alternatives available. Over time, the number of contestants is also likely to shrink. Health care assets are highly specific; they have few alternative uses, unused skills atrophy. Thus, the losers of the initial bid are unlikely to stay around for subsequent bids. As the bidding processes become routine the negotiators form relationships and understandings about the terms of the contract, scrutiny becomes less and the competitive edge to the process can be lessened if not corrupted. Monopolistic forces in health care are strong and are likely to re-emerge.

Although the market is the major disciplinary force to be used in the new system, other disciplines are imposed to ensure greater accountability for clinical and financial decisions. The main target for the New Right is the doctor whose professional power is seen as a major impediment to the operation of markets. His or her power and autonomy is to be severely eroded. The work of doctors is to be subjected to 'medical audit'; which, though apparently now welcomed by doctors, limits their power and autonomy. They are to be exposed to the possibility of locally agreed salaries and their entrance into the merit payment system is to depend upon their being able to deploy managerial as well as clinical skills.[4] But most importantly they are to be made more accountable for financial decisions. It is the agency role of doctors which causes concern. Because of their allegiance to patients and their clinical freedom they are seen to be responsible for waste. Doctors are to be brought to heel: 'Those who take decisions which involve spending money must be accountable for that spending. Equally those who are responsible for managing the services must be able to influence the way in which resources are used' (HMSO, 1989a). 'Resource management' is the method chosen to ensure clinical accountability.

This is a process of management accountability and budgeting introduced after the Griffiths report on management in the National Health Service (HMSO, 1984). It was initially introduced in the form of clinical or management budgeting intended to ensure greater responsibility for use of resources. Under this system, clinical budget holders were charged for the use of all hospital facilities by patients in their care – theatres, cleaning, catering, drugs and personnel. The introduction of this system into the British health service represents a complete change in the culture of the National Health Service which initially strove to distance doctors from the costs of treatments (Roberts, 1989a). This 'distancing' meant that costs of treatments were not known either to doctors or managers. There was no way in which costs could be attributed to an individual doctor or patient. This lack of data on costs and prices is a feature which many used to billing systems find difficult to grasp. It was a design feature of a system which intended to give care based upon 'need'. Such costs and prices, however, are essential data for a more market-oriented system. Thus, after a number of largely unsuccessful trials, the management budgets scheme was relaunched in 1987, under the more 'user friendly' title 'resource management'. Sites were chosen for experiments. It was agreed that only if the work proved to be in the interests of patients would it be extended more generally. Now it is proposed that the system should be extended rapidly after only the most cursory evaluation: 'It is too early to judge probable achievement levels. Most sites have not fully implemented plans' (Department of Health, 1989).

It is difficult to overestimate the importance of 'resource management' to the new proposals. It is essential for the development of internal markets. It is essential for any subsequent privatization of the system. Its importance is acknowledged by the Government:

> There is at present only a limited capacity to link information about the diagnosis of patients and the cost of treatment. The government believes that the best way to remedy this is by extending and accelerating the existing Resource Management Initiative. (HMSO, 1989a)

This potential is explicitly recognized by the Secretary of State for Health at this time, Kenneth Clarke:

> One product of the initiative will be, in effect, a billing system. As individual treatment costs become available, the task of health authorities and family doctors in effectively searching out the best buy for patients, whether from existing NHS hospitals, the new self-governing hospitals or the private sector will be eased, as will cross-charging for treatment between hospitals and health authorities. Such information is needed to run the competitive market in health care which the NHS White Paper sets out. (Department of Health, 1989)

It is even more clearly stated in what are called the Technical Guidance Notes: 'there is a need for interim broad brush costing models from 1990–1 onwards which allow costs to be allocated to groups of patients so that hospitals can with confidence trade in the market place' (Department of Health, 1989). So 'resource management' is the essential informational apparatus for market provision of welfare. It may well play a role as important to social markets in welfare as 'double-entry bookkeeping' was, according to Weber (1968; discussed by Giddens, 1981, p. 117), to the development of capitalism.

In addition to opening up the health sector to the market-place, the proposals include a further attack upon monopolies in the form of trade unions and bureaucracies in the health sector and in local government. Trade union interests in the National Health Service are to be weakened by provisions which allow local wage bargaining. This will erode nationally negotiated wage structures and trade union power. It extends to the health sector the policies which have been introduced into other sectors of British industry.

There will be:

local discretionary payments to nurses to help with particular local staff shortages . . . (HMSO, 1989a, 2.1)

NHS Hospital Trusts should be free to settle the pay and conditions of their staff including doctors, nurses and others covered by national review bodies. (HMSO, 1989a, 3.9)

The performance pay arrangements are being extended to senior and middle managers . . . (and) . . . include an explicit local flexible element . . . so that managers can react to local recruitment problems. (HMSO, 1989a, 2.1)

Negotiations are already underway to introduce flexibility into the administrative and clerical pay scales. This will be based on a national pay spine, but will allow local discretion to take account of market conditions. (HMSO, 1989a, 2.21)

These proposals leave groups of workers with poor bargaining skills vulnerable to exploitation in all but the most buoyant labour markets. Ironically, in the buoyant markets the proposals suggested are likely to create a spiralling rise in wages as the competing sectors attempt to attract staff. Hence it may be a very costly change. The proposals may also affect geographical equity, as the British Medical Association (1989) has indicated.

The BMA argues that:

The proposed abandonment of a national remuneration structure for hospital doctors will further endanger the optimum spread of consultants and other hospital staff, both geographically and by specialty. This spread of staff has been one of the most impressive achievements of the NHS and has won international recognition. The introduction of 'market forces' would inevitably damage this principle.

and further insists that:

An even spread of consultants both geographically and by specialty has been essential in maintaining equality of provision of patient care. If self-governing hospitals were to offer greater financial rewards, it would inevitably lead to a concentration of high quality staff in a few affluent areas which would result in a two-tier service.

Local authorities' power is drastically curtailed. There will be no local authority representation in the new management structure. In this respect the public is effectively disfranchised, and is to be represented in future by non-executive directors chosen 'for the contribution they can personally make to effective management'. Health authorities, at all levels, will operate within tight hierarchical management structures. These changes are said to be an attempt to depoliticize health care. But as the appointments are made largely by the Secretary of State, it is likely to increase the political nature of management and the centralization of power.

These schemes may or may not squeeze inefficiency and waste from the system. The evidence from the United States does not look very promising. It would appear that as firms seek business, the costs may be reduced – but as some are over-optimistic when fixing contracts initially, they subsequently face financial problems and leave the industry. In later rounds, anxiety about quality increases and costs of monitoring rise. The system appears to stabilize with fewer firms and higher costs in later rounds of negotiation (Gardner and Scheffler, 1988).

Whether or not they achieve more efficiency, it is the change in 'culture', the central *ethic* of the system, which is of greater concern. Though avowedly patient need is still the central concern of the Government, the proposed system would in fact be powered by self-interest. The key question is whether 'self-interest' will improve efficiency or result in a deterioration of the quality and equity of services.

In 1989, the British Medical Association collected its concerns about the proposed reform of the NHS in a report, in a national newspaper advertising campaign, and in leaflets, many of which have been distributed through general practice surgeries. The report expresses concern about the effect of the new incentives upon quality. The Government's proposals are seen as likely to distort priorities in hospitals, causing them to concentrate upon 'profitable services' including 'private patients and patients from other districts', at 'the expense of the needs of local people'. They fear that the services in hospitals will be less comprehensive and the concept of the District General Hospital, built up so carefully to offer a comprehensive range of care locally, will be at risk. They also foresee commercial pressures forcing the use of 'non-permanent non-consultant staff' at the 'expense of high-quality care' and fear that some hospitals will be vulnerable to market pressures and will not survive.

The BMA's fears are well founded. In the new system, hospitals *must* seek to be profitable in the market-place. The market, in so far as it is effective, *will* force hospitals which wish to survive to consider their 'product-lines' and choose the most profitable, and use the cheapest methods of production. This is precisely what the introduction of market forces is intended to achieve.

We should add that the same motivations may also lead to the selection of patients who are least costly to treat: it may lead to 'adverse selection'. The likely problems of adverse selection are formidable. Whilst patients exercising choice will seek general practitioners who provide high-quality care, general practitioners will seek patients who do not strain budgets. Government prohibition and loss-limitation arrangements are unlikely to modify this behaviour. Practices will face great risks if they accept potentially expensive patients (Scheffler, 1989). Relationships between doctors and patients cannot be enforced. There must be arrangements for incompatible parties to resolve their contract. Incompatibility with expensive patients will be easy to acquire.

There are also incentives within the proposals for doctors not merely to improve efficiency but to change patterns of care in ways that will affect quality: there is scope for 'moral hazard'. General practices may take more work on themselves rather than use hospital services. Similarly, within hospitals, consultants may decide not to refer patients for tests or treatments to keep within their budgets. Some of these changes may reduce waste and even sometimes improve care, but others will involve increased risks to patients.

The agency relationship which we have discussed earlier in relation to doctors and patients is likely to become ever more diffuse. Many professionals may be involved in decisions about treatment but few will be keen to accept budgetary responsibility. General practitioners referring a patient to hospital will have to pay the bill, yet they will have little control over its size. Individual doctors will be reluctant to give blank cheques to colleagues when referring patients. They are advised in the Working Papers (HMSO, 1989a) to get a quotation before referring patients. There are several problems with this approach. One is the time taken to arrive at a decision and its effect upon patients. Others relate to the strategies which doctors and hospitals may use to protect themselves against unforeseen costs (Enthoven and Kronich, 1989). They might, for example, raise the charge to ensure they do not lose; or they might reduce the care to keep within the contract price. The extent of these problems will depend upon the number of non-standard cases likely to be encountered, the nature of the contract struck with hospitals and the way in which hospitals manage such cases within the resource management framework.

In recent years great efforts have been made to rid fiscal systems of tax 'havens' and loopholes which enable some to escape paying taxes. In the proposed reforms to the health service, in the meantime, the Government has introduced a vast range of ways and incentives to providers to protect themselves from providing care. This replaces a system which, though not perfect, had few such incentives.

The system proposed increases the transaction costs of running the health sector. It increases the number of transactions that take place within an organization by separating into contracting units relationships between departments which had previously been routine, cooperative and continuous. Each contract includes administrative and billing costs, which even with advances in computer technology will not be insignificant. It creates an 'administrative jungle' which Bevan (1952) had sought to avoid. The new systems involve the development of new skills. The contracting procedures required for the new market-oriented system will be quite difficult to manage. And the public-sector hospitals will contract at a disadvantage compared to private-sector hospitals, for they will not be allowed to 'cross-subsidize' – a usual business practice – and must use costs based on resource use when bidding, i.e. not what the market will bear. It will take some time for staff to become adept at using such a system, to select the 'best buy' or place the 'best bid'.

In spite of all services still being available to those who need them without charge, there is a number of ways in which equity will be adversely affected by the new proposals. The relaxation of the Resource Allocation Working Party formula, added to the contracting-out method of provision, will fundamentally affect geographical structural equity. The variety of providers which market systems spawn is likely to result in a very uneven pattern of care throughout the country. Individuals who know how and are able to select a good general practice will, as now, obtain the best treatment, but there will be greater gains and penalties attached to such choices. These are likely to have an impact upon the life chances of the most vulnerable patients. These inequalities are likely to be compounded by adverse selection of patients and by greater inducement for patients, especially the elderly who will gain tax incentives to take out private health insurance.

Patients' choice, of which we hear much in the policy document, is not likely to be enhanced (Roberts, 1989b). They will get more information from hospitals about their treatment and from general practices about their services. People will be able to change their doctor slightly more easily; and can have a cosy chat with their doctor about where they might go to obtain non-urgent treatment. This latter choice is the one most talked about by supporters of the White Paper. But this choice is a chimera. There is no extension of choice. There is a contraction. General practitioners always had the right to refer patients anywhere they wished within the United Kingdom. This right was eroded as resource constraints have caused health services to fall far behind the demand for their services. Now, although doctors who opt out will retain that choice, subject to their budgetary constraints, those who do not 'opt out' will have to send their patients to those hospitals with which the local health authority have placed contracts. They will merely be consulted about their preferences. Thus, these doctors, and their patients, have less choice.

Medical audit is the one element in the proposals which may contribute to improvements in patient care. This initiative will take time to develop and in the absence of external monitoring may not be very rigorous.

Conclusion

The proposals in the White Paper effectively dismantle the National Health Service (HMSO, 1989a). The proposals introduce a structure which will facilitate subsequent privatization. The market will have been segmented, the assets evaluated, product lines developed, and an information system capable of being used as a billing system will be in place. Whilst the present ministers may protest that privatization is not their aim, future ministers are unlikely to feel so constrained. As some self-governing hospitals grow and flourish, it is highly likely that they will wish to become fully independent of the National Health Service. And what minister of the New Right would deny them that freedom?

The proposals may or may not increase efficiency. But any increase in operational efficiency which may be encouraged by the Resource Management Initiative or competition amongst providers may be swallowed up in increased transaction costs. The benefit in efficiency from the introduction of audit and budgetary accountability, or from the scale effects arising from greater specialization were all possible under the existing framework of the National Health Service.

The proposals offered bring into the realm of the market mechanism aspects of health care which for over forty years in the United Kingdom had been organized according to a completely different ethic. They are unpopular with the vast majority of the British people who have a high regard for the National Health Service. Bevan (1952) warned that: No Government that attempts to destroy the Health Service can hope to command the support of the British people . . . No political party would survive that tried to destroy it.' Yet the Government appears to be intent upon its radical deconstruction of the National Health Service. If the changes are introduced, how far they will change the pattern and quality of health care will be a matter for subsequent analysis. It is a leap in the dark. It is, as the most recent Social Services Select Committee Report suggests, an act of faith by the marketeers (HMSO, 1989b). Future analysis will have to explore how various actors in the system react to incentives and economic pressures. Many behaviour patterns, reliant as they are on social relationships, may prove difficult to change in many instances, but in other cases the new economic reality may well force changes upon behaviour and values. It is perhaps this possibility which causes greatest concern. Buchanan (1988, p. 103) discusses this problem:

> to the extent that we care to view our interactions as market transactions they may actually come more closely to approximate the model by which we seek to explain them ... if we change our conception of ourselves profoundly we may change ourselves.

The proposed changes, if they are implemented, may change more than the structure of the NHS.

Notes

1. The National Health Service is funded mainly from general taxation, 88 per cent. The funds are distributed to regional and district health authorities which are responsible for providing the services. The general practitioner is the point of entry into the service, for non-emergency care. People register with a general practitioner who is paid mainly by capitation fees. The general practitioner can treat patients in the surgery or visit them at home, and he or she can refer the patient to any hospital or any other clinician in the country. This system, apart from some charges for prescriptions for drugs, dentistry and optician's charges (a large proportion of the population is exempt from these charges) is free at point of service.
2. For further discussion of Cheung's IEA paper (1978) see pages 8–11 of this book.
3. This proposal echoes earlier radical changes introduced into education by the Thatcher administration. Schools who wish to can be managed independently of local authorities. All head teachers now have to manage a budget for their schools.
4. A system by which doctors are rewarded additional payments by peer review for perceived professional merit.

References

Abel-Smith, B. (1978) *National Health Services, The First Thirty Years*, London: Her Majesty's Stationery Office.

Abel-Smith, B. (1981) 'Health care in a cold economic climate', *The Lancet* 14 February.

Arrow, K. (1963) 'Uncertainties and welfare economics of medical care', *American Economic Review* **55**, 941–73.

Ashley, J. S. A., P. Pasker and J. C. Beresford (1972) 'How much clinical investigation?', *The Lancet* 22 April.

Bevan, A. (1952) *In Place of Fear*, London: Heinemann.

Bosanquet, N. (1983) *After the New Right*, Cambridge: Polity Press.

British Medical Association (1989) *Special Report on the Government's White Paper 'Working for Patients'*, SRM **2**.

Buchanan, A. (1988) *Ethics, Efficiency and the Market*, Oxford: Clarendon Press.

Bunker, J. P. (1982) 'Evaluation of medical technology strategies: proposal for an Institute for Health and Evaluation', *New England Journal of Medicine* **306**, 687–92.

Burton, J. (1978) Epilogue to S. N. S. Cheung *The Myth of Social Cost*, London: Institute of Economic Affairs.

Cheung, S. N. S. (1978) *The Myth of Social Cost*, Hobart Papers, London: Institute of Economic Affairs.

Cochran, A. (1972) *Effectiveness and Efficiency: Random Reflections on Health Services*, London: Nuffield Provincial Hospitals Trust.

Communicable Disease Reports (1988–9) Weekly reports, London: Public Health Laboratories Service.

Department of Health (1989) *Resource Management Initiative*, London: HMSO.

DHSS (1976) *Sharing Resources for Health in England*, Report of the Resource Allocation Working Party, Department of Health and Social Security, London: HMSO.

DHSS (1980) *Inequalities in Health Care, Report of a Research Working Group*, London: Department of Health and Social Security, HMSO.

Downie, J. (1958) *The Competitive Process*, London: Duckworth.

Edwards, F. C., R. I. McCallum and P. J. Taylor (1988) *Fitness for Work*, Oxford: Oxford University Press.

Enthoven, A. and R. Kronich (1989) 'A consumer choice: health plan for the 1990s', *New England Journal of Medicine* **302** (1).

Fein, R. (1971) 'On measuring economic benefits of health care programmes' in *Medical History and Medical Care*, Nuffield Provincial Hospitals Trust, Oxford University Press.

Gamble, A. (1986) 'The political economy of freedom' in R. Levitas (ed.) *The Ideology of the New Right*, Cambridge: Polity Press.

Gardner, L. B. and R. M. Scheffler (1988) 'Privatization in health care: shifting the risk', *Medical Care Review* **45** (2), 215–53.

Giddens, A. (1981) *A Contemporary Critique of Historical Materialism*, London: Macmillan.

Green, D. G. (1986) *Challenge to the NHS*, Hobart Paperback 23, London: Institute of Economic Affairs.

Hansard (1989a) 10 February, columns 415–16.

Hansard (1989b) 21 February, column 973.

Hayek, F. (1949) *Individualism and the Economic Order*, London: Routledge & Kegan Paul.

HMSO (Her Majesty's Stationery Office) (1984) 'National Health Service Management Inquiry, First Report of the Social Services Committee: Griffiths National Health Service Management Inquiry Report', London: Her Majesty's Stationery Office.

HMSO (Her Majesty's Stationery Office) (1988) *Social Services Select Committee, 5th Report*, London: HMSO.

HMSO (Her Majesty's Stationery Office) (1989a) *Working for Patients*, London: HMSO.

HMSO (Her Majesty's Stationery Office) (1989b) 'Social Services Committee Eighth Report, Resourcing the National Health Service: The Government's plans for the future of the National Health Service', London: HMSO.

Ignatieff, M. (1984) *The Needs of Strangers*, London: Hogarth Press.

Le Grand, J. (1982) *The Strategy of Equality*, London: Allen & Unwin.

Levitas, R. (ed.) (1986) *The Ideology of the New Right*, Cambridge: Polity Press.

Marshall, A. (1904) *The Principles of Economics*, 8th edn, London: Macmillan.

Mooney, G. and A. McGuire (eds.) (1988) *Medical Ethics and Economics in Health Care*, Oxford: Oxford University Press.

Petty, W. (1676) in 'Anatomy lecture', *The Petty Papers, Some Unpublished Writings of Sir William Petty*, edited by the Marquis of Lansdown (1927) from the Bowood Papers, London: Constable.

Roberts, J. A. (1989a) 'The National Health Service in the UK: from myths to markets', *Health Policy and Planning*, **4** (1), 62–71.

Roberts, J. A. (1989b) *Choice in Health Care*, London: Department of Public Health and Policy, London School of Hygiene and Tropical Medicine.

Scheffler, R. (1989) 'Adverse selection: the Achilles heel of the NHS reforms', *The Lancet* 29 April, 450–2.

Smith, A. (1776) *The Wealth of Nations*, reprinted 1981, Harmondsworth: Penguin.

Sohl, P. (1988) 'Financing of medical services and medical ethics' in G. Mooney and A. McGuire (eds.) *Medical Ethics and Economics in Health Care*, Oxford: Oxford University Press.

Weber, M. (1968) in Günther Roth and Claus Willich (eds.) *Economy and Society*, New York: Bedminster Press.

Whitehead, M. (1987) *The Health Divide*, London: Health Education Council

Williamson, O. (1975) *Markets and Hierarchies: Analysis and antitrust implications*, New York: Free Press.

Williamson, O. (1985) *The Economic Institutions of Capitalism*, New York: Free Press.

Young, H. (1989) *One of Us*, London: Macmillan.

5

Looking after the cubs

Women and 'work' in the decade of Thatcherism

Miriam E. David

Department of Social Sciences, South Bank Polytechnic, United Kingdom

Introduction

After a decade of Thatcherism have women's lives inside and outside the 'family' really been transformed? Much of the Thatcher rhetoric would suggest that the opportunities for women to be enterprising in the public world of 'work' or paid employment are now as great as they are for men. In this paper I wish to investigate to what extent this is now the case or, on the other hand, whether women are still 'handicapped', as Illich declared they were almost a decade ago, in their ability to participate in the world of work. Illich's (1983) argument was that women had the handicap of family and domestic responsibilities.

The recent celebrations of Mrs Thatcher's tenth anniversary as Prime Minister focused on the one hand on her as grandmother and on the other as tigress, with her accepting this epithet with the additional comment that 'they look after their cubs very well indeed'! Both of these images suggest that the public world has been feminized to the extent that grannies can now be prime ministers and that the job of a prime minister involves the motherliness of caring for the cub-pack. Are these, however, nothing more than the continued attempts of a Prime Minister to portray herself as unique and at one and the same time appeal to female imagery and/or voters? Or is it really the case that the public world of work has been transformed to such an extent that not only can women compete on a par with men, but also that 'womanly values' now dominate the culture of work, albeit that they are not the conventional values of the contemporary nuclear family but those of wild animals in the jungle (Eisenstein, 1984).

The mixed economy of welfare

Before Mrs Thatcher became Prime Minister in May 1979, there was a so-called bipartisan political consensus on how the economy should be managed. In the post-war era, both the Tory and Labour parties shared broad agreement that government should ensure a mixed economy through the provision of social policies. The welfare state would provide social and/or economic support for those deemed unable to or incapable of participating in the world of work. In defining these welfare policies, there was an assumption that everyone lived in nuclear families, or, if they did not, should be provided with social services or cash support as if they did (Land and Parker, 1978). This, however, was about the limit of the broad agreement. There were considerable differences between the political parties about how to implement such welfare.

Some of the initial aspects of the welfare state were designed by a coalition government towards the end of the Second World War. However, the broad programme of the welfare state to cover education, social security, social services, housing and health came to be seen, in general rhetoric, as the achievement largely of a socialist government. But both Tory and Labour parties subscribed to the initial concept that the welfare state should support families in maintaining and caring for their members. The ideological underpinning of this was stated starkly and clearly by Lord Beveridge in his report to the Government in the throes of war. His statements have received widespread attention, as quoted by Hilary Land:

> In the next thirty years housewives as mothers have vital work to do in ensuring the adequate continuance of the British race and of British ideals in the world . . . maternity is the principle object of marriage . . . During marriage most women will not be gainfully employed . . . (Beveridge, quoted in Land, 1976, p. 117)

As Land went on to demonstrate:

> The economic relationship of a substantial proportion of married women was not one of total and permanent dependence on their husbands even in 1945. Since the end of the Second World War married women have joined the labour force in steadily increasing numbers and have acquired an economic status of their own, albeit an inferior one to men, for a woman's average full-time wage is still only half that of a man, and discrimination against women in employment is by no means limited to those with little skill or education. (Land, 1976, p. 117)

The origins of the modern welfare state lay in a sharply sexually divided labour market and family. The roles of housewife–mother were very clearly distinguished from those of father–breadwinner. As the welfare state developed, a gradual shift occurred from the initial notion of male breadwinners earning a family wage to that of the State at least attempting to underpin the family through the provision of financial benefits and social services. By the 1960s, this expenditure by the State was widely referred to as the 'social wage' (Adams, 1981), a term for public provision of services and benefits to families – education, housing, income maintenance and social security, personal social services and health. The term 'social wage' gives some indication of how the State's role had come to be seen; providing for the economic and social support of families, traditionally dependent on wages, particularly the family wage.

In the 1960s, the Labour Government began to extend its concepts of welfare to embrace some notion of equal opportunities. The root notion underpinning the original concept of the welfare state had been that of equality of opportunity, but this tended to mean equal access to public services rather than equal opportunities to participate as consumers or providers or workers. It was this latter notion that was developed in the 1960s. In the first place, the notion was developed for individuals as citizens on the basis of their social class or home backgrounds, rather than their gender. This borrowed from developments in the United States. People, usually men, from poor or working-class backgrounds, began to be afforded more opportunities in education, in housing, in employment, etc. This idea began later to be applied to assess how well racial or ethnic minorities had fared in particular in access to and participation in the education system.

As regards women's equal opportunities, however, these were only taken up as a result of pressure from the 'second wave' women's movement from the 1960s (Oakley, 1981). In 1969, the women's liberation movement formulated four policies as 'demands' on the State: equal pay and equal work, equal educational opportunities, twenty-four-hour nurseries and abortion on demand. Some official consideration had been given to this last 'demand' through the 1967 Abortion Act, although many, especially those in the women's movement, did not consider that it went far enough (Greenwood and Young, 1976). The Labour Government had also given some consideration to the question of equal pay, as a result of pressure from a women's trade union strike in 1968. The Equal Pay Act was passed in 1970 with a staggered programme of implementation to 1975. The other questions of equal work, child care facilities and equal educational opportunities for girls and women were not explicitly addressed by the Labour Government in this period (Coote and Campbell, 1982).

In the 1970s, however, some aspects of these 'demands' were further addressed, partly as a result of further pressure from a growing women's movement. In particular, attempts were made to set a general framework for sexual equality in public life by, first, a Tory and, second, a Labour policy document, which extended the Tory proposals. These resulted in the 1975 Sex Discrimination Act passed by a Labour Government, which sought to outlaw intentional and indirect discrimination on the basis of sex and related issues of marital status. This act also attempted to extend definitions of equal pay and equal work opportunities. However, substantial areas of social policy were specifically excluded; namely social security and taxation questions (David and Land, 1983). It also did not fully define concepts of equal pay for equal work. It has subsequently been frequently criticized, even by the quango which was set up to monitor and evaluate the progress of the implementation of the legislation – the Equal Opportunities Commission (EOC) (Coote and Campbell, 1982). In other areas of public policy – namely employment, education, housing and health, as well as access to public services, such as banking – the new rules of sex discrimination were intended to apply.

However, the procedures set up to deal with such issues differed markedly from the traditional uses of the law in Britain. The system had recently been set up to deal with industrial complaints with only quasi-judicial status. As regards education, the procedures entailed making application first to the relevant local education authority (LEA), second to the Department of Education and Science (DES) and only then to the traditional legal system through the county courts. The general procedure, however, for employment and other public policy questions, was to apply to an Industrial Tribunal, newly constituted and composed of a mix of lawyers and lay people drawn from industry and the trade unions. The burden of proof of sex discrimination rested with the applicant, not the defendant. An appeals system was also developed which was also distinctive, with review going to an Employment Appeals Tribunal (Gregory, 1987).

Moreover, the creation of the Equal Opportunities Commission itself built in some quasi-judicial procedures, with the ability for it also to take up test cases of sex discrimination by issuing special non-discrimination notices, and by supporting special cases at Industrial Tribunals. However, as noted by Coote and Campbell (1982), the EOC has been very wary of proceeding by this method of monitoring employers and has taken up very few cases of sex discrimination. According to Gregory's study, it has been less effective than the Commission for Racial Equality (CRE), set up a year after the EOC, in taking up cases of discrimination or in succeeding in reducing discrimination (Gregory, 1987, Ch. 6). Similarly, the effectiveness of the Equal Pay Act has been limited in reducing the differentials between men and women, particularly in work that is regarded as the same. There have been a number of campaigns to improve on the definitions of equal pay for equal work in the legislation, largely building on the examples in the European legislation. However, the British Government, especially under the Thatcher administrations, has assiduously refused to adopt the conventions of equal pay for equal value.

All of the legislation so far referred to was developed within the so-called liberal or social-democratic framework, dealing solely with attempts to achieve equal opportunities in public life. As has frequently been noted by feminist writers (Pascall, 1986; New and David, 1985) this has left untouched the relationships between men and women in the privacy of the family, and the ways in which such relationships may affect and be affected by sexual divisions in the public world of work and politics (Anthias and Yuval-Davis, 1989). And as already noted, the areas of social policy covered were limited and did not cover those of social security and income maintenance where sharply differentiated roles between men and women continued to apply, despite modifications to the social security system, through legislation in the 1970s. A particularly important change here was the transformation of the new system of family allowances and child tax allowances into a new scheme of child benefits, payable for every dependent child in a family (Land, 1977, 1983). Family allowances were one of the first of the welfare state benefits to be implemented and, after considerable political debate, were paid to the mother to help with the costs of caring for children (Land, 1975). Child tax allowances were deductions from the father's taxable income, on the assumption that mothers did not earn sufficient to benefit from such tax allowances (Land, 1978b). On the assumption that mothers were still primarily full-time housewives, it was agreed after some considerable argument that child benefits, too, should be payable to mothers, not fathers. In fact, this continued to illustrate the assumption that men and women did not share the same roles either in the private family, or in the public world of 'work'. Women's unpaid work in the family, especially caring for children, was at least recognized as requiring some form of financial support (Land, 1983).

However, this recognition did not extend to consideration of how to equalize men and women's participation in paid employment, when there were children to care for. The women's movement's 'demand' for 'twenty-four-hour nurseries' was intended to draw attention to the unequal division for labour in the family, especially where there were dependent preschool children (Segal, 1983). This issue was never seriously addressed. A Labour Government initiative to provide equal educational opportunities between children from different home backgrounds and socio-economic circumstances, rather than between boys and girls, was developed in the late 1960s, borrowing from the American experiences with the 'war on poverty' (Higgins, 1976). The aim was to provide early childhood education for children from poor home circumstances in order to enable them to start compulsory schooling on a par with children who were not from culturally or educationally deprived backgrounds.

Some psychological theories in currency at this time suggested that children's educational development was best enhanced by the involvement of their parents in their learning experiences and by social mixing, that is mixing with children from different economic and social circumstances (Bronfenbrenner, 1974; Poulton, 1983). The development of educational priority area (EPA) projects providing early childhood education sprang from these twin aims of prevention and parental participation (Halsey, 1972). This was even extended, in the early 1970s, by a Tory Government in which Mrs Thatcher was Secretary of State for Education. As part of her educational initiative entitled 'Education: A framework for expansion' (1973) she set about increasing the amount of state provision for nursery education, especially for 4-year-olds but also for 3-year-olds. Provision was to be made available by a staggered programme to 1980, for all parents who wanted it, relying on both social mixing and also parental involvement (David, 1980).

The assumptions underpinning these developments were that such education was in the interests of children, not that it would enable their mothers to be involved in the labour force as if they did not have children (Aplin and Pugh, 1983). Indeed, the hours of such schooling did not coincide with the conventional hours of the working day, even if they were for a full school day. Although the women's movement has always articulated demands for preschool provision as if schooling were unproblematic from the point of view of parental involvement in paid employment, the compulsory education system was not designed to cater to the needs of working parents (David, 1984). The length of the school day and the school year reflects a mixture of theories and demands. On the one hand, it has been assumed that young children's needs are best served by a relatively short period of concentration. On the other hand, the negotiations of teachers' unions have successfully achieved a short working day, and a year which approximates that of further and higher education, rather than the conventional working year. Strober and Tyack (1980) have argued that, for the United States, a short teaching day and academic year was the result of the need for seasonal agricultural labour. Teachers and children could often fulfil that need. Both the length of the school day and the school year require that parents be available within the conventional working day and the 'normal' working year to take responsibility for their schoolchildren (David, 1984). Given the gendered notion of parental responsibility on which compulsory schooling hinges, this has meant, in practice, that mothers are not freely available to take paid employment on a par with working men. They have other 'vital work' (New and David, 1985).

Indeed, this sexual division of parental responsibility both for child care and schooling began to be recognized as an obstacle to achieving equal opportunities in paid employment by the labour movement. In 1977, the Trades Union Congress (TUC) set up a working party to look into the question of provision for the under-fives, which recommended a comprehensive system of care for preschool children. Yet the working party wrote: 'If women's particular role as a parent is fully recognised, and women need to take fairly lengthy periods of leave to have children and may then work part-time afterwards, then they cannot conform to the traditional male pattern of employment' (TUC Working Party, 1977, p. 108). But the 'traditional male pattern of employment' is still seen as *the* feature of the world of work, and the 'natural' division between men and women is still the dominant view. In a review of the arguments of the American women's movement for day care, Steinfels showed that many feminists also accepted that view. They wanted to 'open . . . up present economic structures to women' rather than to challenge them. She went on (1976, p. 26):

> Its thinking tends in the direction of encouraging women to adopt the . . . male dominated work ethic. Its three major demands (abortion on demand, free twenty four hour day care, equal pay for equal work) are directly related to freeing women from their sex-role occupations and allowing them to participate equally with men in the labour market. It is interesting to note that two of the three demands are concerned with motherhood and only one with the situation at the workplace. Day care is a crucial ingredient in a view of women's liberation that focusses on integrating present economic structures. It does not simply propose that women should have childrearing responsibilities with men . . . but . . . that women should have no greater childrearing responsibilities than do men *in our present society* [my emphasis]. Day care, in effect, would fulfil the functions women presently fill.

Compared to other demands of the women's movement, the demand for day care was relatively unsuccessful. Coote and Campbell noted that it failed to win 'funds from government, from charitable trusts and from individual donors' (1982, p. 40). In contrast, appeals for money for women's refuges were often successful: 'people (usually men) who had money at their disposal were evidently unmoved at the thought of mothers and children needing nurseries' (Coote and Campbell, 1982, p. 4). However, the women's movement rarely went beyond this in its thinking. Nava, speaking with all the benefit of hindsight, has been very critical of those socialist-feminists who, in the early days of the contemporary women's movement, argued for 'more nurseries, launderettes and municipal restaurants rather than the entry of men in the domestic sphere' (Nava, 1983, p. 69). She went on:

> the idea that men *must* take an equal part in childcare, and that this was *not* a
> trivial demand . . . seemed daring and exhilarating. It seemed a blindingly
> simple solution to the apparently irreconcilable needs of mothers, for time and
> young children, for the kind of loving and consistent care rarely available in
> nurseries . . . Yet . . . an equal division of labour and responsibility between
> men and women in the domestic sphere was not always priority or even
> considered in the emerging women's liberation movement. (Nava, 1983, pp.
> 70–1)

Indeed, the priority focused *not* on issues of child care but women's status. Extra demands of the women's movement were formulated, such as the campaign for legal and financial independence. This campaign *was* more successful, in that changes in the divorce laws and in the systems of social security and taxation resulted. These all gave women, especially married women, some limited access to more financial resources, but that did not relieve them of, nor allow them to share, the care of family members, especially that of children. Child care remained primarily women's responsibility and women's paid employment was fitted in around that. It is this system that has been built on in the 1980s, leaving issues of the sexual divisions in the private family and their consequences for the public world of paid employment and the market untouched.

The Thatcher era

By the end of the 1970s there had been considerable changes in the ways in which the welfare state defined the roles and work of women, especially those in families, as mothers and wives. However, it had not transformed the relationship between the sexes to such an extent that men and women shared parental responsibilities for child care alike in families and that women participated in the labour force on a par with men. As Illich (1983, p. 46) noted:

> women are discriminated against in employment only to be forced, when off
> the job, to do a new kind of economically necessary work without any pay
> attached to it . . . outside of and along with wage labour, which had spread
> during the nineteenth century, a second kind of unprecedented activity had
> come into being. To a greater extent and in a different manner from men,
> women were drafted into the economy. They were deprived of equal access to
> wage labour only to be bound with even greater inequality to work that did not
> exist before wage labour came into being.

Not that Illich, however, wanted to transform this system to one in which men and women shared both family and public responsibilities, making it more egalitarian. He went on to argue that:

> In one culture men may build shelters, make fences or terrace a hill; in another these tasks are assigned to women. But only from women does bodily life come into the world . . . the special space (and the time that corresponds to it) that sets the home apart from nest and garage is engendered *only* by women, because it is they who bear living bodies . . . By being turned into economic producers . . . women, like men, are deprived of the environmental conditions that allow them to live by dwelling in a place and, by dwelling to make a home. To the degree that they become more productive economically both men and women become homeless. (Illich, 1983, p. 122)

Illich's whole frame of reference was nostalgia for a bygone age of clear gender differentiation, especially within the family. These views fitted in well with those of Ferdinand Mount, who was one of Mrs Thatcher's first policy advisors on the family. He had been the editor of *The Spectator*, when he was asked by Mrs Thatcher to chair a Family Policy Group for the Cabinet. At the same time, too, he wrote a book bemoaning the role that the State had come to play in the family. He argued passionately for the revival of the privacy of the nuclear family, freed from state controls, on the grounds that the family had survived the vicissitudes of history. In *The Subversive Family* (1983), he wrote:

> The defenders of the family . . . assert always the privacy and independence of the family, its biological individuality and its rights to live according to its natural instincts. It is for this reason that, even in societies where male supremacy is officially total, the family asserts its own *maternal* values [my emphasis] . . . We may hope and expect that as a result the spirit of civic equality may seep through into the private world of marriage and blot out the patches of inequality and consequent resentments that disfigure it. But we should also recognise that these inequalities originally seeped through into marriage from the outside, from the public world. For it is *within* marriage that the notions of equality and openheartedness have existed long before they became part of a political programme . . . The old ideals . . . are opposed to *egotism*, whether male or female. They assume a biological ethic – a series of duties of nest-gathering, nursing, feeding, protecting and teaching, all involving the sacrifice of self. (pp. 240–1)

Mount's views clearly chimed with those of Illich and indeed other writers, even on the Left such as Lasch (1976). He was also an early influence on Mrs Thatcher's policies, in her attempts to reinstate the traditional nuclear family. Mount and other Conservatives believed the family had lost its pride of place previously because of the effect of liberal social welfare and economic policies. Perhaps these views were stated most sharply and starkly by American New Right thinkers, such as

George Gilder and Charles Murray, who also tried to influence the changes to the Right in government policies in the USA (Gilder, 1982, 1983; Murray, 1985, 1989; Peele, 1984; David, 1986).

The solution recommended by all the New Right thinkers and applauded by Mrs Thatcher herself was to reduce the role of what she has called 'the nanny state' and return responsibility for social welfare to the private family. This involved, in the first instance, massive public expenditure cuts in the social service budgets to try to reduce dependence on the 'social wage' or welfare state. Such cut-backs were secured in all aspects of social services, from health to education to income mainte-nance and personal social services. Such reductions in public expenditure were not intended to be neutral between men and women with family responsibilities nor neutral in their effects on families. The aim was specifically to reduce help to families and ensure that family responsibili-ties were properly discharged, privately rather than by government agencies. This was made explicit by Mount (1983, p. 173):

> The family's most dangerous enemies may not turn out to be those who have openly declared war. It is so easy to muster resistance against the blatant cruelty of collectivist dictators . . . It is less easy *to fight against the armies* [my emphasis] of those who are 'only here to help' – those who claim to come with the intentions but come armed, all the same, with statutory powers and administrative instruments: education officers, children's officers . . . welfare workers and all other councils . . . which claim to know best how to manage our private concerns.

Over the previous decade, 'armies' of 'helpers' had developed apace. Ironically as the state system has been cut back, voluntary schemes of 'helpers' have grown, contrary to Mount's expectations. The original schemes began in the late 1960s and early 1970s, as noted above, to provide educational opportunities for preschool children from disadvan-taged families. The model was the US Headstart programme which focused on home intervention and parental participation and support. In Britain, preschool home visiting as means of intervention took off in the early 1970s (Smith, 1980). Over the years there was a marked shift from the early educational emphasis on a child's cognitive and social perform-ance to a focus on family support to underpin the part that parents are to or should play in their children's development. All the preschool home visiting schemes used 'visitors' who visited families with a child or children under 5 in the family's own home. Families who were felt to be 'in need' of a 'visitor' were referred to the schemes by health visitors, social workers, schoolteachers, even by friends of the family itself. Families were then initially visited to assess whether home visiting was the best form of help to meet their needs. Poulton stated that by the mid-1970s the role of home visitor could be defined:

> She [*sic*] was frequently required to offer support to mothers in their childrearing. She was certainly involved in trying to improve the quality of mother–child interaction. She was often modelling adult–child behaviour for mothers to observe and possibly develop for themselves . . . She was acting regularly in liaison with other agencies' field coordinators with 'problematic' families. (Poulton, 1983, p. 2)

The development of home visiting schemes has been well documented and criticized for the ways in which it has imposed on families, with need for social work help, white, middle-class standards of child care (Finch, 1984; David, 1985; New and David, 1985). The schemes did not just aim at families in need despite the gender-neutral rhetoric. They were also aimed specifically at mothers to give them help with their childrearing practices, assuming that such mothers were disadvantaged, inadequate, incompetent and potentially neglectful of their children or lived in areas of multiple disadvantage. Indeed the helpers, be they volunteers in schemes such as the preschool home visitors or in family and community centres, were almost invariably women; chosen for their female 'caring' qualities, to pass on their skills to less 'naturally' equipped women (David, 1985). In many such schemes they were meant to help with domestic chores and family budgeting as well as child care. Some schemes preferred non-professional to professional women, that is teachers, health visitors, social workers, because it was felt that there were less likely to be barriers between them and the parents. Poulton, indeed, argued that 'in all of the schemes there has been strong support from the parents' (1983, p. 22) in that they had the same aspirations for their children as middle-class parents and that this provided the motivation for them to accept the schemes (Poulton and James, 1975; Aplin and Pugh, 1983).

As Edwards has argued, these schemes had two conceptual aims: 'education for prevention' and parental participation (1989, p. 167). The Parliamentary Social Services Select Committee, in its examination of *Children in Care* felt that 'children sometimes have to be received into care because their parents simply lack parenting skills' (Social Services, 1984, p. xxv, para. 48) and saw home visiting schemes as means of countering this. However, the schemes were often officially justified not only on grounds of prevention of family breakdown but also on parental participation, giving parents greater confidence, involvement and consumer rights. For example, Smith (1980, p. 12) argued that participation 'carries notions of a service's responsiveness to its consumers, and of consumers' rights to organise the service as they think best or at least to have a say in how it is provided'.

Certainly this kind of notion was the basis for the expansion of home visiting schemes by Labour as well as Conservative local authorities. However, a recent research evaluation of one project found that this was the least developed side. As Edwards argued:

> Mothers certainly did not see themselves as being 'educated' to replace the visitor in her role but viewed the Project in a 'complementary' light . . . the mothers' confidence in their own ability to tackle the real constraints they saw as operating upon their lives remained untouched . . . Whilst this remains the case, criticisms that the Project is just teaching mothers to be 'good little mummies' remain uncontested. (1989, pp. 178–9)

Edwards, in other words, argued that the chief value was to give mothers a respite or break from 'unremitting child care', hence reinforcing or enabling mothers to return to their 'normal' female caring role. From the opposite perspective, Mount also made this point:

> what is always affronting, offensive and distressing is the simple fact of their *intrusion* into our private space. Our feelings are mixed even in the case of the most helpful of all public visitors. The District Health Visitor who visits mothers with babies is often sweet and sensitive and genuinely useful . . . But (mothers) cannot help being continuously aware that she is there as an inspector as well as an advisor . . . The Visitor – grim, symbolic title – remains an intruder . . . In all the revolts against big government and high taxes . . . resentment has played its part . . . the feeling that the state is introducing into private space more and more and ought to be stopped – is growing. The Visitor is being disputed. (1983, p. 172)

The cut-backs in social services, then, have had the effect of reducing *formal* and statutory help to families through health visitors, social workers, education welfare officers only to be replaced by the burgeoning, and almost entirely voluntary, scheme of home visitors. These voluntary schemes drew on a ready supply of women, mostly middle-class mothers, who either did not choose or could not take paid employment. Some of these mothers were denied paid employment, because of the cut-backs, as social workers, health visitors or teachers; and so participated in their children's education on a daily basis (David, 1984, 1985). Such women volunteered to help in such home visiting schemes, informally teaching less fortunate mothers how to cope, especially on reduced incomes, given the cut-backs in public expenditure on income maintenance. The effects were twofold: one was that mothers were denied the rights to paid employment albeit not of a gender-neutral type; the other was that by being forced into a field of voluntary work they ended up reinforcing gender-stereotyped forms of work, especially caring and motherhood as noted by Edwards above. So the 'nanny state' by being 'rolled back' has created new, more invidious forms of nannying, not at all equal in form or substance. In other words, the work of housewife–mother rather than being reduced by cut-backs was extended and reinforced for many middle-class as well as working-class women. The expectations that such mothers would help cushion the impact of cut-backs in expenditure on education also meant that mothers were not only volunteering to help mothers less fortunate than themselves but also *their own children*.

The burgeoning 'armies' of 'helpers' were not just home visitors but also school aides. This parental help in school was also described as a 'volunteer army' stepping into the 'firing line' (*Times Educational Supplement*, 1985). Her Majesty's Inspectorate (HMI), reporting on the effects of local government expenditure cuts on schools, also noted this:

> The LEAs' provision for education is increasingly being supplemented by *parental contributions of both cash and labour*. Such contributions benefit many schools, but at the same time they also tend to *widen the differences* in the levels of resources available to individual schools and, in turn, in *educational opportunities* available to pupils. [my emphasis] (DES, 1984, p. 29)

Parental helpers, involved in 'help in the classroom', were invariably *mothers*, teaching reading and maths, as well as cookery, playing music, laminating and selling books. But the help itself, as the HMI noted, increased inequalities of opportunity both between the children and between women. In some areas extra resources may have been highly skilled. As the Barclay report (1982, p. 78) pointed out: 'We do of course acknowledge that the volunteer cannot be stereotyped as untrained, inexperienced and unreliable: on the contrary, with unemployment so high . . . volunteers could be highly trained and experienced'. Such parental involvement, of an obviously gendered nature, could not fail to reinforce notions of men's and women's different proper 'work' to the schoolchildren themselves (New and David, 1985), as well as constraining the proper work of the mother volunteers. In this way, both sexual and social inequalities were further reproduced.

The cut-backs in public expenditure were not only designed to roll back the State, they were also destined to prevent further degrees of 'family breakdown'. Many Conservative thinkers have argued, as suggested earlier, that not only had the welfare state created dependency, it had also loosened the familial bonds between men and women and thereby increased the amount of divorce, cohabitation and illegitimacy, such that the nuclear family was no longer the norm. It is indeed the case that the nuclear family is no longer the major form of the family and that many 'families' are lone parent or reconstituted families created by choice, force or divorce. According to the available evidence, such shifts in family form have to do with the social and demographic changes which have transformed the traditional nuclear family from its apparent dominance to a complexity of 'family worlds' (to use the term coined by authors for an OECD publication *Caring for Children*, Centre for Educational Research and Innovation, 1982). As they stated:

> The family microcosm is extraordinarily differentiated and, even limiting the description to those families with children, the typology that can be constructed immediately becomes complex . . . Now if this typology is combined with other parameters, for example socio-economic status or number of active persons, the immense diversity of situations experienced by children is immediately obvious. In other words, there is an *enormous number of different family worlds* in which they may grow up [my emphasis]... changes for the child whose parents have divorced and remarried. Such families are often 'corporations' . . . These observations are important because very often the variety of 'realities' is underestimated. Through stressing the role of the parents, one ends up forgetting about all the others, as if the majority of families consisted of one couple and their children. Certainly, this is the majority situation, in the sense that it applies to a great number of children, but a good number of other situations exist alongside it. (pp. 19–20)

Whether or not the nuclear family as the biological breadwinning father and the biological housewife–mother ever assumed the pre-eminent position afforded it in ideology, clearly there have now been substantial economic and social changes whereby it is no longer even so statistically important. The effect of these social and demographic changes is to produce a variety of family forms either by force or by choice. The decision to divorce or separate may be made by either spouse, whereas mothers may have through force of economic or social circumstances to rear children in situations not of their choosing: in poverty, in liaisons with potentially violent or difficult men, in derelict homes. However, changes in Conservative Government policies have not managed to stem their developments. They seem, on the available evidence, to have exacerbated them.

Not only are the 'family worlds' in which children now grow up clearly more varied than was assumed to be the case in some bygone era, so too are the activities of the parents in such family worlds. As Peter Moss (1989, p. 21) has shown:

> Over the last 10–15 years, *differential unemployment rates* for men with and without dependent children have developed. In 1973, the rate was similar, at three percent. By 1980, *fathers had edged ahead*, with five percent compared to four percent. By 1985 the gap had widened *to 10 percent compared to five percent*. Unemployment was highest among men with a child under five, 12 percent compared to 9 percent for men with youngest child aged five to nine

and six percent for men with youngest child aged 10 or over . . . though the impact of unemployment on men with children is far less than the impact of leaving the labour force on women with children. [my emphasis]

He goes on to argue the contradictory point that:

men's earnings are likely to increase while they have dependent children. Average gross weekly earnings for men increase with age up to 50. Manual workers in their 30s earn on average 24 percent more than workers in their early twenties, while for non-manual workers the difference is 65 percent . . . Any increases in men's earnings are unlikely to offset the loss of earnings experienced by their partners. The initial effect when a first child is born, and when most women leave full-time employment for a period of unemployment, is a massive fall in household income. (p. 22)

In traditional two-parent households, then, as Moss argued, there is, in 1989, likely to be substantial unemployment (one in ten) amongst fathers, and in the early months of childrearing low household income, although this may rise quickly in part due to long hours of father's work.

Since the 1940s, in Britain, as in other countries, there has also been an increase in the number of mothers in employment. By 1985 30 per cent of women with a youngest child aged under 9 were in paid employment. As Martin and Roberts (1984) showed, however, 75 per cent of mothers with a youngest child under 9 worked part-time, which contrasted with 58 per cent of employed women with a youngest child aged 11–15 who worked part-time. Over two-thirds of married women with dependent children worked part-time compared to two-fifths of married women without dependent children and only 13 per cent of non-married women without children (Equal Opportunities Commission, 1988, p. 41). However, the rates of part-time employment for lone mothers were lower. The proportion of lone mothers whose youngest child is under 5 working full-time halved between 1978 and 1984. A higher proportion of lone mothers than married mothers worked full-time although as with lone mothers with younger children, the level of full-time employment has fallen in the period 1978–84, whereas it remained constant for married mothers (Equal Opportunities Commission, 1988, p. 43). However, the level of full- or part-time employment for widows was the same as for married mothers, whereas single mothers had the lowest level of full-time employment and the most dramatic fall in full-time employment between 1977/9 and 1983/5.

The explanation for these differences lies partly in the difficulty lone mothers face in making satisfactory childcare-arrangements in the absence of a partner, for both practical and financial reasons (47 percent of mothers in employment with pre-school children in 1980 reported that they relied on their husband for childcare). The other reason, which accounts particularly for the lower level of part-time employment among lone mothers is the poverty trap created by the Social Security system. Under both the old and new systems, Supplementary Benefit or Income Support is lost pound-for-pound above a fairly low level of earnings. This means it is not financially worthwhile taking paid employment unless it is either below this threshold or substantially above it. (Equal Opportunities Commission, 1988, p. 43)

Lone-parent households where the parent was not employed had the lowest equivalent income level of any households with children, with the exception of two-parent households where both parents were out of work (Moss, 1989, p. 26).

The picture that now emerged of the family is that the parents in the union are not necessarily any longer breadwinner–father and housewife–mother. In a substantial minority, the father may be unemployed; he may not be the biological father but rather a step-parent. On the other hand, he may be forced to work long hours to make ends meet or to make a good household income. In a substantial minority (14 per cent of all families of dependent children in 1985, of which nine-tenths are lone mothers) too, the mother may be a lone parent, rearing children alone; often in conditions of poverty (Glendenning and Millar, 1987). Mothers' chances of long-term, permanent full-time paid employment, whether in lone-parent or two-parent households, are now quite slim, and the costs for women quite considerable (Joshi, 1987). In other words, the changes in family forms have had a major impact on women's working lives, although their patterns of work life still do not mirror those of men. 'The costs of caring', Joshi (1987, p. 130) notes, fall most heavily on women, given 'the social expectations about the female caring role'. Changes in 'family worlds' have further differentiated mothers' and fathers' lives to the extent that lone mothers now make up a substantial proportion of the poor even if they are involved in paid employment of some kind.

Digby Anderson, director of the Institute of Social Affairs, with Graham Dawson, argued for a reversal of these changes in family patterns, especially those which have left women rearing children alone without male support (Anderson and Dawson, 1986). They championed 'the cause of the normal family . . . husband and wife living with their own children, the husband the major earner, the spouses intending and trying to stay together', contrasted with the 'anti-family lobby' which was 'merely disposed to help casualties of the traditional family, such as abandoned wives or children brought up by one parent'. What they meant by the 'anti-family lobby' was the social-democratic political parties of the previous era. This, too, was the object of Mount's attack. Both sets of Conservative thinkers wanted to reduce state interventions in family life to ensure that women would not find it viable to rear children on their own. George Gilder, ideologue of the American Right, to which

Anderson and Dawson also referred, had been crystal clear in stating his belief in the causes of the dilemma:

> Disruption in family life creates disruption in the economy because men need to direct their sexual energies towards the economy and they only do so when they are connected by family duty. Marriage creates the sense of responsibility men need. A married man . . . is spurred by the claims of family to channel his otherwise disruptive male aggressions into his performance as a provider for his wife and children. (Quoted in Eisenstein, 1982)

The first Thatcher administration, then, tried to reduce the 'nanny state' by cut-backs in public expenditure on social services aimed at resuscitating the traditional nuclear family and penalizing those women rearing families alone. The initial effects, as noted above, were the reverse – increasing forms of part-time employment and voluntary work with families.

The second Thatcher administration tried to change the governmental infrastructure for the delivery of social services and, in particular, to reduce social services supports to families, especially shifting the responsibility from statutory to voluntary organizations. This became known in 1986 as 'Care in the community'. Edwina Currie, as Junior Minister of Health, for example, tried to ensure 'self-help' schemes for families in her exhortations on 'self-help family centres' as part of the project of helping the community to care. The effects were, as noted above, to add to the burgeoning voluntary 'helper' projects.

The third Thatcher administration has developed more explicit alternative social policies to those of the social-democratic era. These, too, are particularly significant for women's lives inside and outside the family, although all were expressed in gender-neutral terms. The two most significant – the Education Reform Act 1988 (ERA) and the Children Act, which received royal assent in 1989 – mark the apotheosis of Thatcher's social policies. First, the Education Reform Act 1988 demonstrates how far the Thatcher Government has moved away from any commitment to equal opportunities. In the social-democratic political consensus, as noted above, education was the cornerstone of any policy to achieve equality of opportunity, whether on class, race or gender lines. The ERA 1988 seeks to ensure that parents have a major involvement in running their children's schools, whether their schools opt out of local authority control as a result of a parental ballot or the schools remain within local authority control. Schools which remain will still have to implement schemes of local management of schools (LMS) which means that the governing bodies, made up chiefly of parents, will be responsible for the financial management of schools. The implications of these changes are that differences in resources to schools on the basis of parental means will be accentuated rather than reduced, highlighting effectively class differences in schools, along the lines that the HMI previously noted. Secondly, the expertise required for parental involvement in the management of opt-in or opt-out schools is clearly not intended to be gender-neutral. The vast majority of mothers do not have the business or financial management skills to run schools. In the poorer schools, of course, they may still be required as 'parental helpers'. But as noted above a large proportion of mothers of schoolchildren are forced into low-paid employment, and unable to help either in the classroom or with the financial management of schools. So massive disparities between parents of schoolchildren on gender and class lines are likely to develop.

Moreover, the Children Bill does not try to reduce social or economic inequalities between parents. No provisions have been included for the improvement of child care for *all* preschool or school-age children. The Education Reform Act presaged this eventuality by not including provision for early childhood education in its sections (despite Mrs Thatcher's personal commitment to this sixteen years ago as Secretary of State for Education). The Children Bill, although heralded as a major reform of child care legislation, appears only to be an attempt to tidy up legislation for children who are not in traditional nuclear families, namely those who are subject to the care of local authorities (public law) or those who are in families going through divorce or legal separation (private law). The new legislation aims to invoke a new principle of parental responsibility for children 'at risk' or in situations of marital breakdown. The concept is to be applied to parents by virtue of being mothers or married fathers, for non-marital fathers and grandparents to acquire by agreements, for local authorities through court orders and for guardians who might acquire responsibilities for children by a signed agreement.

The specific impetus for this legislation was, on the one hand, the increase and volume of marital breakdown and divorce and the effects on children and, on the other, a series of cases of child abuse and deaths of children subject to local authority care. Three individual cases were particularly significant – all of little girls killed by their step-fathers, namely Jasmine Beckford in Brent, Kimberly Carlisle in Greenwich and Tyra Henry in Lambeth – and the scandal over the extent of child sexual abuse in Cleveland where 123 cases were reported in four months in 1987. Both Blom-Cooper and Butler-Sloss, the two leading lawyers who headed two of the public inquiries into these cases, stressed in their reports the notion of child protection through more careful legal definition of social work and family duties (Blom-Cooper, 1986; Butler-Sloss, 1988).

The effect of these cases was to produce a very legalistic approach to child care, rather than one based on notions of social welfare and the attendant necessary resources to achieve adequate care. The Children Bill was seen as a pressing issue given both the spate of child abuse inquiries, the Blom-Cooper concept of the inadequacy of social workers' definitions of their role and the growing complexity of the law with regard to divorce settlement. The specific pressure, however, came from those concerned about defining legal rights and duties for parents, children, local authorities and others involved in providing child care. In order words, it was pressure to ensure that those families which did not conform to the traditional nuclear family would as nearly as possible imitate or mirror it in their legal and consequent social responsibilities. Hence the centrality in the new law of the concept of parental responsibilities whether for parents or those given responsibility *in loco parentis*. As a corollary, the other general principle in the bill was 'the child's welfare'. But this was defined in an incredibly narrow way to cover the child only in regard to care and contested family proceedings, when deciding any question of upbringing or property. Local authorities retain responsibilities for children in need and, where consistent with this, to promote their upbringing by their families. To do this they have a duty to identify the child and publicize their services, to take reasonable steps to prevent neglect or abuse, to provide home help, holidays, family centres with counselling and other services to keep children in their families 'as they consider appropriate'. This latter term is also used for local authority provision of day care for the under-fives in need, facilities for childminders and for older children. However, there are no resources associated with these provisions in general terms.

The emphasis, then, in the bill is on clarifying court proceedings for a child's welfare, not for providing generally for social welfare. There is a clear shift towards legalizing the procedures in courts and for social workers. Social workers will clearly become more involved in assessment of children at risk and defining the kinds of ways such children can be helped. But as Parton and Parton (1989) have argued, there is:

> a new approach to children and families which is qualitatively different in rationale and approach. Much of this is symbolised by the emergence and emphasis on the notion of child protection. In essence the approach argues that, for those families identified as high risk or dangerous, it is suggested their children be removed on a long-term, preferably permanent, basis. For those deemed to be low-risk, at the so-called 'soft-end', the role of preventative, supportive work becomes a minimal one, reserved for the few families where assessment is problematic. Such a residual, individualistic policy, it is argued, would not only enable social service departments to use scarce and expensive resources more effectively but would minimise state intervention and intrusion into family life. (p. 39)

It is certainly the case that the bill emphasizes the privacy of the family and the limited legalistic role that social work intervention should take. The emphasis is on parental and children's rights, posed in gender-neutral terms, rather than on the resources available to all families. There is a clear shift from the social welfare model to a more judicial one. The ideology underpinning it seemed to have been well stated by Mount as noted above. There is very little emphasis on social work support to families and, where there is, it is on voluntary, home visiting arrangements, extending the 'self-help schemes' started in the mid-1980s. In other words, the bill itself has reinvigorated the notion of the privacy of the (genderless) family, coping on its own. Social work support for such families becomes minimized, and instead social workers are expected to help to root out more serious cases of need and risk of danger.

A further testimony to the way in which the privacy of the family is reasserted is through the lack of attention to the general kinds of support that *all* families need in order to care for children properly. There is no attention given to the question of resources necessary for *all* children. Indeed all the social security measures that exemplify the welfare state have been eroded or changed by the Government so that there are virtually no universal financial measures of family support (Land and Ward, 1986). The bill, itself, does not address this nor the question of child care services, such as comprehensive day care for the under-fives or after-school and holiday play facilities. It appears that the framers of the bill do not assume them to be necessary for adequate family child care (New and David, 1985). They are left, again, to the vagaries of market forces or self-help schemes.

In recent years, however, private business and industry have begun to develop schemes of child care for under-fives, for the children of their women workers. But, given the Government's reluctance to see this as necessary to the conditions of work for mothers, and the punitive systems of taxation that are still imposed on work-place nurseries, it is unlikely that this system will grow rapidly. It is more likely that if changes do occur, that the system of taxation will be altered to enable parents to have a tax benefit to contribute to the costs of child care. The Conservative ex-chairman [*sic*] of the EOC, Baroness Platt of Writtle, recently stated her preference for a scheme of vouchers to contribute to the costs of child care for the under-fives. She considered that schemes of community nurseries or work-place nurseries are not suitable for many mothers who would not wish to travel far with a young child. Her preference would be for the vouchers to be used either for child-minders or home-based nannies, maintaining the traditional forms of maternal child care. She also argued strongly, not for changing the traditional patterns of male employment, but for a new system of 'career breaks' for mothers of young children, with potential careers in science, engineering and technology.

This would enable such women to remain attached to their place of employment and receive regular up-dating whilst also caring for young children.

The EOC, whilst Baroness Platt was chairman, had already developed such a policy of 'career breaks' to ensure that professional women's talents in the sciences and engineering were not wasted and that their value to industry was recognized.

The effects of these schemes are that some professional women are able to work in engineering, successfully achieving the EOC's WISE (women into science and engineering) campaign and thereby becoming token 'male' professionals. However, this leaves untouched the whole system of child care which remains the sole responsibility of women, whether as biological mothers or mother surrogates as child-minders, nannies and nursery nurses (New and David, 1985). In other words, some small number of mainly middle-class women are able to benefit from such schemes, largely at the expense of the great majority of more working-class women and totally ignoring the male half of the population; except that a small number of largely male employers might reap the benefits of such additional talent in their own work-force. The form of the changes has been to increase sexual and social inequalities in both the private family and the labour market, reversing trends of the previous three decades.

Conclusions

It is clear that the decade of Thatcherism has had a tremendous impact on women's lives both inside and outside the family. However, that impact is not quite as Thatcherite rhetoric has led us to believe. It is the case that the opportunities for women, including many who are mothers of dependent children, to participate in the largely male form of the labour force have been increased. However, that has not freed such women from their primary responsibilities for dealing with the care of their children. Either they have been afforded 'career breaks' or have been forced to shoulder what is now conventionally known as the 'double burden', looking after both the home and employment. When in paid employment, despite the provisions of the Equal Pay and Sex Discrimination Acts, women are still discriminated against in terms of pay and often in conditions of employment, particularly promotion. In any event, the vast majority of mothers are involved in part-time rather than full-time employment, which is usually different from male work.

The majority of women, however, have had to shoulder the responsibilities for the care and maintenance of their children in the privacy of the family in even less supportive conditions than was the case under the social democratic welfare state. There now are far more lone-parent families whether by force or choice (one in seven of all families), and such mothers, together with those in two-parent households, are provided with fewer resources and income supports from government than in the past, before Mrs Thatcher came to power. Moreover, the levels of education and social service are more meagre; mothers' contributions the greater. The Thatcherite welfare state has indeed changed the commitment to equality of opportunity, to one of commitment to privacy and freedom from state control. On the available evidence this is likely to continue to render women's lives on the whole more difficult. However, the diversity between families masks the real effects of such policies. 'Looking after the cubs' is still the task that confronts the majority of mothers, who are unable to 'do it very well indeed' because of the lack of social and economic support afforded them, either from their partners in the privacy of the family or from the State, to give them choices over the mix of care and paid employment.

Bibliography and references

Adams, P. (1981) 'Social control or social wage: on the political economy of the welfare state' in R. Dale *et al.* (eds.) *Education and the State*, Vol. 2, *Politics, Patriarchy and Practice*, Brighton: Falmer Press.

Anderson, D. and G. Dawson (eds.) (1986) *Family Portraits*, London: Esmond.

Anthias F. and N. Yuval-Davis (eds.) (1989) *Women–Nation–State*, London: Macmillan.

Aplin, G. and G. Pugh (eds.) (1983) *Perspectives on Pre-School Home Visiting*, London: National Children's Bureau.

Barclay, P. M. (1982) *Social Workers: Their roles and tasks*, London: Bedford Square Press and National Council for Voluntary Organisations.

Blom-Cooper, L. (1986) *A Child in Trust: The report of the panel of inquiry into the circumstances surrounding the death of Jasmine Beckford*, London Borough of Brent.

Bronfenbrenner, U. (1974) *Is Early Intervention Effective? A report of the longitudinal evaluation of preschool programme*, Washington DC: Office of Child Development, US Dept of Health, Education & Welfare.

Butler-Sloss, Lord Justice E. (1988) *Report of the inquiry into Child Abuse in Cleveland, 1987*, Cm 412, London: HMSO.

Campbell, B. (1988) *Unofficial Secrets*, London: Virago.

Centre for Educational Research and Innovation (1982) *Caring for Children*, Paris: OECD.

Children's Legal Centre (1989) 'A Bill for Children' *Briefing*.

Coote, A. and B. Campbell (1982) *Sweet Freedom*, London: Picador.

David, M. (1980) *The State, the Family and Education*, London: Routledge & Kegan Paul.

David, M. (1984) 'Women, family and education' in S. Acker *et al*. (eds.) *World Yearbook of Education 1984: Women and education*, London: Kogan Page.

David, M. (1985) 'Motherhood and social policy: a matter of education?' *Critical Social Policy* **12**, 28–43.

David, M. (1986) 'Moral and maternal: The family in the right' in R. Levitas (ed.) *The Ideology of the New Right*, Oxford: Polity Press.

David, M. and H. Land (1983) 'Sex and social policy' in H. Glennerster (ed.) *The Future of the Welfare State*, London: Heinemann.

DES (1984) *Report by Her Majesty's Inspectorate on Effects of Local Authority Expenditure Policies on Education Provision in England, 1983*, London: HMSO.

Edwards, R. (1989) 'Pre-school home visiting projects: a case study of mothers' expectations and experiences' *Gender and Education* **1** (2), 165–83.

Eisenstein, H. (1984) *Contemporary Feminist Thought*, London: Counterpoint.

Eisenstein, Z. (1982) 'The sexual politics of the New Right: on understanding the crisis of liberalism for the 1980s', *Signs: Journal of Women and Culture* **7** (3), 567–88.

Equal Opportunities Commission (1988) *Women and Men*, London: HMSO.

Finch, J. (1984) 'The deceit of self help: pre-school playgroups and working class mothers', *Journal of Social Policy* **13**

Gilder, G. (1982) *Wealth and Poverty*, New York: Buchan & Enright.

Gilder, G. (1983) *Sexual Suicide*, New York: Basic Books.

Glendenning, C. and J. Millar (eds.) (1987) *Women and Poverty*, Hemel Hempstead: Harvester Wheatsheaf.

Greenwood, V. and J. Young (1976) *Abortion in Demand*, London: Pluto.

Gregory, J. (1987) *Sex, Race and the Law*, London: Sage.

Halsey, A. H. (1972) *Educational Priority*, London: HMSO.

Higgins, J. (1976) *The Poverty Business*, Oxford: Martin Robertson.

Illich, I. (1983) *Gender*, London: Marion Boyars.

Joshi, H. (1987) 'The costs of caring' in C. Glendenning and J. Millar (eds.) *Women and Poverty*, Hemel Hempstead: Harvester Wheatsheaf.

Land, H. (1975) 'Family allowances' in P. Hall *et al*. (eds.) *Change, Choice and Conflict*, London: Heinemann.

Land, H. (1976) 'Women: supporters or supported?' in D. Barker and S. Allen (eds.) *Sexual Divisions and Society*, London: Heinemann.

Land, H. (1977) 'The child benefit fiasco' in *The Yearbook of Social Policy in Britain 1987*, London: Routledge & Kegan Paul.

Land, H. (1978a) 'Who cares for the family?' *Journal of Social Policy* **7**, 3, 257–84.

Land, H. (1978b) 'Sex role stereotyping in the social security and income tax systems' in J. Chetwynd and D. Hartnett (eds.) *The Sex Role System*, London: Routledge & Kegan Paul.

Land, H. (1983) 'Who still cares for the family?' in J. Lewis (ed.) *Women's Rights Women's Welfare*, London: Croom Helm.

Land, H. and R. Parker (1978) 'United Kingdom' in S. Kamerman and A. Kahn (eds.) *Family Policy*, New York: Columbia University Press.

Land, H. and S. Ward (1986) *Women Won't Benefit*, London: NCCL.

Lasch, C. (1976) *Haven in a Heartless World*, New York: Basic Books.

Lewis, J. (1986) 'Anxieties about the family and the relationship between parents, children and the state in 20th century England' in M. Richards and R. Light (eds.) *Children of Social Worlds*, Oxford: Polity Press.

Martin, J. and C. Roberts (1984) *Women and Employment: A Lifetime Perspective*, London: HMSO.

Moss, P. (1989) 'The indirect costs of parenthood' *Critical Social Policy* **24**, 20–38.

Mount, F. (1983) *The Subversive Family*, Harmondsworth: Penguin.

Murray, C. (1985) *Losing Ground: American social policy 1950–80*, New York: Basic Books.

Murray, C. (1989) *In Pursuit of Happiness and Good Government*, New York: Basic Books.

Nava, M. (1983) 'From utopian to scientific feminism' in L. Segal (ed.) *What is To Be Done about the Family?*, Harmondsworth: Penguin.

New, C. and M. David (1985) *For the Children's Sake: Making child care more than women's business*, Harmondsworth: Penguin.

Oakley, A. (1981) *Subject Women*, London: Fontana.

Parton, C. and N. Parton (1988/9) 'Women, the family and child protection' *Critical Social Policy* **24** , 38–50.

Pascall, G. (1986) *Social Policy: A feminist analysis*, London: Allen & Unwin.

Peele, G. (1984) *Revival and Reaction: The Right in contemporary America*, Oxford: Clarendon Press.

Poulton, L. (1983) 'Origin and development of pre-school home visiting' in G. Aplin and G. Pugh (eds.) *Perspectives on Pre-School Home Visiting*, London: National Children's Bureau.

Poulton, L. and T. James (1975) *Preschool Learning in the Community: Strategies for change*, London: Routledge & Kegan Paul.

Segal, L. (ed.) (1983) *What is To Be Done about the Family?* Harmondsworth: Penguin.

Smith, T. (1980) *Parents and Preschool*, London: Grant McIntyre.

Steinfels, M. O'Brian (1976) *Who's Minding the Children?*, New York: Harper Torchbooks.

Social Services (2nd Report) (1984) *Children in Care*, **1**, London: HMSO.

Strober, M. and D. Tyack (1980) 'Why do women teach and men manage? A report on research in schools' *Signs* **5** (3), 494–503.

Times Educational Supplement (1985) 15 October, p. 8.

TUC Working Party (1977) *The Under Fives*, London: TUC.

PART 2

Australia*

* The following three chapters were completed before the narrow victory of the Australian Labor Party, under the leadership of Mr Bob Hawke, over the Liberal and Country Party opposition, in the Federal Election of 24 March 1990.

Minor editorial changes have been made to acknowledge that the Hawke Government is now in a fourth term of office, but it has not proven possible, within existing time constraints, to comment on the election campaign itself, to take into account the reduced size of the ALP majority, or to speculate on its likely effects.

6

Jam every other day
Living standards and the Hawke Government 1983–9

Rob Watts

School of Community Services and Policy Studies, Phillip Institute of Technology, Melbourne, Australia

> 'The rule is, jam tomorrrow and jam yesterday, but never jam *today.*'
> 'It *must* come sometimes to jam today', Alice objected. 'No, it can't',
> said the Queen. 'It is jam every other day: today isn't any other day.'
> (Lewis Carroll, *Through the Looking Glass*)

Introduction

Since March 1983, Australia has had a Federal Labor Government. At the centre of the Hawke Government's electoral strategy and of its economic and social policy has been an often redefined 'social contract' with the Australian labour movement. Around the so-called Accord, the Labor Government has been able to pursue a set of 'economic rationalist' programmes.[1] This approach has emphasized wide-ranging deregulation of the financial and banking systems, and a major reduction in the scale of Federal Government economic and social interventions. The objectives of both the Accord and Federal Government policies have been to 'integrate' Australia into the global market, to expand exports, restructure industries through industry plans, redesign both unions and industrial awards, and to increase investment. Central to all of these objectives was a simultaneous assault on inflation and unemployment by reducing the cost of labour through wage restraint, or cuts, a strategy designed to promote renewed investment without fuelling increased inflation. What the Labor Government offered, at least in its rhetoric, was 'restraint with equity'. Wage-earners and low-income households were offered compensations for their sacrifices through the promise of increased social expenditures and tax cuts. This chapter addresses one central question:

what have been the major effects of the Hawke Government's policies on Australian living standards? Given a number of conceptual issues – referred to later – and the proximity of this analysis to the events under review, this paper can offer only a preliminary assessment of the intentions of government policies against its achievements, defined here in terms of changes in living standards. It does so by beginning with an account and assessment of the policy context (and its effects), bequeathed by the Fraser Government (1975–83) to its Labor successor. This is necessary if only because it may draw attention to certain continuities in policy between apparently opposed party commitments. A detailed account of the Hawke Government's policy is not offered here, nor is any attempt to justify the view of that policy as a free market policy. Readers are referred to excellent accounts elsewhere (Stilwell, 1986; Indecs, 1987; Johnson, 1989; Maddox, 1989). The major focus of this paper is an assessment of the impact of policy measures on Australians' living standards.

It is important, indeed necessary, to locate the Hawke years (1983–9) against the achievements of the Fraser years (1975–83). Against that popular view in Australia which has represented Labor parties as parties of reform and progress and the non-Labor parties as parties of resistance, pragmatism and reaction, it is useful to observe real continuities in policy (Beilharz, 1989, pp. 132–49). In an important sense, the Hawke Government not only inherited but enhanced the transformation of Australia's political culture begun under the Fraser Government and has moved against the post-war consensus which had seen government and capital as harmonious partners. Importantly, where the Fraser Government's rhetoric was often inflammatorily monetarist, the Hawke Government has willingly adopted programmes and policies only dreamt of by Fraser, as this Government set out to prove once and for all that, unlike its Laborist predecessors, it would be a rational and effective economic manager which would restore Australian capitalism to health.

The Fraser years: 1975–83

Spokespeople for Fraser's Government now claim that they anticipated the rigour of Thatcherism or Reaganomics. In practice, as Hughes (1980, p. 137) points out, the Fraser Government cultivated the rhetoric of Friedmanite monetarism, but its practice was always qualified by both Fraser's physiocracy and by his suspicions of an overly deregulated economy, especially in the banking sector (Ayres, 1987, pp. 137–54). What characterized the actual policy substance of the Fraser years was a mix of initially consistent attempts to fight inflation, first through a mix of wage restraint and wage freeze policies, and then by increasingly stringent fiscal restraints by cuts in government expenditure. This phase lasted from 1976–7 to 1980–1. Thereafter, as his electoral stocks ebbed, Fraser drove his Government away from fiscal restraint oriented to achieving a balanced budget and back towards a half-hearted deficit budget-financed expansionary policy, combined with a fierce campaign to impose a wage freeze. It proved a highly unstable policy mix. These ambivalences are fully revealed in Fraser's record on welfare cuts.

Nominally a 'New Right' Government, the Fraser Government's actual achievements were often sharply at variance with the popular conception of it as an 'anti-welfare' government (Graycar, 1982). It is certainly the case that small-spending, but highly visible, departments or programmes, including housing, Aboriginal affairs, child care and urban development, all came in for early and severe expenditure cuts (Scotton and Ferber, 1979). Yet the Fraser Government was not able to wind back the major areas of welfare expenditures. Claus Offe has spoken about the welfare state as an 'irreversible achievement' (Offe, 1984, p. 13). Offe is suggesting that state expenditures are now embedded in so many economic and social processes that, 'New Right' fantasies notwithstanding, these expenditures cannot be fundamentally reduced without threatening the collapse of the whole social order. This point may be more controversial than Offe allows for; it may still be too early to say that the evidence is available to test his claim.

On a variety of indicators, the Fraser Government was at best able to slow down the momentum in expenditure increases and then only between 1979 and 1981. As Table 6.1 suggests, Fraser presided over a general increase in the share of Commonwealth money being spent on welfare. Likewise, as Table 6.2 indicates, the Fraser Government presided over a general increase in the proportion of total economic resources (defined here as Gross Domestic Product) being spent on welfare activity. Both Tables 6.1 and 6.2 suggest that the Fraser Government restrained the *rate of increase* in welfare expenditures between 1978–9 and 1981–2 before it blew out again in the last budget.

Against these two indicators, another measure suggests something of the restraint which the Fraser Government *was* able to achieve. It is a fair generalization, making certain assumptions about what to include in it, that the so-called 'social wage' declined on a *per capita* (or head of population) basis during the Fraser years.

The 'social wage' is a highly debatable idea or concept designed to identify the value to Australians of a very wide range of social expenditures by governments (Harding, 1982; Jones, 1979). It includes not only welfare spending, but also spending on health and education, and depending on who is doing it, it may include money spent on roads,

Table 6.1 All social security and welfare expenditure by Commonwealth governments as a percentage of total budget outlays 1972–83

Year	Percentage of TBO	$ Billion (10^9) nominal
1972–3	20.6	2.1
1973–4	20.3	2.4
1974–5	20.8	2.7
1975–6	23.0	5.0
1976–7	26.4	6.3
1977–8	27.8	7.4
1978–9	27.9	8.1
1979–80	27.7	8.7
1980–1	27.3	9.9
1981–2	27.8	11.5
1982–3	28.8	14.1

Source: *Budget Statement No. 1, 1983–84*, p. 58.

Table 6.2 Social security and welfare expenditures as a percentage of gross domestic product 1972–83

Year	Percentage of gross domestic product
1972–3	4.9
1973–4	4.8
1974–5	6.0
1975–6	6.9
1976–7	7.7
1977–8	8.2
1978–9	7.9
1979–80	7.7
1980–1	7.6
1981–2	7.8
1982–3	8.8

Source: *Budget Statement No. 1, 1983–84*, p. 59.

transport, recreation, film-making, cultural activities and urban development. (It can also include the money spent on administering these services.) According to Ken Davidson, the value of a broadly defined 'social wage' on a *per capita* basis declined between 1975–6 and 1982–3 (Davidson, 1986). In 1975–6 the social wage, says Davidson, was worth $5,867 per head of population (in 1986 dollars). By 1982, it had declined to $5,069 *per capita* (in 1986 dollars). This can certainly be explained, as David Peetz has done, by the fact that real total outlays over a range of

Table 6.3   Federal expenditures on the social wage 1975–6 to 1982–3 (in constant 1979–80 dollar terms)

Outlay	Expenditures 1975–6 ($000)	1982–3 ($000)	Change (%)
1 Education	2,671	2,714	1.6
2 Health	4,165	3,232	−22.4
3 Social security	8,281	9,255	11.8
4 Housing	793	509	−35.8
5 Total of 1–4	15,910	15,710	−1.3
6 Urban and regional	543	05	−88.0
7 Culture and recreation	357	381	−6.7
8 Urban transport	48	0	−100.0
9 Consumer protection	5	4	−20.0
10 Legal aid	23	42	82.0
11 Total of 1–10	16,886	16,202	−4.1
12 Payment to states–social wage	2,693	3,118	15.8
13 Total of 11–12	19,579	19,320	−1.3
14 Number of households	4,118	4,531	10.0
15 Real outlay per household at 5	3,864	3,467	−10.3
16 Real outlay per household at 13	4,754	4,264	−10.3

Source: Peetz (1985), p. C14.

social wage items were either unchanged or even declined (Peetz, 1985). As Table 6.3 suggests, big proportional cuts were inflicted on health, housing, transport and urban development expenditures. (By a simple arithmetical calculation, Peetz points to a 10 per cent cut in the value of the 'social wage' (as defined by Peetz) for each Australian household.) It should be noted that Peetz's calculations rest on a very generous definition of what expenditures are to be included in the 'social wage'. Equally, it is clear that the proportional cut inflicted as the first four big spending portfolios was relatively small, as was the scale of cuts inflicted on the much smaller areas of expenditure which Peetz cites.

It could certainly be objected that some items in Peetz's social wage were not designed to improve *all* Australians' living standards, even of those Australians on or below the poverty line; subsidies of a handsome nature to film-makers hardly qualify as a welfare measure as that term is ordinarily used. And, in defence of the Fraser Government, it can be pointed out that well-targeted expenditures in the field of social security (i.e. money designed to be given to low-income earners) did enjoy an over-all, *real* 11 per cent increase during the Fraser years.

Yet equally these increases were mostly for reasons outside the control of this or any government. Against various attempts to reduce social expenditures (for example, by de-indexing benefits from increases in the cost of living), the Fraser Government confronted the consequences of an ageing Australian population and the increased eligibility of ageing Australians for the old-age pension (EPAC, 1986). It also confronted the consequences of its own 'fight inflation first' policy, in steep increases in the numbers of unemployed people and in the average duration of unemployment; both produced unplanned increases in unemployment benefit expenditures.

On the one hand, then, the Fraser Government scarcely lived up to its own fierce rhetoric, demonstrating more often than not a mixture of unsympathetic and conservative policies affecting minorities or poorly organized interest groups, and of the electoral pragmatism for which Australian Liberal Governments are well known. (This failure to deliver on its rhetoric generated its own crisis of credibility amongst its 'natural' supporters.)

On the other hand, and this testifies to the fragmentary and con- tradictory tensions which surface in times of crisis, the Fraser Govern- ment, in casting about for a solution to the economic crisis, presided over a significant redistribution of national income away from the low- and middle-income earners and towards the already advantaged. (That this could be so testifies to the fact that *welfare expenditures*, which *increased* during the Fraser years, contributed relatively little to the over-all economic welfare of most Australians.) This redistribution of national income occurred as a result of a mixture of inflation, taxation policies, fiscal restraint and attempts to cut budget deficits, big increases in unemployment, and a consequent rise in the incidence of poverty, and as a consequence of real wage restraint through a retreat from full-wage indexation (Stretton, 1987; Norris, 1985). Economic recession tends to be bad for those already vulnerable in an unequal society because of their place in a class and gender society where schooling, jobs and incomes are not equally distributed. Unemployment was a major destructive force of many Australians' living standards. Between November 1975 and December 1982 the unemployment rate increased by 117 per cent to affect (officially) 672,000 Australians. (Another 386,400 people were estimated to be members of the 'hidden unemployed', whilst an additional 224,000 wanted work, but could not obtain it (Manning, 1982).) In 1982 the average (median) income of men and women who became unemployed had been, before unemployment, $222 per week and $178 per week respectively. The single adult rate in 1982 was around $64 per week with 'add-ons' for dependants. (In 1982 the *real* value of unemployment benefits was 22 per cent lower than it had been in 1975.) The unemployed were one obvious group whose living standards nose-dived under Fraser. Women, especially single parents and other low-income women, have, as Cass (1985) shows, borne the brunt of policy changes in the last two decades.

Wage-earners, of course, in comparison with those of their number who became unemployed, remained relatively advantaged. Yet amongst wage-earners, the combined impact of inflation, wage restraint (even with partial wage indexation for some of the Fraser years) and macro-economic policy meant a significant reduction in real earnings under Fraser for nearly half (and the bottom half at that) of wage-earners.

As ABS (1983) indicates, both male and female employees in the bottom half of wages distribution lost, in real terms, their share of available income; indeed, the lowest-paid workers, in the bottom decile lost between 10 and 13 per cent of their initial share between 1975 and 1982. Conversely, workers in the top 20 per cent of wage income gained most during these years.

In effect, for the bottom 40 per cent of male workers and for the bottom 50 per cent of female workers, they were worse off after six years of Fraser Government, whilst the higher-income groups enjoyed a higher real increase the greater their share of income. (It should be noted that the increase in income inequality which is suggested here reflected the growth in the rate of part-time employment which grew faster than full-time employment.) If we widen the focus slightly to include all sources of income, which includes everyone from welfare beneficiaries, wage-earners and that smaller group of the self-employed, and owners of capital (in a variety of forms), then we get a vivid picture of a major, and hardly surprising, redistribution of national income away from the low-income groups and towards the highest-income groups.

Table 6.4, which distributes the population into approximate groups of 10 per cent in terms of share of national income, shows clearly that in terms both of nominal and real changes the lowest 30 per cent of income-earners between 1978–9 and 1981–2 lost in real terms what small share of income they had initially had, whilst the top 20 per cent of income-earners added to the share of income. Under Fraser, Australian income distribution became even more unequal than it had been when his Government assumed office. To put this point in a slightly different way, Ken Davidson has estimated that non-wage-earners (whose income came from property, rentals, dividends, profits, etc.) enjoyed under Fraser a rise in their average annual household income from $27,735 in 1975–6 to $37,900 in 1982–3 (ABS, 1984; Peetz, 1985).

Finally, a very expansive view offered by the important and sophisticated work done by Keith Norris begins to track down changes to the living standards of a wide variety of Australian households differentiated by the composition of households and the size of source of household incomes (Norris, 1986a). Norris has constructed a set of indices for the living standards of some sixteen types of Australian households on varying levels of income which takes into account the inputs of wages and

Table 6.4   Australian income distribution: individual mean (average) annual income of decile classes

Decile	People on percentiles	Mean annual income		Real change (%)
		1978–9 ($)	1981–2 ($)	Nominal change (%)	

Decile	People on percentiles	1978–9 ($)	1981–2 ($)	Nominal change (%)	Real change (%)
Lowest	0–9	390	500	28	–4
2nd	10–19	1,610	1,900	18	–11
3rd	20–29	2,680	3,400	17	–5
4th	30–39	3,540	4,800	36	2
5th	40–49	5,230	7,100	36	2
6th	50–59	7,300	9,900	36	2
7th	60–69	9,080	12,600	59	4
8th	70–79	10,790	15,100	40	5
9th	80–89	12,190	18,700	42	7
Top	90–100	20,700	29,400	42	7

Source: ABS, (1984).

social security payments, the value of the social wage minus the subtractions of taxation.

Norris finds that some households enjoyed an increase in their living standards (e.g. two-income childless households and single high income-earners), whilst others stayed still (e.g. married couples on the Aged Pension or the single parent with one child on a Supporting Parent Benefit), whilst for others there was a decline in their living standards, such as the single adult unemployed person. Norris's work, subject as it is to some significant methodological quibbles, nonetheless indicates that we need to be discriminating in our assessment of changes to living standards, at the same time as he suggests something of those changes.

This then was the Australia bequeathed by Fraser to Hawke. The Hawke Government took office in a society fractured by economic crisis, with the political process increasingly unable to manage that crisis, and in a society dominated by a demonstrable increase in income inequality, and by a partial decline in living standards. Fraser's own efforts to rein in the 'welfare state' had been at best an ambiguous effort, even if his Government's policies had also begun to drive a wedge between the haves and the have-nots.

The Hawke Government, 1983–9

In assessing the effects of the Hawke Government's policy since 1983, it seems indubitable that it has combined a number of elements in an electorally appealing amalgam. In particular, it has practised the free marketeers' commitments to deregulation and market-driven outcomes, cleverly packaged within an Australian version of corporatist industrial restructuring and that partiality for equity which labour parties have long claimed to be uniquely equipped to deliver. In this way the Hawke Government has avoided that extravagant rhetoric directed against 'Big Government' (characteristic of the Fraser, Thatcher and Reagan Governments) even as it has systematically set about reducing public-sector outlays, in ways which its predecessor might only have dreamed of doing.

Any interpretation of the Hawke Government should of course acknowledge the assumptions underpinning such a critique. Two points can be made. First, it is important to note with Mishra and others that the Keynesian provenance is now historically defunct. Accordingly, there is little point to arguing from such a paradigm so as to find the Hawke Government wanting. Equally, this author, and others, has found the Australian experiment in corporatism unconvincing. New styles and forms of democratically and environmentally sustainable economic and social policy will need to be invented[2] if we are to have a sustainable and just future.

Secondly, it is apparent that neither the critique offered here nor the sense of alternatives which informs it presupposes either the prior existence, or desirability, of big government, whether Keynesian, socialist or corporatist. That is, the political framework underpinning this interpretation does not privilege traditional Keynesian or socialist models of government interventions.

In common with other post-Second World War capitalist societies, Australia's political culture *appeared* to operate within a loosely defined Keynesian policy framework which allowed a complementary role for government (see Smyth, 1989). Yet unlike its welfare state counterparts in northern Europe, the scale and scope of the Australian public sector was always in the middling to lower end of comparable OECD countries. Australia, for example, has long lacked a comprehensive national health service. Its means-tested, tax-based social security system has likewise long been silent about citizen rights. As Castles (1989) suggests, Australia, in terms of its taxation, public-sector outlays and national planning capabilities, has always been a laggard. Post-war affluence and growth from 1945 to 1975 camouflaged fundamental weaknesses in the 'mixed economy'. In reality, Australia was a staples-based economy vulnerable on the world-commodity market, and operating a branch plant industrial sector, which all came unstuck after 1974. The violent ideological shift against the Keynesian consensus was at least as vehement in Australia as elsewhere: my only point is that we should not overstate the case for seeing in the period since 1975 a major assault on a *powerful* public sector.

The central features of the Hawke Government's policy drive can be quickly summarized. (See Maddox, 1989, and Johnson, 1989, for more detailed accounts.) Six main thrusts can be discerned:

1. Deregulation of the banking sector with admission, after four decades of a closed shop, of large numbers of major foreign banks.
2. Deregulation of the currency and foreign exchange markets with a free-floating Australian dollar.
3. Commitment to systematic reduction in industrial tariffs so as to 'expose Australian industry to the rigours of international competition'.
4. Deregulation of the housing market with most interest rates for home purchase set by the market.
5. Some privatization of government-run enterprises, including munitions and shipbuilding operations with increasing promotion of the principle of privatization.

6. A sustained drive, first outlined by Hawke in the so-called Trilogy of Commitments of 1984:
   (a) to reduce the scale and ratio of government deficit as a proportion of GDP;
   (b) to reduce the scale and proportion of government outlays as a ratio of GDP;
   (c) to reduce the scale of government tax revenues. In this last respect, there has been a ruthless consistency in the Hawke Government's policy.

Finally, all of these policies have been successfully coupled to the Government's use of Australia's unique wage-fixing system through the Arbitration (now the Industrial Relations) Commission to impose significant wage cuts by unlinking wage increases and cost-of-living increases.

All of these policy objectives have been implemented as part of the Accord, an agreement between the Government and the union movement which has tied one of the major social groupings, which might have been expected to react violently against much of this policy, into an embrace with that policy.

The Accord refers to the original agreement between the Australian Labor Party and the Australian Council of Trade Unions (ACTU) signed in February 1983 and ratified by a special union conference (see Stilwell, 1986, pp. 11–15). This was a bipartite agreement, which would later be extended to include business. The Accord has subsequently come to refer to a general framework of agreements, and a commitment to mutual consultation, between the Labor Government and the ACTU, especially around wages policy as well as to the inclusion of union and business representatives in various tripartite forums such as the Economic Planning and Advisory Council (EPAC). It is this which has generated much discussion around the theme of 'corporatism', and the question of how much this corporatism is an agent of or an obstruction to political and social transformation (Beilharz, 1983; Stewart, 1985). In 1990, after a historic fourth Federal Election victory by the ALP, much of this commitment to mutual consultation around wage-fixing, although battered and bleeding, is still in place if only because the ACTU remains convinced that it can continue to lobby a Labor Government to make it behave like one.

We should observe simply that the original Accord has been successively modified or renegotiated by the following:

1. The National Economic Summit of June 1983.
2. The announcement of the Government's commitment to the Trilogy of Commitments of 1984.

3. The negotiations which followed the Tax Summit of August 1985 and
    led to the Accord Mark II of September 1985.
4. Finally, the major revision in Government policy as outlined in June
    1986 and May 1987 mini-Budgets.

Stilwell (1986), and Watts and Beilharz (1990) have summarized much of
this redefinition of the Accord.

In much that follows, reference is made to the impact of 'economic'
policy on 'social policy'. Yet it is extremely difficult – and probably
impermissible too – to detect or draw a neat dividing line between
'economic' and 'social' policy. In a capitalist economy, the economic
decisions of corporations, small businesses or governments invariably
affect the quality of people's lives, whilst social and welfare policy is
equally powerfully compromised and constrained by the ground rules
which sustain the reproduction of the political economy of a capitalist
economy. One of the consequences of a capitalist economy, in which the
State is heavily implicated, both as circulator of capitals and as agent of
legitimation, is that the distinction between the 'social' and the 'economic' dissolves on closer inspection. However, for pragmatic reasons the
focus here is not primarily on the development of employment, wages or
macro-economic policies, even as we acknowledge the profound implications of such policies for people on welfare. The focus is very much more
in the impact of so-called 'social wage' expenditures on the living
standards of Australians, especially for those initially most disadvantaged
by their location in the dominant class and gender relations of Australian
society. In this respect the interconnections between the Accord as
economic policy framework and the Accord as social policy framework
are profoundly important.

As a social-economic policy framework, the architects of the Accord
set out to restore full employment by 'restraining' real wage growth in the
hope that this would control inflation or price increases, at the same time
as promoting economic growth via renewed business investment (Mc-
Donald, 1985). This, it was believed or hoped, would take place because
'wage restraint' would allow a redistribution of national income away
from wage-earners and towards business in the form of increased profits
which a socially responsible business sector would use to invest in new
enterprises and hence new jobs. In effect, redistribution of national
income in a more, and not a less, unequal direction was at the heart of the
Accord's recipe for economic recovery. How this could be reconciled
with the Accord's stated commitment to equity and to redistributing
income and other resources to the most vulnerable Australians is the
essential contradiction *and* mystery of the Accord. It should be noted that
the unequal redistribution of national income has taken place, that the

new investment in productive, high-value-added industry has not, and that the economic and social crisis continues to deepen. As Davidson indicates, the Hawke Government has presided over a very rapid redistribution of income; the average household income for those households earning income from profits, property and rentals increased by $10,000 to $47,000 in only three years, whereas an equivalent increase took seven years under the Fraser Government. The coincidence of the maldistribution of income and continuing crisis may of course point to an underlying explanatory logic.

At the macro-economic level the central objective of the Government's policy has been to provide Australian business with the opportunities and incentives to rebuild exports, productivity and growth through reinvestment and aggressive marketing. One of the constraints to be removed in 1983 was a rise in wages in evidence by 1981–2. The Accord, with a primary emphasis on 'voluntary' wage restraint, agreed to by the union movement, and ratified through Australia's central wage-fixing system, was to be the instrument of this policy. It has worked spectacularly and to serious effect on the wages of Australian workers and, by implication, on their living standards.

The chief effect on this Hawke Government's wages policy has been a steady onslaught on Award rates of pay, producing a systematic reduction in average weekly earnings of 1985–6.[3] The net effect of this has been a real decline in total earnings by wage-earners, the bulk of whom continue to be full-time (male) wage-earners, alongside an increasingly significant female work-force, although still predominantly engaged in part-time wage labour. Treasury reports indicate (Treasury, 1989) where in the early 1980s total real wage earnings increased, by 1985–6, real wage earnings were shrinking.

As a consequence of what began as a policy of wage 'restraint' (1983–5) and became a programme for wage-cutting (1985–9), labour costs have declined to the level, in real terms, they were at in the late 1960s, a point illustrated in Table 6.5. This in part reflected the clear policy commitment embedded in the Accord strategy which accepted that the wage share of national income had got out of hand under both the Whitlam Labor and Fraser Liberal Governments and that previous rates of wage increases were responsible, in varying degrees, for inflation, unemployment and declining rates of investment.

In effect, the Hawke Government has presided over and facilitated a major redistribution of national income away from wage-earners and in favour of capital. This redistribution is suggested in a crude way in Table 6.6, where the shares of gross domestic product going to capital and to wage-earners is represented.

As a consequence of a major cut in wages, national and international

Table 6.5   Percentage change in unit labour costs

Year	Nominal	Real
1980–1	11.2	0.5
1981–2	14.4	2.7
1982–3	11.4	0.3
1983–4	2.1	−4.3
1984–5	4.1	−1.8
1985–6	6.2	−0.8
1986–7	6.4	−1.0
1987–8	5.5	−2.1

Source: *Economic Roundup*, March 1989.

Table 6.6   Changes to distributional share of profits and wages 1980–8

Year	Corporate gross operating surplus share (%)	Wage share (%)
1980–1	13.2	62.5
1981–2	11.4	64.0
1982–3	10.9	64.6
1983–4	12.7	62.2
1984–5	13.3	61.7
1985–6	13.4	60.3
1986–7	13.2	59.8
1987–8	13.8	59.0

Source: *Economic Roundup*, March 1989.

investors have been handed a rare opportunity to invest their additional income in new capital equipment, new buildings and infrastructure so as to boost employment. In theory, the Accord's objectives envisaged such an outcome, though ironically capital has chosen not to invest in high-value-added industrial or developmental projects, preferring instead shorter high-yield speculative investment. Even more ironically, much of the capital equipment, for example electronic data-processing equipment, has been purchased overseas, one effect of which has been to worsen the overall balance-of-trade deficit, which has made Australia increasingly a debtor nation.

Even so, it is clear that whatever factors other than Federal Government policy might be drawn on to explain it, the Hawke Government has largely claimed the credit for one of the few real economic bright spots of its period in office. Unemployment has undoubtedly been brought down from the Australian post-war high of 10 per cent in 1983–4. By any account, this is an achievement, and one which has to be taken into account in assessing the impact of policy on living standards. Unemployment by itself is a major factor in reducing the standard of living, and other things being equal, wage employment will be a major contributor to the income component of living standards. As Table 6.7 suggests, both the numbers and proportions of the unemployment rate have been reduced, especially since 1986–7.

Yet a more careful analysis should provide cause for more qualified praise. In particular, we should note, as in Table 6.8, that growth in employment has been greatest for part-time workers, whilst the duration of unemployment has evened out through the late 1980s. Further, when the growth in employment is disaggregated by industry, some of the underlying difficulty of accepting a simple picture of employment growth is recognized. Few of the mainstream productive sectors have recorded any significant or constant growth (Table 6.9), whilst the majority of growth has taken place in construction as well as in a range of the service industries, including retail, business services, community services and recreational services (this last reflecting the boom in Australia's tourism and hotel trade as the Australian dollar has plummeted even as Australia's pioneering image has attracted increasing numbers of high-value currency-bearing tourists).

On balance, then, it seems that a combination of policy-driven and market-driven factors have combined to create a significant number of new jobs without seriously eroding an apparently durable and historically high plateau of long-term unemployment. On this count the Hawke Government's actual record is spotty.

In 1989, therefore, the presumed nexus between wage cuts, reinvestment and a major reduction in unemployment has yet to be decisively achieved. In the meantime, real wages have been cut, as the architects of the Accord indicated would have to take place if economic recovery was to be realized. In effect, real wages/unit labour costs have been cut to the levels they were at in the late 1960s. In the context of the Accord, this policy objective, defined only as 'wage restraint', was acknowledged as was the effort to offer compensation to all through tax reform and social wage increases and protection for low-income earners.

This is, however, a Government which has proclaimed its commitment to protect both low-income-earners' living standards and the real living standards of all wage-earners. What are the achievements of the Hawke Government's social policy measures?

Table 6.7   Unemployment in Australia 1981–8

| Year | Full-time job seekers | | | Total unemployed Including part-time (000) | Unemployment benefits recipients |
	15–19 years	20+	Total		
1981–2	17.4	4.7	6.1	6.1	419.7	332.0
1982–3	23.4	7.6	9.3	8.9	619.4	538.8
1983–4	25.7	8.2	10.0	9.5	674.8	619.5
1984–5	23.1	7.3	8.8	8.5	613.8	581.9
1985–6	21.4	6.6	8.0	7.9	585.8	559.2
1986–7	22.4	7.1	8.5	8.3	634.6	575.1
1987–8	20.5	6.7	7.8	7.8	609.6	501.8

Note: In Australia, the unemployment rate and the work-force participation rate are calculated on the basis of regular household surveys: the last column records the numbers of people who have met the eligibility and income test so they may receive unemployment benefits.

Source: *Economic Roundup*, March 1989.

Table 6.8   Growth in work-force participation rate and average duration of unemployment 1980–8

Year	Participation rate (%)	Full-time workers (rate of change) (%)	Part-time workers (rate of change) (%)	Average duration of unemployment (weeks)
1980	61.6	2.2	5.7	31.2
1981–2	61.3	1.2	1.3	32.9
1982–3	60.9	–2.9	4.4	42.0
1983–4	60.8	0.7	1.8	46.0
1984–5	60.9	2.2	5.3	46.9
1985–6	61.7	3.3	6.5	46.9
1986–7	62.0	1.6	5.4	41.7
1987–8	62.3	2.4	5.8	46.9

Source: *Economic Roundup*, March 1989.

Table 6.9 Employment growth in selected industries 1981–8

Year	Food beverages	Metal products	Other manufacturers	Construction	Finance services	Community services	Recreational services
			(% change on previous year)				
1981–2	2.6	3.0	−1.0	−2.8	4.5	1.5	2.2
1982–3	2.2	−10.5	−7.8	−8.2	0.9	1.4	0.7
1983–4	0.2	−6.1	−1.6	−6.2	4.3	4.4	2.3
1984–5	−3.3	1.2	1.5	11.3	5.2	5.0	5.0
1985–6	−1.8	−2.5	−0.3	3.2	9.3	3.3	3.9
1986–7	−0.5	−3.1	0.3	4.8	4.9	5.0	5.5
1987–8	4.3	4.2	2.7	0.7	6.5	1.9	8.3

Source: *Economic Roundup*, March 1989, p. 49.

Social wage compensations in a context of wage cuts

It is plain that the primary objective of the Accord was the restoration of 'full employment', and social policy expenditures, or the so-called 'social wage', were seen either as 'trade-offs' or as a compensation to wage-earners practising 'wage restraint', but suffering real wage cuts. (The Accord defined the 'social wage' as 'expenditures by governments that affect the living standards of the people by direct income transfers or provision of services'; cited by Stilwell, 1986, p. 166.)

In specific terms, the Accord identified a number of basic social policy objectives:

1. To maintain real income standards and to improve them to the maximum feasible extent.
2. To extend provisions to redress gaps and anomalies in welfare coverage.
3. To foster social equity by striving to improve the relative position of the most disadvantaged.
4. To take urgent action to restore the position of recipients of unemployment benefit.
5. To develop the automatic indexation provisions (and restoration of the relative value of pensions) to the basic rate of 25 per cent of average male earnings.

In addition, the Accord spoke about the commitment to reintroducing a national health insurance scheme (Medicare), the need to improve child care and to extend family income supplements, as well as the addition of a rental subsidy. The sum intent of these statements appeared to be the redistribution of income in a moderately equitable way – an impression confirmed by the apparent commitment in the Accord to taxation reform. We should turn, therefore, to this aspect of government policy to assess whether living standards attacked by real wage cuts have in fact been sustained by 'social wage' expenditures.

Within Australia there has been a mixed evaluation of the successes and failures of the Hawke Government's policy. Initially, and up to late 1985, the general tendency was summed up by Peetz's enthusiastic assessment that the 'relative position of low income earners has been significantly improved by changes in the tax and social wage balance from 1982 (to 1985)' (Peetz, 1985). Likewise John Mathews enthused about the introduction of Medicare, tax reform and 'real improvements in education, housing and child care (as) gains in the social wage' (Mathews, 1986). Yet by 1986–7, commentators were no longer quite certain. The Victorian Council of Social Services (VCOSS) and the Australian

Council of Social Services (ACOSS) slammed the 1986–7 federal budget, whilst Stilwell saw a 'steady erosion of social reform tedencies' as a consequence of the Government's economic policy obsessions with deficit reduction. The assessment offered here certainly suggests that there is little here for the Hawke Government to be crowing about; some of the early improvements have been cancelled out by a policy of fiscal restraint imposed after 1985. There are indeed close parallels with the record of the Fraser Government.

The general trend evident in the Hawke Government's social expenditures has been for modest increases between 1983 and 1985 followed by a major attempt to rein in those expenditures. On any kind of comparison, the record of the Hawke and Fraser Governments suggests at best a spotty commitment to maintaining social expenditures and no commitment at all to egalitarian-redistributive objectives.

Within the context of a budgetary policy oriented to restraint, it should be acknowledged that the one clear positive social policy achievement of the Hawke Government has been the reintroduction of a universal health insurance scheme. It is a progressive reform, especially for the 2 million people without private health insurance up to 1984 and the 20 per cent of that group who reported that they lacked ready access to medical insurance and to hospital care. It has involved major expenditure growth for the Federal Government (Table 6.10), with some 37 per cent of total health outlays going to finance the medical and hospital benefits scheme.

Medicare has helped to reduce hospital and medical insurance costs for those on average weekly earnings. Contrary to received opinion, Medicare is probably not likely to have been responsible either for the drastic increase in waiting lists for hospital beds or for the continued spiral in health costs. If consumers of health care now have a high measure of economic security, the essential negative achievement of Medicare is its systematizing of the use of tax monies (through the 1.25 per cent Medicare levy) to augment the already advantaged economic status of doctors. The combination of constitutional prohibition on controls over doctors' fees and the arrogant assertion of 'professional autonomy' has turned Medicare into a massive tax-funded benefit fund for an already privileged, conservative and economically irresponsible occupation. Equity in this instance has come off a bad second against 'efficiency'.

After Medicare, the record of the Hawke Government becomes increasingly ragged. In the area of cash benefits through the social security system, the Hawke Government, after modest increases, began to rein back the proportion it allocated of its total outlays to social security from 29.1 per cent (in 1983–4) to 28.0 per cent (1984–5), 27.4 per cent (1985–6), 27.4 per cent (1986–7) and 28.9 per cent (1987–8).

Table 6.10 Federal health expenditures 1976–89

Year	$ million	% of TBO
1976–7	2,544	6.4
1977–8	2,701	10.1
1978–9	2,902	10.0
1979–80	3,165	10.0
1980–1	3,636	10.1
1981–2	2,905	7.05
1982–3	3,417	7.0
1983–4	4,401	7.8
1984–5	6,128	9.6
1985–6	6,870	9.8
1986–7	7,499	10.0
1987–8	8,213	10.5
1988–9	10,790	13.1

Source: *Budget Statements, No. 1*, 1989–90.

Table 6.11 Social security payments as a percentage of total budget outlay (TBO) and of gross domestic product (GDP) 1976–89

Year	Social security as percentage of TBO	Personal benefits as percentage of GDP
1976–7	26.5	8.9
1977–8	27.8	9.1
1978–9	28.0	8.8
1979–80	27.9	8.6
1980–1	27.5	8.5
1981–2	27.9	8.7
1982–3	28.9	9.8
1983–4	29.1	10.1
1984–5	28.0	10.2
1985–6	27.2	10.0
1986–7	27.3	8.1
1987–8	28.6	7.9
1988–9	28.9	7.3

Source: *Budget Statements No. 1, 1989–90.*

This pattern is represented in Table 6.11, which indicates that whilst the proportion of federal expenditures going to social security benefits has been stabilized, as a share of the total economic cake, this expenditure has declined dramatically. By the late 1980s, personal benefits as a proportion of GDP were at a very low level indeed.

The Government has combined restraint, some improvement in targeting expenditures and tougher eligibility and reporting procedures which has put added stress on already disadvantaged beneficiary groups such as unemployment beneficiaries and single parents. This last strategy represents the Hawke Government's acceptance of an apparently widespread belief that Australia's social security system has been abused by dole cheats; it was obsessively present in the 'Mini Budget' statement of May 1987. In a context where 2 billion dollars was predictively to be cut from the August 1987 budget, much of it from social wage portfolios, additional money was allocated for field surveillance activities.

Generally, we should also note that where the Fraser and Hawke Governments have sponsored apparent increases in social security, it has often been more of an involuntary response than an act of spontaneous generosity. In general all governments since the early 1970s have seen a constant press on social security expenditures simply because of the big increase in the numbers of eligible applicants for old-age and unemployment benefits, whilst the introduction of new benefits has likewise seen a big increase in expenditures as a result of an increase in claimants.[4]

In areas such as children's services, there has been partial implementation of the relevant commitment in the Accord, as the Hawke Government did begin to restore resources to an area battered by Fraser restraint. The Hawke Government seemed to agree with arguments that adequate child care services released more women back into educational or training programmes, or into part- or full-time wage labour. By 1984, major increases had been delivered although they were accompanied by a tightening of income testing for subsidized child care services. The then Minister (Grimes) argued in 1985 that as most users were 'middling income' earners, these users should pay more for their service. Further cuts in subsidies for child care were announced in May 1987 (Brennan and O'Donnell, 1987).

In respect of larger expenditure areas, which can involve potentially great electoral costs for governments intent on restraint, the Hawke Government has been as cautious as its predecessor. Thus declining numbers of children below 18 years of age have encouraged the Government to look for savings in spending on family allowances. In November 1985, family allowances were restricted to student children which became available only in association with means-tested student allowances to 18 years old. The 1986–7 budget saw hundreds of millions saved via the introduction of a partial means test for applicants with children over the age of 16. Further means-testing of family allowances followed in May 1987 with a $50,000 income cut-off being imposed. With respect to old-age benefits, the Hawke Government has introduced an income test on those applicants over 70 years and reintroduced an assets test on all pensioners. Its decision in August 1986 to delay payment of

Table 6.12 Public sector indicators 1978–89

Year	Commonwealth deficit/surplus (Commonwealth % of GDP)	Total Commonwealth budget outlays as % of GDP
1978–9	3.1	27.1
1979–80	1.6	26.0
1980–1	0.7	27.3
1981–2	0.3	27.7
1982–3	2.7	29.7
1983-4	4.2	31.0
1984-5	3.2	31.2
1985-6	2.4	29.5
1986–7	1.0	28.5
1987–8	−0.7	26.5
1988–9	−1.7	24.4

Source: *Budget Statements, No. 1*, 1989–90.

Consumer Price Index (CPI)-related pension increases was a blatant cost-saving measure which won it scant praise.

As Sheila Shaver (1989) has suggested, underlying both the Fraser and the Hawke Governments' approaches to social policy has been a partly consistent attempt to achieve over-all expenditure constraint and to diffuse the political costs of this objective. As Table 6.12 indicates, the Hawke Government has been able to achieve budget surpluses since 1987; for 1989–90 it anticipates a $10 billion surplus. This surplus has been achieved by a consistently successful exercise to wind back federal expenditures since 1985 from around 30 per cent to under a quarter of GDP by 1989. The essential point to be made is that whatever might be thought generally about the strategy of reducing the scale of government spending, some of the cost of doing this has been borne by the lowest income-earners.

It is certainly no matter for self-congratulation by this Government that, since gaining office, no category of benefit recipient has improved its position (between March 1983 and March 1987), *vis-à-vis* the 'poverty line'. As Table 6.13 indicates, all groups of beneficiaries experienced a slow erosion in their economic position against this bench-mark between 1983 and 1988. In particular this table suggests that between 1981–2 and 1985–6 poverty claimed above-average increases in its incidence amongst two-parent families with more than two children (10 per cent increase) and amongst single people increases of between 13 per cent and 34 per cent.

Table 6.13 Comparison between pensions and poverty lines

Beneficiaries	Pensions and allowances (%)	1981-2 poverty line ($)	% difference from poverty line	Pensions and allowances ($)	1983-4 poverty line (%)	% difference from poverty line	Pensions and allowances (%)	1985-6 poverty line ($)	% difference from poverty line	Pensions and allowances (%)	1987-8 poverty line ($)	% difference from poverty line
Single persons												
Unemployed	77.25	87.90	−12.1	102.10	118.50	−13.8	112.10	164.70	−31.9	112.70	169.97	−34.0
Unemployed	40.00	87.90	−54.5	50.00	110.00	−57.8						
Unemployed (Pensioner)	64.40	87.90	−26.7	88.20	118.50	−25.6	135.50	164.70	−17.7	135.50	169.97	−20.2
Couples with												
one child	128.80	124.50	+3.5	170.30	167.90	+1.4	210.10	220.30	−4.5	210.10	227.35	−7.5
two children	144.05	153.80	−6.3	191.55	207.40	−7.6	242.35	264.90	−8.5	246.10	273.38	−9.9
three children	161.55	183.10	−41.4	215.05	246.90	−12.9	271.85	309.40	−12.1	277.10	319.30	−18.2
three children	180.55	213.40	−15.0	240.05	286.40	−16.2	302.85	353.90	−14.4	308.10	365.22	−15.6
four children	199.95	241.60	−17.2	265.05	325.90	−18.7			–			–
Single parent with												
one child	100.50	118.60	−15.3	133.53	160.00	−16.6	174.30	211.50	−17.5	178.05	218.27	−18.4
two children	118.10	147.90	−20.1	156.85	199.58	−21.4	203.80	256.0	−20.3	209.05	264.19	−20.8
three children	137.00	177.20	−22.7	181.85	239.00	−23.9	234.80	300.50	−21.8	240.05	301.12	−22.5

Note: Pensions and allowances include all benefits, rent rebates, as applicable to each family.

Source: Based on Institute of Applied Economic and Social Research Poverty Line Data.

For Australians already powerfully disadvantaged by being unemployed, the failure of the Hawke Government to tackle the problem of poverty in the midst of a radical redistribution of income ought to be and is a disgrace. It makes little sense to plead that under Fraser no headway was made against poverty or that any attack on poverty must wait until economic recovery has taken place. It is plain that social reform has been at best a second- or fourth-order priority of the Hawke Government as this Government embraces 'economic rationality' and 'fiscal restraint'. The ALP has yet to discover what it might have been expected to have already understood. Where a social contract between labour, business and government with a mild version of 'corporatism' worked up until 1974 on a set of shared rules and expectations (about growth, stable wages and healthy profits) the post-1974 crisis has destabilized this contract. The Accord has sought somehow to operate as if none of this has happened and that a win–win consensus could be forged. This can at best only be legitimating fiction, since the real point of the Accord is to assist in the redistribution of national income in capital's favour so as to encourage accommodation of 'economic recovery', while 'social justice' can be only a fantastic, because contradictory objective. For 'social justice' to become more than a 'spray on' social placebo, there must be a genuinely egalitarian commitment informing a set of interlinking social investment, social security, labour market and national economic policies. The very reliance on a market-sponsored economic solution has seen wayward investment decisions on absence of equity, and a failure to address the underlying problems of a dependent economy, as signified by high interest, inflation and unemployment rates, by mounting national indebtedness and a trade balance in increasing debit.

Living standards since 1983

If we are to try to summarize the net effects of this diverse range of economic and social policy inventions in terms of impacts on living standards, it must be conceded that we do not – currently – have a compelling way of discussing living standards.

There can be no doubt that the concept of 'living standards' or 'standard of living' is a highly vexatious matter for economists and social policy analysts alike (see Hutton, 1988). The vexatious character of the concept is revealed clearly in the attempts to define or measure 'living standards' especially for 'poor' or 'low-income' individuals or other social units, with the presumed objective being either to establish a constant standard of living, or minimum tolerable standard of living (i.e. a spending pattern 'necessary for an average family to participate in society') (Henderson, 1975, p. 112).[5]

Much of the extensive literature on living standards had as its goal the empirical definition of a population alleged to be in poverty. In Australia we have seen attempts spanning some twenty years by Henderson (1967, 1975) to Manning (1982) to deal with the severe restrictions and taxonomic difficulties involved in establishing 'poverty lines', 'equivalence scales' and the like. In this context, Manning's conclusion that: 'the standard of living is a subjective concept, and there is therefore no single objective way to measure differences in the cost of a constant standard of living' (Manning, 1982, p. 1) is probably unexceptionable.

More recently, an alternative, largely unexplicated, notion of living standards has been inserted into policy debates which does not simply focus on expenditure patterns or on the value of certain baskets of goods and services. The newer approach tends to equate 'living standards' with the net result, *after* we add together the usual forms of 'private income' (wage income, profits, superannuation and dividends) plus direct government benefits (pensions, allowances, plus indirect government benefits – the so-called 'social wage') minus direct and indirect government revenue raising through the taxation system. That is, this exercise attempts to track down the effects of both inputs (i.e. wage and other income) plus direct and indirect government benefits, as well as the 'negative' effect of taxation, and has been provided by the work of Norris, and in a different way by Whiteford *et al.* (1988).[6] What this approach attempts to do is to capture the distributional effects of government interventions, taking account of both taxes and benefits.

At this stage, a simple critical review is all that is possible. It is imperative, if debate is to take place in Australia, that a more adequate conceptualization and measurement of indicators of living standards is developed.

My point of critical engagement with EPAC, Peetz and Norris has to do with their largely uncritical use of the concept of the 'social wage' as one of the key contributors to Australian living standards. The 'social wage' can be contrasted with 'wage incomes' which are earned by individuals who enter into a labour contract with an employer. Yet it is not clear either what kinds of social expenditures ought to be included or how to sort out the differences between the individual and/or household recipients of such expenditures, or how to sort out the differences between direct cash benefits, for example (a pension), and indirect services, such as schools or hospitals. By common consent most writers include in the 'social wage' expenditures on social security and welfare, education, health and housing; others include spending on roads, transport, urban planning, recreation and even subsidies offered to film-makers.

Table 6.14 Government social wage expenditures as percentage of total budget outlay 1975–88

Year	A: Social wage expenditure ($m)	B: Total budget outlays	A as % of B
1975–6	11,153	21,787	51.2
1976–7	11,458	24,047	47.6
1977–8	12,598	26,690	47.2
1978–9	13,328	28,934	46.0
1979–80	14,134	31,470	44.9
1980–1	16,110	36,020	44.7
1981-2	17,286	41,206	42.0
1982–3	20,236	48,792	41.7
1983–4	24,101	56,430	42.7
1984-5	27,991	63,712	43.9
1985-6	30,404	69,917	43.5
1986–7	32,484	74,748	43.4
1987–8	36,462	78,119	46.6

Source: *Budget Statement, Number 1*, 1986–7.

If we begin with the general range of social expenditures which are frequently added up to produce the so-called 'social wage' (which here includes education, health, social security, housing, regional development and cultural and recreation spending), we can build up a simple picture of how much federal governments since 1975 have put into such portfolios; see Table 6.14. In this aggregating of 'social wage' expenditures, a pattern of restraint, growth and restraint linking the Fraser and Hawke years is plainly evident.

If we turn to the more sophisticated use made of the social wage by writers such as Peetz and Norris, then two simple, but quite critical, problems must be acknowledged. Firstly, we could note the difficulty in counting the value of the 'social wage' granted the three levels of government in Australia (Commonwealth, State and local), all of which contribute to these expenditures in different measure. Complexity mounts when trying to assess the impact of the 'social wage' on living standards. The difficulty, readily acknowledged by Norris, is the very large and diverse combination of income levels and sources of income available to a range of different kinds of 'households', which for the ABS embraces 'households' of one person up to households with parents and children. Each of these kinds of households has different needs and aspirations; each has different levels of income with which to try to meet those needs. Each has, in short, different living standards, and measuring the impact on these diverse standards of policies is a very large task.

Far more fundamentally difficult, however, is the imputing of the social wage, which entails adding up the value of the social expenditures and then dividing it up on a *per capita* basis, implying that each Australian gets so many thousands of dollars in social benefit.

By and large, the essential difficulty which Peetz and Norris generate for themselves is that they have to end up *imputing* the value of the social wage, that is, rather abstractly dividing up the total social wage expenditure amongst the total number of households. This begs very serious questions. For example, not all households have equal access to the value of the Commonwealth Government's expenditure on schools or on higher education. Norris's work, in assuming that this is in fact so, can therefore rather simply end up giving each household so many thousands of dollars' worth of educational service which we know to be unequally distributed in reality. Equally the distribution of the health expenditure on an actual as against an imputed basis suggests that we cannot simply impute the value of the increase in the 'social wage' which the introduction of Medicare in 1984 entailed. (Indeed to follow Davidson here the value of all social wage increases between 1983 and 1986 (in 1986 $ terms) meant that Hawke had only restored $600 of the $800 cut, on a per household basis, from the 1975 social wage.) That is to say, the actual distribution of social wage expenditures is not equally distributed, as Norris implies, amongst all households. Its actual distribution can confirm already existing patterns of advantage and disadvantage as the facts of the distribution of educational expenditures suggest, where for example over half of the Commonwealth money spent on secondary schools goes to the one-third of schools in the private sector. The method of imputing the value of the social wage therefore seriously conceals the actual distributive effects of the social wage and its actual effect on different kinds of families' standards of living. I would suggest that this difficulty really means we cannot agree at this stage with Norris that the Accord has preserved the living standards for certain families. His conclusion, based on a distribution amongst some sixteen different family types of the combination of changes to wages, the social wage and taxation, is worthy of attention.

Norris would suggest that between 1980 and 1985 there has been some modest increase in living standards. All households with children, and aged pensioner householders, saw some increases in their living standards over these years. These households in the first five groups, whose income came from wage earnings, increased their total living standards by between 1 and 3.8 per cent. Married couples dependent on a pension did a little better whilst three kinds of single-person households suffered a decline. The one apparent major beneficiary of change was the single unemployment benefit recipient who enjoyed a 14.9 per cent increase in their living standards: it should be pointed out that the 1985 value of this benefit was still less than it had been in 1975. Norris also attempted to assess the respective contribution made to changes in living standards of the following:

1. Annual changes in gross earnings on benefits.
2. Changes in disposable income.
3. Changes in the social wage.

For those households which Norris has done this for, it seems that Medicare has been the biggest contribution to social wage increases, whilst wage restraint has entailed that wage-earners have lost out as their wages lag persistently behind price increases. Finally, then, Norris's work which is a sophisticated and important essay deserving of wide discussion is possibly misleading in its overly sanguine assessment of the impact of government policies on living standards. Certainly more refined empirical research is called for on this vital question.

Conclusion

Since the mid-1970s Australia has with other comparable societies been host to crisis. Governments have struggled, largely without success, to manage that crisis. In this sense, both Liberal and Labour governments have attempted, via various policy approaches, to generate growth, sustain profits and restore investment and to do so without seeming to cast too stark a light on the inequities involved in this. The governments of Fraser (1975–83) and of Hawke (1983–9) have given greater and greater legitimacy to the rhetoric of deregulation, privatization and the apparently 'natural' laws of the market-place. The objective measures of crisis have not, however, gone away.

Since 1983 ordinary Australians have begun to feel the full impact of this more or less coherent strategy. Real wages have been cut. Cuts to living standards have in general not been compensated for, this in a context where neither inflation nor unemployment, each producing major effects for people's living standards, has been brought under control. The reduction of public-sector expenditure in specific areas such as education has seriously compromised the 'social wage' and its capacity to sustain living standards for low income earners. Neither tax reform nor the much-touted higher targeting of means-tested social security benefits has done much to lift incomes above the poverty line. Like its predecessor, the Hawke Government has found itself caught in a cross-fire of contradictory demands. The pragmatics of electoralism lead it towards a politics of consensus even as its acceptance of much of the rhetoric of the free marketeers is tempered by its need to be seen as something like a Labor Government. Nonetheless, there can be little doubt that on balance the Hawke Government has facilitated a significant shift into the policy terrain designed by a resurgent pro-capitalist discourse and that in consequence the living standards of Australians as a whole have been seriously affected.

Notes

1. The Accord has not yet generated a significant body of critical literature. The best is Stilwell (1986), whilst Maddox (1989) and Johnson (1989) pick up on its political impact. See also Carney (1989) for an assessment of its impact on industrial relations.
2. Much of the critique of the Hawke Government here is based on a positive and new vision of economic and social policy which is perhaps too pithily encompassed in Melbourne Economics Group (1989).
3. In Australia, with its centralized wage-fixing system, federally registered unions operate under industrial awards, a form of contract specifying rates of pay and terms and conditions for workers. See Carney, 1989, pp. 146–68.
4. As EPAC has argued, the use of a 'decomposition analysis' suggests that increases in social security expenditures are largely driven by increases in the numbers of applicants and not directly by increases to the value of benefits.
5. When trying to define and/or measure living standards, the difficulties in the way to achieving a desired degree of objective, measurable and consensually compelling measures usually include reference to:
    (a) the diversity of actual spending patterns and variability in consumer's choice;
    (b) lack of consistency between experts and/or the poor/low-income groups as to what ought to be in a basket of desired goods and services;
    (c) the actual heterogeneity of household types (including in Australia – everything from single-person households, couples, nuclear families and the immense range of life-cycle characteristics;
    (d) changes in the household and/or life-cycle needs of social groups over time;
    (e) empirical difficulties involved in finding out what households actually spend their incomes on, the kinds of income (wage income, social wage income) and outgoings (taxes of varying kinds).
6. This method has been applied by the Australian Bureau of Statistics in ABS (1984–5).

Bibliography and references

ABS (Australian Bureau of Statistics) (1983) *Weekly Earnings of Employees (Distribution)*, ABS Cat. No. 6310.0, Canberra: AGPS.
ABS (Australian Bureau of Statistics) (1984) *Income and Housing Survey: Income of Individuals, 1981–82*, ABS Cat. No. 6502.0, Canberra: AGPS.

ABS (Australian Bureau of Statistics) (1984–5) *Household Income and Expenditure Survey 1984–85*, ABS Cat. No. 65307-0, Canberra: AGPS.

Ayres, P. (1987) *Malcolm Fraser*, Sydney: Heinemann.

Beilharz, P. (1983) 'The view from the summit', *Arena* **64**, 19–25.

Beilharz, P. (1989) 'The Laborist tradition and the reforming imagination' in R. Kennedy (ed.), *Australian Welfare: Historical sociology*, Melbourne: Macmillan.

Brennan, D. and C. O'Donnell, (1987) *Caring for Australian Children*, Sydney: Allen & Unwin.

Carney, S. (1989) *The Accord and Industrial Relations*, Sydney: Sunbooks.

Cass, B. (1985) 'The changing face of poverty in Australia', *Australian Feminist Studies* **2**.

Castles, F. (1989) 'Welfare and equality in capitalist societies', in R. Kennedy (ed.) *Australian Welfare*, Sydney: Allen & Unwin.

Davidson, K. (1986), cited in L. Ross *et al.*, 'Labor's Accord: why it's a fraud', *Socialist Action*.

EPAC (1986) *Growth in Australian Social Expenditures*, Canberra: Economic Policy Advisory Council, AGPS.

Graycar, A. (ed.) (1982) *Retreat from the Welfare State*, Sydney: Allen & Unwin.

Harding, A. (1982) 'An introduction to the social wage', *Social Security Review*, December. **7**, 11–15.

Health Issues Centre (1987) *Medicare: A Double Edged Sword*, Melbourne: HIC.

Henderson, R. F. (1967) *People in Poverty*, Melbourne: Longman Cheshire.

Henderson, R. F. (1975) *First Main Research: Commission of Enquiry into Poverty*, Canberra: AGPS.

Hughes, B. (1980) *Exit Full Employment*, Melbourne: Oxford.

Hutton, S. (1988) 'Testing Townsend: explaining living standards using secondary data', Mimeo, University of York.

Indecs (1987) *State of Play 4*, Sydney: Allen & Unwin.

Johnson, C. (1989) *The Labor Legacy*, Sydney: Allen & Unwin.

Jones, E. (1979) 'Fraser and the social wage', *Journal of Australian Political Economy*, **5**, 57–69.

McDonald, D. (1985) 'The Accord and the working class', M. Ed. Thesis, University of New South Wales.

Maddox, G. (1989) *The Hawke Government and Labor tradition*, Melbourne: Penguin.

Manning, I. (1982) 'The Henderson poverty line in review', *Social Security Review*, June.

Mathews, J. (1986) 'The Accord and politics', in D. Knight (ed.) *Moving Left*, Sydney: Pluto.

Melbourne Economics Group (1989) *New Economic Directions for Australia*, Melbourne: Centre for Australian Social Policy Analysis.

Norris, K. (1985) 'The accord and living standards', mimeo, Perth: University of Western Australia.

Norris, K. (1986a) 'Taxes, transfers and the social wage', mimeo.

Norris, K. (1986b) *Living Standards in Australia, 1980–86*, Perth: University of Western Australia.

Offe, C. (1984) *Contradictions of the Welfare State*, Oxford: Blackwell.

Peetz, D. (1985) *The Accord and Law Income Earners*, Wages and Incomes Policy Research Paper, Number 7, Canberra: Department of Employment and Industrial Relations.

Scotton, R. B. & H. Ferber (eds.) (1979) *Public Expenditure and Social Policy in Australia, The Fraser Years 1975–78*, Melbourne: Longman-Cheshire.

Shaver, S. (1989) 'Sex and money in the fiscal crisis' in R. Kennedy (ed.) *Australian Welfare: Historical Sociology*, Melbourne: Macmillan.

Smyth, P. (1989) *A Legacy of Choice: Economic thought and social policy in Australia, the early post war years*, Social Welfare Research Centre Discussion Papers, University of New South Wales.

Stewart, R. G. (1985) 'The politics of the Accord, does corporatism explain it?', *Politics* **20**(1), 55–64.

Stilwell, F. J. (1986) *The Accord and beyond*, Sydney: Pluto.

Stretton, H. (1987) *Political Essays*, Melbourne: Georgian House.

SWRC Paper to Child Poverty in Australia Conference, Melbourne.

Treasury (1989) *Economic Roundup, March 1989*, Canberra: AGPS.

Watts, R. (1989a) 'In fractured times: the Accord and social policy under Hawke, 1983–1987' in R. Kennedy (ed.) *Australian Welfare Historical Sociology*, Melbourne: Macmillan.

Watts, R. (1989b) 'Politics or paralysis: review of Maddox and Johnson on the Hawke Government', *Arena* **87**.

Watts, R. and P. Beilharz (1990) *A Powerful Social Engine? Australia and the Accord under Hawke*, Sydney: New Left Publications.

Whiteford, P., B. Bradbury and P. Saunders (1988) 'Inequality and deprivation among families with children: an exploratory study'.

7

Deregulation, youth policies and the creation of crime

Mike Presdee
Department of Youth Studies, Christchurch College,
Canterbury, United Kingdom

Since 1985, there has been an almost total preoccupation in Australia with things economic, that has permeated through all levels of government and the bureaucracy, covering all areas of administration, from the structure of banking and methods of taxation, through to defence, education and child care. Yet there has been little thought given to how these major changes achieved in economic life have affected, and will continue to affect, the ordinary everyday lives of Australians, and how ordinary Australians are 'making sense' of the deregulatory policies that are changing both the material and cultural conditions of their existence.

The Australian Labor Government, through embracing policies aimed at producing a form of 'people's capitalism', has raised popular expectations that have contributed to the formation of a culture that is essentially 'individualistic, competitive, efficient and affluent' (Seabrook, 1979). When the economy collapsed in 1986 with the fall in world commodity prices, there was a cultural acceptance, on the part of the more conservative forces of labour, of a deregulated economy, partially privatized, and guided only by the 'hidden hand' of the market. Market forces were now seen as able to make both private, and public, enterprises more competitive. The agenda quickly emerged of transforming not only airlines but also institutions of education into being efficient economic organizations.

Coupled with this was a continuing strongly held belief that poverty can be 'managed away', by pursuing the path of increased efficiency and effectiveness on the part of the major institutions of society, and moreover that this would in itself in some way herald the beginnings of social justice. It appears now that poverty is no longer a result of economic relationships, but a by-product of bad management, especially on the part of the bureaucratic welfare state.

The fact that these policies have created massive corporate success with new records of corporate profit has given both confidence, and comfort, to those conservative workers made insecure in their traditional class positions by the sudden and deep recession. This has produced a split in Australian society that has forced large sections of the working classes into poverty, where they languish, unrepresented and overcontrolled: and has in many ways added to the creation of crime.[1]

The culture of affluence

Australians have all, in recent years, become far more aware of what is going on in the courts of our Corporate Kings. Fed by all sections of the media with the complete and intricate details of the private lives of our own *Dynasty*, we are informed of the twenty-first birthday parties of their offspring, their marriages and their latest art acquisitions; and we have made a national sport out of watching them bob up and down in their expensive Hi-tech yachts. We know of Alan Bond's 'Irises' as if they were bought for the nation. And we watched on television the Labor Prime Minister and the Cabinet trek to the home of Kerry Packer through a corridor of glitz to celebrate with him his daughter's twenty-first birthday.

The Labor Government, more than any government, has brought to the centre stage these Corporate Masters, so that we might all gain spiritual sustenance from both the size of their economic success, and the 'rightfulness' of their social behaviour. It now seems, as one newspaper editorial put it, that the Labor Government has made 'the interests of Mr. Hawke's "rich mates"' one of its chief interests (*Advertiser*, 1987a). The process has developed to the point where the once Chancellor of the Exchequer in Thatcher's Britain, Nigel Lawson, recently felt able to cite Australia's fiscal policies as a justification for his own policies, that unabashedly benefited the affluent over and against the poor (*Advertiser*, 1987c).

Now thousands of tourists take boat trips up the Swan River in Perth to marvel not at the beauty of their natural surroundings, but to take in the evidence of the wealth of their nation and wonder at the conspicuous consumption that clings to the side of the Swan. The commentary of one of the trips explains:

> The house of John Roberts that you can see cost A$5½ million for the land and A$5 million for the house, the air-conditioning alone cost A$250,000. The house that you can see there, with the limestone base, is the home of Kevin

Parry. We've been reliably informed that it has just been revalued at
A$6½ million.

Since the world stock-market 'readjustment' (or 'crash' depending on
whether you 'lost' or 'gained'), we have been fed even more detailed
accounts of the lives of our entrepreneurs. Indeed there was, initially, an
almost touching consideration for the plight of the rich, with advice being
offered by psychiatrists and counsellors as to how they might all cope with
the reality that they were down to their last few millions. The Press ran
stories about the rich at the races, after the crash, explaining how they
coped with the logistics of the Melbourne Cup carnival. The Hyatt
Hotel's best 'suite' in Melbourne was booked out for the week at A$1,300
a night and Budget Chauffeur Services' fleet of thirty-five limousines was
fully booked at A$1,100 a day, as was its fleet of twenty-five Mercedes,
Jaguars and Ford LTDs, at only $550 a day. Nick's Wine Merchant in
Melbourne expected to 'shift' a million dollars' worth of champagne in
the week, with Dan Murphy Cellars reporting that it wasn't unusual for
someone to buy A$9,000 worth of bubbles for a single party (*The Herald*,
1987).

South Australia boasted its own 'post-crash' celebration with its 'better
than ever' four-day Grand Prix extravaganza that produced an orgasm of
drinking and dying,[2] as tens of thousands watched millions of dollars'
worth of cars decrease in value at A$3.125 a minute, throughout the
two-hour race (*The Australian*, 1987c). During the week, organizations
and politicans watched over the struggle between large corporations and
the tourist industry, as the corporations scrambled to block-book in
advance as many luxury rooms for next year that they could, until the
Premier of the State called for a more rational approach, and for all to
share. After all, this was the International Year for the Homeless. The
Adelaide Hilton – eager to play its role in providing accommodation for
the homeless rich – opened its 'yellow ribbon' floor with the expressed
purpose of allowing the extremely wealthy to retain their separateness
and to keep them from being soiled by the 'ordinariness' of others.

In Melbourne, Brents Toyshop in Toorak Road sold at least two
motorized toy Porsches in October – a snip at only A$5,500 each (*The
Herald*, 1987).

In the last financial year we have read of the media musical monopoly
game that has done little to change what we hear, read and see, but has
somehow magically created vast wealth for individuals. Kerry Packer
made a profit of $79.5 million overnight by selling his stake in Hill Samuel
(UK) to the TSB group, and since the 'crash' there has been a 'flurry' of
activity with our new national heroes continuing to compete in their quest

for further wealth. After the crash, John Spalyins moved into the British insurance industry at a cost of A$158 millions. Alan Bond moved into gold for A$750 million and 'played' with Allied Lyons. Kevin Parry bought Television Satellite Services and Larry Adler was reported to be 'all cashed up' and wondering what to do with a billion dollars (*Times on Sunday*, 1987). Chris Skase managed to keep the A$2 billion Quintex leisure empire intact after divesting certain companies before 'Black Monday', and Bob Hawke reminded us that the businessmen who had built up successful export enterprises were 'national heroes' and de-scribed Alan Bond as one of the 'most outstanding exports from Pommie land' because 'risk takers . . . create employment and opportunities for tens of thousands of Australians' (*The Australian*, 1987a). There was no mention of workers as heroes or of the thousands of United Kingdom migrants who had given their working lives to the steelworks and car factories of Australia.

Daily, the real estate pages showed us how the property boom was benefiting us all as we saw how much we had all made from the homes we live in, as we all scrambled at auctions to pick up a bargain at half a million or so. In Sydney, in one week alone, fifteen properties went for over A$1 million and were all snapped up within a week of coming on to the market. There was no mention as to whether the purchasers were factory workers or QCs, although the fact that ABC current affairs reporter Max Walsh was half-a-million lighter was thought to be newsworthy. Again, since the 'crash' property prices have continued their high public profile, measured in both press coverage and millions of dollars. The largest residential sale of 'crash week' took place in Sydney where sixty-three residences were sold for more than A$20 million and Jones Lang Wootton recorded a sales record of A$400 million for the ten days directly following the 'crash' (*The Australian*, 1987b). October was a record month for Gold Coast dealer Max Christmas who celebrated crash month with a new high of A$42.5 million in sales and the Benton Corporation was congratulated 'publicly' in a full-page advertisement in *The Australian* for paying a record price of A$106.6 million for number 327–43 Collins Street in the central business district of Melbourne (*The Australian*, 1987c).

The stock-market crash has made more visible the culture of our designated national heroes but has little altered the way in which they live, nor indeed the way in which they accumulate the wealth created by others. There has simply been a move from one market to another as 'cash' looks for stable and growing markets. Since 'Black Monday', a series of record prices has been paid for a motley collection of scrap metal, canvas, paper and rocks, that when presented as cultural commodities demand millions of dollars on the open market.

October: 54.99 carat Rhodes diamond record price – *US$3.85 million*
   followed next day by
64.83 carat stone – new record of *US$6.38 million*
Gutenberg Bible – record price of *A$7 million*
November: Van Gogh's 'Irises' – record price *A$79 million*
Picasso etching – record price *A$864,700*
Bugatti Royale car – record price for a car *A$14.2 million*
March: Ashoka diamond *A$5.36 million*
April: World's most valuable diamond expected to fetch over
   A$11 million

In January 1988 the whole country listened and looked at the opening of Australia's first complete housing estate for the extremely rich, as 50,000 people attended the finale of the A$15 million five-day opening of the Sanctuary Cove resort. The Resort's brochure, adorned with the bottom half of a bikini-clad young woman and a large glass of champagne, informed us that 'Sanctuary Cove is unashamedly elitist . . . protected by its own Act of Parliament. In a world which seems to have gone mad, in a society in which crime and violence have become commonplace, this kind of peace of mind is priceless.' All for a starting price of A$885,000 through to A$1.5 million.

As Chase AMP implores us in double-page spreads to line up for A$20,000 worth of credit with the heading 'FOR PEOPLE WHO WANT IT ALL NOW', we need not wonder that welfare workers complain about the recipients of social security payments falling into the 'millionaire for a day' syndrome, as they spend all their money virtually as soon as they get it (*Sunday Mail*, 1987).

The culture of affluence now dominates the way in which we make sense of our new, deregulated economic world, creating a moral code, designed for affluence, that understands the experience of wealth as sensuous in itself, to be savoured, revelled in and rejoiced. Wealth is no longer understood as a measurement of value created by workers, but is now seen as being discovered by the prospectors of capitalism. Wealth is now something that lies dormant until discovered by the creativity of the entrepreneurial mind, and excavated by workers under the watchful eye of management. In this society enterprise is everything, and inexhaustible wealth waits to be liberated.

The reality for a large proportion of the citizenry is, of course, vastly different from the world described in the new enterprise-minded mass media, as welfare agencies pick up the casualties of the new culture of efficiency and affluence. The latest report on bankruptcies shows that for the first time the number of individual bankruptcies has overtaken the number of business bankruptcies, with household debts rising by over 500 per cent in a decade and bankcard debt rising by 42 per cent in a year (*Advertiser*, 1987b).

Young people have been just as vulnerable with the South Australian Legal Aid service for example advising 135 young people aged between 18 and 20 during 1988 about their debts: with some young people being so in debt that they needed advice about personal bankruptcy proceedings. The budgeting advice service of the South Australian Department of Community Welfare also found that the young people who came for advice averaged debts of about A$1,000 with one young person owing A$5,000 in credit card and bank loans (*Advertiser*, 1987a). And the '2nd storey' multiple youth services centre in the middle of Adelaide's Rundle Mall shopping centre has been forced to introduce a Breakfast programme for young people, in a desperate attempt to divert them from prostituting themselves for subsistence money. A more modern version of the old soup kitchens, whose re-emergence in Canada is discussed in Chapter 9 by Graham Riches.

The experience of young people

As the rift widens between how the Government thinks people live, and the everyday reality that many experience, so a cultural confusion confronts large numbers of youth. There has been a fundamental misunderstanding by this Government about how young working-class people live: their expectations, hopes, fears, their happiness, their desperation. The present governing group of Parliament, Peak Unions and Corporate Capital, presents itself as a grey, sombre-suited, wall of conservatism (the very picture of propriety), who are under the misapprehension that young people need to be coerced into the new, sparkling, corporate economy.[3] If the young resist the power of 'rationality' then they should suffer all the controls needed to render them both socially and politically impotent. It is only by enforcing control mechanisms that the unacceptable social side-effects of economic deregulation can be masked and portrayed as a moral, rather than economic, question. In this way the regulation of young people is separated from the question of employment.[4] From this society, that has as its spiritual driving force the legal, or illegal, acquisition of individual wealth, we can expect not only an unconstrained rise in so-called legal economic activities, but also a corresponding rise in illegal activities. As the prospects of poverty begin to bear down over more and more young people, so we can expect cultural responses that will be considered rational by the young, and illegal and irrational by our 'leaders'.

Youth poverty

Unemployment still remains the greatest threat to the social development of young people. In South Australia the rate of unemployment for 15- to 19-year-olds hovers between 25 and 30 per cent, still above the national average of between 16 and 20 per cent, a figure that is now beginning to rise once again, at both state and federal levels. Cities, like that of Elizabeth, 14 km north of Adelaide, have particularly suffered high youth unemployment for about eight years. The 1981 census felt fit to describe fully what was happening there:

> These areas of Elizabeth which were settled by young nuclear families during the migrant boom years of the 1950's and 1960's, and which have been heavily dependent on jobs in the depressed manufacturing sector of the economy, have now sadly become affected by unemployment especially of school leavers . . . Here youth unemployment exists in combination with high levels of total unemployment, low levels of labour force participation by married women, low incomes of those who do have work, with high percentages of single parent families. Under these circumstances it is hardly surprising that welfare workers describe a sub-culture of despair amongst unemployed young people.

In the city of Elizabeth, local employment office figures show a rate of 40 per cent for the same age group, a figure which excludes any 15-year-olds who rarely register at the employment office.[5] A more realistic unemployment rate for Elizabeth is more likely to be in the region of 50 per cent of all those above the age of 15 eligible for work, a situation that has changed little in seven years. Surprisingly whilst the 15- to 19-year-old labour force has reduced significantly in South Australia, from 78,300 in 1981 to 69,500 in 1987, youth unemployment has become both higher and entrenched.

I have carried out a close study of the responses of young people in Elizabeth to these long periods of poverty and inequality. These are reported in detail elsewhere (see Presdee, 1984, 1985, 1987; White, 1987a, 1987b, 1987c).[6] The general lesson of these studies is that one should not underestimate the ability of sub-cultures to take even the most entrenched structural inequality and numb it into normality, creating for those involved a much-needed sense of being part of 'the wider world', of 'fitting in' and of being 'normal'. Sub-cultures have the potential to capture the 'different' and 'routinize' it into the normal and necessary. This alternative sense of normality has the potential to confront the dominant culture, disrupting its rhythm and order. In this way sub-cultures resist the outer world, and protect the social world of their members as they create new senses of the same economic reality that is experienced by us all. Competing views of the world, containing as they do different politics, come into being and present a threat to the existing dominant understandings and meanings made of society. It is just this process of 'making meaning' that politicians and political economists find so hard to understand. It is their failure to do so that has led them to the belief that improvements in training opportunities and schooling will, on their own, persuade young unemployed people to give up their 'hedonistic' lives of leisure and suspend their involvement in the culture of affluence, whilst they are retrained and reschooled, ready for life on the dole at 18 rather than 16.

This offer of a reduction in income by the removal of the dole for 16- and 17-year-olds is one that a great number of young people are likely to reject, forcing even more young people to attempt to survive a consumer society from the conditions of poverty. As Frank Maas has suggested, the policy proposals introduced in the 1988 May economic statement 'seem destined to exacerbate rather than reduce problems such as family conflict and young homelessness' (Maas, 1987) and, we might add, increase crime. The present situation points significantly to disaster when we consider that in January 1988 there were 60,000 16- and 17-year-olds 'not at school, not at a tertiary institution' and looking for work (ABS, 1988). But the Social Services in Canberra had, on 29 January, given only 25,126 job search allowances, which rose only slightly to 26,055 on 11 March at a time when young people had already re-enrolled at school.[7] Even allowing for the vagaries of statistical sampling techniques and the new thirteen-week waiting period for 'dole' eligibility, there is still a staggering 30,000 plus young people without work, without a wage and without income. There seems to have been a naive assumption, even though all the evidence shows otherwise, that all young people live happily at home, with parents who not only care, but, more importantly, are competent, and cope. Social policies that rely for their success on business practices such as money incentives or disincentives have the potential to create casualties that could prove even more costly in the long run. Unlike business, human services cannot simply 'write-off' those that are no longer needed, or take to the scrap-heap the inefficient bits of humanity that seem unable to fit the new systems.

Youth responses: school absenteeism, unemployment and crime

In an attempt to gain a greater understanding of the reactions of young people to the restructuring of their lives taking place in the late 1980s, I undertook a further series of investigations into the everyday lives of unemployed young people in Adelaide.

1. Young people from the Northern suburbs of Adelaide were closely interviewed.
2. Workers with youths, interviewed in a number of settings, gave 'case studies' of young people who had been helped by their agency.
3. Ten street youths were interviewed in depth.
4. A group of twenty young women involved in a special 'at risk' project in a northern suburbs high-school were interviewed.
5. The November 1988 Adelaide confidential 'youth phone-in weekend' project was especially designed to question young people about the effects of the new job-search allowance.

The official extent of juvenile crime in South Australia and its connection with unemployment has been well documented by the South Australian Office of Crime Statistics. The crime figures for the period 1 January–30 June 1986 reveal a 3.4 per cent increase compared with the previous six months. Of 4,856 appearances in court, the great majority were for relatively minor property crimes, such as shop theft (57.9 per cent), breaking and entering (11.6 per cent) and offences against order (9.2 per cent). Under 1 per cent of all juvenile appearances involved an offence defined by the Department of Community Welfare researchers as a crime of violence (*Crime and Justice in South Australia*, 1982), and perhaps the most striking statistic is that 46.1 per cent of young people appearing before courts were unemployed, whereas 72.3 per cent in front of aid panels were in the student/apprentice category.

The situation for young women 'offenders' is worse than that of young men with 55 per cent of young women 'offenders' being unemployed, compared to 45 per cent of young men. The figure for 15- and 16-year-old 'young women unemployed offenders' was dramatically high, being 68 per cent and 70 per cent, with the corresponding figure for young men being 48 per cent and 54 per cent.

The stress on young unemployed women is quite clear, as those without dole payments figure highly in the 'offenders' figures. And it is these conditions of continuing high unemployment that the present Government has created for thousands more Australian youths.

The high unemployment areas of the outer western, southern and northern suburbs of Adelaide account for almost 70 per cent of all offences dealt with by the children's court, with the regional area of Elizabeth making up 36.6 per cent of the total. This, coupled with a high frequency 'court and panel appearance' rate of 42.7 per 1,000 in Elizabeth, 51 per 1,000 in Port Adelaide (against 4.6 for the middle-class eastern suburbs area of St Peters), shows clearly the class nature of criminalization.

(It is not my intention here to discuss the added problem of race that faces, for example, the city of Elizabeth, but we should be aware of the over-representation of Aboriginals in all the figures, especially young Aboriginal women.)

The fact that the greater number of panel appearances are from young people, still at school, is little comfort when we consider the state of absenteeism in schools, and the statistical connection between absenteeism and crime. The increasing number of truants shows the extent of the failure of present educational policies (especially for working-class young people), as 15-year-olds choose unemployment without the dole over the exciting learning environment of school and further education. There has been a continuing failure by politicians, bureaucrats and academics to understand the effects that schooling has on a vast number of young people, who have struggled with not just the content of the curriculum but with the very nature of the institutional form of schooling itself that stands as an instrument held over and against them. The cultural effects of being actively part of something that you do not understand, and cannot understand, becomes layered into the structures of everyday life, laid down in the minutiae of social interaction. It is difficult, if not impossible, for pupils to make sense of questions of class, race and gender. The human pain of being powerless and unknowing, of being a confused recipient instead of an active participant, is experienced constantly but rarely fully understood. There seems little point for working-class youth in schools in opting for more of the same, and there is little surprise that they vote with their feet.

For those working with young people, the enormity of the gap between policy expectations and the real social conditions of people, created in them a real sense of helplessness. As one youth worker pleaded when interviewed:

> How do you get a kid into a training programme who can neither read or write, a kid that hasn't been to school since they were 7 years of age? They have played truant, the system has never been able to find something that is applicable to them. When they turn 15, miraculously they can read and write? No way! No way! They have lived out on the streets for donkey's yonks going from foster family into care, to out on the streets, to the salvos, God knows where – they've been all round the place, they've never had chance to stop to learn, and they don't want to, some of them, that's the other thing, you've got to get back to that choice stuff, you can't take choice away from a human being, it's almost an existential argument isn't it, because if they choose not to choose they still make a choice.

> *Question*: But aren't we dealing here with just a small minority of young people?

Answer: 'What's a small minority, I mean, uh, between 15 and 19? When you consider my major client group is 15 to 19 years. I see forty kids a week in that age group of which a percentage would probably be – oh, 2 per cent would be at school, it's a joke, it's not a minority. I'm talking about majorities here, I'm talking about kids that – in the month of July I saw 6 10- to 14-year-olds, 116 15- to 19-year-olds, 38 20- to 24-year-olds, and 115 mums and dads, you tell me, and of those 7 per cent were at school, it's a hoot.'

Without exception, all the young unemployed people that were interviewed had truanted from school at some time, so beginning an early pattern of 'offending'. Truanting was a response to problems faced within the school, with young people rarely truanting to do specific things, but simply to steal both time and space for themselves in which they could, for a short period, be autonomous, be free and be themselves, thus escaping, even for a short period of time, the rules, regulations and regimentation of schooling.

'I hated science, every science lesson I went down the school creek and sit in the tunnel – they got a tunnel there, or we go up the shops – we used to go down the shops and pinch smokes.' (Wendy, 15)

'The first time [I truanted] I went into Adelaide with a couple of friends. It was really funny because they found out we were wagging an' that so the police in Elizabeth sent out, it was so funny, sent out a message to police in Adelaide, and we were walking along. There was three of us and this guy had a really short haircut and there was two policemen were standing there and we walked right past them, and they said, and one of the police said 'Ha, ha, look at his hair', like we was messing around, and they were looking for us, and they never realized it was us. It was so funny and we mucked around in Adelaide all day – it was nothing exciting – we went down the Torrens.' (Sue, 17 – left school at 15)

'Another time I sat in a tree all day – I was not going to school – I did not want to go to school – That's where I stayed – in a tree.' (Ann, 16 – left school at 15.)

Already Chris, 13½ and still at primary school, is 'wagging' regularly and spending her time 'scoring for my brother' and Deb aged 14½ last went to school one-and-a-half years ago.

In Rachel's case there is an attempt to work out what is going on; to work out why they are responding to their education in the way that they do:

Answer: 'Yeh, like, he's nice to me but at the start of the year [term?] like he said, like, if we had a problem with our maths, like, if we said "could you help us, please", he says, "I'll help you with all of the class, uh, we'll go over it again but we'll help you with all of the class". But I just want to get helped "individual" but he won't, he just said "I'll help you with all the class", and I went up to him, I think it was yesterday, yeh, it was yesterday, I said "could I have some more, um, help with some fractions cause I'm really messed up with fractions". And he said "we'll go back over it today, tomorrow" and I'm there, I said no, I want some individual work and he's there, "well we'll try okay", and that you know I can't go home and tell my parents cause I . . . and he doesn't listen anyway cause my mum went to the, um, interviews and he doesn't listen, he just says "oh what do you think about it", you know, and cause he's an advanced teacher that's what he'll do, he'll just teach that's it, you know, if you're not good enough then he won't help you, that's just his kind of attitude, and it's not on because you know you can't help it if you can't do something, and I feel so small when I go and tell other people if they can help me you know and there's a girl and they say "oh go and tell S . . ." you know and I say, oh they don't know how you feel like, I just feel embarrassed and I don't want to go to my boyfriend and say, oh could you help me with this you know I mean they probably wouldn't mind but inside you that's what minds, you know like I say, oh, nah, I just go and see somebody and never get around to it.'

Question: 'So, do you ever feel like you don't want to come to school, take a day off?'

Answer: 'Lately I have, when, um, I had a lot of problems with my friend, my best friend, she didn't come to school. I really wanted her to come to school, I was really trying to make her, she finally came and, um, lately I, I don't know, I just sort of everything was coming on top of me, I didn't feel like coming to school. I just feel like running away into a little hole.'

Question: 'What do you do when you wag school? What type of things do you do?'

Answer: 'I just go to Adelaide, just go down the train station just stay there or we used to go cause I got Uno cards now and I used to go with this girl called T. . . and just go with her and just sit there and play Uno all day and talk. It's not much fun. It's boring really, we don't do much.'

There is little doubt that the rates of absenteeism are increasing in South Australia, with attendance officers reporting an increasing problem. The pattern and reasons are complex, but there are significant differences in daily rates between working-class schools, such as Port Adelaide at 6.9 per cent and middle-class schools such as Marryatville with just 1.7 per cent. The latest study undertaken by the Adelaide regional office estimates that 8,500 students are absent for more than one term a year and that on any one day 18,000 children may be absent for a variety of reasons. It is clear that a great majority of these would be absent with parental knowledge although not necessarily under the direct supervision and care of parents.

Young women are more often absent than young men, a pattern that starts in the late primary school and becomes exceptionally marked by year ten (Elburn, 1987).

It is when young 15-year-olds, especially young women, finally leave school that the battle for an income, for survival, begins in earnest. It appears that no matter how hard they try, in the end the way in which an income is achieved matters less and less. In each of my interviews every young person had broken some legal regulation, in some way, in their fight for survival. Although most had never been caught, they had, between them, been guilty of the following:

1. Non-attendance at school.
2. Vandalism.
3. Drug use.
4. Underage carnal knowledge.
5. Drinking.
6. Smoking.
7. Breaking and entering.
8. Shop-lifting.
9. Prostitution.
10. Driving offences.
11. Non-declaration of taxable income.

'I'd left school and I wasn't on the dole and wasn't getting any money whatsoever. So I had to get money somehow – from friends, borrowed from friends, hassle kids at the shops – not bash them, just say give us your money or we're going to get you into so much trouble.' (Sue)

'I used to steal out of Mum's purse all the time – if I went to a friend's place, I'd steal out of their mum's purse. I just needed the money. I wasn't getting any money. Mum would buy me a packet of smokes. I just had to have money.' (Ann)

'I've been to court just for pinching . . . flogging stuff. It was cause I liked them, it was for my bike, a pair of pedals. I was with my two mates but they never knew I done it.' (Rod 14¾, left school)

The extent that 'subsistence crime' is increasingly becoming a part of the lives of 'non-street' young people was examined through the confidential phone-in weekend held in November 1988. On this weekend young people were requested, through all forms of the media, to answer a number of questions concerning their employment situation and specifically whether they were receiving any subsistence allowances and if not, how they acquired money and how they spent their time. All but two of those questioned were in the wealthless, under 18-years category, and out of a total of forty-three, 55 per cent were receiving the reduced job search allowance of A$25 whilst 18 per cent received no income at all.

The most important factor of the phone-in was that 68 per cent of those interviewed were from stable homes having lived for some time with one or both parents or a relative. They were not from that group of young people whose lives were in such confusion that they were without homes and without families. These young people were living out the beginnings of adult life from a position of poverty, knowing that they could neither face, nor enter, in an acceptable way, any part of the education and training system. The pressures on relationships that resulted from being both unemployed and without subsistence confronted and consumed their everyday life, posing the single most important problem of their social existence. At a time when they are at their most vulnerable they are rendered both useless and wageless and are unable to form relationships from any position of status or autonomy. Nearly 70 per cent of those interviewed stated they had problems with families and friends, created by being wageless, whilst 54 per cent had problems created by being jobless.

Already over 50 per cent of this sample were committing crimes in order to subsist, involving breaking and entering, drug dealing, begging, prostitution and the cash economy. With relationships under stress all around them, these young people are clearly 'at risk' of becoming homeless, defenceless and exploited. The conditions in which they now exist contain all the ingredients for human tragedy on a grand scale, that could with a more flexible policy be avoided. It is not enough to give help when the young become homeless, when relationships have already broken down – what is needed are policies that recognize the needs of young people and allow for the development and maintenance of existing relationships.

This precise pattern was unravelled by Mary (16) who had never succeeded at school, had truanted but not often, had left school at 15 with no income at all and *clung to the future of 'dole' at 16*. The removal of this allowance, the only hope she had, finally finished her home life, and five months before this interview she left home and lived for four weeks on the banks of the River Torrens. After losing a great deal of weight and in a depressed state she was taken in by friends. Five months later she took an overdose and cut her wrists:

> I tried to O/D once cause I couldn't hack it no more. I wasn't getting no money, no food, there was nothing, no family, I was just shaking and everything – pulse was up and I was sweating and going dizzy and I tried to slash my wrists and I got marks on my wrist – I tried to cut my wrists before. It was three or four weeks ago, we had a party drinking beer and everything and everything got to me because I was sort of drunk and I got a piece of glass and started cutting my

wrist. [Why?] Oh, I don't know, no money still, no money, no family – nothing. It's hopeless all the time. (Mary, 16)

At times the 'event' of breaking and entering served both the purpose of providing an income and of structuring the day. Like the fullness and richness of radio cricket commentaries the descriptions of breaking-in were vivid and precise.

> One time I was with one of my girlfriends. We went to this meeting at the shops and no one had any money whatsoever and this girl who was there, she was really trying to get into the group, sort of thing, and she was saying we could all trust her, and she said she'd left the window open. There was a guard dog there but because it was her house she went and got the dog, an' that, and there was about five guys and two of us girls – I stood at the letterbox and was watching, and that, pretending I was waiting for someone, and she went and opened the window and they cut the wire and they just forced it open, and I remember hearing this scream go bang! crash! and she goes 'Oh there goes my ornament, gone' – or something like that – um, no lights were turned on and she led them through to where there was this, like a jewellery box or something – some sort of box where this money was kept – they were going away on holiday and they'd saved it all up.
>
> We only took 50 – we only took 50 cause we were scared that if we did get caught it would be worse. (Sue, 17)

In all cases they came to regard stealing as a disease. Something they had to be cured of, something that they were battling against in a brave effort to accept their poverty, to accept the bottom of the pile, as they began the painful process of learning to be poor.

> I, I don't do it no more – I can handle being without money – I can handle it now. If I'm broke I just come here – I don't steal no more. (Sue)

> I got done for smashing windows at school – four months ago it was, it was over at the North Primary school I was looking for my lighter cause I dropped it – night time – the cops came over and my friend smiles a bit and the copper says 'Smack!' knocks him to the ground and he goes 'Don't laugh at me'. I'm alright now, my soccer coach is a policeman. If I've got no money I just stays at home. (David, 17 – left school at 16)

Never, in six weeks, did any of these young people suggest that they might return to school. Several had tried to go back, and failed once more. Several had finished CYSS schemes and further education courses, and they had all got skills that, although unmarketable, they clung to as examples of their individuality, their creativity, their humanity.[8]

> I've got a thing about Egyptology – I've written masses about it and I'm always reading about it. I've got no maths though. I need an education: so I'd like to go

back, but then I couldn't keep up with it unless I did my year 8 and year 9 all over again, but I don't think I could do it – I could do Egyptology – I went for a job in the Museum in the Egyptology department but I didn't get it. (Ann)

I was thinking of, about doing industrial sewing cause I'm a good sewer – I make skirts an' that for me sister. (Wendy, 15).

My sister designs clothes – she's got a whole book that thick of clothes' designs – she's going to do a fashion parade and I'm going to be a model. They say I've got the right face for it. (Chris)

I've got no talent, an' that. I've just got skills and sports, but no talent. My mum's got no talent either, she's 40 years old and still plays netball. (David, 17 – played soccer for South Australia)

I put my name at the CES[9] and I done a CYSS course – retail sales – I went for an interview at John Martins but I didn't do too good cause it was my first interview. She said I got good eye contact – next time just try a bit harder and don't be so nervous, cause I was stumbling over my words, an' that. (Sally, 15)

As their high expectations for their new independence and their hopes for a life of work and social activities recede into the poverty of unemployment, so new ways of filling the day with normal activities becomes important. The loss of the regulated work day with its richness of social life and social rhythms drives most young unemployed people to the extremes in their quest for an income, or what an income might buy. A workless life means the loss of the very 'reason' for living itself, the loss of the essence of working-class life, pushing young people into the unknown world of marginal labour, where they are exposed to the extremes of exploitation and personal danger.

I went for a couple of jobs as a waitress. Fake name, fake age. Then I thought . . . the peek-a-boo girls (peep show) an' that, and I thought should I, shouldn't I. It'll be extra money, anybody can do that sort of thing – but I didn't end up doing it – I got an interview and said I was 25 – I got to Adelaide but I chickened out. (Ann)

This guy I was seeing had an older brother who was 35 and was setting up an escort agency and he was going to get me a car an' that – I would have done that cause I knew he would treat me right. At that time I was really desperate – I would only have had to do it two or three a day. (Sue)

When I was on the run I slept with guys but I wasn't getting paid. The guys were protecting me a lot – you know – they really protected me heaps. (Ann)

Young women and the cash economy

There is little doubt that young unemployed women are more susceptible to working in the cash economy than young men, driving young women to accept both illegal conditions and illegal work. Even the most respectable businesses were found to have accounting practices that dealt frequently with only cash transactions. One young woman, after completing a further education beauticians' course, got work at a nail-sculpting salon, only to find that she was paid in cash, no pay-slip, no tax – no questions asked. When she and her friend asked for a proper pay-slip they quickly found themselves on the dole and again back into training in a CYSS course. Another young woman worked for six months at a baker's shop and only demanded a pay-slip when the family realized something was wrong. She found herself quickly joining the unemployed statistics! During this study I encountered a range of jobs which were part of the cash economy including: waitressing, swimming lessons, nursing, tennis coaching, telephone selling and child care centre work and I found that market-places were used often for cash earnings but the most institutionalized method of all was the 'vice' industry. The extent that young women work in the general area of 'vice', i.e. photographic studios, stripping, peek-a-boo, prostitution, is difficult to ascertain, but there is a generalized feeling from the police, bureaucrats, street-workers, and young women themselves that this is an area of work that has increased in the last two years and is still expanding.

In a recent report in South Australia, the head of the Children's Interest Bureau stated: 'Young prostitutes often have . . . petty criminal records for offences other than prostitution, usually committed in order to survive. They are runaways and have low educational achievement and are often unemployed.' She went on to report that the 'Federal government's decision to cease dole payments to 16- to 17-year-olds will further disadvantage an already alienated group' (McGregor, 1987).

In the Victorian *Inquiry into Prostitution* (1985), it was estimated by the police that there were 180 young people involved in prostitution in that state whilst Hancock's research for the same enquiry showed 67 per cent of a sample of 63 young women had left school and 85 per cent of those were unemployed. The Fitzgerald enquiry in Queensland has been told of a 16-year-old who worked at 'Fantasy Photographic' agency during her school holidays, earning up to $1,800 a week (*Advertiser*, 1987d).

The recent debate in South Australia has been about whether organized underage prostitution exists. With the exception of reports of two such establishments, one in Port Adelaide and one at Dry Creek, there is little evidence of any organized approach. However, there is no doubt that young women, rather than underage women, are more desired by 'businesses', their services cost more, and they are in greater demand by clients, with some establishments specializing in young women, as against underage women. It is doubtful whether the niceties of a legally defined age bracket have any effect on young women's responses. Just because they reach the age of 18 does not mean they feel less exploited, less helpless, less vulnerable: or for that matter more able, all of a sudden, to cope. By only concentrating on the legally underaged, a great deal remains unrecognized, invisible and beyond concern.

The 1986 'prostitutes of South Australia' phone-in of 108 calls showed that 54 per cent were under 21 when they started working, whilst the Victorian report showed only 34 per cent under 20, from a sample of 90. However, workers were now working longer with 54 per cent working two years or more, whilst in 1979 only 22 per cent worked longer than two years (*Inquiry into Prostitution*, 1985).

In the last year, there has been an explosion of escort agencies in Adelaide with 112 agencies now in existence and 22 brothels. The South Australian vice squad estimates around a hundred 18- to 20-year-olds to be working in the business and there seems little doubt that ages are getting lower, and harder to detect, and that prostitution, like war, is something experienced by the young: both young men and young women.

> My wage was only 40 odd dollars – I didn't know anybody [having just run away to Melbourne] I started to go out. I started meeting people and I think it was in a pub in Coburg, and some old guy came over and offered me some money, and I said no. The next night there was this young guy, so I took it and that's how I started – it wasn't organized or anything – I wish I'd done it properly – it was the company I liked.
>
> I didn't care about the morals of it, I think I was too young – I was only 15. It was A$20 then – now I think they got a bargain – a 15-year-old for A$20. I was drinking an' that – it just seemed to happen. (Jane)

By the age of 15 Jane had run away to Melbourne, married at 16, become pregnant, lost her child, went to Perth: started to work as a stripper before being tempted by the money available in escort agencies.

The other young women Jane worked with had the following histories that connected them, inevitably, with the young women I had interviewed in Elizabeth.

1. Left school 2nd year High. Almost illiterate.
2. Worked Hindley Street at 14 – little schooling (described as no schooling).
3. Just started working. Left school at 15, worked in a supermarket six days a week for $180 – living in a flat and started to shoplift.

4. Left school at 15. Ran away from home at 14 – slept around in exchange for housing. Became pregnant – stayed in single mothers' home. State housing emergency list – slept in park with baby. Now working to buy a home.

For these young women there is a sense of 'belonging' – bringing to them the normality of a working life that they have never had before. 'Even now some of the girls don't like the work but they like being part of something. The girls who work together get quite friendly – they like to belong' (Jane). And Sue, in Elizabeth, who had flirted with the idea herself of joining an escort agency, got the same feeling of 'belonging' from the drop-in centre that now held her life together.

> Do you ever watch *Cheers* – the song in that is magic, it goes – 'Sometimes you need to go where everybody knows your name' I walk into this place and I feel welcome – we all know each other and we all care about each other, we muck around and we – you know – have a laugh and do really weird things . . . we all belong.

For many young women living on the street, that sense of 'belonging' is something that still eludes them. At the age of 16 having been 'provided' for by education policies, income policies, employment policies, training policies, control policies, they appear confused, abused and broken and their 'talk' about themselves is a measurement not, as they see it, of their own failure, but the failure of policy:

Cathy . . .
'I hate me.' 'Others hate me.' 'People say things to me just to be nice and underneath, they're thinking I'm stupid.' 'People only like me when they want something.'

Marie . . .
'No one will believe me.' 'It was my fault.' 'I deserve to be punished.' 'I'm dirty.'

Diane . . .
'I'm stupid.' 'I'm really crazy.' 'It's all my fault.' 'I should have looked after my mum, so she wouldn't resent me . . . sort of thing.'

Vanessa . . .
'I'm not a person. Because mum didn't think I "was there" (I was just there to do things for her) I thought I wasn't there . . . because I couldn't see anything . . . I didn't seem to know what was going on around me.' 'I'm disgusting, dirty, a slut.'
'I was called a fat slut by mum and my sisters . . . so I imagined myself cutting off hunks of flesh down to the bone . . . to get rid of myself.'

'If I look at someone or they look at me . . . they will know how disgusting I am.'

'Nobody wants to look at me and come near me unless they want to bash me up or . . . you know.'

'I'm only around to do things for people and to let people do things to me. I thought that because I couldn't feel nothing.'

'I was that close to becoming a prostitute in . . . but a voice inside me – which I could barely hear – stopped me.'

The struggles facing 15-, 16- and 17-year-olds have had little effect on persuading them to return to the realms of education and training. They have, after all, all failed there already. To attempt to solve the low school retention rates of 16-year-olds, and thereby youth unemployment, by the use of financial disincentives will only create further personal poverty and hardship.

The present Australian Government's policy of starving young people back into education is just as likely to drive as many young people into the vagaries of the cash economy and crime, as it is likely to drive young people into the experience of traineeships. We can assume that the withdrawal of the dole will create a bigger pool of 'at risk' young people virtually overnight, creating a nightmare for the social services throughout the country.

From young people themselves have come both the warning, and the evidence, if we care to look and to listen. Whilst politicians and administrators peddle the politics and economics of 'competition, efficiency and affluence', they should look deeper, beyond the image-world of the new Australian 'enterprise culture' and become aware of the struggle for survival, the struggle for creativity, and the struggle for humanity, that many young Australians are now engaged in. There will be little thanks for youth policies that neglect the creation of work and thereby encourage the *de facto* creation of crime.

Notes

1. For a wider discussion see Taylor (1987).
2. The Road Safety Unit at Adelaide University showed the accident rate during the Grand Prix week increased considerably.
3. The term 'Peak Unions' refers here to the Australian Council of Trade Unions (ACTU), which is at the 'peak' of the trade union organization.
4. For a major discussion of this view, see Presdee and White (1987).
5. Figures supplied by Elizabeth Commonwealth Employment Service June 1987.
6. The same arguments for British working-class youth are spelt out by Paul Willis (1977, 1979, 1984a, 1984b).

7. The 'job search allowance' replaced unemployment (dole) payments for 16–17-year-olds, who now can claim A\$25 (£11) per week as payment towards the cost of searching for a job. Young people still have to 'sign on' and complete unemployment forms and undertake interviews at their 'job centre'. Many have simply not done so and are therefore without subsistence. In extreme cases of family hardship a further A\$25 can be claimed.
8. Community Youth Support Scheme (CYSS) provides short work 'skills and training' programmes, as well as 'life skills' courses.
9. Commonwealth Employment Service (CES) is the network of employment offices run by government, where the unemployed both 'sign on' and get help in finding either work or training programmes.

References

ABS (Australian Bureau of Statistics) (1988) Cat. No. 6203.0, Table 11, Canberra: AGPS.
Advertiser (1987a) 7 October, Adelaide.
Advertiser (1987b) 11 October, Adelaide.
Advertiser (1987c) 27 October, Adelaide.
Advertiser (1987d) 18 November, Adelaide.
Crime and Justice in South Australia 1 January–30 June 1982, No. 20, Series A.
Elburn, T. (1987) 'The management of student absenteeism. A trial in the Adelaide area, 1987', Adelaide Area Office, Education Department.
Inquiry into Prostitution, Victoria, October 1985, pp. 97–108, Chapter 13, 'Social and economic responses to prostitution'.
Maas, F. (1987) 'The abolition of junior unemployment benefits – who should bear the cost?', *Youth Studies Bulletin* **6** (3).
McGregor, S. N. (1987) *Prostitution and Children in South Australia*, Children's Interests Bureau, South Australia.
Presdee, M. (1984) 'Youth unemployment and young women', *Radical Education Dossier* **23**, 4–7.
Presdee, M. (1985) 'Agony or ecstasy: broken transitions and the new social state of working-class youth in Australia', Occasional Papers No. 1, South Australian Centre for Youth Studies, Magill Campus, South Australian College of Advanced Education.
Presdee, M. (1987) 'Class, culture and crime and the new social state of Australian youth', paper presented at the Australian Criminology Institute Bi-annual Conference, Canberra.
Presdee, M. and R. White (1987) 'Priority one down under: Australian youth policies in the 1980's', *Youth and Policy*, August.
Seabrook, J. (1979) *What Went Wrong? Working people and the ideals of the Labour Movement*, London: Victor Gollancz.
Sunday Mail (1987) 4 October, Adelaide.
Taylor, I. (1987) 'Putting the boot into a working-class sport: British soccer after Bradford and Brussels', *Sociology of Sport Journal* **4**, 171–91.
The Australian (1987a) 26 September.
The Australian (1987b) 31 October–1 November.
The Australian (1987c) 14–15 November.
The Herald (1987) 22 October.

Times on Sunday (1987) 1 November.

White, R. (1987a) 'No space of their own: young people, law and the street', Occasional Papers No. 2, South Australian Centre for Youth Studies, Magill Campus, South Australian College of Advanced Education.

White, R. (1987b) 'Spaced out crime and the crime of no space: young people and car theft', paper presented to Australian and New Zealand Society of Criminology, Melbourne, August.

White, R. (1987c) 'The 1987 budget and young people: how to blame and train the victims', unpublished paper, SACAE, September.

Willis, P. (1977) *Learning to Labour: How working class kids get working class jobs*, Westmead: Saxon House.

Willis, P. (1979) 'Shop-floor culture, masculinity and the wage form' in J. Clarke, C. Critcher and R. Johnson (eds.) *Working Class Culture: Studies in history and theory*, London: Hutchinson.

Willis, P. (1984a) 'Youth unemployment 1: a new social state', *New Society* 29 March, 475–7.

Willis, P. (1984b) 'Youth unemployment 2: ways of living', *New Society* 5 April, 13–15.

8

Violence, public policy and politics in Australia

Russell Hogg
Charles Stuart University, Bathurst, New South Wales, Australia

David Brown
University of New South Wales, Sydney, Australia

Law and order is beginning to assume a significant role in Australian politics. It has been one of the major issues in recent state elections in New South Wales, Victoria and Western Australia. The mid-term manifesto released by the federal Liberal–National Coalition in December 1988 (entitled *Future Directions*) signals a serious attempt to make it a critical issue in Australian national politics and one which will work electorally for the Right.

One reason for the attempts by the conservative political parties in Australia to popularize law and order, and other social issues such as the family and immigration, is the unprecedented electoral success enjoyed by the Labor Party in the 1980s, both nationally and at a state level. The Hawke Labor Government, first elected in 1983, has been re-elected twice since, and faces another election in the first half of 1990 with strong prospects of being re-elected. Many argue, partly correctly, that the electoral difficulties confronting the conservative coalition parties stem from the fact that the Hawke Labor Government has promoted and implemented conservative free market and deregulatory policies, leaving the conservatives in something of a political and policy vacuum. To distinguish themselves, and build an electoral majority, the Coalition parties have sought to graft apparently popular, neo-conservative themes (on the family, immigration, crime, etc.) onto a free market economic programme, much as conservative parties in Britain and North America have done in the last decade. Law and order has thereby gained at least part of its currency in Australian politics at the present time.

The one electoral success that *might* be claimed for such a strategy has been in the state of New South Wales in 1988, when the Greiner Liberal–National opposition tipped out a Labor Government which had been in power for twelve years. Law and order was a major issue in that election and has been central to the programme of the Greiner Government, as has been privatization and deregulation of the economy. However, it is far from clear that such a strategy is likely to bring electoral success for the Coalition nationally, as long as Labor is perceived to be more competent at managing the economy.

Whilst there is little doubt as to the important role that free market ideologies are playing in contemporary Australian political debate, the role they are playing and are likely to play in the actual formation and implementation of government policies, and the effects of these policies, are separate questions. To some degree, free market ideology has become as much of a mirage for its critics as for its slavish devotees. Frequently, attention to the details of policy and its implementation is subordinated to generalized claims about the supposed triumph of economic liberalism and in some accounts the emergence of an 'author-itarian populist' politics. [1,2] In this paper we try to resist this tendency. We also try not to exaggerate the place of law and order in contemporary Australian politics and avoid the simple transposing to the Australian context of British analyses of Thatcherism. The paper examines some dimensions of interpersonal violence in Australia, and seeks to identify some of the related features of social relations, public policy and political culture which impinge on these patterns of violence.

Violence in Australia

Australia is a federal state, within which the major responsibility for law and order rests with the state and territory governments rather than the national Government, making it dangerous to generalize about the issue for the country as a whole. What happens at a local level, especially state government level, is of critical importance.

The federal nature of the Australian state has also created problems for the production of reliable national crime data. Bearing this major qualification in mind, the following can be fairly confidently concluded with regard to recent crime trends.

1. All the major categories of crime, except homicide, have experi-enced major increases over the 1970s and 1980s.
2. The most dramatic increases have occurred in relation to violent offence rates (about 400 per cent for serious assault and perhaps as much as 300 per cent for rape/sexual assault, although estimates for the latter are confounded by probable changes in reporting be-haviour: Wilson, 1989; Mukherjee, *et al.*, 1987; Robb, 1988).

3. Less dramatic, but still sizeable, increases have occurred in robbery, burglary and car theft rates, which all about doubled between the mid-1970s and mid-1980s (Mukherjee, *et al.*, 1987, pp. 15–18).

This chapter concentrates on the issue of violence. It has been an issue of considerable national concern in the late 1980s, following two multiple public slayings in Melbourne which led to the establishment by the Federal Government of a National Committee of Inquiry on Violence.

In Australia, as in similar cultures, most violence occurs in *private*, despite the massive popular focus on street crime and violence. Important dimensions of public policy and the political culture have contributed to the widespread evasion of this fact and the reproduction of the invisibility of many of the victims most affected by patterns of violence. They have also helped shape the patterns of violence and the experiences and options of its victims. Before examining these issues we need to consider some of the data on violence in more detail.

Official crime data and the only two national victim surveys conducted in Australia to date suggest that there is a strong social symmetry between violent offenders and their victims: in particular, that both tend to be disproportionately male, young, lower class, unemployed and black (ABS, 1986, pp. 39–40; Braithwaite and Biles, 1986; Robb, 1988). Some of this work also suggests that alcohol plays a major role in much violent crime (see also Australian Institute of Criminology, 1989).

Whilst such data present a disturbing picture of the interaction between masculinity, alcohol and violence, a closer examination might focus attention on other dimensions of violence. In particular, the general picture obscures the extent to which the *impact* of violence is disproportionately focused on working-class women and children and Aboriginal Australians. The general picture overlooks two things: first, the levels of *hidden* violence against particular groups. Although more focused, localized and methodologically sensitive studies are required adequately to measure and analyze hidden violence against particular groups in Australia, the survey research that has been done on family violence suggests that such violence occurs at a much higher rate than has hitherto been officially recorded (Johnson *et al.*, 1982; Mugford, 1989; Waldby, 1985).

Secondly, official accounts do not examine the differential *impact* of violence on differently placed victims. Jock Young (1988), writing in Britain, has argued that the impact of crime has to be considered in relation to four related factors: *risk* of being victimized; *vulnerability* to the effects of crime, including the capacity or power to mitigate those effects; the *compounding* of the effects of crime through interaction with other problems and disadvantages suffered by the victim; and the location of victimization within particular patterns of social *relationships*. It is not simply a matter of measuring the incidence of violence, but of recognizing its differential impact on unequally placed victims. Such impacts cannot be disentangled from the social relationships within which violence occurs and which it frequently serves to enforce and reproduce.

In the remainder of this section we will look at two areas of concentration of violent victimization in Australian society, and the links between such patterns of violence and wider social relations.

Family violence

Research on homicide in NSW provides a useful window onto the social relations of violence, partly because of the availability of detailed data as to the context of fatal attacks and partly because homicide constitutes merely one end of a continuum of violent interpersonal conduct. Interestingly, the degree to which adult males are disproportionately the victims of violence (noted above) drops when we move from non-fatal to fatal attacks. Women were the victims in over 36 per cent of homicides committed in NSW between 1968 and 1986 (Bonney, 1987; see Wallace, 1986), as against only around 25 per cent of reported serious assaults (Robb, 1988). They were twice as likely to be victims of homicide as suspects. And 68 per cent of female victims were killed by other family members (compared with 28.4 per cent of male victims: Bonney, 1987, p. 26). This has to be placed alongside the further finding that 43 per cent of homicides were intrafamily and 54 per cent of these involved spouses (a further 20 per cent involved friends or acquaintances and only 18 per cent strangers). In over 80 per cent of the cases in which the suspects were females, the victim was a family member (48 per cent of these being the male spouse and 46 per cent offspring). There was evidence in half the spouse killings of a prior history of domestic violence and this rose to 70 per cent in cases where women had killed their husbands. (It should be noted that this is probably an underestimate especially as regards male to female spouse killings.) These patterns of homicide for the last twenty years do not represent a major shift from the patterns that prevailed earlier in the century. Family and spouse homicides have been the most prevalent throughout and spouse homicides the most prevalent of these (Wallace, 1986, pp. 86–93; Allen, 1982, 1985).

Knowing that women are usually the victims of the most serious form of violence in the context of domestic relationships may strongly suggest that they are frequently the victims of lesser forms of violence in these contexts as well. As a high price may be paid for 'betraying' marital relationships (about 46 per cent of husbands who killed their wives were separated from them or in the process of separation at the time of the homicide), it would hardly be surprising if the vast majority of incidents of intimate violence falling short of homicide were not reported to the authorities (also see Allen, 1982, pp. 5–6). For these reasons, victim surveys are also likely to leave untouched many of these instances of violence.

The same points might be made with regard to the victimization of children. The homicide study referred to above found that 85 per cent of child victims (under 9) were killed by a parent. Again the frequency of such forms of victimization is massively underestimated in official statistics and victim surveys. The risks and effects of victimization are closely associated with its conditions of relative invisibility which include most importantly the hierarchies of power within which it occurs, namely adult–child relations in particular, and most frequently parent–child relations.

It seems that the more we are able to delve into hidden violence against women and children the more we would discover: first, that such violence is much more frequent than either the official picture or general victim surveys suggest; secondly, and by way of a corollary, that it is dispropor-tionately hidden from public view; and thirdly, that this is because it is disproportionately domestic or quasi-domestic in nature. Another way of putting this is to suggest that much violence against women and children is normalized, legitimized and trivialized. This is true, not only in the domestic setting, but also in work and other relations.

What is important from our perspective in this chapter are the connections between patterns of such violence and the dominant frameworks of public policy and social intervention.

As we indicated in our earlier reference to Jock Young's work on victimization, the use of force in interpersonal relationships has to be considered in relation to other dimensions of power – economic, social and political – as they impinge on those relationships. This is not to suggest a unitary or monolithic process is at work – for example, that the systematic under-policing of domestic violence is simply a function of '*the* patriarchal state', conceived as some general and pregiven essence that underpins and governs all social policy. Donzelot's analysis of the interaction of apparatuses of social government and families reflects more closely the position we would take (Donzelot, 1979; see also Rose, 1987). Different agencies and practices (public and private) interact with the family for different purposes and using different methods, which conform to no unitary or overarching principles of social organization. Moreover, such agencies and practices interact *differentially* with diffe-rent family members in pursuing their objectives.

A whole range of agencies is involved, or potentially so, in the organization of relations of force within families, including other family members, the criminal law, police and magistrates, family law, marriage guidance agencies, education authorities, doctors, social workers, refuges, etc. (see Johnson *et al.*, 1982, p. 45). This means, for example, that changes in divorce laws and effective access to divorce may influence such patterns of force, by allowing some women at least to leave such relationships or to reconstruct them (Golder, 1985, pp. 202–3; Allen, 1982, p. 19, 1985). Similar points may be made about access to the labour market, social security, child care services, etc.

There may be definite connections that can be traced across these different arenas of public policy and social intervention, but there are dangers in simply positing an analysis in terms of a generalized collusion or a succession of models of intervention (criminal, welfare, medical-psychological, etc.) which are more or less equally patriarchal in nature and effects. The growth of what is often referred to as the 'psy complex' (Rose, 1985) is frequently seen as a way of obscuring the causes of, and responsibility for, family violence, and in particular promoting the blaming of the victim. The implication of some feminist arguments is that a 'return' to a criminal model of intervention is more appropriate. There are, no doubt, particular examples which support such an analysis. However, it is by no means clear that agencies and forms of intervention (such as counselling, family therapies, etc.) that are directed at the management and adjustment of family conflicts in ways that seek to avoid overt pathologization and segregation are working simply in accord with some patriarchal agenda. The reality is that such measures are likely to be favoured by, and more accessible to, many victims of violence over resort to the criminal law. It is possible to argue for their expansion without engaging in 'victim blaming' and whilst also arguing for more satisfactory responses on the part of police and criminal courts.

None of this detracts from the fact that where violence against many women and children is concerned, the factors identified by Young – of risk, vulnerability, compounding and the wider patterns of social relationships within which the actors are located – often tend to be mutually reinforcing. Material dependency on economically, socially and physically more powerful adult men ensures that many women and children are likely to be placed at greater and more persistent risk, are more vulnerable to violence and its consequences and that this will compound their position of relative powerlessness.

This is especially likely to be so for those women and children who are otherwise economically and socially vulnerable. Our argument is not that violence is confined to the poor, or simply that poverty causes violence. The available contemporary and historical evidence with regard to domestic violence in NSW suggests, on the contrary, that it transcends class and other social boundaries (O'Donnell and Craney, 1982; Allen, 1982; Johnson *et al.*, 1982). However, such research also suggests that the *duration* of violent relationships and the *frequency* of violence within them vary in accord with such factors as the employment status of the woman, whether she is skilled or unskilled and whether there are children in the relationship (O'Donnell and Craney, 1982, pp. 60–5; Allen, 1982, p. 19; 1985). The economic and social resources and constraints on victims thus clearly affect their ability to influence their situation directly, supporting the arguments of Young referred to above. In this process, the criminal law is an extremely remote factor. It is the capacity to leave a relationship (or exercise sufficient leverage to reconstruct it on more favourable terms) that is important. Thus, most solutions are more or less non-legal or civil in nature. They depend, amongst other things, on the material situation and power of victims, which is not simply a matter of individual condition, but a function of social policy in areas such as employment, education and training, child care and income maintenance.

More research is needed on these connections in the Australian context, but what data we do have support the view that a strong connection exists between domestic violence, poverty, dependency and welfarism. That is, both the economic conditions of poverty and the dominant social policies directed at their alleviation have tended to perpetuate the patterns of family violence discussed above, as well as other aspects of the crime problem in Australia.

In the 1980s the principal sources of poverty in Australia have been the growth in unemployment coupled with changes in family structure. In 1971 the official unemployment rate in Australia was 1.6 per cent, in 1976 4.4 per cent and in 1986 9.2 per cent (ABS, 1988, p. 50). It has dropped to about 6.5 per cent as of 1989. However, the average duration of unemployment has also increased significantly, from about seven and a half weeks in the early 1970s to over fifty-six weeks for males and over thirty-seven weeks for females in 1987.

As is the case in other countries, unemployment is highly unequally distributed across the populace. The increase in unemployment that has been most serious in its social implications has been in relation to families with dependent children, both sole- and two-parent families. This, along with changes in family structure, has been the principal contributing factor to a situation in which in 1987 almost one in five of Australia's children under age 16 lived in families whose main source of income was state welfare (Graycar and Jamrozik, 1989, pp. 16–17; Cass, 1989), compared to about 4 per cent in 1973.

In the decade from the mid-1970s to the mid-1980s, Australia's sole-parent population grew by 73 per cent (Raymond, 1987, p. 31). At the 1986 census one-parent families had the lowest of median family incomes. The vast majority of sole parents are female (about 88 per cent as of 1985) (Raymond, 1987, p. 32). Of female sole parents, 89 per cent were in receipt of some form of welfare benefit in 1985 (Graycar, 1987, p. 2). The vast majority of these (about 86 per cent) were at some stage married, or living in a *de facto* relationship (Graycar, 1987, p. 3). It has been estimated that in the financial year 1985–6 about 43 per cent of sole-parent households were living below the poverty line after paying housing costs (Graycar, 1987, p. 7). About 60 per cent of female sole parents are not in paid employment (Social Security Review, 1986, p. 6).

These data highlight the concentration of poverty in the 1980s amongst those women and children who do not have as their principal means of support a wage income. The potential interaction of such economic conditions and patterns of family violence should be apparent. Women, especially those with children, are thus frequently confronted with the options of remaining in a violent relationship or joining, or becoming more deeply entrenched in, the welfare class. There is some evidence to suggest that domestic violence is one significant reason why women find themselves in receipt of sole-parent benefits (Frey, 1986, p. 7; see also Graycar, 1987). However, welfare provides meagre material support, imposes a stigma on its recipients and, through measures such as the cohabitation rule, constantly aims to force women and children back into relations of domestic dependency. The finding referred to above – that it is women who are unemployed, lacking labour market skills and who have children that suffer violent relationships for the longest periods – is hardly a surprising one.

The serious increase in child and family poverty has also contributed to a cycle of poverty and deprivation for a sizeable group of youth in Australia, by seriously retarding their educational opportunities and hence their employment prospects and contributing to high levels of youth unemployment and homelessness (Human Rights and Equal Opportunity Commission, 1989; Graycar and Jamrozik, 1989, pp. 230–5).

It is also clear that violence, including sexual violence, against children and young persons in the family is a major factor in the high levels of youth homelessness and poverty (and related forms of predatory crime) that currently prevail in Australia. As limited provision (in terms of housing, income support, etc.) is made for youth in this position, they are frequently confronted with the choice between poverty (and possibly violence) within their families and poverty, homelessness and effective criminalization outside them (Human Rights and Equal Opportunity Commission, 1989, pp. 43–58; Girls in Care Project, 1986, pp. 83–99).

The assumption of dependency and the limited and residual forms of social support that are provided outside the labour market and the family structure thus contribute not only to the perpetuation of child abuse, but also to those secondary forms of predatory and expressive crime that are directly associated with the available escape routes from abusive family relationships (e.g. homelessness and street hustling).

It is likely that these conditions are currently producing a distinct underclass within Australian society with limited investment in its major social and economic institutions and for whom various forms of street crime, prostitution, hustling, etc., are becoming a way of life (Presdee, 1989; White, 1989, Chapter 7, above).

As we indicate in more detail in the next section, the dominant tendencies within the political culture and related patterns of social policy in Australia have served to underwrite the dominance of the dependent family and the male wage as the primary mechanisms of material support. In so doing, they have also provided some of the conditions of existence of the most pervasive forms of violence in Australia.

Aborigines, violence and public policy

The pattern of relationships between Aborigines, welfare measures and violence is one of distinctive and tragic proportions.

Of those Australians living in poverty, Aborigines (about 1.5 per cent of the population) constitute as a group the poorest, most oppressed and most criminalized and imprisoned section of the population. As of 1986 unemployment amongst Aborigines and Torres Strait Islanders was 35 per cent, almost four times that of the general population (ABS, 1988, p. 50). When in work they earn on average half the income of white Australians. They are also massively disproportionately represented amongst the homeless population and the educationally disadvantaged, and have a male life expectancy of about 48 years compared to the white male life expectancy of 72 years (*Sydney Morning Herald*, 1987).

The rate of Aboriginal imprisonment is about ten times that of the general population and in some states it is much higher. Aborigines are disproportionately concentrated in particular states and territories and generally within rural rather than urban areas. Racism and law and order have been perennially linked within local law-and-order politics in many country and some urban areas throughout Australia.

The homicide rate amongst Aboriginal Australians is one of the most obvious indicators of the way in which welfarism and violence interact to produce, and reproduce, conditions of dispossession, marginality and intracommunity conflict. The homicide study in NSW, referred to above, found that the rate at which Aborigines appeared as suspects in homicide cases in the period 1968–86 was over eleven times that of the general population. They were over-represented amongst victims by a factor of more than seven. Over 87 per cent of Aboriginal victims of homicide were killed by other Aborigines (Bonney, 1987, p. 14). In some Aboriginal communities the incidence of homicide is much higher (Wilson, 1985). Much research has, quite properly, concentrated on the massive over-representation of Aborigines in the institutions of white justice. However, the greater outrage is possibly the toll in Aboriginal life and well-being that has been exacted historically, and continues to be, through the economic and cultural devastation wreaked on Aboriginal communities, a situation within which both welfare and penal agencies play a major part. Paul Wilson, in a study of violence on a number of Aboriginal reserves in Queensland in 1979–81, concluded:

> that violence and death is such a common occurrence in black communities that every family, directly or indirectly, suffers the consequence of murder or serious assault. Often multiple tragedy affects the same family, with a violent death occurring more than once in a generation. (Wilson, 1985, p. 5)

There is a mutually reinforcing relationship between welfarism, penality and the conditions (of poverty, alcoholism, violence, etc.) that historically they have produced and sustained in Aboriginal communities. In particular, the high levels of intracommunity violence are compounded by the futile and frequently violent consequences of penal intervention by white authorities. A national Royal Commission into Aboriginal Deaths in Custody established in 1987 found that in the period 1980–8 21 per cent of the persons who died in police or prison custody were Aboriginal, whilst they constituted less than 1.5 per cent of the Australian population (Royal Commission into Aboriginal Deaths in Custody, 1988, p. 90). The toll in Aboriginal life thus continues whilst the 'justice' process does its work.

The life of one Aboriginal man, Malcolm Smith, whose death was the subject of a report by the Royal Commission, typifies the historical and continuing interaction of welfarism, punishment and violence in the lives of Aboriginal people (Royal Commission into Aboriginal Deaths in Custody, 1989). Malcolm Smith died in prison custody in early 1983 several days after locking himself in a prison toilet and shoving the handle of an artist's paint brush into his left eye such that only the metal sheath and bristles were left protruding.

Malcolm Smith had been taken from his family in 1965 at age 11 as part of the then policy of child welfare authorities in NSW of removing Aboriginal children from their families on a wholesale basis. This policy prevailed from the beginning of the century, during which time thousands of children were removed (Royal Commission into Aboriginal Deaths in

Custody, 1989, pp. 17–19, 73; Read, 1983). Malcolm Smith did not see his family for another eight years, during which time he spent a combined total period of time of eight months outside juvenile institutions. In the remaining nine years of his adult life he only spent a matter of a few more months outside of prison. His final sentence was for the manslaughter of his sister's white boyfriend who had allegedly been bashing her. These events severely breached his relationship with his family and precipitated his death less than two years later.

The story of Malcolm Smith contains a great many elements common to the experience of Aboriginal Australians. It demonstrates the role that white officialdom, especially welfare and penal agencies, has played in directly destroying the lives of Aboriginal people and creating the conditions in which they take the lives of other members of their communities.

We have sought in this section to summarize some of the evidence with regard to the dominant patterns of interpersonal violence in Australia, emphasizing the complex interaction of social and economic conditions with such violence and its unequal distribution and impact. We are not proffering a simple causal analysis between poverty and violence. The origins of violence are diverse and complex. They include, but are not restricted to, social and economic factors. However, we argue that economic and social marginality affects the capacity of individuals, families and communities, at mainly an informal level, to mitigate the incidence and impact of violence and reconstruct the social relations within which it occurs. They can be said to perpetuate and exacerbate patterns of intrafamily and intracommunity violence without this in any way reducing to the simple argument that poverty causes violence.

We will now turn to the dominant political and public policy traditions which contribute to these conditions of marginality and the patterns of violence associated with them.

Politics and public policy in Australia

In the 1960s Donald Horne coined the term 'the lucky country' to describe Australia (Horne, 1966). Perhaps more than any other, this term has entered the popular lexicon and consciousness, although not in the ironic sense intended by Horne. Needless to say, this luck did not extend to all Australians, as became clear within the decade after the publication of *The Lucky Country*, which saw a major poverty inquiry reveal that over 10 per cent of Australians lived below a stringently drawn poverty line and a further 8 per cent were less than 20 per cent above it (Commission of Inquiry into Poverty, 1975, p. 6).

However, there was some foundation to the popular currency of 'the lucky country'. In the 1960s Australia was the sixth richest country in the world in *per capita* terms. It had enjoyed a very high level of employment since the Second World War (with less than 2 per cent unemployment at any given time), comfortable levels of economic growth and low inflation (see Castles, 1988, pp. 14–16). Australia had also enjoyed for a long time a very high level of owner occupation in housing which had been promoted and supported by government policy, especially in the tax area, and at the expense of public housing.

The 'lucky Australians' were those in full and secure employment who owned or were purchasing their own homes. This success story belongs in important respects to the 'new liberal' consensus fashioned in the early part of the century in a political settlement between anti-free trade liberals and the emergent labour movement. This political settlement was anything but liberal in the classical nineteenth-century sense, being statist, interventionist and in vital respects collectivist. It was organized around a number of factors: an economy abundant in natural resources, high levels of protection for Australian industry, a white Australia policy which sought to insulate the domestic labour market from the competitive effects of cheap immigrant labour and an industrial arbitration system directed at securing high levels of unionization and safeguarding the wages of full-time male workers. The labour movement was a committed partner in this political consensus, founded on protection, regulation and wage justice (see MacIntyre, 1989, pp. 20–32). Herein lie some of the differences between Australian labourism and European social democracy.

The social democratic tradition in western Europe has been associated with the expansion of the rights of citizenship, including social rights embodied in the public provision of social welfare measures such as housing, health care and income maintenance. The emphasis, at least formally, has been on equality and universalism. Australian labourism, and its foundations in the 'new liberalism' of the early twentieth century, has, on the other hand, emphasized the expansion of rights relating to paid employment, from which benefits to those not in the labour market were to flow indirectly. This provided the foundation for what has been called 'the wage-earners' welfare state' (Castles, 1985).

> Labor's determination to ensure that the wealth-producer received the full fruits of his labour rendered superfluous any large-scale supplementation of market outcomes. The provision of public housing or public health, for example, was quite overshadowed by private provision catering to the 'provident' working man. (MacIntyre, 1986, p. 5)

Industrial arbitration and other aspects of public policy were organized around a gender-based division of labour, within which the welfare of all or most within society was to be secured through the protection of male wages, calculated to meet the needs of the male household head and his family. The family wage principle, coupled with legal restriction on the employment of women and children, reflected and reinforced the assumption that women were to be confined to the domestic sphere. Where they entered the labour market they were to be paid at a much lower rate than males (MacIntyre, 1989, pp. 23–4, 30–1).

The white Australia policy similarly institutionalized a racial bar within the social and economic fabric of Australian society. This complemented the systematic legal denial of citizenship to the Aboriginal population (a position that was only formally terminated in 1967).

As MacIntyre indicates, this gender- and racially based division of labour and economic rewards crucially shaped the scope of social welfare provisions, producing an essentially residual conception of social policy.[3] It was premised upon 'the dependence of the female and the permanence of the family' and the guarantee of full male employment (MacIntyre, 1985, p. 58). Those who were not directly or indirectly supported by a wage were to be beneficiaries of a generally means-tested and comparatively meagre system of state welfare (and private charity). An examination of comparative social welfare expenditures over this century demonstrates the very limited nature of the Australian welfare state by comparison with most of the western European countries (Castles, 1988, pp. 30–3).

Whilst the reconstruction of the welfare state in the post-Second World War period entailed significant extensions of welfare provision, the basic commitment to a 'workers' welfare state' remained, as did the commitment to the peculiar Australian brand of social policy residualism (Castles, 1988, p. 17; Watts, 1987; Butlin *et al.*, 1982, pp. 193–4). Bipartisan commitment to Keynesian macro-economic policies was added to the existing political repertoire, consisting of high levels of industry protection (see Ewer *et al.*, 1987, pp. 5–25) and state wage regulation through the arbitration system. These arrangements helped sustain high levels of (male) employment and economic prosperity for most Australians until the early 1970s. Their electoral and party political popularity was not surprising. The post-war conservative electoral dominance of national politics (from 1949 till 1972) was founded upon a pragmatic acceptance of this basic policy framework and an ability to take advantage of the favourable electoral implications, in the face of a divided and often disorganized Labor opposition (Sawer, 1982).

The degree of protection and prosperity that these institutional arrangements secured for Australia concealed the fundamental vulnerability of the Australian economy to international economic forces

(Castles, 1988, pp. 36–60). With the end of the long post-war economic boom, the growth in unemployment and inflation, and the intensification of international competition and economic interdependence, the structural weaknesses of the Australian economy have been exposed. The resultant problems have been at the centre of national politics since the early 1970s. There has been a serious decline in the role of manufacturing in the economy and in manufacturing employment (Ewer *et al.*, 1987, pp. 26–51; Gilmour and Hunt, 1989, p. 13) and a growing balance of payments crisis (Schott, 1988).

The beginning of this period of economic decline coincided, ironically, with the return of the first post-war Labor Government in national politics. The attempts of the Whitlam Government to bring about a social democratization of Labor – through the expansion of social provision in education, housing, social welfare and health (including the introduction of a national health care service), the urban environment, legal aid, etc.; the final abandonment of the remnants of the 'white Australia' policy; and a commitment to national Aboriginal land rights legislation – were interrupted first by economic events, and then by the political events they set in train.

Under Malcolm Fraser, Whitlam's conservative successor, there was an initial and quite radical shift to monetarism, although this was heavily tempered by electoral pragmatism. Nevertheless the priority given to reducing inflation led to the more than doubling of unemployment and the substantial retrenchment of many of the Whitlam reforms by the time of Fraser's defeat in 1983 at the hands of the current Prime Minister, Bob Hawke (Castles, 1988, pp. 26–7; Patience and Head, 1979).

The Hawke Government: a crisis of labourism?

By the time of the election of the Whitlam Government many of the nostrums of labourism dating from earlier in the century were in disrepute and were, to one degree or another, targets of that Government's reformist programme. These included some of the major institutional supports for racism, sexism and economic protectionism and isolationism. With the benefit of hindsight these reforms can be seen as part of a broader sweep of social and economic change, whose unfolding, and its effects, continues to dominate Australian politics.

These include the globalization of the Australian economy and the consequent serious decline in the relative international position of the Australian economy, reflected in particular in a large and growing foreign debt, serious balance of payments problems, the decline of manufacturing industry and the end of 'full' employment. On the more positive side, the participation of women in the paid labour force has continued to grow (Graycar and Jamrozik, 1989, p. 19) and there has been an increasing individual and political assertiveness on the part of women, racial, ethnic and sexual minorities, as well as other issue-oriented social movements (environmentalists being the obvious example). Significant amongst the changes in the social structure of Australian society have been changes in the patterns of family formation and dissolution, in particular the growth in the number of sole-parent families, both absolutely and as a proportion of all families with dependent children (from about 7 per cent in 1969 to 14.6 per cent in 1986: Graycar and Jamrozik, 1989, pp. 193–4). The majority of these are women separated or divorced from a spouse or *de facto* spouse.

We have discussed earlier the implications of some of these changes for patterns of marginality, poverty and violence in Australia, and in particular amongst certain groups – women, children, youth and Aboriginal Australians. They are also severely testing the viability of the foundations of Australian public policy discussed in the previous section, which have assumed the primacy of male wages and the dependent family as sources of social support.

These changes and related issues have occupied a central place in the public arena throughout the period of the four Hawke Labor Governments. Many of its responses to them have invited the retort from Labor supporters that it has abandoned Labor principles and traditions and adopted the policies and strategies of its political opponents, especially a passion for economic liberalism and free market solutions (see, for example, Maddox, 1989).

There are a number of problems with this view. At a general level it is arguable that the popularity of free market policies, as distinct from the rhetoric, has been exaggerated. And certainly the viability of a thoroughgoing government programme of free market policies has been overstated, by left commentators as well as the right. Reappraisals of the Thatcher Government suggest that political pragmatism and the policy U-turn have been a more distinctive feature of its performance than any consistent adherence to the principles of the free market (see Gamble, 1988, especially pp. 120–8; Hirst, 1989, pp. 11–39).

There is a number of aspects of the performance of the Hawke Labor Government which have earned it the reputation of being conservative and free market in orientation. The principal ones include the general priority it has given to 'sound' economic management over social reform, its specific commitment to a 'trilogy' of constraints on public expenditure, the size of the budget deficit and levels of taxation, its deregulation of exchange rates and the financial sector, and the (to date unsuccessful) moves by sections of the parliamentary leadership towards the privatization of some public enterprises (Castles, 1988, pp. 27–8). Others have emphasized the apparent increases (rather than reductions) in social and economic inequalities under Labor as the crucial measure of its failure as a *Labor* Government.

There is no doubt that in all these respects the Hawke Government hardly accords with the traditional ideal of a Labor government. However, the record is more mixed and unclear than many critics allow. The Government has certainly sought to target welfare expenditures much more closely on the needy (Watts, 1989; Shaver, 1989). But it has also significantly increased employment (by about $1\frac{1}{2}$ million jobs since 1983) and thereby reduced unemployment, introduced a child poverty package which, it is generally agreed, will substantially reduce family poverty (Brownlee and King, 1989; Cass, 1989), reintroduced a national health care scheme, substantially increased child care places, introduced a number of labour market and training programmes directed at the most disadvantaged groups in the labour market, committed itself to substantially expanding support for homeless and other disadvantaged youth, generally expanded the numbers in all parts of the education system (see generally Commonwealth of Australia, 1989; Minister for Employment, Education and Training, 1989) and introduced sex discrimination and affirmative action legislation.

For those looking for a consistently radical programme and rhetoric, these and other Labor reforms, when taken with the overt economic caution and selective deregulatory measures, appear very tame. However the Hawke government's record of reform certainly distinguishes it from the Fraser Government and any likely successor government of the Right. Any widening disparities in wealth and income that have been experienced are at least partly a consequence of the growing internationalization of the Australian economy. Whilst criticism may properly be levelled at specific policies aimed at facilitating this process, it is hard to resist the view that for cultural, social, political and environmental reasons, as much as for mere economic ones, the greater integration of the Australian economy into the world economy is a necessary and unavoidable step. It cannot be looked upon as simply a right-wing, free market strategy. In any case its origins lie, not with Hawke Labor, or even with the Fraser Government, but probably with the Whitlam Government's 25 per cent across-the-board tariff cut in July 1973 (Ewer *et al.*, 1987, p. 20).

The centrepiece of the Hawke Government's programme was, and remains in vital respects, an Accord with the peak council of trade unions (the Australian Council of Trade Unions, or ACTU), organized around orderly wage adjustments, price control, enhancement of the social wage, and an active investment and industry policy (Stilwell, 1986). Whilst the focus of the Accord has, under the influence of worsening economic conditions, shifted largely to the terrain of restrictive wages policy, the strategy, and the political relationships entailed, are obviously corporatist rather than free market in nature, and constitute a shift within Australian political life of major significance. The Labor Government has also been a strong defender of a regulated labour market against those on the right who wish to dismantle or emasculate the arbitration system. Despite the many failings and disappointments, therefore (in areas like industry policy, for example: Ewer *et al.*, 1987, pp. 105–9), the Hawke Government's record on economic and social reform is a mixed one. Far from being simply and consistently deregulatory, it has recognized the importance of state regulation (e.g. in relation to the labour market, education, training, and research and development) and the responsibility of government for economic and social outcomes. In substance, it is no more free market in orientation than was the last Labour Government in Britain before its defeat by Thatcher in 1979, and the record of the Hawke Labor Government certainly compares favourably in most respects with that of the Callaghan Government (see Coates, 1979).

If it is appropriate to talk of a 'crisis' of labourism in Australia, it must be assessed at least as much in positive as in negative terms. Those who invoke 'traditional' Labor ideology on the underdog and minorities in order to inpugn the record of the Hawke Labor Government in relation to Aborigines and ethnic minorities (Maddox, 1989, p. 6) simply suffer a chronic amnesia. This does not make the record of the Government on such issues a satisfactory one, but the actual conditions for radical reform in such areas, as in the economy and society at large, have little to do with a defence of many of the tenets of traditional labourism. Similarly, the Government's strategy for economic modernization, whatever criticisms might be made of specific aspects of it, does not represent an abandonment of labourism in favour of the free market and deregulation. It preserves some of the features of the former (often conservatively), utilizes some aspects of the latter (often positively) and in a limited way has initiated some new and desirable directions in economic and political strategy (the potentialities of the Accord, if not their realization, being amongst the most significant).

Violence and law-and-order politics in Australia

The failure of the major political parties to address satisfactorily the issue of violence in Australian society is bound up with a failure to address the conditions of economic, social and political marginality of certain social groups in the society. Although the social and criminal justice policies of the major political parties do vary significantly as they relate to these issues, the dominant tendency is to deny the connection between violence and social policy. This is compounded by the division of powers and responsibilities between national and state governments in a federal state.

It is not the case, as studies of hidden crime indicate, that crime and violence are simply lower-class phenomena. However, public institutions of criminal justice and definitions of crime have tended to focus on lower-class crime. This is not simply a one-way process of the State imposing its definitions on select groups. It is also crucially a function of the fact that inequalities affect access to alternative solutions – such as leaving a violent relationship, relying on family and other social supports in periods of crisis, etc. The resources for informally sanctioning and managing conflict are unequally distributed and these inequalities are, not surprisingly, associated with other social and economic inequalities.

The conditions which cast certain categories into positions of extreme economic and social marginality in Australian society also expose them to increased risks of victimization–criminalization. Victims are frequently stigmatized as much as offenders by the intervention of the criminal law. Where family relationships are concerned, the economic consequences of criminalization are likely to be visited as heavily upon the family as the individual offender. Thus, the effect of criminalization, most baldly apparent in Aboriginal communities, is often to reproduce and exacerbate conditions of poverty, dispossession and violence. Addressing the problems of crime and violence necessitates addressing the conditions of marginality of its most frequent and vulnerable victims.

It needs to be remembered also that the relation between economic and social marginality and victimization is also mediated by a range of more specific factors, such as the availability of firearms and patterns of alcohol use. Popular ideologies of crime often serve to disconnect patterns of violence from these cultural and situational factors and associated public policies as much as they do from wider social and economic policy debates.

State and Federal Labor Governments have generally sought to improve the response of the legal processes to the victims of family violence, whilst providing financial support for crisis services, such as refuges, and increasingly are coming to recognize the interrelationship of issues such as public housing and domestic violence (Department of Prime Minister and Cabinet, 1988, pp. 35, 37–8; Stubbs and Wallace, 1988). The Hawke Government has initiated both a National Committee of Inquiry on Violence and a specific public education campaign on domestic violence. Many of its economic and social policies are likely to alleviate some of the more severe conditions of poverty (and hence positively contribute to the reduction of violence). However, the tendencies towards greater selectivity in social policy and the frequent lack of integration of social and economic policies are likely to leave some of the structural conditions of poverty and violent victimization (such as many factors affecting female and child dependency) intact.

For Aboriginal communities the principal measure for securing a level of economic self-determination and autonomy from the traditional and destructive relationship with state welfare and other agencies is the recognition of land rights. Although granted in limited forms by some state Labor governments, the Hawke Labor Government quickly abandoned its commitment to national land rights legislation, which would have begun to redress the situation of Aborigines, especially in states such as Queensland and Western Australia.

These major limitations apart, it needs to be reiterated that perhaps the major positive feature of the Hawke era has been the general shift in the perspective of the labour movement, especially the trade union movement, towards a more self-consciously political and progressive role in relation to economic and industry policy, the social wage and social policy, and advocacy on behalf of those who have traditionally been marginalized within a movement which concentrated its attention on defending the interests of male wage-earners. This reflects not only a greater concern for social equity but also a changed conception of political strategy – a move from a defensive, economistic posture to adopting a social leadership role within Australian society (see, for example, ACTU/TDC, 1987). These concerns could hardly be said to encompass the issues of violence and marginality discussed in this chapter, but they generally augur well in terms of creating some of the political conditions for more satisfactory responses to such problems, through enhanced policies in areas like employment, training, child care, etc.

If it can be said that Labor Governments of the 1980s have sought to address problems of violence in a way which frequently avoids their connection with wider questions of social and economic policy, the philosophy and policies of the conservative political parties often come close to denying the existence of the most pervasive forms of violence and poverty, except as dimensions of individual pathology, alien intruders on the terrain of normal and healthy family life. Of course, just as we have questioned the political viability of free market economic policies, we would also query whether many of the priorities and evasions to be found in much conservative rhetoric on the family, law and order and race can actually be sustained by governments of the Right. It is probably becoming increasingly impossible, for example, for political parties of any kind in Australia simply to ignore issues such as domestic violence and those areas of social policy (child care, housing, etc.) which bear directly on the lives of many women.

The New Right in Australia

There is a number of works available which examine the emergence in Australia of what is frequently referred to as the 'New Right' (see Sawer, 1982; O'Brien, 1985; Coghill, 1987). For the most part, New Right thinking in Australia consists of a grafting on of moral and social conservatism to a free market economies, although there are important differences on some major issues, like immigration.

The clearest political articulation of these positions is to be found in the manifesto of the Liberal–National Coalition launched in 1988 and entitled *Future Directions*. This document is organized around a commitment to a free economy, the defence and strengthening of the family and the galvanization of one nation, 'one Australia' (Liberal–National Parties Coalition, 1988).

Central to the document is the commitment to privatization and deregulation of the economy, including the labour market. However, the areas where the conservatives have sought to distinguish their position most from that of Labor are on social issues.

At the centre of New Right ideology as articulated in *Future Directions* (hereafter *FD*) is the family. The family as the basic unit of society, 'the prime source of individual security, has come under attack' (*FD*, p. 7). The Right sees the family as the major site for 'restoring people's control over their own lives'. Government policy, far from supporting the family in the face of challenges to it, has aided the process by which it is being undermined. However, Government is simply one of a number of forces directed, purposefully or inadvertently, at undermining the family. The others include the familiar right-wing rogue's gallery of 'social engineers', 'educational theorists', 'pressure groups' and 'special interest groups', all of whom are said to have sought to have their own interests prevail over those of the ordinary, self-reliant individual and their family:

> When the traditional family unit is undermined, as it has been, self reliance tends to be lost and responsibility tends to disappear, both to be replaced be a dependence, often long term, on the government and manipulation by social engineers. It also provides the setting which leads young people to the treadmill of drug abuse and crime. (*FD*, p. 15)

As this passage indicates, one of the most powerful metaphors for this decline is crime. 'The safety and security of law-abiding individuals, their families and their property has deteriorated alarmingly in recent years' (FD, p. 16). The answer is to strengthen the family at the expense of government (which 'seemed to be more on the side of the criminal than the victim') and to enhance the fight against violence, drug abuse, child pornography, etc. The last is to be done primarily by maximizing the financial and physical resources of law enforcement.

There is no recognition anywhere in *Future Directions* that violence is predominantly a problem *within* the family, rather than one which threatens it from without. The acknowledged problems which afflict families – like divorce and break-up – are induced from the outside. Government 'actually encouraged families to break up rather than stay together; for example, by enticing young people to leave the family home or to forgo further education in order to take up welfare benefits' (*FD*, p. 16). Welfare thus promotes the breakdown of the unit which is the principal transmitter of shared norms and values and of a sense of individual responsibility and self-reliance. This is the source of dependency and crime, as individuals are encouraged to live off others and to indulge their appetites without the need for discipline and effort.

Several themes, familiar in New Right ideology in Britain and the United States, are welded together here. First, there is the populist dimension. The Right claims to speak on behalf of ordinary, decent Australians and their families. Secondly, the causes of the ills which threaten the fabric of the lives of these ordinary Australians, including crime, drugs, family breakdown, etc., are firmly attributed to the 'liberal establishment', a 'new class' of 'social engineers', welfare bureaucrats, progressive educationalists and the like (Edgar, 1986, 1989). Thus, the liberal social-democratic orthodoxy is turned on its head. The measures ostensibly directed at ameliorating conditions of marginality (such as social welfare provisions) are treated by the Right as the major source of problems of crime and violence.

'The family' is here treated as a self-contained unit within which individual freedom and responsibility are realized. The notion that families frequently function systematically to do the opposite to their members, to brutalize them, constrain their freedoms and run roughshod over their 'rights', is evaded through the familiar liberal assimilation of the interests of all household members to their (usually male) heads. The rights and freedoms of individuals within families are thereby treated indivisibly and equated with the health, or ostensible health, of family units. The distribution of power and rewards within families is never placed in issue. 'Restoring people's control over their lives' amounts to restoring the primacy of traditional familial relationships, even where this so obviously means restoring some people's control over other people's lives.

The interaction of welfarism, the family and violence thus receives an interesting twist in New Right ideology. Evidence of conflict and breakdown in families, and of their social effects (such as sole parenthood, poverty, youth homelessness, etc.) is treated as indicative, not of problems within family relationships themselves, but of the corrupting effects of outside forces, particularly allegedly generous welfare provisions. The answer is to remove these incentives, to ensure that the alternatives to family life are rendered far less attractive for its members. One effect of such a programme would be further to privatize the necessary means of material support of women and children in particular, and hence increase poverty amongst them. In so doing, it would also increase the vulnerability of these groups to violence by restricting the means available to them to escape such violence.

Law and order can only be recruited to the defence of traditional institutions so long as crime is successfully represented as an alien force threatening those institutions from without. The view has to be sustained, therefore, that crime is something which happens *to* families, not *within* them. Adherents of the New Right also confront the problem that the untrammelled free market, by its very nature, tends towards the dissolution of traditional social relations and ways of life, towards the industrialization of family life and the erosion of national cultural, as well as economic, boundaries. They seek to maintain a disconnection between economic change and its social consequences. Solutions to crime and other social problems are thus sought in an intensification of penal controls and a bolstering of legal authority.

We should not mistake the emphasis on legal authority for a commitment to legality or the rule of law. In the context of debates about economic and social regulation and redistribution, the 'rule of law' is invoked as the necessary foundation of a free society. Its rationale is to limit the power of the State to intervene in the lives of its citizenry by ensuring that there is a universal framework of rules which apply equally to all and within which individuals are free to pursue their own ends. Thus, it is not the role of the State to redistribute rights from one section of the population to another.

However, when it comes to crime and law and order the relation between law and freedom is turned on its head. When John Howard (then leader of the opposition) argued in the 1986 Alfred Deakin Lecture that the appropriate role of the State was 'to protect the life, liberties and property of its citizens' he was supporting an extension of the coercive capacities of the State against those who threaten these things. He was arguing for a shift in emphasis within the organization of the legal system away from the rights of suspects to the extension of policing and penal powers. Thus, he observed:

> In recent years there has been an unhealthy obsession with the rights of the criminal – rather than with those of the victim of crime and his or her family . . .

The primary obligation of government is to ensure that its citizens can live freely without the threat or reality of violence.

In the context of debates about law and order, the primary threat to freedom ceases to be the State and becomes 'the criminal' whose rights, moreover, have in the view of conservatives been given precedence over those of the victim. Counter-posing the rights of 'criminals' and the liberties of victims in this way promotes a tendency to enhance the policing powers and capacities of the state (not only to investigate and apprehend, but also to designate who is 'criminal', undesirable, etc.) at the expense of independent, open and accountable legal processes. The rights of citizenship, universally guaranteed within the ideology of 'the rule of law' (in order to guarantee a realm of freedom for the individual from state interference), are to extend only in a modified form to 'criminals'. 'Criminals' exist prior to any legal process for designating them as such, and are themselves responsible for forfeiting their rights to full citizenship. The critical emphasis in New Right law-and-order discourse, therefore, is not on the rule of law or legality, but on coercive state authority. The solicitude shown by the New Right for economic freedoms and rights does not necessarily extend to other legal, civil and political rights and liberties. The defence of freedom does not imply hostility to authoritarianism.

Moreover, it falsely equates the extension of coercive power with the expansion of the freedom of the citizen from criminal and violent interference. There is no doubt that this equation has considerable popular currency. It underpins a law-and-order discourse that is predominantly focused on punishment and law enforcement to the exclusion of the many social and economic factors whose relevance to patterns of violence we have emphasized in this chapter. However, the evidence is that within the feasible economic and political limits for reforming criminal justice policies, any adjustments are, in themselves, likely to have limited effects on the incidence of crime and violence.

Another central plank of *Future Directions* is 'one Australia'. Here again, the same bunch of 'woolly-minded idealists and their friends in the bureaucracy' have under the leadership of Labor Governments pursued:

policies which divide Australia . . . policies towards Aboriginal Australians have sought to elevate Aboriginal people into a nation within a nation; and their policies for immigrant Australians have turned the original aims of multiculturalism back on themselves and elevated the differences between us over the similarities we share. (*FD*, p. 89)

In this context, the notion of 'equal access to common services' for those in need serves to dent the historical processes of dispossession and exclusion which have ensured that Aboriginal Australians occupy a position that is wholly marginal to economic, social and political institutions. Again, such a discourse effects a disconnection between social and economic processes and policies and the material position of a particular section of the population. The source of the problem lies not with historical and continuing policies towards Aboriginal communities, but to those mischievous or misguided forces who seek to divide the country by pointing to the effects of such policies and demanding policies supportive of self-determination.

Images of divisiveness can very quickly become associated with a threat to the existing order of things and hence become allied to law-and-order strategies within which criminality and disorder are widely taken to be the province of particular racial, ethnic and cultural groups within society. Within Aboriginal communities their traditional relationship with welfare and policing agencies has ensured that their dispossession and marginality have been taken as evidence that they are the divisive element in black–white relations. Legal authority and national identity can readily join hands to ensure that those who resist 'one nation' are sanctioned for their divisiveness. The point also has some relevance to the position of ethnic minorities in Australia, some of whom have been targeted as prone to various forms of criminality and antisocial activity.

There is considerable doubt as to whether such a government of the Right will be elected nationally in the coming few years and whether such rhetoric on family, nation and social order provides anything like a viable programme for national government in Australia. However, there is no doubt that many of these populist themes – especially law and order – can have electoral purchase at a state level, as demonstrated by the election of the Greiner government in NSW.

The New Right in government: the NSW Greiner government

In March 1988 the Liberal–National Coalition won government in NSW after twelve years of a Labor government. Law and order was a major issue in the election and the Coalition promised to stop rising crime rates and restore public confidence in the justice system by introducing a series of tough legislative, policing and penal policies. The Labor government oscillated between playing down the law-and-order issue and seeking to match the rhetoric and promises of the opposition in the run-up to the election. The one major area in which Labor promised radical reform was that of firearms control. This galvanized a variety of forces into a powerful gun lobby and apparently proved to be one of the major issues on which electoral support swayed to the Coalition, especially in crucial rural and outer urban electorates.

The government led by Nick Greiner has initiated a radical retrenchment and overhaul of the public sector, including the privatization of some government enterprises, services and assets and the 'corporatization' of others, deregulation of public controls in a range of areas, serious cuts to public expenditure and services, the widespread introduction of the 'user-pays' principle and increases in charges in a range of areas.[4] At the same time, it has adopted a tough law-and-order stance.

The foundations for such changes were laid in the first of a series of reports prepared by private consultants which deal with various aspects of the public sector. This *Report on the State's Finances* (NSW Commission of Audit, 1988, hereafter the Curran Report) adopted an essentially free market view of the role of the state, condemning the growing size of the public sector so as to lay the foundation for 'a significant downsizing of Government, based upon a review of the services and activities in which the Government should be engaged' (p. 65). According to the report the appropriate role of the State lies in the provision of 'the social infrastructure needs of the community' (p. 67), the typical example provided being that of law and order.

The report examines in some detail rising law-and-order expenditures over the last decade, indicating that these have far outstripped increases in the other major areas of public expenditure (including education, health and transport, pp. 14–21). The rising relative expenditures on law and order are implicitly understood to be a natural consequence of growing levels of reported crime (pp. 18–19) and the agencies of criminal justice therefore exempted for the most part from the demands for efficiency applied to other areas of state administration. The exceptions to this are what are referred to as 'soft areas' such as legal aid and rehabilitation in prisons (p. 58).

Within the law and order budget there has been a very selective retrenchment of these 'soft' areas, including the curtailment of salaried legal aid services; the closure of thirty local court houses, reducing the number and accessibility of chamber magistrates who traditionally fulfil a legal aid advisory role, especially in relation to matters such as apprehended domestic violence orders (Johnson *et al.*, 1982); the cutting of welfare, education and training programmes and probation and parole positions within Corrective Services; and attacks on procedural safeguards in the prosecution process.

At the same time, the coercive and custodial resources within the law-and-order portfolios have been maintained or in some cases considerably enhanced. A major prison-building programme is being undertaken. The numbers of police are to be increased by 1,600 (about

7–8 per cent) over the first three years of the government's term in office. However, the law-and-order bureaucracies have not been freed entirely from the fiscal constraints being imposed elsewhere in the public sector.

Police powers under street offences legislation were significantly increased with the liberalization of the definition of some existing offences, the creation of new offences (such as the offence of 'violent disorder') and the making of all these offences imprisonable. There is little doubt that these provisions will be used, as such provisions have been in the past, to police and gaol Aborigines disproportionately in the rural towns of NSW.

These changes in the distribution of powers and resources within the law-and-order area reflect, and seek to reproduce, a popular understanding of law and order in terms of an enhancement of the coercive power of the State. Moreover, implicit in these developments is the decisive location of 'the crime problem' on the domain of the street, and especially amongst youth. They are coupled with substantial cut-backs in social services in other areas, such as housing, child care, public transport and education. Education has also witnessed a political and ideological offensive centred on discipline and the 'restoration' of traditional standards in education.

Problems of crime and violence are disconnected from social and economic relations, and even from such obvious situational factors as alcohol use and abuse. In a very clear example of the contradictions within neo-conservative ideology, the government is proposing a substantial deregulation of hotel licensing hours such that they would be permitted to open up to nineteen hours a day, and in some cases twenty-two hours. This is being coupled with a crackdown on underage drinking through an increase in penalties directed at both publicans and drinking minors themselves (*Sydney Morning Herald*, 1989a). Such forms of deregulation seek to eschew any responsibility for the social consequences of the patterns of alcohol use they facilitate and encourage, by elsewhere intensifying the rhetoric and practice of penal individuation and discipline against the bearers of those consequences.

The area in which the articulation of law and order to a wider right-wing ideological and political discourse is most discernible in government social policy is in the areas of child welfare and juvenile justice policies. In a deeply symbolic move the new government changed the name of the Department of Youth and Community Services to that of the Department of Family and Community Services. At the same time it transferred the major women's policy unit out of the Premier's Department into the Department of Family and Community Services. As one commentator put it: 'in one swoop, it seemed, the "community" had been redefined as "families"; welfare returned to its proper relation to the family unit; and women removed from the foreground of "political" issues to the familiar hinterlands of charity and the family' (Burchell, 1988, p. 26).

In the lead-up to the NSW election the opposition consistently sought to portray the Department (and the government) as siding with children against parents and thus as an agency of family breakdown, a depiction of welfare services exactly in line with that to be found in the *Future Directions* document discussed above. The Greiner government has sought to correct this by significantly increasing the legal power of the Department and police to exercise control over children and juveniles. A number of measures have been taken which seek to dissolve the separation between the criminal and welfare jurisdictions of the Children's Court and the Department, a separation which had formed a critical principle underlying the reforms of the 1970s and 1980s. Police powers to apprehend homeless children have been increased and there have been attempts to reintroduce truancy as a status offence. The Department has at the same time curtailed its provision of community-based residential care and established secure institutions for juveniles detained under care provisions. The number of institutional places provided is set to double (*Sydney Morning Herald*, 1989), institutional regimes have been substantially toughened and the powers to transfer juveniles to adult prisons have been increased.

These substantial increases in the coervice role of the Department have also to be considered alongside departmental cuts in child care expenditure, the closing of a quarter of the local offices of the Department, cuts in staffing, cuts in funding to community welfare agencies and the abolition of child protection workers (who have a specialist responsibility in relation to child abuse).

These changes reflect a deep-seated ambivalence about violence where it disturbs neo-conservative assumptions about the family and social welfare. In NSW we are witnessing the working through in practice of some of the major ideological tenets of neo-conservatism to be found in *Future Directions*. We have sought to indicate earlier some of the ways in which welfare and punishment, care and control, have been closely allied to each other within social policy discourse and practice in Australia. This has been particularly so in relation to children and juveniles. The limited, residual and frequently punitive nature of substitute forms of care underlines the assumption that children belong with their families and that the role of the State is to reinforce family responsibilities and authority. A punitive policing orientation to youth seeks to bolster this familial ideology, if not the functionality of particular families. It rests on the view that priority should lie with controlling the propensity of unsupervised youth for disorder and crime rather than the social and familial conditions – of poverty, violence and conflict – which have frequently been the root cause of their homelessness and public visibility.

On the right, affirmation of the family and family values becomes the vehicle for a particular construction of the problem of violence, within which the issue of private violence *within* the family gives way to a focus upon the problem of disorder, violence and danger which resides in the public realm. As we have suggested earlier, though, there are definite limitations to these evasions under current conditions, due to the growing political and electoral assertiveness of women on such issues.

The Greiner government's policies with regard to Aborigines are also in line with the philosophy outlined in *Future Directions*. The major focus of attack is the land rights legislation implemented by the previous Labor government, which the current government wants to repeal and replace with the 'mainstreaming' of services to Aborigines. Thus, the intention is to restore Aborigines in NSW to their more traditional relationship of dependency on state welfare services, which themselves are being drastically cut. This has to be considered alongside what are likely to be the effects of the government's general law-and-order policies on Aborigines, who have always been massively over-represented in court appearances for street offences, in police gaols, prisons and juvenile institutions (New South Wales Anti-Discrimination Board, 1982; Cunneen and Robb, 1987).

At a time of massive homelessness and of a worsening of all those conditions which are likely to increase levels of interpersonal conflict within poor families and communities (including the curtailment of public provision in housing, child care and other welfare services), the promise of right-wing policies on family and welfare is illusory. They amount to a recipe for increased private violence and intensified public discipline. However, they may secure other temporary ideological effects. By attempting to salvage the image of the family as the primary source of support and authority, they effectively deny any genuinely communal responsibility for what happens within families. Thus, violence, homelessness and poverty all become the responsibility of the individual, who thereby becomes a fit subject for state discipline.

Conclusion

Without resiling from what we have suggested above are the likely effects of New Right social and law-and-order policies on the level and impact of violence, we would seek to reiterate three points by way of conclusion.

First, there are dangers in exaggerating the effectivity of the New Right (just as there are in underestimating it). There are very definite limits on the realization of much New Right rhetoric as viable government policy. For example, the fiscal discipline that the Greiner government is currently imposing on public expenditures in NSW carries implications for the wasteful expansion of prison budgets, at a time when the NSW prison population is at its highest ever level, with massive prison and gaol overcrowding and serious court backlogs (Hogg, 1988). There is no doubt that, in the first instance, this has led to a serious deterioration in living and working conditions in the prisons and police cells. However, this in turn has led to protests by prisoners, prison officers and lawyers. The minister himself recognizes the limits beyond which such developments will rebound on the government, displacing the image of appropriately stern discipline with that of incompetent administration. Despite the recent passage of legislation facilitating a substantial increase in the sentencing powers of the judiciary, he has argued that the legislation should not be used to increase sentences.

Secondly, because governments and political movements of whatever persuasion cannot exercise full control over political and reform agendas and the conditions for realizing them, the terrain of social change always tends to be much more complex, contradictory and open than can be gleaned through the lens of any given political ideology. The Greiner government in NSW has introduced freedom-of-information legislation (albeit of a very weak kind) and legislation dealing with incitement to racial hatred and it has supported quite progressive and far-reaching reforms of the NSW Police Force which were initiated under Labor, but whose principal author is the current Commissioner of Police. Such changes are not to be dismissed and there is a grave danger of political analyses, such as many of those which have addressed the phenomenon of the New Right with an eye primarily to its ideological dimensions, promoting a monolithic and essentialist view of the political process, without the necessary attention to local detail and strategy.

Finally, the purchase of the Right on law and order has to be considered in the light of the general defensiveness of the Left, both of its organizations and individual commentators, on issues of crime, violence and law and order. This variously takes the form of denying that the problem is as bad as it appears, of pointing to the problems with crime statistics or of making favourable comparisons of Australian rates of violence with those of countries such as the United States. If the Left is not to be left floundering on the margins of popular debate about law and order, it will be necessary to do better than this. A recognition that some forms of violence in Australian society are pervasive and incalculably damaging in their effects on victims must be clearly located within a political programme which realistically addresses some of the crucial conditions of existence of these forms of victimization. In so doing, some of the denials and contradictions of New Right positions on law and order need to be exposed and exploited, and the assumption that the issues are the natural property of the Right finally laid to rest.

Notes

1. Francis Castles, amongst others, has made the point regarding the limit-ations of economic liberalism as a practical doctrine of government: 'Under democratic rule the pressures for greater social protection are always present. Hence, contrary to the guiding notions of economic liberalism, democratic capitalism is necessarily and unavoidably the progenitor of big government.' (1988, p. 2)
2. For the major contributions to the debate about 'authoritarian populism' in Britain see Hall (1980) and Hall and Jacques (1983). For an example of an attempt to transpose these forms of analysis to the Australian context see Corns (1989).
3. The residualism in question is of a distinctively Australian kind, as Castles in particular has argued:

    Whether successfully or not, the Australian state has been utilised as a mechanism for securing social policy goals through the control of wage levels and the regulation of trade, and given that strategy, welfare has been residual not in the sense that social policy intervention has been minimal, but rather because redistribution through transfer payments and social wage benefits has been a subsidiary goal of public policy. (1989, p. 67)

4. 'Corporatization' refers to the organization and management of public enterprises and utilities according to strict market criteria and as a precursor to their privatization.

Bibliography and references

ABS (Australian Bureau of Statistics) (1986) *Victims of Crime, Australia, 1983*, Canberra: AGPS.

ABS (1988) *Census 86 – Australia in Profile*, Canberra: AGS.

ACTU/TDC (Australian Council of Trade Unions/Trade Development Commission) (1987) *Australia Reconstructed*, Mission to Western Europe, Canberra: AGPS.

Allen, J. (1982) 'The invention of the pathological family: a historical study of family violence in N.S.W.' in C. O'Donnell and J. Craney (eds.) *Family Violence in Australia*, Sydney: Longman-Cheshire.

Allen, J. (1985) 'Desperately seeking solutions: changing battered women's options since 1880' in S. Hatty (ed.) *National Conference on Domestic Violence – Proceedings, Volume 1*, Sydney: Australian Institute of Criminology.

Australian Institute of Criminology (1989) *Alcohol and Crime*, Trends and Issues in Crime and Criminal Justice, no. 18, Canberra: Australian Institute of Criminology.

Bonney, R. (1987) *Homicide 2*, Sydney: NSW Bureau of Crime Statistics and Research.

Braithwaite, J. and D. Biles (1986) 'Victims and offenders: the Australian experience', in R. Block (ed.) *Victimisation and Fear of Crime: World perspectives*, Washington, DC: US Department of Justice, Bureau of Justice Statistics.

Brown, D. (1988) 'Post election blues: law and order in NSW Inc.' *Legal Service Bulletin* **13**, 99.

Brownlee, H. and A. King (1989) 'The estimated impact of the family package of child poverty' in D. Edgar, D. Keane and P. McDonald (eds.) *Child Poverty*, Sydney: Allen & Unwin and the Australian Institute of Family Studies.

Burchell, D. (1988) 'Now it's really back to basics' *Australian Society* June, 26.

Butlin, N., A. Barnard and J. Pincus (1982) *Government and Capitalism*, Sydney: Allen & Unwin.

Cass, B. (1989) 'Children's poverty and labour market issues: confronting the issues' in D. Edgar, D. Keane and P. McDonald (eds.) *Child Poverty*, Sydney: Allen & Unwin and the Australian Institute of Family Studies.

Castles, F. (1985) *The Working Class and Welfare*, Sydney: Allen & Unwin.

Castles, F. (1988) *Australian Public Policy and Economic Vulnerability*, Sydney: Allen & Unwin.

Castles, F. (1989) 'Welfare and equality in capitalist societies: how and why Australia was different' in R. Kennedy (ed.) *Australian Welfare*, Melbourne: Macmillan.

Coates, K. (ed.) (1979) *What Went Wrong – Explaining the Fall of the Labour Government*, Nottingham Spokesman.

Coghill, K. (1987) *The New Right's Australian Fantasy*, Fitzroy: Penguin.

Commission of Inquiry into Poverty (1975) *Poverty in Australia, an Outline*, Canberra: AGPS.

Commonwealth of Australia (1989) *Towards a Fairer Australia: Social Justice Budget Statement 1989–90*, Budget Related Paper No. 8, Canberra: AGPS.

Corns, C. (1989) 'Claiming the victim territory: the politics of law and order', paper delivered at the Australian Law and Society Conference, 12–14 December, La Trobe University, Melbourne.

Cunneen, C. and T. Robb (1987) *Criminal Justice in North-West New South Wales*, Sydney: Bureau of Crime Statistics and Research.

Department of Prime Minister and Cabinet, Office of the Status of Women (1988) *A Say, a Choice, a Fair Go – The Government's National Agenda for Women*, Canberra: AGPS.

Donzelot, J. (1979) *The Policing of Families*, New York: Pantheon.

Edgar, D. (1986) 'The free or the good' in R. Levitas (ed.) *The Ideology of the New Right*, Oxford: Polity Press.

Edgar, D. (1989) 'Culture vulture', *Marxism Today* May, 18.

Ewer, P., W. Higgins and A. Stevens (1987) *Unions and the Future of Australian Manufacturing*, Sydney: Allen & Unwin.

Frey, D. (1986) *Survey of Sole Parent Pensioners' Workforce Barriers*, The Social Security Review, Background/Discussion Paper No. 12, Canberra: Commonwealth Government.

Gamble, A. (1988) *The Free Economy and the Strong State*, Melbourne: Macmillan.

Gilmour, P. and B. Hunt (1989) 'Australian manufacturing – the role for better management', *Current Affairs Bulletin* **66** (5), 12.

Girls in Care Project (1986) *Girls at Risk*, Report to the Premier of NSW.

Golder, H. (1985) *Divorce in 19th Century New South Wales*, Kensington: University of NSW Press.

Graycar, R. (1987), 'A legal response: a limited solution', paper presented to the National Human Rights Congress, 26 September.

Graycar, A. and A. Jamrozik (1989) *How Australians Live*, Melbourne: Macmillan.

Hall, S. (1980) 'Popular–democratic vs authoritarian populism: two ways of "taking democracy seriously"', in A. Hunt (ed.) *Marxism and Democracy*, London: Lawrence & Wishart.

Hall, S. and M. Jacques (eds.) (1983) *The Politics of Thatcherism*, London: Lawrence & Wishart.

Hanmer, J. and E. Stanko (1985) 'Stripping away the rhetoric of protection: violence to women, law and the state in Britain and the U.S.A.', *International Journal of the Sociology of Law* **13**, 357–74.

Hirst, P. (1989) *After Thatcher*, London: Collins.

Hogg, R. (1988) 'Sentencing and penal politics: current developments in NSW' in *Proceedings of the Institute of Criminology, No. 78: Sentencing*, Sydney: Sydney University Law School.

Horne, D. (1966) *The Lucky Country: Australia in the Sixties*, Melbourne: Penguin.

Howard, J. (1986) 'The new challenge of liberalism: hope through freedom, choice and incentive', the 1986 Alfred Deakin Lecture.

Human Rights and Equal Opportunity Commission (1989) *Our Homeless Children*, Report of the National Inquiry into Homeless Children, Canberra: AGPS.

Johnson, V., K. Ross and T. Vinson (1982) 'Domestic violence: cases before chamber magistrates', in C. O'Donnell and J. Craney (eds.), *Family Violence in Australia*, Melbourne: Longman-Cheshire.

Liberal–National Parties Coalition (1988) *Future Directions*, Canberra: Liberal Party of Australia and National Party of Australia.

MacIntyre, S. (1985) *Winners and Losers*, Sydney: Allen & Unwin.

MacIntyre, S. (1986) 'The short history of social democracy in Australia', *Thesis Eleven* **15**, 3–15.

MacIntyre. S. (1989) *The Labour Experiment*, Melbourne: McPhee Gribble.

Maddox, G. (1989) *The Hawke Government and Labor Tradition*, Melbourne: Penguin.

Minister for Employment, Education and Training (1989) *Employment, Education and Training – Key Trends and Government Initiatives*, Submission to the Economic Planning Advisory Council, Canberra: AGPS.

Mugford, J. (1989) *Domestic Violence*, National Committee on Violence, Report No. 2, Canberra: Australian Institute of Criminology.

Mukherjee, A., J. Walker, T. Psaila, A. Scandia and D. Dagger (1987) *The Size of the Crime Problem in Australia*, Canberra: Australian Institute of Criminology.

New South Wales Anti-Discrimination Board (1982) *Study of Street Offences by Aborigines*, Sydney: New South Wales Anti-Discrimination Board.

NSW Commission of Audit (1988) *Focus on Reform – Report on the State's Finances*, Sydney: New South Wales Commission of Audit.

O'Brien, P. (1985) *The Liberals*, Melbourne: Penguin.

O'Donnell, C. and J. Craney (1982) 'Domestic violence and sex and class inequality', in C. O'Donnell and J. Craney (eds.) Family Violence in Australia, Melbourne: Longman-Cheshire.

Patience, A. and D. Head (1979) *From Whitlam to Fraser*, Melbourne: Oxford University Press.

Presdee, M. (1989) 'Made in Australia: youth policies and the creation of crime', in D. Edgar, D. Keane and P. McDonald (eds.) *Child Poverty*, Sydney: Allen & Unwin and the Australian Institute of Family Studies.

Raymond, J. (1987) *Bringing up Children Alone: Policies for sole parents*, Social Security Review, Issues Paper No. 3.

Read, P. (1983) *The Stolen Generations*, Aboriginal Children's Research Project, NSW Ministry of Aboriginal Affairs, Occasional Paper No. 1.

Robb, T. (1988) *Police Reports of Serious Assaults in New South Wales*, Sydney: NSW Bureau of Crime Statistics and Research.

Rose, N. (1985) *The Psychological Complex*, London: Routledge & Kegan Paul.

Rose, N. (1987) 'Beyond the public/private division: law, power and the family', *Journal of Law and Society* **14** (1), 61.

Royal Commission into Aboriginal Deaths in Custody (1988) *Interim Report*, Canberra: AGPS.

Royal Commission into Aboriginal Deaths in Custody (1989) *Report of the Inquiry into the Death of Malcolm Charles Smith*, Commissioner J. H. Wootten, Canberra: AGPS.

Sawer, M. (ed.) (1982) *Australia and the New Right*, Sydney: Allen & Unwin.

Sawer, M. (1983) 'State interventionism and coalition governments, 1949–66' in B. Head (ed.) *State and Economy in Australia*, Melbourne: Oxford University Press.

Schott, K. (1988) 'Debts and deficits – is Australia solving its economic problems?', *Current Affairs Bulletin* **65** (7), 17.

Shaver, S. (1989) 'Sex and money in the fiscal crisis' in R. Kennedy (ed.) *Australian Welfare*, Melbourne: Macmillan.

Social Security Review (1986) *Survey of Sole Parent Pensioners' Workforce Barriers*, Background/Discussion Paper No. 12.

Stilwell, F. (1986) *The Accord and Beyond*, London: Pluto Press.

Stubbs, J. and A. Wallace (1988) 'Protecting victims of domestic violence?' in M. Findlay and R. Hogg (eds.) *Understanding Crime and Criminal Justice*, Sydney: Law Book.

Sydney Morning Herald (1987) 7 November.

Sydney Morning Herald (1989a) 1 May.

Sydney Morning Herald (1989b) 30 June.

Waldby, C. (1985) *Breaking the Silence*, A report based upon the findings of the Women Against Incest Phone-In Survey, Sydney: Honeysett.

Wallace, A. (1986) *Homicide: the social reality*, Sydney: NSW Bureau of Crime Statistics and Research.

Watts, R. (1987) *The Foundations of the National Welfare State*, Sydney: Allen & Unwin.

Watts, R. (1989) '"In fractured times"': the Accord and social policy under Hawke', in R. Kennedy (ed.), *Australian Welfare*, Melbourne: Macmillan.

White, R. (1989) 'Making ends meet: young people, work and the criminal economy', *Australian and New Zealand Journal of Criminology* **22** (3), 136.

Wilson, P. (1985) *Black Death White Hands*, 2nd edition, Sydney: Allen & Unwin.

Wilson, P. (1989) 'Sexual and violent crime in Australia' in *Current Affairs Bulletin* **65** (10), Sydney.

Young, J. (1988) 'Risk of crime and fear of crime: a realist critique of survey-based assumptions', in M. Maguire and J. Pointing (eds.) *Victims of Crime: A New Deal?* Milton Keynes, UK: Open University Press.

PART 3
Canada

PART 3

Canada

9

Market ideology and welfare reform
The breakdown of the public safety net in the new Canada

Graham Riches
University of Saskatchewan, Canada

This chapter will examine the application of market ideas to welfare policy in Canada in the 1980s. It will explore changes in unemployment insurance and social assistance at both the federal and provincial levels of government. This is necessary as social welfare in Canada, while principally a matter of provincial constitutional responsibility, is at the same time subject to the exercise of considerable power and influence by the Federal Government.

The Federal Government achieves this partly through its control over monetary and fiscal policy and partly through its use of existing federal powers in relation to such areas as unemployment insurance, veterans' affairs, Indian social welfare, immigration policy, corrections and citizenship services (Armitage, 1988, p. 87). It can also call upon its broad spending powers and its right to make payments to individuals as in the case of family allowances and old age security (Armitage, 1988, p. 87); or it can choose to support provincial programmes through a range of transfer payments (Armitage, 1988, pp. 88–9). Only Quebec in terms of social spending has achieved an independence not generally shared by the other provinces.

Our first concern here is with the extent to which the Federal Government's 1984 and 1989 commitments to deficit reduction and to a recovery led by the private sector have influenced the introduction and application of welfare reform in Canada. Of particular interest will be the findings of a number of national commissions and inquiries which also helped shape the context for the reform of unemployment insurance and social assistance.

Second, using a case study approach, the introduction of welfare reform in Saskatchewan between 1984 and 1989 by a provincial government openly and unapologetically committed to neo-conservatism will be analyzed. This case study will assess the application of market-driven principles to that province's social assistance programme and consider its social effects.

Finally, the implications of the breakdown of Canada's public safety net will be considered in light of the broader changes which the Federal Government is likely to be seeking in the field of social welfare as it moves to implement the Free Trade Agreement signed in January 1989 between Canada and the United States.

Food banks, the market and welfare reform

Food banks have quickly become the symbols of the cost legitimacy of the welfare state in Canada. The first food bank was established in Edmonton, Alberta, in 1981. By 1989 130 were reported to exist across the country (CAFB, 1988), with many being organized on ideas borrowed from United States food bank organizations (Riches, 1986, p. 18). Food banks are centralized warehouses or clearing houses registered as non-profit charitable organizations which collect, sort and distribute food (either donated or shared), free of charge, to frontline agencies providing supplementary food or meals to the hungry. They represent the response of community-minded citizens to the growing plight of the hungry in Canada, many of whom are public welfare recipients whose monthly benefits are inadequate to meet their basic needs. The emergence and institutionalization of food banks is an essential starting point for examining the social impact of free market ideas upon Canada's public safety net.

The rise of the food banks has demonstrated that the federal unemployment insurance programme and provincially run social assistance schemes are no longer responding to the needs of the poor and jobless. The public safety net has, indeed, collapsed. Food banks are now providing substitute forms of relief to hundreds of thousands of destitute Canadians (Riches, 1986, p. 42). In the face of stubbornly high levels of unemployment and significant economic restructuring (Ternowetsky, 1988, pp. 20–1), private welfare and public begging have re-established themselves as part of the new economic reality of the 1980s.

However, the problem has been more than one of system overload. While it may be premature to claim that the welfare state is being dismantled, it is clear that the increasing application of free market ideas has been reasserting the idea that 'social policy' is a residual field of the state rather than a central institutional value (Guest, 1986, p. 235). In other words there has been a retreat to the nineteenth-century idea that the family and the private market are the 'normal channels' for meeting social need and that publicly provided social security should not be maintained as the first line of defence (Guest, 1986, pp. 1–2).

Evidence for this change can be traced back to the mid-1970s in terms of fiscal restraint and the shift to privatization (Mishra, 1988, p. 2; Ismael and Vaillancourt, 1988, p. 221; Riches and Maslany, 1983, pp. 36–46). Such policies were espoused both federally and provincially and by all political administrations including the Liberals, the Progressive Conservatives and the New Democratic Party. Moreover they were introduced during a period of worsening economic conditions. The clearest and most dramatic examples of the application of these policies provincially have been in British Columbia and Saskatchewan. In 1983 British Columbia's newly elected Social Credit Government, briefed by the Fraser Institute, a neo-conservative think-tank based in Vancouver, surprised an unsuspecting electorate by declaring a budget of stringent restraint 'designed to get the people off the backs of business' (Magnusson *et al.*, 1984, p. 12). In 1984 the province of Saskatchewan introduced welfare reform as a major strategy for cutting social spending, reducing public dependency on the social assistance rolls, reasserting the traditional work ethic and privatizing welfare. The costs of social and economic change were to lie where they fell: on the backs of the poor.

It has also been evident that the achievement of federal power by the Progressive Conservatives in 1984, followed by their re-election in 1988, indicated a new direction for social welfare policy reflecting a recommitment to market principles. The emphasis clearly echoed the neo-conservative arguments put forward by right-wing pressure groups such as the Fraser Institute and the National Council on Business Issues. Indeed, if the Federal Government's commitment to its strategy of deficit reduction, a recovery led by the private sector and free trade with the United States is sustained, over the long term there are likely to be major implications for social policy and the welfare state. The most recent examples have been the 1989 budget decisions to attack the universality of family allowances and old age security benefits, to restrict further unemployment insurance eligibility and to eliminate entirely the Federal Government contribution to the funding of unemployment insurance itself. As Resnick has noted, neo-conservatism:

> invokes individualism against collectivism, and repudiates the principle of
> equality (both of opportunity and condition). It rejects the redistributionist ethic
> of the welfare state and the interventionist role of government. It evokes
> populism and traditional morality in defending the social order of capitalism.
> (1984, p. 138)

Neo-conservative ideas for reforming welfare are clearly directed at imposing private market solutions upon systems of public welfare. Broadly understood they seek to develop policies which tie social programmes such as unemployment insurance and social assistance more closely to the demands of business and private capital, to perceived changing labour market needs and to the creation of a large and available pool of low wage labour. The task is to create a more competitive and dynamic economy. The major obstacle to turning the economy around is held to be the size and growth of the federal deficit. It is this which has to be curbed. Given that social spending leading to unnecessary welfare dependency is regarded as a major factor in causing government deficits, neo-conservatives argue that welfare policies have to be reshaped in order to fit the new economic reality.

Welfare reform in Canada, as in the United States which provided the original well-spring of ideas (Schram, 1982, p. 1; Goldberg, 1987, p. 1), has aimed therefore to reduce welfare dependency by moving people off the unemployment and social assistance rolls and back into the labour force. It has done this by requiring welfare recipients to enter employment and training programmes and to work for welfare benefits. Other goals have included the reallocation of scarce resources to those most in need, cutting welfare expenditures, reducing benefits, imposing more stringent eligibility requirements and discouraging fraud and abuse (Rofuth, 1987, p. 12). The essential task has been to reassert the primacy of the traditional work ethic and to make people self-sufficient. In this way welfare reform of the 1980s differed from earlier attempts in the 1970s in both Canada and the United States which sought to reduce poverty by major expansions of cash welfare (Leman, 1980, p. xiii).

Welfare reform's long-term objective has been to develop a more efficient and selective public safety net which, in the case of unemployment insurance and social assistance, would enhance employability. As such it would help promote the conditions for social policy harmonization between Canada and the United States in light of the Free Trade Agreement (Guest, 1988, p. 97; Warnock, 1988, p. 153). For those denied eligibility, welfare reform has simply reasserted the logic of 'residualism' and the market-place: individuals and families would be responsible for their own welfare and, if they could not manage, the church or the food bank was just around the corner.

Yet, while neo-conservative thinking is clearly the major inspiration for these ideas in Canada, it is perhaps debatable whether the New Right or New Business agenda has been fully accepted and applied by Ottawa and the provinces, with the possible exception of British Columbia and Saskatchewan. While it is not difficult to detect the increasing influence of market ideas upon federal social policy, it is not entirely evident that they have become dominant.

In fact, the Federal Government has been harshly criticized by the corporate community for not severely curtailing social programme spending in its 1989 budget. Thomas d'Aquino of the Business Council on National Issues recently stated:

> Let's be brutally frank. The budget was a disappointment. The deficit is up and taxes are up and there will have to be further taxes...the sad consequence of this budget is that the public was ready for deep spending cuts but Ottawa lost its political nerve and wasted an opportunity it will not enjoy later in its term. (*Globe and Mail* 1989c)

Clearly what this suggests is that the Federal Government is subject to a greater array of constraints in terms of implementing a forceful neo-conservative agenda than those who advocate such a path might realize.

It is surely the case that the nature of Canadian federalism combined with historical pressures to create and maintain political and constitutional harmony in a linguistic and culturally bifurcated state act as powerful brakes upon both the reactionary and indeed progressive tendencies of federal and provincial politicians. National unity is not something which any federal politician can afford to cast aside lightly. By the same token the fact that the popular vote in the 1988 fall federal election was strongly opposed to free trade with the United States, and by implication supported Canada retaining its traditional and collective commitment to publicly funded social programmes, may have acted as a check on the Federal Government moving ahead to full implementation of the neo-conservative agenda. This is not to say that market ideas were not to be strongly advocated as important principles in guiding both the economy and welfare reform, but rather that their application has been more muted.

Market ideas and welfare reform: national implications

While food banks have become the new symbols for social welfare in Canada, there can be little doubt that deficit reduction, the private sector led recovery and free trade remain the rallying cries for the Federal Government's economic agenda. These policies were clearly set out in Finance Minister Wilson's November 1984 economic statement (Department of Finance, 1984a, 1984b) and the May 1985 budget papers (Department of Finance, 1985). As Ternowetsky points out:

> The scenario presented in these documents rests on the basic assumption that the motor of economic growth is the private sector which will reinvest its profits and create jobs for Canadians ... Before growth and employment can reach

their potential the government forcefully argues that the deficit must be reduced and controlled. The source of Canada's economic and employment problems lies in the deficit and its adverse impact on the private sector's investment and job creations decisions. These two pillars of lowering the deficit and creating conditions for a private sector led recovery hold the key to economic growth and job creation in Canada. (1986, p. 42)

These arguments have been forcefully reasserted in the April 1989 budget address. Despite the fact there is little evidence to support the view that the federal deficit and social spending are out of control, the Government has clearly resolved to pursue its goal of applying free market ideas to Canada's economic and social agenda. In this regard it is useful to note that the National Council of Welfare, an advisory body appointed by and reporting to the Federal Government, states in a recent report that, between 1984 and 1989, the Government had substantially reduced the deficit and significantly reduced social spending. It points out that in real dollar terms while public debt charges have grown from $27.5 billion in 1984–5 to an estimated £33 billion in 1989–90, the annual deficit in the same period declined from $47 billion to $29 billion. Social spending in terms of old age pensions showed a steady real increase but unemployment insurance, established programme financing (health and post-secondary education), the Canada Assistance Plan and family allowances either remained flat or declined (NCW, 1989, pp. 1–3).

To place the 1984 commitments in context it is important to recall that at that time the Canadian unemployment rate stood at 11.4 per cent with provincial rates varying between a low of 8.2 per cent in Manitoba to a high of 20.3 per cent in Newfoundland (Statistics Canada, 1984). Unofficial estimates put the number of jobless Canadians at over 2 million (Rotstein, 1985, p. 13). The length of time that people were out of work was increasing. By 1984 10 per cent of the unemployed had been jobless for over a year. In 1980 only 3.8 per cent had been similarly affected (Statistics Canada, 1985, p. 141). Between 1981 and 1984 the official poverty rate had increased from 14.7 per cent to 17.3 per cent (NCW, 1988, p. 7). While nationally it is true that unemployment and poverty rates have since declined and Canadian job creation was impressive, in 1989 most regions of Canada were still suffering from the effects of the worst recession of the post-second World War period. While Ontario's economy boomed and became overheated, the Maritimes and the West continued to suffer disproportionately. The free market recovery was not of universal benefit.

In terms of the public safety net the trends were ominous. Nationally, unemployment insurance case-loads had grown on average by 67 per cent between 1981 and 1984 (Statistics Canada, 1981, 1984) with social assistance cases climbing by 37 per cent (Health and Welfare Canada,

1984). The western Canadian provinces, particularly Alberta and British Columbia, experienced the sharpest increases as their resource-based economies were badly hit by the recession. It was of little surprise therefore that food banks first emerged in the West.

Against this background the Tories swept to office in 1984 on a platform promising 'jobs, jobs, jobs!' The private sector led recovery and deficit reduction, as the device for curbing high inflation, were quickly introduced as the key economic strategies. Advocacy of free market principles was riding high. At the national level, support for these policies was to be found in the work of three major federally appointed inquiries.

The first and doubtless the most significant was the Report of the Royal Commission on the Economic Union and Development Prospects for Canada, otherwise known as the Macdonald Report, after its Chairman Donald Macdonald. While the report had initially been commissioned by the Liberal Government of Pierre Trudeau in 1982 it reported to the new Conservative administration in August 1985. On achieving office Prime Minister Brian Mulroney lost little time in appointing his Deputy Premier Erik Nielsen to conduct a major review of all federal programmes and expenditures, including social welfare. This came to be known as the Nielsen Task Force Report and was also published in 1985. The third report was that of the Commission of Inquiry on Unemployment Insurance headed by Claude Forget which completed its work in November 1986.

From the perspective of applying market principles to social welfare policies there was a considerable convergence of opinion which emerged from the reports. The one exception was the Forget Report which contained a significant minority report written by two representatives of labour organizations serving on the Commission. Yet the official voices favoured principles which reflected market-driven welfare reform.

Income security

The Macdonald Commission report will long be remembered as the most significant economic and political document in recent Canadian history. Not only does it recommend a strong reliance on competitive market forces in developing the Canadian economy, it also reintroduced the idea of free trade with the United States to the Canadian political agenda (1985, pp. 382–4), an idea which was to be realized only four years later. It is within this context that it is important to consider Macdonald's views on social policy. While the report itself did not discuss the welfare reform issue as such, it did deal with the relationship of income security to unemployment and labour market issues in terms of the role played by unemployment insurance (1985, pp. 585–616). It also considered the need for a guaranteed annual income which it termed a Universal Income Security Program (UISP). This was to replace a wide range of federal income support programmes including family allowances and federal contributions to provincial social assistance payments (1985, pp. 794–6).

Yet it has been observed that for Macdonald, 'economic interests are primary, social interests are secondary' (Ross, 1986, p. 10). The major task of the income security system appeared to be that of returning, and, if necessary, of *requiring* unemployed persons to return to the labour force (Macdonald, 1985, p. 542). In this, the report's major recommendations reflected a commitment to welfare reform. On the one hand they proposed a Transitional Adjustment Assistance Programme (TAAP) which would assist out-of-work Canadians to acquire job skills and achieve labour force mobility (1985, p. 616). And on the other hand for those no longer employable they recommended the UISP which was designed to ensure a minimum income below which no one would fall (1985, pp. 794–801).

However, there were deep-seated problems with both approaches. TAAP, which was to be financed by eliminating extended regional unemployment insurance benefits (Patterson, 1987, p. 70) offered no guarantees to workers that they would find permanent jobs in their own communities. The jobs could be thousands of miles from their homes. With the high levels of provincial unemployment rates it was not difficult to understand why people were reluctant to accept such a proposal. At the same time the UISP recommendation pitched the level of its benefits to match those of current social assistance rates thereby ensuring the long-term perpetuation of poverty.

One underlying problem of these policies, which is reflected in neo-conservative approaches to welfare reform, is that any change in the system must either be financed out of existing funds or on the basis of a shrinking budget. Another is the longstanding fear that if unemployment benefits or social assistance rates are raised to adequate levels then the work incentive will be destroyed. What has therefore to be maintained and enforced is the doctrine of less eligibility.

Macdonald's recommendations for reforming the welfare system reflected the federal view that social spending was too generous in Canada and that the real agenda must be deficit reduction and the private sector led recovery. Moreover as Ross notes:

the recommendations, coming as they do from a strict economic perspective, provide a prescription for an ailing system that will not open up fresh opportunities for the poor to participate in Canada's social, cultural, political and economic activities. It will perpetuate their dependency on the society that grudgingly maintains them at poverty levels, and the few dollars that the poorest families may receive will not compensate their being left outside the mainstream of Canadian society. (1986, p. 13)

Unemployment insurance

These reflections could also be aptly applied to the majority recommendations of the Forget Report on unemployment insurance (1986) and to the recent 1989 Federal Government proposals for reshaping Canada's unemployment insurance programme. In their different ways they both carry forward the message of welfare reform, namely that the unemployed should be returned to the work-force as quickly as possible but in ways that would impoverish the unemployed in the process.

Three assumptions could be said to have informed Forget's majority report. First, it expressed the view that unemployment insurance in Canada was no longer focused on responding to the short-term interruptions of earnings which the programme was originally designed to meet (1986, pp. 20,181). Second, it argued, along with Macdonald, that unemployment insurance had been too generous and was in fact contributing to high rates of unemployment (Forget, 1986, p. 90). Third, changes needed to be made to programme benefits to reassert work incentives and to ensure that labour market efficiency was maintained (1986, p. 182). The introduction of the annualization of benefits, the elimination of regionally extended benefits and support for measures aimed at returning the unemployed to the workforce through increasing and advancing their mobility and training were advanced as reform policies. The intention was to return unemployment insurance to its original and more actuarial insurance principles (Guest, 1988, pp. 97–8).

However, as one observer commented, the majority report could provide no assurance that 'large numbers of people, especially those who need the most assistance, will not endure greater hardship as a result of the proposed changes' (Patterson, 1987, p. 72).

Labour, speaking through the minority report, denounced the Commission's analysis and recommendations. In general they believed the current system to be fundamentally sound (1986, p. 466). They argued strongly against the annualization of benefits which they said would result in devastating benefit cut-backs for more than 78 per cent of current claimants (1986, p. 455). What they wished to see was an extension of unemployment insurance as social insurance and as a programme that was more responsive to the real needs of the unemployed (1986, p. 469).

However, their wishes were not to be fulfilled. The report itself was released amidst considerable controversy and perhaps because of that no action was taken by the Federal Government with respect to its recommendations. It seemed as if the heat had gone out of the debate. Yet shortly after the Conservatives' re-election in the fall of 1988, the Federal Government announced plans to make significant changes to unemployment insurance. The proposals reflected the Federal Government's commitment to deficit reduction and the private sector led recovery as the way to achieve welfare reform.

The intention was to reduce the federal contribution to the unemployment insurance fund by as much as $1.3 billion which, taking into account employer and employee contributions, amounted to 10 per cent of the total cost of the programme in 1988. These savings were to come from reducing the length of benefit entitlement periods and by extending the amount of time a person must work before qualifying (*Globe and Mail*, 1989a, p. 1). Further savings were anticipated based on an expected increase in employer/employee contributions. For those quitting their jobs without just cause the penalties would be tightened. Savings made in these areas would be used to fund a variety of training schemes aimed at reducing dependency and returning workers to the labour force.

In other words while the method for reforming unemployment insurance differed from that proposed by the Forget Report, the intent was nevertheless the same: to cut benefits and remind people that they would be better off working; to use the money saved to create worker training schemes without being able to guarantee employment; and to make no new money available for implementing the proposals. There was no political objection to the idea of employment and training schemes, but as the then Liberal leader John Turner said in the House of Commons: 'Why is the government forcing unemployed people on welfare to pay for what should be government training programs?' (*Globe and Mail*, 1989a, p. 2).

Yet no politician in Canada should have been surprised at the proposals, for they closely followed the welfare reform policies that had been evolving both federally and provincially with respect to social assistance programming since at least 1984.

Social assistance

The release in 1985 of the Nielsen Task Force study on the Canada Assistance Plan (CAP) predated those of the Macdonald and Forget commission reports. CAP which was established in 1966 is the federal–provincial cost-sharing arrangement for provincial social assistance programmes.

The report noted a steady increase in the proportion of people

receiving social assistance for unemployment-related reasons and reported that by 1985 'provincial case loads now include from 30 per cent to
70 per cent in "employables" [*sic*]' (Nielsen, 1985, p. 5). Given that
Canada was experiencing its worst recession since the end of the Second
World War this fact was hardly surprising.

Nielsen recommended that the only way to reduce case loads of
individuals on welfare was to provide a range of employment and training
programmes which would require the participation of the federal
ministries of Health and Welfare Canada, Canada Employment and
Immigration and provincial ministries of social services and manpower
(Nielsen, 1985, p. 17). In making these proposals the report refers to
United States' experience and to policies already being implemented in
the provinces of Prince Edward Island, Newfoundland and Saskatchewan
(Nielsen, 1985, p. 16).

This proposal along with the provincial initiatives in welfare reform
were later reflected in the signing of *employability enhancement accords*
between the Federal Government and the provinces, with the first one
being signed by the province of Saskatchewan in 1986. The purpose of the
accords was to divert cost-shared funding from the Canada Assistance
Plan to support subsidized employment, training and job readiness
schemes for employable people on social assistance.

In practice what this meant was that fully employable welfare
recipients had their benefits cut in order to pay for training and short-term
work experience. This was the device used in order to cut welfare
expenditures, reduce dependency and require people to accept low-
paying jobs. It was the same formula which was to be applied in 1989 to
reform unemployment insurance.

It can be seen, therefore, that during the 1980s in Canada neo-conservative ideas regarding the relationship between an economy driven by
a recovery led by the private market sector and the need for social welfare
policy to reflect and contribute to this enterprise have been actively
implemented. Not only have they been acted on by the Federal
Government, they have also been clearly articulated by a series of
nationally commissioned studies and reports.

On examining the effects of welfare reform at the provincial level, it
becomes possible to appreciate the extent to which it has contributed to
the breakdown of public welfare in Canada and the further impoverishment of the already poor.

Reforming social assistance: the provincial agenda

Welfare reform was the name given in 1984 by the Saskatchewan
Government to its policy of reforming the province's social assistance

programme. While other provinces such as Quebec and British Columbia have introduced similar reforms (Willms, 1987, pp. 10–12; Shragge, 1988, pp. 13–19) and Ontario has just completed a major review of its social assistance system (SARC, 1988), there are particular reasons for considering the Saskatchewan experience.

First, welfare reform in Saskatchewan represented an unequivocal commitment by a government committed to neo-conservative ideas to re-order public relief in the shape of market principles. As such it formed a key part of the overall government agenda of privatization which has been increasingly implemented since the Progressive Conservatives achieved office in 1982 (O'Sullivan and Sorensen, 1988, pp. 75–93; Martin, 1988, pp. 6–8). The private sector was viewed as the major stimulant to economic growth (Saskatchewan Finance, 1982, p. 7) and diversification (Saskatchewan Finance, 1989, p. 11). It followed that perceived government waste and inefficiency was to be eliminated through cutting public services or else through the contracting out of public services to the private sector. In the Government's second term of office the privatization of the province's major crown corporations, including its public utilities, was strongly advanced. Such policies were seen by the opposition New Democratic Party as a direct assault on the social democratic heritage of Saskatchewan.

Second, in the broader context of Canadian federalism the championing of free market principles by a Saskatchewan Government is politically significant in that since the Second World War the province has had a long history of electing social-democratic parties to office. The Cooperative Commonwealth Federation (CCF) held power from 1944 to 1961 and again, as the New Democratic Party (NDP), between 1971 and 1982. In Canadian eyes the province has been regarded not only as the homeland of socialism in North America but most particularly as the birthplace of medicare.

The CCF concluded its Regina Manifesto of 1933, 'No C.C.F. government will rest content until it has eradicated capitalism and put into operation the full programme of socialized planning which will lead to the establishment in Canada of the Cooperative Commonwealth' (McNaught, 1971, p. 249). Since the election of the Progressive Conservatives in 1982 the tables have been turned. Premier Devine, like Prime Minister Thatcher in Britain, has committed himself to eradicating socialism from the province (*Globe and Mail*, 1989, p. 6). Not only does he rely on the neo-conservative think-tank of the Fraser Institute based in Vancouver to advise his Government but he also employs the services of a former member of Margaret Thatcher's Policy Unit; Oliver Letwin, the head of the International Privatization Unit of N. M. Rothschild and Sons, and Author of *Privatising the World* (Letwin, 1988), is a frequent visitor to Saskatchewan. Indeed Saskatchewan, along with Quebec and British Columbia, is noted by Letwin to be developing an exciting programme of privatization (Letwin, 1988, p. 19).

Third, while Saskatchewan could not be regarded as a significant economic player in the context of the Canadian political economy, it is nevertheless one province which has often been looked to for its progressive social leadership. This has given the debate about welfare reform in the province, in the broader context of privatization, a special significance. If it is possible to bring about such a fundamental change in social policy in a province well known for its espousal of social democratic ideas, then it would suggest that the application of market principles to the welfare state in Canada has been broadly accepted. While the outcome of that debate remains an open question, the fact remains that Saskatchewan has become a testing ground for these ideas. It is not possible to say if the choice is a deliberate one – in the sense that Thatcher's United Kingdom Community Charge (Poll Tax) was first applied in Scotland – but it is clear that if the neo-conservative agenda can triumph in Saskatchewan then it will have won a significant ideological battle.

The origins of welfare reform in Saskatchewan lie in a study of the Saskatchewan Assistance Plan (SAP) commissioned by the province's new Minister of Social Services in 1982 and published in October 1983 (Adams, 1983). The report's major recommendations reflected the new economic agenda. They were to reduce welfare dependency by moving people into jobs and training; to streamline an unnecessarily complicated administrative structure; and to make greater use of the private, non-government and voluntary sectors.

Welfare reform as a specific government policy was introduced in March 1984 with a second stage being implemented in 1987 (Saskatchewan, 1984, 1987). Its overriding objective was to reduce welfare dependency. It aimed to do this by moving long-term fully employable social assistance clients into work and training programmes. Workfare was introduced. As an inducement for people to enter the work and training programmes, benefits were first reduced. If social assistance recipients then refused to participate in the schemes, quit work or failed to complete courses, their benefits were cut off and they were also denied the right to re-establish eligibility. In other words the receipt of welfare was made conditional upon their being willing to work, to look for work or accept training.

While the aim of providing work and training was publicly accepted it soon became evident that the real intent of these policies was to move people into government subsidized short-term, low-wage jobs. This would remove them from the welfare rolls and, in time, recycle them back to unemployment insurance, where they would be of no cost to the provincial exchequer. Fully employable people became the new class of undeserving poor.

Its second objective was to provide equitable benefits for people unable to work. Equity was to be achieved by cutting benefits to the single long-term unemployed and by freezing overall benefits at 1984 levels for all other recipients. The $9 million saved from the cutbacks were invested in the workfare programmes as wage subsidies to employers. As in the case of the proposed changes to the unemployment insurance programme by the Federal Government five years later, no new money was put into the work schemes. Indeed to support their endeavour Saskatchewan became the first province to sign an *Employability Enhancement Accord* in 1986 with the Federal Government. This enabled the Saskatchewan Government to divert funds originally earmarked for social assistance benefits to these projects. It was clearly a case of robbing the poor to pay the poor.

Welfare reform's third aim was to make the social assistance programme more efficient and effective. This was to be achieved by increasing programme control and accountability for expenditures and by improving standards of service provided to clients. The intent was to automate and computerize the social assistance delivery system. Tighter eligibility requirements, verification units, surveillance, home visits, spot checks and requiring recipients to pick up their cheques as opposed to having them delivered in the mail were introduced. Standardizing benefits and computerizing the assessment process were designed to produce a more cost-efficient programme with less room for error, by staff and clients alike. The programme became less responsive to individual circumstances.

An additional objective was to reduce error and fraud. This reflected the neo-conservative antipathy for perceived welfare dependency and the belief that everyone on welfare was a scrounger and was out to milk the system (Higgins, 1981, pp. 125–9). Despite the fact that studies have shown that welfare abuse in Canada is minimal (Hasson, 1981, p. 132; Hickel and Campbell Mackie, 1988, p. 24), the allegation of abuse became a highly successful method for making the public believe that benefits were too high and social spending should be cut. Despite the fact that the Government had introduced a policy whereby welfare clients were required to pick up their cheques (as opposed to receiving them in the mail) in order to curb welfare abuse (Saskatchewan Social Services, 1986, p. 1), two years later a new Minister of Social Services was still complaining that one in ten people on welfare was a cheater (*Leader Post*, 1988). Not only did such a campaign blame the victim, it also preached that the poor must be punished. It thereby became a useful device for persuading financial aid workers that their central task was to screen people out rather than help clients claim their legitimate entitlements.

What then have been the outcome and consequences of welfare reform? One question is whether welfare dependency has been reduced by people moving into stable and well-paid employment. The Saskatchewan Government claims that its work and training programmes have led to 2,000 people leaving the welfare rolls between 1984 and 1989 (Saskatchewan Finance, 1989, C10). Between 1985 and 1988 $25 million was spent creating 4,893 job placements for social assistance clients in 1,516 approved projects (Saskatchewan Social Services, 1985–8, p. 9). In addition a small number of New Careers Corporation jobs were provided in provincial parks. The job placements were in private business, local government and non-profit agencies.

These sound like attractive statistics until it is realized that these placements represented only 16 per cent of the fully employable SAP case load for those years. The majority of the jobs were of 20–3 weeks in length – just long enough to recycle workers back onto unemployment insurance. Overall social assistance case loads have declined by 9.5 per cent since 1985 but the fully employable case load continues to represent 25 per cent of all unemployed persons in the province.

Between 1985 and 1988, approximately one in five of the fully employable case load participated in some form of adult basic education, upgrading or job training (Saskatchewan Social Services, 1985–8). Clearly for some these are worthwhile schemes. The question remains, however, whether the training really did translate into full-time employment and decent wages. In fact, Saskatchewan was the only province which saw the size of its labour force and the number of employed persons decline between 1987 and 1988; and was one of only two provinces, the other being Manitoba, which experienced an increase in unemployment (Saskatchewan, 1988).

Indeed, five years after the introduction of welfare reform, provincial social assistance case loads remained 20 per cent higher than when the Government achieved power in 1982 (Saskatchewan Social Services, 1982–8). There was, therefore, little reason to believe that 'welfare dependency' has indeed been significantly reduced, a finding that is consistent with a number of US studies (Rofuth 1987, p. 20; Morris and Williamson, 1987, p. 49; Karger and Stoesz, 1989, p. 118).

But while dependency has not been reduced, poverty has increased. The pursuit of workfare and the diversion of funds to pay for these schemes has resulted in a significant erosion in the value of welfare benefits. At a time when family and child poverty had been growing in Saskatchewan (NCW, 1988, pp. 12, 28), welfare cuts coupled with inflation had succeeded in reducing the real purchasing power of SAP benefits between 1981 and 1989 by 54 per cent for single employable persons; and by 29 per cent for single- and two-parent families (Riches and Manning, 1989, p. 6).

In 1989 a single employable person was only entitled to received $375 a month. After rent and utilities have been paid, he or she was left with a real basic allowance of $65 a month or $16 a week for food, clothing, household, travel and personal expenses. The real basic allowance for a single mother with two children was $26 per person per week; and for a husband/wife family with four children $23 per person per week.

In addition, the increasing practice of recovering welfare overpayments can further reduce the amounts received in the real basic allowances. One third of those on social assistance have money deducted from their welfare cheques for 'overpayments' (*Leader Post*, 1989), for advances against household expenses and for duplicate assistance in the form of emergency food vouchers or Salvation Army meals. People are sometimes denied assistance altogether and are referred to the food bank. From the middle to the end of every month there are many people who simply have no money. They are destitute. They must resort to public begging. Despite the fact that social assistance rolls have declined by 9.5 per cent since 1985, food bank usage has risen by 51 per cent. Food banks have become one of the major consequences of the Government's strategy to privatize social services in Saskatchewan (O'Sullivan and Sorenson, 1988, p. 85).

Many have been denied or cut off financial assistance for refusing or being unable to participate in job search training programmes or for failing to pick up their welfare cheques. Through the application of a range of stringent eligibility tests, the province has ensured either that claimants' basic needs have not been adequately met or that their right to establish eligibility has been denied.

What these findings suggest is that the real intent of welfare reform is to use the spur of poverty to make people accept short-term low-wage labour; or to be punished by having to accept a real basic allowance which does not even permit subsistence living. Given also that workfare is being funded by monies previously used to pay higher welfare benefits, welfare reform essentially finances itself by robbing the poor to pay the poor. Its prime objective has been to save money and cut case loads at any costs.

The breakdown of the public safety net: social effects and implications

The introduction of a market-based welfare reform has been a key federal and provincial social policy strategy agenda in Canada in the 1980s. Its origins lie in the neo-conservative commitment to reduce the size and scope of government, to reduce the deficit and to stimulate a recovery led by the private sector. To bring this about, social spending and public dependency had to be cut and welfare policy made more responsive to the needs of private capital and the labour market. Despite the fact that welfare state expenditures are not profligate in Canada, and in fact have been held down in recent years, welfare reform has been chosen as the policy device for implementing the business agenda for social spending.

Promises to reduce welfare dependency and expand training and employment opportunities doubtless enjoyed broad public support. Few politicians, jobless people and progressive thinkers disagreed with these objectives, especially given the high levels of poverty and unemployment in Canada being experienced in the early 1980s. Yet it is difficult to argue that the promises have been fulfilled. Perhaps in Ontario with its booming economy and an unemployment rate down to 5.3 per cent, it may seem as if the restimulated private sector has led the rest of Canada out of the recession. But in the Maritimes, Quebec and the West unemployment rates still hover, on average, between 12.8 per cent and 8.2 per cent. In this context it is difficult to conclude that welfare reform has been little more than a labour market strategy for managing high levels of unemployment and preserving a large pool of low-wage labour.

This argument is certainly tenable if one views welfare reform as being part of the longer-term free trade agenda with the United States. To enable Canada to compete on an equal footing with its neighbour to the south will require the establishment of 'a level playing field'. To achieve this, social policy harmonization will be necessary between the two countries. For Canada this would imply a leaner and more selective safety net.

Food banks were the early warning signals of this impending Americanization of Canada's welfare state. The advent of welfare reform served to confirm the increasing application of market principles to Canada's system of social security and the implementation of residual and voluntarist solutions.

There can be little doubt that applying market ideas to the reform of unemployment insurance and social assistance has contributed to the collapse of these two pillars of the public safety net. The purchasing power of welfare benefits has been seriously cut back. Current family welfare rates represent only 63.1 per cent of Canada's most conservative poverty line (NCW, 1988, pp. 66–9). Eligibility criteria continue to be tightened and people are even being denied the right to establish entitlement. People's basic needs are not being met.

Given the fact that welfare rates remain high despite the decline in the jobless rate in the late 1980s (NCW, 1989, p. 3), it would appear that employment and training schemes targeted at social assistance recipients have not led to any significant reduction in welfare dependency. In fact the funding of these schemes from existing welfare dollars has contributed to the erosion in the value of the benefits themselves and has led to the further pauperization of the already poor. Destitution and public begging have returned to Canada. Food banks themselves are turning people away and cannot guarantee adequate substitute relief. The fact is that many social assistance clients are without any income for many days each month. More ominously children up to the age of 16 years constitute between 35 and 50 per cent of those using food banks, a clear indication that child hunger has emerged as a significant social problem (Riches, 1986, p. 43).

It is not, therefore, inappropriate to speak of the breakdown of Canada's public safety net. Since the early 1980s the universalist values which have strongly influenced the development of the Canadian welfare state have been under constant attack from market ideas. Yet, it should be said that what the future holds for the development of social security in Canada is not altogether clear.

While the Federal Government may indeed wish to pursue its twin policies of deficit reduction and the private sector led recovery, and in so doing increasingly subject Canadian social policies to the discipline of the market-place and a closer harmonization with those policies of the United States, the achievement of these objectives may prove more difficult than the Government thinks. Indeed, it would likely be a grave political mistake for any federal administration fundamentally to attack the universality of medicare, family allowances and old age security. If the cause of national unity is not in itself sufficient reason to eschew such an approach, then the politically expedient need for any federal government, in a country as large and diverse as Canada, to be active and be seen to be active in developing and providing nationally accessible human services which meet the social needs and rights of Canadians from coast to coast is likely to be the best guarantor of their retention.

In terms of unemployment insurance and social assistance, the lessons of the 1930s remain to guide politicians at both the federal and provincial levels. It should not go unnoted that during the Great Depression it was provincial premiers, mayors, business and labour leaders as well as two federal commissions and the unemployed who argued that the Federal Government should assume responsibility for the unemployed (Struthers, 1983, p. 209). Given that unemployment insurance is today a Federal Government constitutional responsibility, and that it also pays half the cost of provincial social assistance payments, it may indeed prove difficult for the Federal Government to avoid these obligations by trying to off-load them onto either the provinces or the private sector. One thing is indeed clear. If Ottawa strictly adheres to its new policy of withdrawing federal funding from unemployment insurance and insists on it having a more limited actuarial base with more restricted eligibility criteria, it will at some point have to face provincial demands for increased financial assistance in dealing with expanding social assistance rolls. And, as we have tried to show earlier, there is little evidence to suggest that welfare reform has successfully handled the problem of welfare dependency. The growing institutionalization of food banks is one strong sign of that.

In the longer term the idea of the guaranteed annual income is put forward by bodies such as the Macdonald Commission (1985, pp. 794–801) and the Canadian Council on Social Development (1986, p. 1) as the answer to the problems of the collapsing safety net. However, without a shared commitment by all levels of government and by business and labour to full employment and adequate incomes it is unlikely that a guaranteed income policy would be either affordable or adequate. Certainly the Macdonald proposals recommended income levels similar to that of current social assistance rates. As such these would only serve to institutionalize poverty and would be unable to give real assistance to the growing vulnerability of the working poor and the unemployed.

It is clear that market ideology has strongly influenced the development of Canadian social security policy in the 1980s, and the evidence discussed in this chapter suggests that such thinking has contributed to the collapse of the public safety net. Such a conclusion no doubt appears alarmist and contentious to many Canadians, who undoubtedly see themselves as fair-minded and compassionate people with an array of social programmes far in advance of those of their neighbours to the south. Yet how else is it possible to explain the persistence of food bank line-ups from one end of the country to the other? But there are grounds for believing that there are political limits to the extent to which market principles can be applied to Canada's social programmes. What is missing in the meantime from the contemporary scene in Canada, quite crucially, is a commitment by any organized political grouping to full employment and adequate incomes as a national goal.

Bibliography and references

Adams, D. (1983) *A Productive Welfare System for the Eighties: A review of the Saskatchewan Assistance Plan*, Regina: Saskatchewan Social Services.

Armitage, A. (1988) *Social Welfare in Canada*, Toronto: McLelland & Stewart.

CAFB (Canadian Association of Food Banks) (1988) 'Goals and objectives' *Brochure*, Toronto.

Canada, Ministry of Supply and Services (1986) *Commission of Inquiry on Unemployment Insurance*, Ottawa: Ministry of Supply and Services.

Canada/Saskatchewan (1986). *Accord on Employability Enhancement for Social Assistance Recipients*, Ottawa, 4 July.

Canadian Council on Social Development (1986) 'WIN: work and income in the nineties'. *Overview* **4**, (1), 1–4.

Department of Finance (1984a) 'A new direction for Canada: an agenda for economic renewal', presented by the Honourable Michael Wilson. Ottawa: Department of Finance.

Department of Finance (1984b) 'Supplementary information', Tables in the House of Commons by the Honourable Michael Wilson, Ottawa: Department of Finance (8 November).

Department of Finance (1985) 'Securing economic renewal' *The Budget Speech*, Ottawa: Department of Finance.

Department of Finance (1989) April Budget.

Forget Report (1986) *Commission of Inquiry on Unemployment Insurance*, Ottawa: Ministry of Supply and Services.

Globe and Mail (1989a). 'Jobless Insurance Gets Massive Overhaul', 12 April, Toronto.

Globe and Mail (1989b). 'Editorial', 18 April, p. 6, Toronto.

Globe and Mail (1989c) 23 May, p. 8, Toronto.

Goldberg, G. (1987) 'The illusion of welfare reform and some new initiatives', paper presented at the International Conference on Social Welfare, Rome (September).

Guest, D. (1986) *The Emergence of Social Security in Canada*, Vancouver: University of British Columbia Press.

Guest, D. (1988) 'Canadian and American income security responses to five major risks: a comparison', In G. Drover, (ed.) *Free Trade and Social Policy*, Ottawa: Canadian Council on Social Development.

Hasson, R. (1981) 'The cruel war: social security abuse in Canada' *Canadian Taxation*, **3** 114–47.

Health and Welfare Canada (1984) *Inventory of Income Security Programs in Canada 1981–1983*, Ottawa: Health and Welfare Canada.

Hickel, R. S. and P. Campbell Mackie (1988) *A Review of Economic Security Programs: Final report*, (Stevenson, Kellog, Ernst and Whinney). Prepared for Honourable Clayton Manness, Minister of Finance, Manitoba Government (30 March), Winnipeg.

Higgins, J. (1981) *States of Welfare*, Oxford: Basil Blackwell.

Ismael, J. and Y. Vaillancourt (1988) *Privatisation and Provincial Social Services in Canada*, Edmonton: University of Alberta Press.

Karger, H. J. and D. Stoesz (1989) 'Welfare reform: maximum feasible exaggeration' *Tikkun* (2) 23–5, 118–22.

Leader Post (1989). 'Manitoba ruling may affect Saskatchewan welfare policy', 24 January, Reginar.

Leader Post (1988). 'Welfare ripoff: cheating is a way of life for many recipients', 21 April, Reginar.

Leman, C. (1980) *The Collapse of Welfare Reform: Political institutions, policy and the poor in Canada and the United States*, Cambridge: MIT Press.

Letwin, O. (1988) *Privatising the World: A study of international privatisation in theory and practice*, London: Cassell.

Macdonald Commission (1985) *Royal Commission on the Economic Union and Development Prospects for Canada*, Ottawa: Ministry of Supply and Services.

McNaught, K. (1971) *The Pelican History of Canada*, Harmondsworth: Penguin.

Magnusson, W., *et al.* (1984) (eds.) *The New Reality*, Vancouver: New Star Books.

Martin, P. (1988) 'Reshaping Saskatchewan: Grant Devine – the new Tommy Douglas', *Saskatchewan Business* **9**, (6), 6–8.

Mishra, R. (1988) 'Riding the new wave: social work and the neo-conservative challenge'. Paper presented to the 10th International Symposium, Social Workers World Conference, International Federation of Social Workers, Stockholm, Sweden (26–30 July).

Morris, M. and J. B. Williamson (1987) 'Workfare: the poverty/dependence trade off', *Social Policy*, **18** (1) 13–16, 49–50.

NCW (National Council of Welfare) (1988) *Poverty Profile 1988*, Ottawa: National Council of Welfare.

NCW (National Council of Welfare) (1989) *Social Spending and the Next Budget*, Ottawa: National Council of Welfare.

Nielsen Task Force Study (1985) *Service to the Public: Canada assistance plan, a study team report to the task force on program review*, Ottawa, Ministry of Supply and Services.

Ontario, Community and Social Services (1988) 'Transitions', Report of the Social Assistance Review Committee, Ontario: Ministry of Community and Social Services (September).

O'Sullivan, M. and S. Sorenson (1988) 'Saskatchewan' in J. Ismael and Y. Vaillancourt, (eds.) *Privatisation and Provincial Social Services in Canada*, 75–93, Edmonton: University of Alberta Press.

Patterson, J. (1987) 'What do you do in the absence of an adequate framework for Social Policy? On the Commission of Inquiry into Unemployment', *Canadian Review of Social Policy/Revue canadienne de politique sociale* **18** 69–73.

Resnick, P. (1984) 'The ideology of neo-conservatism', in W. Magnusson, W. K. Carroll, C. Doyle, M. Langer and R.B.J. Walker (eds.) *The New Reality: The Politics of Restraint in British Columbia*, pp. 131–43, Vancouver: New Star Books.

Riches, G. (1986) *Food Banks and the Welfare Crisis*, Ottawa: Canadian Council on Social Development.

Riches, G. and L. Manning (1989) 'Welfare reform and the Canada assistance plan: the breakdown of public welfare in Saskatchewan, 1981–1989', Working paper Series No.4, Social Administration Research Unit, Faculty of Social Work, University of Regina.

Riches, G. and G. Maslany (1983) 'Social welfare and the New Democrats: personal social service spending in Saskatchewan, 1971–81', *Canadian Social Work Review*, 33–54, Ottawa.

Rofuth, T.W. (1987) 'Moving clients into jobs: Pennsylvania and Massachusetts take conservative and liberal approaches to a common problem', *Public Welfare* (Spring), 10–21.

Ross, D. (1986) 'The Macdonald Commission and the poor', *Perception* **9** (3), 10–13.

Rotstein, A. (1985) 'Repairing the fences', *Canadian Forum* (March) **LXIV**, 747, 13–18.

SARC (1988) *Transitions: Report of the Social Assistance Review Committee*, Toronto: Ministry of Community and Social Services.

Saskatchewan (1984) 'Dirks outlines welfare reform package', *News Release*, Social Services 84–228 (March).

Saskatchewan (1986) 'Dirks announces initiatives to curb welfare abuse', *News Release*, Social Services 86–154.

Saskatchewan (1987) 'Welfare Reform', Saskatchewan Finance (June).
Saskatchewan (1988) *Monthly Statistical Review*, **14**, 12 (December), 3.
Saskatchewan Finance (1982) *Budget Address* (November, March).
Saskatchewan Finance (1989) 'Challenges and opportunities', *Budget Speech Papers* (March 30).
Saskatchewan Human Resources (1989) *The Saskatchewan Labour Market*, Regina: Saskatchewan Human Resources, Labour and Employment.
Saskatchewan Social Services (1981–8) *Monthly and Quarterly Bulletin of Statistics*, Regina: Saskatchewan Social Services.
Schram, S. (1982) 'The myth of workfare', *Catalyst* **13**, 49–60.
Shragge, E. (1988) 'Welfare reform: Quebec style or poor law reform act – 1988?', *Canadian Review of Social Policy/Revue canadienne de politique sociale* **22** (November), 13–19.
Statistics Canada (1981, 1984) *Unemployment Insurance Act, Catalogue 73-001*, Ottawa: April–June Quarterly.
Statistics Canada (1984) *Canadian Statistical Review*, Ottawa: Statistics Canada.
Statistics Canada (1985,1989) *The Labour Force, Catalogue 71-001*. Ottawa: Statistics Canada.
Struthers, J. (1983) *No Fault of Their Own: Unemployment and the Canadian Welfare State 1914–1941*, Toronto: University of Toronto Press.
Ternowetsky, G. (1986) 'Federal spending on the private sector, profits and the creation of unemployment: another side of the unemployment insurance review', *Canadian Review of Social Policy/Revue canadienne de politique sociale* **14/15** (May), 41–61.
Ternowetsky, G. (1988) 'Unemployment, employment, the declining middle and the expanding bottom: the challenge for social work', *Canadian Review of Social Policy/Revue canadienne de politique sociale* **22** (November), 20–5.
Warnock, J. (1988) *Free Trade and the New Right Agenda*, Vancouver: New Star Books.
Willms, S. (1987) 'Work for welfare: British Columbia's initiative', *Canadian Review of Social Policy/Revue canadienne de politique sociale* **18** (May), 10–12.

10

Freezing the free market in Northern Canada

Peter J. Usher
Box 4815, Station E, Ottawa, Ontario K15 5H9, Canada

The Canadian north lies at the extremity of the contemporary economic world. Since the seventeenth century its economic life has been steered by several states or versions of capitalism, none of which resembles the 'free market' policies now so widely advocated in the western democracies.[1] If such 'free market' policies were to be fully implemented in the north without any off-setting measures, they would result not only in reduced living standards, village depopulation and social disorder, but also lead to a sharp decline in the volume of economic activity generally. There are, however, severe constraints on any Canadian government moving very far in that direction in the north, even if fully committed to such policies on a national level.

Seen on a map, Canada is as tall as it is wide. Since almost all Canadians live within easy driving distance of our southern border with the United States, 'the north' is often taken to refer to almost all of the country. This discussion, however, is centred on the Northwest Territories and Yukon, the two northern jurisdictions which, because of their territorial political status, have limited self-government, and whose land and most natural resources are controlled by the Federal Government in Ottawa. Together they account for 40 per cent of Canada's land mass but much less than 1 per cent of its population, and have been called, justly, Canada's colonies (Coates, 1985).[2]

Although both visionaries and buccaneers have described the north as a treasurehouse of riches, the more common view of its place in our national life has been that of a cold storage room; a reserve of space and resources that might come in handy when we need it. It is thus both opportunity and liability; in contemporary terms, a *problem* of economic development. The objective of this discussion is to show why the various

255

solutions advanced have not included, and are not likely to include, the contemporary bundle of free market policies.

Background

The northern territories consist entirely of the arctic (tundra) and subarctic (boreal forest) environments, and are bounded by sea coasts frozen over for most of the year. Winters are long and intensely cold, and permafrost (permanently frozen ground) is normally found below the thick layer that thaws each summer. Under these conditions biochemical processes are slow, biological productivity is but a fraction of that in more temperate environments, and the degradation of the environment by human activity and pollution is a major concern.

While mineral and energy resources exist in no less abundance in the northern territories than in other parts of Canada (or the world), these are typically much more costly to extract and transport owing to the engineering requirements of cold and ice, distance from markets and the difficulty of attracting labour. The north continues to be a very high-cost environment, exceeded only by Antarctica and the deep ocean bottoms. Comparative advantage, the *sina qua non* of free market economics, is virtually non-existent in the north.

The entire population of the north could be seated at a single major outdoor sporting event. The indigenous peoples (Inuit, Dene and Metis) account for a large proportion of the resident population (more than half in the Northwest Territories). Most are scattered in about seventy small villages (most without road access), typically of 500–1,500 inhabitants each. The non-Native population, in contrast, is concentrated in a few regional centres, modern communities equivalent to small towns in the south. This pattern has persisted for many decades and seems unlikely to change. The Northern population as a whole constitutes an insignificant market, and at most locations it is lower than the threshold level of commercial viability for all but the most rudimentary enterprises.

Not surprisingly, few investors, whether large or small, have seen the north as an attractive place to put their money. From the conventional economic perspective, the problem of northern development is not whether or how to regulate capital but how to get it there in the first place.

Since the arrival of Europeans, the expansion of the northern economy (in the provinces as well as the territories) has been fuelled by a succession of staple exports: furs, whale oil and baleen, minerals, timber and energy. Most were developed by large private corporations granted exclusive resource rights and state aid, or by Crown corporations (see, for example, Nelles, 1974; Rea, 1968; Zaslow, 1988).[3] Competitive or 'free market' development has been the exception: whaling in the Arctic, commercial fishing on the inland lakes, the modern fur trade at times and the Klondike gold rush of 1898. All of these could be entered initially with minimal capital and modest technology; none lasted long as such. Under competitive and unregulated conditions, resources were often rapidly depleted. Producers faced growing impoverishment from rising costs and declining prices, and even the merchants fared poorly under competitive conditions.

The post-Second World War era in the North was characterized by two major thrusts. On the one hand, the development of mineral and energy resources, by then identified as the key to the North's economic future, was promoted by all levels of government through the provision of tax incentives, subsidies, physical infrastructure and social overhead costs. Major energy or extractive projects, requiring billions of dollars and years of planning to bring to fruition, were to be undertaken by consortia of giant international corporations having the technical and organizational capacity to operate in such a difficult environment. Since these projects would promote national growth and generate public revenues, they received the political and financial support of governments.

On the other hand, the passage of general welfare legislation and the development of specific government programmes aimed at improving the standard of living of the Native population provided a basic safety net for all. Governments belatedly recognized that the Native population could no longer be sustained by hunting, fishing and trapping alone, and sought to assimilate them as rapidly as possible into the industrial future that was thought to be at hand.

The cooperation of state and capital in resource development and the provision of infrastructure has thus been the dominant economic strategy in the Canadian North for most of this century. The implementation of social democracy in Saskatchewan between 1944 and 1964 differed somewhat in emphasis and innovation from the initiatives taken in other provinces, but all jurisdictions regardless of political party in power have subscribed to a resource-extractive and export-led programme of northern economic development.

The contemporary economy

The prevailing development strategy has only partly fulfilled the hopes of its advocates, and at the same time led to some significant problems. Although some individual resource-extractive enterprises have been highly profitable, the public costs have been high in terms of both direct government expenditures on infrastructure and subsidies, and indirect expenditures on mitigating the adverse effects of development. Although touted as a means of improving Native people's economic well-being, only recently, and as a consequence of considerable public and government pressure, has there been any significant Native employment in the resource sector. Resource development has generally proceeded more slowly than expected, and as a source of public revenues has contributed little to the total public expenditure levels. The northern economy continues to be weakly integrated internally, highly dependent on imports of labour, capital, goods and services, and thus highly vulnerable to external shocks.[4]

A distinctive bimodal economy has emerged in the North.[5] On the one hand there is an urban-style wage economy in a few larger centres, in which a large proportion of workers are highly skilled and well paid. The labour force, mostly non-Native and short-term resident, is employed mainly in public administration and services, and to a lesser extent in resource extraction and defence.

On the other hand there is the village or Native economy. It is not a rural economy in the conventional sense: almost no one lives permanently outside a village, there is no scattered farm population making its living on small private plots of land. The village economy is sustained instead by hunting, fishing and trapping which occurs over vast tracts of communal lands and waters. These are supplemented by local wage employment and government transfer payments, as well as some direct links to the industrial economy.

The changing political context

Both the goals and the methods of economic development in the North have been modified significantly since the early 1970s. This change is a result of growing resistance within the North, as well as of the limited success of post-war policies from southern perspectives.

Since at least 1970, the Federal Government's northern development policy has recognized on paper, if not always in practice, that local needs and aspirations, environmental concerns and national sovereignty in the Arctic have at least as great a claim on public policy as (and may not always be consistent with) large-scale mineral and energy development. Since 1974, northern megaprojects have all been made subject to public review procedures, the most notable of which was the Mackenzie Valley Pipeline Inquiry (Berger, 1977).[6] The Federal Government also acknowledged the various outstanding aboriginal land claims in the North, and the growing political power of Native people to pursue those claims. Several have been formally resolved or are under active negotiation: the pattern has been to establish new administrative and economic institutions under the control of Native people, and to provide them with preferential access to certain economic opportunities as well as fee-simple title to large tracts of land (Abele, 1987; Dacks, 1981). These have been important gains for northerners (limited though they may be when compared to original objectives), achieved through intense political struggle.

Since the late 1960s, the focus of resource development in the territorial North has been on oil and gas. Energy megaprojects were promoted by the Federal Government as providing greater and more lasting economic benefits than mines, and in the 1970s, when North American self-sufficiency seemed worth paying any price for, Arctic oil development seemed imminent.[7] It required, however, massive investment by major foreign-owned oil companies. In response to strong nationalist sentiment, the Federal Government created a national oil company (PetroCanada) and the National Energy Policy to spur the pace and reap some of the benefits.

Since the mid-1980s, oil prices have made Arctic development seem less attractive, and both the multinationals and PetroCanada are less active there. As the dream of rapid development has faded, so too has the dream of financing northern government through resource royalties and taxes. During the 1980s, federal expenditures rose nearly fourfold, much of this in grants to multinational oil companies under the Petroleum Incentives Program (which accounted for virtually all of the rise in territorial gross domestic product). Federal Government revenues from the North, on the other hand, are less than 20 per cent of expenditures and are rising slowly.

The Federal Government's problem is that big capital has withdrawn from the development partnership. The much-vaunted economic 'take-off' to growth and development has not occurred. Casting about for substitute partners in the private sector, the Federal Government sees only small and mostly resident business, hence its rather astonishing recent conversion to renewable resource development and tourism as the basis for a northern economic development strategy (DIAND, 1988).

The emergence of a new vision

It is under these circumstances that a new consensus has emerged among northerners — Native and non-Native alike — not only about the need for greater autonomy but also about the economic and political directions necessary for the future. Important sources of division and conflict remain, and the consensus may prove fragile, but few would have anticipated this convergence of views a decade ago. The new consensus centres around the following points.[8]

First, and perhaps most important, there must be some means of stabilizing the northern economy and insulating it as much as possible from uncontrollable external shocks. Following the sharp decline of oil and gas development in the recession of the 1980s, it is now widely recognized within the North that neither the Federal Government nor the multinationals can be expected to provide the necessary solutions.[9] Instead, economic diversification is now seen as both necessary and possible, and this can come about only through northern initiative, although it requires federal support.

The old development philosophy no longer serves the northern interest, even as perceived by the local economic élite. The new emphasis is on import substitution, local preference, self-reliance and self-sufficiency. Diversification is to be encouraged by government support through performance incentives, subsidies and the use of regulatory powers. The use of Crown development corporations may increase, especially with respect to economic development ventures in the smaller communities.

Secondly, there is a much greater recognition of the importance of subsistence activities, especially as pursued by Native people in the smaller communities. Food from the land is one of very few sectors of real self-sufficiency. The promotion of this domestic sector requires maintaining the integrity of the land and resource base, and security of access and tenure, through active resource and environmental management, innovative property and management systems, and the provision of producer subsidies and programmes.[10]

The acknowledgement of the place of the domestic sphere is part of a now widespread recognition of the importance and viability of a mixed economy, based on a balance between staple export development, a healthy domestic sphere and continued high levels of public investment, to meet the social and cultural as well as the narrow economic needs of the North. The need for government investment will not decline in the foreseeable future; the debate focuses instead on the most desirable direction of this investment and on how to obtain maximum local control over it.

Few northerners now regard the multinationals as either the only or even the most desirable mechanisms by which development and diversification will occur. There is much greater emphasis on locally based enterprise, and hence (not surprisingly) much talk of the need for an entrepreneurial culture. However, some of the largest pools of local capital are those held by Native development corporations that have come into being through the claims settlement process. These only partially resemble profit-making corporations. They are constitutionally recognized entities which have special responsibilities to their shareholders (claims beneficiaries) beyond the narrowly economic. Also, they cannot be sold to non-beneficiaries and hence cannot be 'privatized'.

Finally, self-reliance and prosperity in the smaller communities rely primarily on the development of renewable resources, whether for domestic provisioning, commercial sale and export, or as a base for tourism. Because this resource base is so vulnerable to competing forms of development and to pollution and degradation, a key objective is control over and active use of resource and environmental management tools for both conservation and economic ends. The capabilities and uses of public regulatory authority are highly valued by many. These facts give life to the concept of sustainable development in the North, and their implementation is a central focus of public policy debate there. Part of that debate involves the maintenance of communal aboriginal property rights *vis à vis* superimposed western private property rights in the system of land tenure and resource management.

This consensus is by no means complete, nor is it overtly or conventionally 'social democratic' in nature, despite the election of two successive social democratic governments in the Yukon Territory. New forces and prospects, perhaps especially a major development initiative, could fracture it.

First, there is a strong streak of anti-government, anti-bureaucratic feeling in the North, which is shared by the resident non-Native small business class and the Native population. The former especially expresses this through a populist free market rhetoric. The small and recently developed, but growing, Native entrepreneurial class has also adopted a pro-business stance. The emergence of a Native economic élite has been fostered by government economic assistance programmes as well as by the insistence by the Federal Government, in aboriginal claims negotiations, on the establishment of corporate structures to handle the land and money assets of beneficiaries.[11] There are Natives and non-Natives alike who yearn for 'the good old days' when megaprojects promised a quick pay-off.

Secondly, there is a widespread resentment about the implementation and effects of social programmes in the North. The sedentarization of the Native population in the 1960s came about chiefly through massive government investment in housing and public services, and the extension of welfare state programmes to circumstances in which these payments formed the core of personal income rather than supplementing it. A common view among non-Native northerners is that these circumstances, along with government acting as employer of first resort in the absence of a private sector, have created a culture of welfare dependency among

Native people which is inimical to productive work and enterprise. This can be changed only through private enterprise and 'real' economic development replacing government activity.[12] Yet many Native people also resent certain social programmes on the grounds that these were forced upon them with no consideration of local needs or ways of doing things, and eventually robbed them of their independence.

Behind the rhetoric, however, there is for the most part a sober recognition that, whether people like it or not, the northern economy is government-driven and will remain so for a long time. What northern business needs, therefore, is not government abdication from the market-place but government support there. This is accompanied by a growing realization that the smaller communities are now permanent, and home to a large part of the northern population. Neither mega-projects nor small business can alone solve their economic problems. With the prospects for most forms of commercially profitable enterprise in the communities dim, the best that can be hoped for is financial viability: break-even or non-profit operations run on cost-accounting principles. Because this view of economic reality is now apparently shared by the Federal Government, the short-term outlook for maintaining and even implementing the consensus would seem to be at least fair.

Sources and effects of free market policies

The chief obstacles to implementing the new northern vision are the restricted constitutional authority of the two territories, their dependence on federal grants for the bulk of their operating budgets and the effects of nationally implemented free market policies. The most obvious expressions of these policies are deficit reduction initiatives involving tax reforms and programme cuts, the Canada–United States Free Trade Agreement (hereafter referred to as the FTA), and the removal of government from the market-place through deregulation and privatization. The North is more insulated than most of the country from some of the effects of these policies, while being more exposed to other effects.

The Federal Government has abandoned its traditional policies of regulation and government involvement in the areas of transport, communications and utilities. While this has led to major restructuring in the country as a whole, the North has been largely unaffected. Air is the sole mode of transport to most northern points: it can be neither abandoned nor made competitive. Some Crown corporations in utilities and surface transport have been sold, but most were purchased by the territorial governments or Native corporations. Their functions, too, cannot be abandoned.

The North is much less well insulated from the effects of tax reform. Recent Federal Government initiatives in this area include levelling out graduated income tax rates in favour of high earners, and of shifting the overall tax burden from income to consumption, in the form of a new VAT-type Goods and Services Tax. The effects will be especially noticeable in the North, where Native people's incomes are lower, and prices are high (as much as twice southern levels in the small communities, especially for such essentials as heat, utilities and transport — all of which will be subject to the new tax). Northerners could now pay double the tax, as well as double the price, that Canadians living in the South pay for the same consumer items.

The major regional effects of the FTA on the North are anticipated to include the following:

1. Limiting government's ability to play a directing role in the economy by such commonly used means as subsidizing input costs to industry, imposing local processing requirements prior to export and local preference in procurement and investment opportunities.
2. Reduction of the effectiveness of certain benefits negotiated by aboriginal groups in claims settlements, especially pertaining to economic benefits and resource rights, by limiting government control and opening the way to legal challenges to preferential access and other rights.
3. Opening the system of subsidies to the domestic economy to legal challenge because of its close linkages to commercial activity and trade.

Not all of these effects are spelled out in the FTA at present, but will depend on the outcome of forthcoming subsidy negotiations with the United States (Abele and Usher, 1988). The philosophical basis of the agreement, however, is clearly to replace economic strategies based on public control and incentives, and import substitution, with market forces and open access.

This leaves the expenditure-cutting side of deficit reduction as the policy initiative most likely to have severe adverse effects on the North. However, the cuts most likely to affect the North will not be those introduced and promoted as 'short-term pain for long-term gain', but through the slow starvation of programmes through lack of funding to which the Federal Government will still claim a commitment in principle.

Thus, direct reductions in social programmes, which are already occurring nationally, will have the least important income effects in the North. Personal income, and indeed community viability, is much more heavily dependent on government spending on public services and infrastructure than on transfers to persons. Yet it is the key expenditure areas such as the federal-territorial or Native economic development agreements, federal grants to the territorial governments, Native peoples' programmes, and the implementation of Native claims agreements, that are the must vulnerable to cut-backs, precisely because they are regional or sectoral rather than national in scope.

To date these reductions have come slowly, for two reasons. One is that few of these programmes are being frontally attacked either ideologically or practically. Modifications, and failure to increase funding levels, are the norm, rather than the slashing and abandonment of programmes (see, for example, Department of Supply and Services, 1986; Abele and Graham, 1988). The other is that the gradual and continuing process of devolution of responsibilities from the Federal to the territorial governments means that some programmes and expenditures are cut from the books of the former while being taken up by the latter.

The North is thus at least temporarily insulated from many direct cuts, because of devolution and because of the fixed formulas by which federal funding is provided to their operating budgets as a whole. In the longer run, however, it remains to be seen whether the territorial governments will be forced to do their own budget cutting when these funding arrangements are negotiated.

The prospects

Free market policies are no more able to generate economic development, even in the most conventional sense (let alone provide for the North's needs), now than in earlier times. Free market rhetoric is no less common in the North than elsewhere, but there is a widespread recognition that an exclusive reliance on market forces, especially in combination with any significant withholding of public investment, can only perpetuate the old boom–bust cycle, and would condemn the smaller communities to permanent impoverishment. If the present consensus in the North dissolves, it will be because some will find the old strategy of an industry–government alliance for megaprojects once again attractive. No political or economic interest group advocates, or would support, government withdrawal.

It is the Federal Government that holds the purse strings, however, and the Federal Government that wants to reduce its spending. The question is what strategies are open for it to do so. Abandoning the communities seems unlikely, although it is not without precedent. In considering the level of social expenditures in the Arctic nearly forty years ago, the finance minister of the day enquired whether it might not be cheaper to bring the Inuit out of the North and put them up permanently in Ottawa's leading hotel. In the 1950s and 1960s, considerations of efficiency and modernization led to forced resettlement to 'growth poles' and 'reception centres' in many parts of the circumpolar world, including Greenland, Newfoundland and Labrador, and a few cases in the Northwest Territories. There were also some successful cases of resistance, and these programmes have since been discarded in the territorial North.

Community abandonment now seems unlikely to happen by official policy in the territorial North and especially the Arctic. One reason, and perhaps the most important, is sovereignty. With Canada's authority over the Northwest Passage and offshore Arctic waters under challenge (chiefly from the United States), the unsettling of the Arctic would send an inappropriate message to other circumpolar nations. There is an increasing military presence in the North, which would be even harder to justify to a somewhat sceptical public if combined with civilian withdrawal.

Another reason is the complex constitutional, legal and moral obligations that Canada has entered into with its Native people. They live disproportionately in the North and in small communities and reserves. These locations are thus the home and hearth of aboriginal society and culture in the modern day, and could not be abandoned without serious disintegration and disorder. There have been and will continue to be reductions in programme expenditures, and failures by the Government to live up to its obligations. But the Government simply cannot withdraw from these communities, leaving the economy to a non-existent private sector. Behind this may lurk a recognition that the problems created by a too-rapid migration to the larger northern centres would create problems even more costly to fix than continuing the invest in the communities.

Finally, it seems unlikely any level of government can be seen to withdraw from its obligations of environmental monitoring, management and protection. This requires not simply programme expenditures, which are substantial, but also a willingness either to forgo certain types of economic development opportunities, or to render them much more costly. Budget cuts may limit the effectiveness of environmental programmes for the time being, but they will remain in principle and can thus be more easily revived.

The prospects for any thorough implementation of free market policies in the Canadian North are sharply limited by the region's physical geography, economic history and current political considerations. Such indeed is the case throughout the circumpolar world. Alaska, an apparent exception, has a strong private sector because of a national commitment to oil self-sufficiency and a very high level of military expenditure there, as well as more favourable geographical conditions in the southern half of the state. In Canada, free market policies could only be imposed by the Federal Government, and would meet considerable local resistance.

It may well be that the effects of deficit reduction will hit the North hard over the next few years. No one, however, will trumpet this as a triumph of free market policies. When the Federal Government once again feels it has money to spend, it will reassert itself in the North. For better or worse, Canada is committed to northern development, and northern development, whatever the variety, cannot occur without government as partner.

Notes

1. The policies loosely referred to as free market in this context are aimed at the globalization of markets and corporations, and involve eliminating the role of national and local governments in stimulating economic growth by protection or subsidy, in regulating commerce for social purposes, in providing public services, and in maintaining social welfare. In sum they constitute an attempt to restructure the world economy by eliminating restrictions on capital, and should not be confused with economists' theoretical models in which all actors have equal access to the market-place, and governments' role is to ensure such access by preventing monopolies.
2. An equally large part of Canada, the mid-north, is divided among seven provincial jurisdictions.
3. In Canada, the state retains title to all of these resources, rather than selling them to the highest bidder. The effect is that the state, far from taking a *laissez-faire* approach to development, has a direct interest, as manager, in promoting the development of its resources by private capital or, if necessary, itself.
4. See Berger (1977), Brody (1977), Usher (1987) and Watkins (1977) for a variety of critiques of the social, environmental and economic costs of northern development. Between the mid-1970s and the mid-1980s, the amount government paid out in subsidies and capital assistance to corporations was over six times the amount transferred to persons under social programmes. Nearly 80 per cent of these funds was directed to exploration companies under the petroleum incentives provisions of the now-defunct National Energy Program (Weick, in press). For a recent account of the relationship between resource development and Native employment, see Abele (1989).
5. The term bimodal is used here in preference to 'dual economy' because the latter generally implies a disconnection between the two economies, and obscures the fundamental linkages between them in the North. See Usher and Weihs (1989).
6. This was the most wide-ranging and innovative of numerous public reviews of major northern projects, and was an important factor in cancelling the proposed multi-billion dollar investment. The result was seen as a major victory by Native people, environmentalists and nationalists. See Page (1986).
7. In the Yukon Territory, where the mining industry has dominated

historically, by 1982 there was not a single operating mining property for the first time in eighty-five years, and the industry has since been revived only with public assistance. Mining as a whole has been somewhat more stable in the NWT, although most individual mines have had a short life, leading to town-site closures. Rates of employment and training for Native people have been much lower in mining than in oil and gas.

8. Both territorial governments have undertaken major economic policy reviews recently, with public participation. See Yukon (1987) and NWT (1988).

9. The decline resulted not only in the loss of wage employment but also hardship and failure for many small businesses established (often with the direct encouragement of the oil companies) specifically to service the oil and gas boom. This was a major setback to the newly emergent business class in the western Arctic.

10. See, for example, Usher and Weihs (1989). Support programmes to provide cash to domestic producers, similar to agricultural support programmes except that payments are based on a combination of need and effort rather than production, are in place in northern Quebec and are under active consideration in the territorial North.

11. The imposition of a corporate structure has met with some cultural resistance in the NWT as has been the case in Arctic Quebec and in Alaska.

12. Like all enduring myths, it contains elements of truth. It is further argued that these huge expenditures and state intervention in the communities have led to massive dislocation, low education and incomes, social disintegration. This would seem to confirm the diagnosis of the free market advocates, that intervention is inherently counterproductive. Yet these are also the consequences of welfare imposed from above, the loss of control at community level and the absence of economic programmes.

I am grateful to Frances Abele and Ed Weick for their critical review of this manuscript in draft stage.

References

Abele, F. (1987) 'Canadian contradictions: Forty years of northern political development', *Arctic* **40** (4), 310–20.

Abele, F. (1989) *Gathering Strength*, Calgary: Arctic Institute of North America.

Abele, F. and K. A. Graham (1988) 'Plus que ca change ... Northern and Native policy', K. A. Graham (ed.) *How Ottawa Spends, 1988–89: Heading into the stretch*, Ottawa: Carleton University Press.

Abele, F. and P. J. Usher (1988) *A New Economic Development Policy for the North? The impact of the Canada–U.S. Free Trade Agreement*, Ottawa: Canadian Centre for Policy Alternatives.

Berger, T. R. (1977) *Northern Frontier, Northern Homeland: The Report of the Mackenzie Valley Pipeline Inquiry*, Ottawa: Dept Indian Affairs and Northern Development.

Brody, H. (1977) 'Industrial impact in the Canadian North', *Polar Record* **18** (115), 333–9.

Coates, K. (1985) *Canada's Colonies: A history of the Yukon and Northwest Territories*, Toronto: James Lorimer.

Dacks, G. (1981) *A Choice of Futures*, Toronto: Methuen.

Department of Supply and Services (1986) *Improved Program Delivery: Indians and Natives. A Study Team Report to the Task Force on Program Review* Ottawa, Supply and Services.

DIAND (Department of Indian Affairs and Northern Development) (1988) *A Northern Political and Economic Framework*, Ottawa: Supply and Services Canada.

Nelles, H. V. (1974) *The Politics of Development*, Toronto: Macmillan.

NWT (Northwest Territories; Government) (1988) *Directions for the 1990s*, Yellowknife: Northwest Territories.

Page, R. (1986) *Northern Development, The Canadian Dilemma*, Toronto: McClelland & Stewart.

Rea, K. J. (1968) *The Political Economy of the Canadian North*, Toronto: University of Toronto Press.

Usher, P. J. (1987) 'The North: one land, two ways of life', in L.J. McCann (ed.) *Heartland and Hinterland, A Geography of Canada*, 2nd ed. Scarborough: Prentice-Hall, 483–529.

Usher, P. J. and F. Weihs (1989) *Towards a Strategy for Supporting the Domestic Economy of the Northwest Territories*. Background study prepared for the NWT Legislative Assembly's Special Committee on the Northern Economy. Yellowknife: Dept Culture and Communications.

Watkins, M. (1977) 'From underdevelopment to development', in M. Watkins (ed.) *Dene Nation: The colony within*, Toronto: University of Toronto Press. 84–99.

Weick, E. R. (in press) 'The North', in M. Watkins (ed.) *Handbooks to the Modern World — Canada*, New York: Facts on File.

Yukon (Government) (1987) *The Things That Matter*. A report of Yukoners' views on the future of their economy and their society, Yukon 2000.

Zaslow, M. (1988) *The Northward Expansion of Canada, 1914–1967*, Toronto: McClelland & Stewart.

11

Clawback

The demise of universality in the Canadian welfare state

Ken Battle
National Council of Welfare, Ottawa, Canada

Imagine a social programme that operated like this: every family with children would receive a monthly cheque from the government to help with their child-rearing expenses. However, come income tax time, families with incomes above a certain level would have to pay back all of the benefits they had received during the course of the previous year. In other words, the government would use the income tax system to recover all of the benefits it had delivered to higher-income parents through its child benefits programme.

This might seem a peculiar way to run a social programme. Why would the state want to go to the bother and expense of sending out and then collecting back the same amount of cash from some of its citizens? Why would it want to pay upper-income families any child benefits at all, if at the end of the year they had to turn around and return all the money back to the government?

Such a social programme would in effect deliver interest-free loans to higher-income families with children. They could use the money as they see fit from January to December, but come income tax time next spring they would have to pay it all back to the government – without interest. Why would a government want to loan money at zero rate of interest to affluent parents?

Bizarre as it sounds, this is not a mental experiment on social programme design that went awry. Canada's national Conservative Government, led by Prime Minister Brian Mulroney to a second electoral majority in the autumn of 1988, announced just such a give-to-all/take-back-from-the-rich scheme in its April 1989 budget. Although the country's two major income security programmes for children and the aged – family allowances and Old Age Security – will continue to deliver monthly payments on behalf of all Canadians under age 18 and over age 65, the income tax system will be used to collect back all of the benefits paid to parents and pensioners with incomes over $50,000. This schizophrenic scheme has been dubbed the 'clawback' by its critics, who prefer a more graphic term than the government's newspeak bureaucratese 'repayment of social transfers' (Wilson, 1989a).

The clawback proposal marks the end of universality, a long-established and supposedly sacrosanct principle of Canada's federal welfare state. It is the most significant development in Canadian social policy in a generation. Yet, apart from rote and ineffectual attacks on the clawback from the opposition Liberal and New Democratic parties bolstered by more hard-hitting criticism from a handful of interest groups representing the poor and elderly, this fundamental shift appears to be occurring virtually unnoticed by the media and electorate and with no apparent political pain whatsoever to the ruling Conservatives.

I say 'appears to be occurring' and 'no apparent political pain' because the clawback was not yet legislated at the time of writing. The income tax amendments necessary to put the social programme changes into effect are now before the House of Commons (Autumn of 1989), which has just reconvened following its summer recess. The opposition parties will renew their attack in debate; one major national social policy organization (the National Council of Welfare, an advisory body to the Minister of National Health and Welfare) published a scathing critique of the proposals in September; and seniors' groups, armed with the National Council of Welfare's arguments, are mounting a campaign against the clawback on the old age pension. Whether the Tories will back down on their plans or at least amend their proposals remains to be seen: I suspect they will not, since the Government can use its majority to ram the clawback through Parliament, and may not want to be seen as backing down in the face of the same 'grey power' that it bowed to once before in 1985 when the finance minister rescinded his scheme to partially de-index the old age pension.

What makes the Government's 1989 budget all the more remarkable is that – if the clawback goes through, as seems inevitable – the Minister of finance will have managed to effect a veritable sea-change in Canadian social policy, whereas his maiden budget in 1985 provoked a tidal wave of criticism from across the nation simply for proposing a relatively minor amendment to the Old Age Security programme – switching from full to partial indexation of benefit rates. To keep from capsizing after his first venture into the perilous waters of social policy reform, Finance Minister Michael Wilson had to jettison his scheme to partially de-index income security payments to the elderly. Yet he and his government have subsequently proved to be much more adept than they are generally given credit for at fighting the deficit – one of the troika of major Tory policy preoccupations to date, the others being negotiating a free trade agreement with the United States and the Meech Lake constitutional accord with the provinces – through a potent brew of tax increases and social spending cuts, the most recent being the looming and largely unlamented death of universal child and elderly benefits.

This chapter argues that Canada's ruling Conservatives have accomplished their fiscal restraint programme largely by means of a skilful strategy of technical changes to the tax/transfer system that are deliberately arcane and difficult to understand. They have capitalized on the byzantine nature of Canada's labyrinth of taxation and social benefits by further complicating that system and thus attempting – quite successfully, on the whole – to insulate their policies from public criticism and voter resistance. They have cloaked their tax increases and spending cuts in the rhetoric of fairness and compassion for the poor, even though in reality most low- and middle-income Canadians have been hit much harder by Tory restraint measures than have the well-to-do.

The chapter focuses on the imminent demise of universality in the Canadian welfare state through a detailed analysis of changes to the federal child benefits system under the Mulroney administration. However, first I must set the scene by reviewing the Tories' major methods and results in restraining social spending and raising taxes since they took power in 1984.[1]

The technology of fiscal restraint

Although conservative editorialists and the business and financial community think he has not gone far enough, in fact Canada's Minister of Finance has chopped the deficit from $47 billion in the fiscal year 1984–5 to a projected $27 billion in 1990–1 – for a substantial 43 per cent real decrease.[2] The corporate sector is also displeased at the Government's heavier reliance on tax hikes than on spending cuts; for instance, measures announced in the most recent (1989) budget will save some $5.2 billion in 1989–90, of which $3.7 billion or 71 per cent will come from tax increases and $1.5 billion or only 29 per cent from spending reductions. Nonetheless, the Finance Minister has managed to flatten out the social spending curve – despite the relentless pressure of an increasing elderly population on publicly insured health services and social programmes – and to trim overall spending on Federal Government programmes from $107 billion in 1984–5 to $104 billion in 1990–1. And despite the implacable high-interest rate policy of the Bank of Canada, Finance Minister Wilson would appear to have put the breaks on escalating public debt-financing charges, which rose sharply from $28 billion in 1984–5 to $39 billion in 1989–90 but will ease to $38 billion in 1990–1.

Each Tory budget has increased one or more federal taxes. The 1985 budget raised personal income taxes by abolishing the federal tax reduction (which helped low- and middle-income taxpayers), imposing surtaxes and, most important of all in terms of its long-term impact, partially de-indexing the income tax system: tax brackets and personal exemptions are now adjusted only by the amount that inflation exceeds 3 per cent a year, thereby guaranteeing the federal and provincial treasuries billions in extra revenue over time thanks to inflation-induced tax hikes on individual taxpayers. The 1985 budget and each budget since raised federal sales and/or excise taxes. Corporate tax concessions have been trimmed or tightened as well, and the Government recently raised unemployment insurance premiums.

Personal income taxes continue to collect the lion's share of federal tax revenues, rising from 41.3 per cent in 1984–5 to a projected 45.6 per cent of total revenues in 1990–1; the tax take from federal personal income tax went from $36 billion in 1984–5 to $52.7 billion in 1990–1 for a sizeable 46 per cent real increase. However, there has been a significant shift in the tax mix towards consumption taxes: federal sales and excise taxes contributed only 19.9 per cent of federal revenues when the Tories came to power but will rise to 25.3 per cent by 1990–1, and their dollar value went from $17.4 billion in 1984–5 to a projected $29.2 billion in 1990–1 – for a hefty real increase of 68 per cent. The controversial Goods and Services Tax (a form of value added tax), which the Government plans to put in place of the old manufacturers' sales tax in 1991, will accelerate the regressive policy of shifting the tax mix from income towards consumption. Corporate tax revenues rose by 21 per cent from $11.6 billion to $13.9 billion from 1984–5 to 1990–1, but their share fell from 13.2 to 12.1 per cent of total revenues because other taxes went up much more. Overall, federal tax revenues increased by close to one-third, from $87.4 billion in 1984–5 to a projected $115.4 billion in 1990–1 (NCW, 1989a, Table F, Figures 12 and 13).

The Finance Minister's tax changes have not created the fairer tax system that he promised.[3] On the contrary, most lower-income Canadians – especially the working poor – are shouldering a more onerous tax burden than they did when the Tories came to power.

Despite the 1986 introduction of a modest refundable sales tax credit for households with incomes under $15,000, federal sale tax hikes have hurt the poor as well as middle- and upper-income consumers. On the one hand, the 1988 income tax reform's conversion of personal tax exemptions and most deductions to credits, was a progressive step. On the other hand, the counteracting regressive changes – lowering the top tax rate from 34 to 29 per cent, introducing a $100,000 lifetime capital gains exemption, doubling the tax deduction for child care expenses, and plans to triple and fully index the tax deduction limit for Registered Retirement Savings Plans – have awarded generous income tax savings to most upper-income taxpayers. The partial indexation of the income tax system has hit lower-income taxpayers proportionately harder than those in higher-income groups and is pushing the taxpaying threshold further and further below the poverty line, adding more and more working poor families and individuals to the tax rolls with each passing year.

The inequitable distribution of income tax increases under the Conservatives is glaring. For instance, a couple with combined spouses' earnings of $20,000 and two children will see its federal and provincial income taxes increase from $175 in 1984 to $822 in 1991, which amounts to a 370 per cent real increase; a middle-income family earning $49,000 will experience a 17 per cent rise in its income taxes from $7,903 in 1984 to $9,099 in 1991: and a wealthy couple earning $123,000 will enjoy a 6 per cent cut in its taxes from $34,775 in 1984 to $34,076 in 1991.[4]

The Finance Minister has promised to protect the poor from the new Goods and Services Tax. Poor and modest-income households will be eligible for a larger refundable sales tax credit. Unfortunately, the boost in the sales tax credit will simply match the increase in the sales tax for most lower-income families and individuals, leaving them with much the same after-credit sales tax burden as before; the happy exception is single-parent families, which will be somewhat better off at first as a result of an adult equivalent credit for one child.[5] The new sales tax credit and its threshold for maximum benefits will be only partially indexed, so that over time, inflation will eat away at the value of the credit, the sales tax burden on those with below-average incomes will mount steadily, and fewer and fewer Canadians will be eligible for the sales tax credit.

The Mulroney Government has not taken a broadaxe to social programmes, but used a scalpel instead. Nonetheless, the Tories have managed to cut ever-increasing millions from the social spending budget even though outlays on income security programmes for the elderly have escalated steadily due to swelling numbers of recipients and the Government's failure to partially de-index the old age pension. As we shall examine in more detail below, the Minister of Finance partially de-indexed federal child benefits. He also reduced federal transfers to the provincial governments for health and post-secondary education. His government is in the process of reforming the unemployment insurance programme; eligibility requirements are being tightened, the duration of benefits reduced, and $2.9 billion in federal funding of the programme shifted onto employers and employees in the form of premium increases.

The partial indexation of child benefits and the personal income tax system and changes in the indexing formula for federal transfers to the provincial governments for health and post-secondary education have reaped enormous fiscal rewards for the Federal Government – in the order of $26 billion from 1986 through 1990, or about the size of the annual deficit. These technical changes have been politically astute as well, remaining virtually invisible to all but a few experts. Most Members of Parliament and the media seem to find partial indexation incomprehensible, so it is not surprising that the Finance Minister plans to use the same technique in the Goods and Services Tax credit and, as we shall see, the clawback on child and elderly benefits.

'Reform' of child benefits, 1985–90

Canada's child benefits system typifies its social security system as a whole, with all its contradictions, complexities, strengths and weaknesses. Before chronicling the tortuous tale of the Conservatives' changes to child benefits over the past five years, it is necessary first to give a brief account and critique of the system which they inherited from the Trudeau Liberals in 1984.

Most Canadians can name only one child benefit – the family allowance or 'baby bonus' as it is popularly termed – but in fact the Federal Government offers parents several programmes which differ in terms of their stated objectives, eligibility criteria, benefit rates, administrative features and distributional impact. In 1984, there were five child benefits – the aforementioned family allowance, the children's tax exemption, the refundable child tax credit, the married equivalent exemption, and the child care expense deduction. (The provincial governments in Saskatchewan, Manitoba and Quebec provide various types of child benefit, but I will not consider them here since this article deals only with federal programmes, which are potentially available to all Canadians.) I first describe each programme separately, and then assess how they fit together as a 'system'. I generally use the past tense in discussing the system as it existed in 1984, even though all of the programmes still operate today, albeit with varying degrees of Tory modification which will be explained later.

Canada's oldest child benefit is the children's tax exemption, introduced during the First World War as part of the personal income tax system – the latter a 'temporary' measure to help finance the war effort that proved too useful to discard after the Armistice. In 1918, as in the mid-1980s, the children's tax exemption was intended to provide a benefit – in the form of income tax savings – to taxpayers with dependent children in recognition of their child-rearing expenses. According to the principle of 'horizontal equity' the children's tax exemption adjusted the income tax burden as between taxpayers with equal incomes but unequal demands on those incomes as a result of the presence or absence of children. It is significant that this first child benefit should be delivered through the income tax system – a vehicle which has played a growing role in Canadian federal social policy over the past decade.

Also spawned by war, the family allowances programme was enacted in 1944 by the Liberal Government of Mackenzie King. Its designers envisaged this monthly cash benefit as serving at least three purposes – recognizing the contribution that parents make to society and the economy by raising future workers, taxpayers and citizens; providing financial assistance to help low- and middle-income husbands/fathers fill the gap between their wages and the costs of providing for their wife and children; and helping smooth the way from a wartime to peacetime economy by putting cash each month in the hands of housewives who, in turn, would recycle the money into the economy and so play their small part in priming the pump in the post-war world of Keynesian optimism. These three objectives can be characterized as the parental recognition, anti-poverty/income-supplementation and economic stimulus purposes of Canada's child benefits system. Presumably the latter rationale – which one rarely hears today, even from welfare state apologists – helped convince Mr King's less enthusiastic cabinet and caucus members to support or at least go along with the use of public funds to subsidize families with children.

The third major federal child benefit is the refundable child tax credit. Introduced by the Trudeau Government in 1978, this programme was designed to provide additional financial assistance to low- and middle-income parents. It is regarded as a significant advance in Canadian social policy because, for the first time, the federal income tax system was used to deliver a benefit not just to taxpayers, but also to poor parents with incomes below the taxpaying threshold. Moreover, instead of providing the benefit in the form of an exemption – which gives the largest tax savings to the well-off – the refundable child tax credit delivers the largest benefit to lower-income families with children, a diminishing amount to those with modest and average incomes, and no benefit to upper-income parents.

The two other child benefit programmes which the Conservatives inherited in 1984 were more limited in reach. The equivalent-to-married exemption gave single parents an income tax exemption for one of their children equal to the exemption for married taxpayers supporting a spouse not in the labour force; the equivalent-to-married exemption was substantially larger than the children's tax exemption (in 1984 they were $3,470 and $710, respectively) in recognition of the extra financial hardship facing single parents. The child care expense deduction provided a tax deduction of up to $2,000 for each child of 14 or under for whom receipted child care expenses are available and was intended to ease the child care costs of parents either in the paid labour force or taking training courses.

Social policy advocates had long criticized the pre-Tory system of federal child benefits as being inequitable, contradictory and overly complex. The root problem lay not so much in the multiple and potentially conflicting purposes of the system – which few observers recognized as a difficulty, though I think it is (for reasons examined later) – as in the delivery mechanisms employed. Underlying this critique is the belief that Canada's child benefits system should be universal in reach – it should serve all parents, regardless of their income - but progressive in impact – lower-income families should receive the largest benefits and well-off families smaller benefits.

The family allowances programme provides a flat-rate monthly benefit on behalf of all children under age 18, regardless of their parents' income. However, since 1973, family allowances have been counted as taxable income in the hands of the parent claiming the children's tax exemption (i.e. the parent with the higher income in the case of two-earner couples), which means that after-tax benefits are smallest for upper-income families. For example, in 1984 the family allowances for one child totalled $359: parents in the top tax bracket (34 per cent at that time) paid federal and provincial income taxes of $189 on their family allowances, leaving them with an after-tax benefit of $170; parents in the middle tax bracket (19 per cent) ended up with an after-tax benefit of $257; and parents too poor to pay tax received the full $359 per child.

In 1984, the refundable child tax credit provided $367 per child under age 18 to families with net income (from both parents) under $26,330; benefits above that level were reduced by 5 per cent, disappearing when net family income exceeded $33,670 for one child, $41,010 for two children and $48,350 for three children. For instance, families with two children and incomes less than $26,330 got the maximum credit of $734, families with net incomes of $30,000 got $550 and those at the $35,000 family income mark received refundable child tax credits totalling $300.

If the child benefits system comprised family allowances and the refundable child tax credit only, it would meet the criterion of universal and progressive, though total benefits – a maximum of $726 per child in 1984 – could hardly be considered adequate to fulfil either the anti-poverty or parental recognition objectives. However, substantial public funds were allocated to the other three child benefit programmes – the children's tax exemption, equivalent-to-married exemption and child care expense deduction – which, because they were tax exemptions, delivered their largest benefit to upper-income parents. The $710 children's tax exemption saved an $80,000 family with two children $660 in federal and provincial income taxes, compared to $506 for a middle-income $40,000 family, $418 for a $20,000 family and nothing at all for a $9,000 family below the taxpaying threshold. So also was the equivalent-to-married exemption a regressive social programme, delivering the largest benefit to the well-off, though in fact relatively few single parents enjoyed an income high enough to produce the maximum tax savings from the programme. The child care expense deduction is regressive not only because it is an exemption, but also by virtue of the fact that higher-income families can afford to spend more on child care (and thus qualify for the maximum $2,000 per child deduction) and are more likely to have their children in child care facilities that provide the receipts necessary to claim the deduction; many lower- and middle-income families also purchase child care, but from care-givers who do not provide receipts because they are working in the informal economy outside the income tax system.

Viewed as a system, Canadian child benefits in 1984 made little sense. Family allowances and the refundable child tax credit are progressive programmes which gear their largest benefit to low-income children, but the children's tax exemption, equivalent-to-married exemption and child care expense deduction were regressive schemes which excluded poor families and awarded their largest subsidy to the affluent. The overall distribution of child benefits resulting from this blend of opposites bore no systematic, rational or defensible relationship to financial need as measured by family income.

Figure 11.1 illustrates the roller-coaster pattern of child benefits in 1984 for two-earner couples at different income levels. Not only does the distribution of benefits show an up-and-down curve that might suggest that a drunkard designed the system, but the highest-income families fared the best. Their generous income tax savings from the children's tax exemption and child care expense deduction far outweighed their smaller after-tax family allowances and lack of the refundable child tax credit. Conservatives no less than liberals and social-democrats would have trouble defending a system that paid $1,913 in child benefits to a $120,000 family yet only $1,405 – over $500 less – to a poor family struggling to get by on an income of less than $10,000.

Measured in dollar terms, the worthy goal of supplementing the incomes of poor and modest-income families clearly took second place to the aim of ensuring upper-income parents received compensation for their child-rearing travails and adjusting their income tax burden *vis-à-vis* equally well-heeled taxpayers with no children to support. While the introduction of the refundable child tax credit in 1978 by the Government

Child benefits ($)

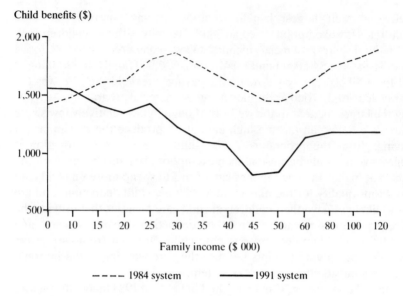

Family income ($ 000)

- - - - 1984 system   ————1991 system

Figure 11.1   *Total child benefits (constant $ 1984), two-earner couples with two children, 1984 and 1991*

of Pierre Elliot Trudeau had made the child benefits system more progressive and had strengthened somewhat its anti-poverty capacity, the Liberals' failure to deal with the regressive elements left the system only slightly less flawed than before.

Another failing of the child benefits system when the Tories took office was its inordinate complexity. Canadians can hardly be blamed for their general lack of knowledge and understanding of so complicated an array of cash transfers and tax subsidies for families with children, let alone the entire ramshackle apparatus of federal, provincial and municipal social programmes.

One programme – the family allowance – was delivered on its own, as a direct income transfer each month, while the other four benefits were delivered once a year by means of the income tax system. Few recipients knew how much child benefits they actually got, and many mistakenly believed they received more than they really did. Since it is a taxable benefit, the family allowance's after-tax value varies according to the higher-income spouse's marginal tax rate; the higher the marginal tax rate, the smaller the after-tax family allowance. The value (in the form of income tax savings) of the children's tax exemption, equivalent-to-married exemption and child care expense deduction also varied according to the taxpayer's tax bracket, except that the value increased with the marginal tax rate – the opposite to the family allowance. Unlike the family allowances and like the other tax-delivered benefits, the refundable tax credit is not a taxable benefit; its value depends not on the individual taxpayer's marginal tax rate, but rather on the interaction between the level of family income (i.e. from both parents) and a special tax rate (5 per cent of income above a threshold) separate from the income tax system's regular tax rates.

To confuse matters even more, the value of four of the child benefits – the family allowance, children's tax exemption, equivalent-to-married exemption and child care expense deduction – depended on their recipient's province as well as level of income. The territories and all the provinces save Quebec – which operates its own income tax system – calculate their income taxes as a percentage of basic federal tax, since the Federal Government collects both its and the provinces' and territories' income taxes through a joint tax form; however, the provincial and territorial rates vary from 43.0 per cent of basic federal tax for the Northwest Territories to 61.0 per cent for Newfoundland. As a result, the after-tax family allowance and the tax savings from the other three benefits varied from one province to another. Moreover, Quebec and Alberta have chosen to vary the federal family allowance rates paid to their families; Quebec varies the rate according to the number of children (the first gets least, the fourth or more get most), while Alberta varies the family allowance rate paid to its children by the age of the child (benefits increase with age).

Thus, although they were ostensibly federal programmes, in fact four of Canada's five national child benefits had a provincial dimension as well. The provinces collect through their income taxes a portion of the family allowances paid out by Ottawa. The provinces paid out, in the form of uncollected provincial income tax revenue, the child benefits delivered by means of exemptions and deductions. Only the refundable child tax credit is a purely federal programme with no provincial implications.

Although they were each paid out on behalf of children, the child benefits were delivered to parents. But even this seemingly innocuous aspect of the delivery of Canadian children's benefits applied another layer of complexity to the system. The monthly family allowance cheque is made out to the mother, but the higher-income parent – generally, still, the father – pays income tax on the benefit. The higher-income parent (read father) claimed the children's tax exemption, but the lower-income parent (read mother) claimed the child care expense deduction. The refundable child tax credit goes to the parent with the family allowance (i.e. normally the mother), but the income of both parents is taken into account in determining the family's eligibility for, and amount of, benefit from the credit.

A final criticism of Canada's pre-Tory child benefits system is its inadequate level of benefits. In 1984, the maximum benefit for poor families (from the two programmes to which they were all qualified, family allowances and the refundable child tax credit) came to $726 a year. While low-income families depended on this money to supplement their meagre incomes, child benefits could hardly be portrayed as a potent weapon in the (undeclared) war against poverty, as readily attested to by the fact that 1.2 million children under age 16 – one child in six – lived in poverty in 1984: $726 a year per child was insufficient to lift many families above the poverty line ($20,010 for a family of four living in a metropolitan centre like Vancouver, Toronto or Montreal), and those whose child benefits did bring their total income over the line still lived on modest incomes.[6]

With child-rearing costs running at around $3,000 a child, Canada's children's benefits only partially offset the financial burden borne by parents. The fact that upper-income parents received more benefits than low- and middle-income families made the relatively low level of child benefits all the more difficult to accept.

Women's lobbies such as the National Action Committee on the Status of Women – an umbrella group representing several hundred women's organizations of varying ideological (mainly Left and centrist) persuasion from across Canada – were and remain highly critical of the low level of child benefits. They argue that child benefits are an important (and in some cases, the sole) source of income for Canadian mothers: a Health and Welfare Canada study found that, in 1984, family allowances and the refundable child tax credit contributed 41 per cent of mothers' income on average; for the 40 per cent of mothers who reported no earnings from paid employment, child benefits provided most (82 per cent) of their income (Laurendeau and Overstreet, 1985). All the more necessary, women's groups contend, to augment child benefits in order better to recognize the child-rearing work that is still largely the domain of mothers.

Given their concern for improving child benefits, one might expect some support from the women's groups for the anti-universalist position which holds that universal child benefits should be replaced with a selective or 'targeted' system which concentrates resources on lower-income families. Yet the National Action Committee on the Status of Women and the Canadian Advisory Council on the Status of Women count among universality's staunchest defenders. An interesting wrinkle in the feminists' position is what I call the 'poor wives with rich husbands' line: according to this argument, universal family allowances should be supported on the grounds that the programme supplies income directly to the mother who, in some cases, has little or no access to her spouse's income, even if the latter is affluent. In this sense, family allowances act as a state-imposed compulsory intra-familial transfer from the husband (whose taxes pay for the programme) to the wife.

Such was the 'system' of children's benefits when the Tories swept into office with their large majority in the autumn of 1984. It did not take them long to announce a review of Canada's income security programmes for children, and the results of that inquiry surprised social policy advocates who feared a deficit-inspired assault – although the final outcome of the Tory review would bear little relation to the initial discussion paper.

In January 1985 the Conservative Minister of National Health and Welfare, Jake Epp, released a *Consultation Paper on Child and Elderly Benefits*. The Government proclaimed three guiding principles for its review; in view of what it actually did to child benefits, these statements are worth quoting in full:

> 1. The concept of universality is a keystone of our social safety net. Its integrity must not and will not be called into question. 2. The concept of a means test to determine eligibility for selective benefit programmes is not appropriate. Eligibility for these programs, such as the Child Tax Credit and the Guaranteed Income Supplement, will continue to be determined on the basis of taxable income. 3. Any savings which may result from programme changes will not be applied to a reduction of the deficit. (Minister of National Health and Welfare, 1985, pp. 5–6)

The Welfare Minister took a more positive view of child benefits than I have provided, assuring Canadians that 'the government regards the present system as a good one, which is working well' and that his purpose was only 'to determine whether modifications or refinements can be identified which would make it work even better' (p. 6). Nonetheless, the Consultation Paper went on to document the regressivity of exemptions and deductions and the resulting irrational distributional impact of the child benefits system, since the children's tax exemption worked at odds to the progressive family allowances and refundable child tax credit. While these insights were by then commonplace among critics, the 1985 Consultation Paper marked an important advance since it was the first time that a Canadian government had publicly acknowledged the inherent incompatibility of progressive and regressive social benefits.

The Welfare Minister's review reaffirmed the worth of several features of Canada's existing child benefits system. First and foremost, it must continue to rest on a solid foundation of universal family allowances, albeit one that is progressive since benefits count as taxable income. The notion of a 'special surtax' on family allowances paid to upper income families should not be ruled out of consideration, but the exemptions and deductions 'are the most regressive components of the existing system and are, therefore, those deserving most careful scrutiny'. Any changes to the system 'should improve benefits for those most in need' and any savings which then remain 'whether resulting from reductions in expenditure or additional revenues' should be applied to social programmes and not used for deficit reduction (pp. 9–10).

The Consultation Paper went on to proffer two options for the reform of Canada's child benefits system. The first, labelled the 'consultation option', reflected popular criticisms and proposals for change. This option would eliminate the regressive children's tax exemption and use the resulting savings to boost the refundable child tax credit from $367 to $595 per child. Since such a large (62 per cent) increase in benefits would elevate the income level up to which (partial) refundable child tax credits would be paid (e.g. for families with two children, from $41,010 to $50,130 in 1985 dollars), the income threshold for maximum benefits would be lowered from $26,330 to $20,500, so that partial benefits under the proposed scheme would disappear at $44,300 or roughly the average income for a family with two children. The family allowance – the bulwark of Canada's child benefits system – would be untouched.

These proposals would produce a more progressive child benefits system. The poorest families would gain $228 per child thanks to the increase in the refundable child tax credit, whereas families with incomes above $50,000 would see an average $318 per child reduction as a result of the elimination of the children's tax exemption. However, many modest-income families with children would be worse off; a two-earner couple with income of $35,000 (more than $7,000 below the average income of $42,279 for a family with two children) would lose about $122 per child. Two-earner couples with incomes as low as $30,600 – $11,679 below the average income – would fare worse under the Consultation Option, and the 'win/lose' point for one-earner families with two children would be as low as $23,000. The provincial governments which, as explained earlier, have a financial stake in federal child benefits, would run away with an estimated $330 million in extra income tax revenue resulting from the abolition of the children's tax exemption; unless the provinces redirected this money into their own child benefits (and only three provinces have such programmes), the federal child benefits system would be effectively cut by $330 million.

Thus the Consultation Paper put forward an 'Alternative Option' which – as soon became clear to social policy advocates – the Federal Government actually favoured, despite touting the changes described in the previous paragraphs as its 'Consultation Option'. (Such doubletalk subsequently proved to be characteristic of the Mulroney Conservatives, who have taken government newspeak to a new high (or low, depending on your point of view) in marketing its social and economic policies to Canadians.)

The so-called 'Alternative Option' would reduce the annual family allowance from $375 to $240 per child; cut the children's tax exemption from $710 to $240 per child; raise the refundable child tax credit from $369 to $610 per child; and lower the child tax credit threshold for maximum benefits from $26,330 to $25,000. These changes would give low-income families somewhat better benefits ($108 per child), but not as much as under the Consultation Option; their larger refundable child tax credit ($610 as opposed to the Consultation Option's $595) would be offset by a one-third reduction in the family allowance (from $375 to $240 per child per year). The child benefits system would become progressive but, again, not as much as under the Consultation Option. From the Government's point of view, the Alternative Option's attractions were purely political: middle-income families would end up about where they were under the status quo, whereas they would lose benefits under the Consultation Option. And while upper-income taxpayers would lose almost as much from the Alternative Option ($284 per child as opposed to $315 under the Consultation Option), they would probably object less to a reduction in their family allowance and children's tax exemption than to losing the children's tax exemption altogether.

Social policy advocates welcomed the Consultation Paper's criticisms of the existing child benefits system but rejected both of the Government's options, proposing instead a third approach to the reform of child benefits which offered the advantages but none of the drawbacks of the Consultation and Alternative Options.[7] Like the Consultation Option, the critics' option would leave family allowances intact as universal, but taxable, benefits and would eliminate the children's tax exemption, redirecting resources from this regressive programme to the progressive refundable child tax credit. However, instead of lowering the family income threshold for the refundable child tax credit from $26,330 to $20,500, the critics would have slightly raised the threshold to $27,000. In addition, they suggested that the definition of income used by the child tax credit – 'net family income' – be amended to disallow the deduction of contributions to private pension plans, Registered Retirement Savings Plans and Registered Home Ownership Savings Plans, since these deductions allowed better-off families to profit from what amounted to an artificial lowering of their actual income and so qualify for more child tax credits than they would otherwise receive. The critics also broadened their review to the child care expense deduction and equivalent-to-married exemption, which they would convert to tax credits. While this third option would have entailed no increase in overall spending on child benefits, it did depend on the Federal Government's negotiating the provinces' agreement to leave their financial windfall (from eliminating the children's tax exemption) in the federal child benefits system – a tactic which the Federal Welfare Minister himself proposed in the House of Commons.

The critics' option would substantially improve benefits for lower-income families, by $228 per child; maintain the same level of support for middle-income families; and make the resulting overall distribution of benefits progressive. Upper-income families would receive only the family allowance, which would remain a taxable benefit. The triad of major child benefits – family allowances, children's tax exemption and refundable child tax credit – would be transformed to a duo – family allowances and an expanded refundable child tax credit. While the social policy groups did not say so at the time, their approach could have paved the way for a further simplification of child benefits in which the equivalent-to-married credit could be merged with the refundable child tax credit and the resources spent on the child care expense deduction/credit eventually reallocated to help finance a better child care system.

The Government referred the Consultation Paper to the all-party Standing Committee on Health, Welfare and Social Affairs which, in turn, held public hearings on the reform of child benefits attended by dozens of groups and individuals and then reported to the House of Commons. In the end, however, all this activity and effort proved to be little more than a charade.

In his May 1985 budget, the Finance Minister ignored the Welfare Minister's January 1985 Consultation Paper and the public reactions it spawned and sailed full steam ahead on what turned out to be a quite different tack. His actions are significant not only for what they did to the child benefits system, but also because they wrested control of a major part of federal social policy fully away from the cabinet minister ostensibly in charge – the Minister of National Health and Welfare – in the process confirming suspicions long held by the critics and advocates that federal social policy is really being determined by the economizing economists of the Department of Finance.

The May 1985 budget proclaimed a phased reduction in the children's tax exemption from $710 per child in 1986 to $560 in 1987, $470 in 1988 and an amount equal to the family allowance from 1989 on. The refundable child tax credit was gradually increased from $384 per child in 1985 to $454 in 1986, $489 in 1987, and $549 in 1988; its threshold (the net income level above which benefits are reduced by 5 per cent) was lowered from $26,330 to £23,500 in 1986 (Wilson, 1985). In themselves, these changes did not depart all that much from the Alternative Option put forward in the Welfare Minister's Consultation Paper issued four months earlier.

The joker in the deck was the decision to abandon the full indexation of child benefits. As of 1986, family allowances were to be adjusted only by the amount that inflation exceeded 3 per cent a year; for example, if the inflation rate was 4 per cent (the average during the 1980s), the family allowance rate would go up by 1 per cent, as opposed to 4 per cent under the old system. This same 'partial de-indexation' formula was to be applied to the children's tax exemption and refundable child tax credit in 1989. The income threshold for the refundable child tax credit was partially de-indexed as well, starting in 1987.

Children's, women's and social policy advocacy groups objected to the Finance Minister's partial de-indexation ploy, recognizing that its purpose and effect would be to cut increasing millions of dollars out of the federal child benefits system as the years went by. Despite the critics' noise and petitions, the media and public showed little interest in the issue, and the Government's large majority guaranteed easy passage of the changes. When questioned, Conservative Members of Parliament parroted their Finance Minister's line that the Government was improving child benefits by raising the refundable child tax credit and reducing the children's tax exemption – after all, isn't that what the social policy do-gooders had been clamouring for all along? – and either sidestepped the partial indexation issue or argued that the fiscal situation precluded the luxury of fully indexed social benefits.

The next significant change to child benefits came with the June 1987 White Paper on Tax Reform which, as part of a sweeping reform of the personal income tax system that was largely inspired by American tax reforms, proposed that the children's tax exemption (slated to be $470 for the 1988 tax year) be converted to a non-refundable credit of $65 per child and that the $3,740 equivalent-to-married exemption – which single parents can claim in respect of one child – be changed to a non-refundable credit of $850 (Wilson, 1987). Responding to criticisms from social policy and women's organizations and both the Commons Committee on Finance and Economic Affairs and the Senate Committee on Banking, Trade and Commerce, the Finance Minister made some minor amendments to his proposals before enacting them. The non-refundable credit for the third and subsequent children was raised to $130 and the refundable child tax credit was boosted by another $35, bringing it to $559 per child for 1988.

Social policy groups supported the conversion of tax exemptions such as the children's exemption and married equivalent exemption to credits, though they would have preferred that the money spent on the children's exemption be redirected to either the family allowance or refundable child tax credit (opinions varied) rather than used to create yet another child benefit programme that, while progressive – measured as a percentage of income, the flat-rate income tax savings from the non-refundable credit is worth more to lower-income families – excludes the poorest families below the tax threshold because the new credit is not refundable. Doubling the non-refundable credit for the third and subsequent children made little sense; why should larger families receive proportionately larger child benefits than the eight in ten families with only one or two children? Naturally the groups applauded the additional increase in the refundable child tax credit.

Interestingly, the 1988 income tax form which contained the tax changes treated the new non-refundable credits as if they were exemptions, as under the old system. For example, instead of listing the basic non-refundable child tax credit as $65, the revenue department listed it as a $388 'exemption' and required the taxfiler to multiply this amount by 17 per cent; God help those without a calculator or with rusty arithmetical skills. The reason for the 17 per cent figure is that the Finance Minister converted most of the personal exemptions and deductions to non-refundable credits at the lowest tax rate (17 per cent after tax reform) so as not to hurt lower-income taxpayers, since a non-refundable credit of $65 produces the same income tax savings as an exemption of $388 (actually, the non-refundable credit should have been $66, but presumably was rounded off at $65).

Why complicate matters by pretending the new non-refundable credits are exemptions and deductions? Revenue Canada may justify this as an attempt to avoid confusing the taxpayer, who has enough difficulty coping with exemptions and deductions, let alone dealing with a new tax concept. The real reason, I suspect, is to avoid giving the impression that taxpayers would lose substantially as a result of tax reform. Those with taxable incomes under $27,500 in 1988 are in the lowest tax bracket (with a 17 per cent tax rate) and actually are no worse off after tax reform since their non-refundable credits bring the same tax savings as the old exemptions and credits. Taxfilers with taxable incomes above $27,500 receive smaller tax savings from the non–refundable credits than the old exemptions and deductions. By pretending that the new non-refundable credits are exemptions, the Government is trying to avoid giving lower-income taxpayers the mistaken impression that they will lose from tax reform and to minimize the impression of loss in the eyes of middle- and upper-income taxfilers. While the former may be a justifiable motive, the latter is not – and is characteristic of the Mulroney Government's reliance on technical trickery to delude the public.

The same year that he implemented one of the most significant tax changes in Canadian history – the conversion of personal exemptions and most deductions to credits – the Minister of Finance took an abrupt about-face on another child benefit: he decided to double the child care expense deduction for 1988 from a maximum of $2,000 to $4,000 for children 6 years and younger and to remove the $8,000 family limit for child care expense deductions. However, the maximum child care expense deduction for children 7–14 years of age was left at $2,000. These changes were sold as part of a new 'national child care strategy' which the Government later abandoned in the face of tough criticism from advocacy groups and problems in negotiating new agreements with the provinces, which are responsible for the design and delivery of child care; the decision not to proceed with the plan caused the Federal Government little anguish, since it saved more than $1.4 billion in new spending than had been allotted to enlarge the supply of child care spaces.

In 1988 the Government added yet another layer to the child benefits system in the form of a $200 supplement to the refundable child tax credit ($100 in 1988 and another $100 in 1989) for children of 6 and under, bringing the maximum benefit to $659 for 1988. (The maximum for children 7 and older remained $559.) The Finance Minister billed this change as part of the Government's child care strategy since the supplement supposedly would help families which lack the receipts required to claim the child care expense deduction. This claim is nonsense, since the supplement is available to all refundable child tax credit families with children under 7, whether or not they spend money on child care. No more convincing was the contention that another $200 a year would supply the kind of help families require to meet their child care needs: what Canadian parents really need is a lot more (affordable) child care spaces, not scarce public funds wasted on bigger tax breaks for the well-off or small increments to the refundable child tax credit.

The clawback on family allowances

The Tories saved their biggest and boldest change to child benefits for last. The April 1989 budget announced a special taxback or 'clawback', as it has been dubbed, on family allowance payments for parents with net incomes over $50,000. (The same scheme is planned for Old Age Security, Canada's other major universal income security programme.)

The clawback is complex, and deliberately so. If the parent who pays income tax on the family allowances (in the case of two-income couples, the higher-income spouse) has net income over $50,000, he or she will be required to repay family allowance payments received the previous year at a rate of 15 per cent (i.e. for every $10 of net income over $50,000, the parent will have to pay back $1 of family allowances). For instance, a parent with two children and net income of $53,000 will repay through the clawback $450 of the family's $786 family allowances. Once net family income exceeds $55,240 for a family with two children, the clawback will take back 100 per cent of family allowances. Families subject to the full (100 per cent) clawback will end up with no benefits from the family allowances programme.

Unless they are accountants or spend their spare time dabbling with their home computer and tax models, most Canadian parents who will have to pay the clawback will have no idea how much family allowances they actually end up with after they pay their income taxes and the clawback. When they file their income tax returns, they will be able to deduct the amount they repay through the clawback from their taxable income. Their after-tax-and-clawback family allowances will equal gross benefits less the sum of (a) federal and provincial income taxes paid on the difference between gross benefits and the clawback and (b) the amount of the clawback. So much for the Finance Minister's goal of 'simplifying' the tax system.

The virtually incomprehensible clawback will add yet another layer to the ramshackle, multi-tiered federal child benefits edifice. It also will discriminate against one-earner families with children and will reach into the back pockets of more and more middle-income parents as time goes by.

The discriminatory effect stems from the Government's decision to base the clawback on individual rather than family income: it will affect taxpayers – not families – whose incomes are above $50,000. A one-earner couple with two children and a net income of $56,000 will be hit by the full clawback and so will forfeit all of its family allowances. Yet a couple with two children in which both spouses bring in income of, for instance, $85,000 ($45,000 from one spouse and $40,000 from the other) will not be subject to the clawback because the higher-income parent's net income is below the $50,000 threshold; instead, this family will pay only the normal federal and provincial income taxes on its family allowances and thus will end up with $469 in after-tax benefits or 60 per cent of its gross payments. (At the extreme, a two-earner couple in which each spouse earned $50,000, for a joint income of $100,000, would avoid the clawback.) A social programme which pays family allowances to a middle-income one-earner family and makes the same family return all of its benefits to the Government, while at the same time allowing a high-income two-earner family to keep 60 per cent of its family allowances, must surely rank high in the dubious achievement hall of fame of public policy. The clawback's tougher treatment of one-income families is all the more difficult to fathom in view of the fact that the 'traditional' (albeit declining) family of dad-in-the-labour-force/

mom-at-home is supposed to figure among the Conservatives' traditional supporters.

The most objectionable characteristic of the clawback on family allowances is that it will catch increasing number of families at lower and lower-income levels over time. The $50,000 threshold above which the clawback applies will be only partially indexed, by the same inflation-over-3 per cent formula which the Finance Minister has applied to child benefit rates and the personal income tax system. In just eight years, the $50,000 threshold will be worth only $39,187, and families with two children in which the net income of the sole earner or the higher-income spouse exceeds just $43,293 will pay back all of their family allowance benefits. To make matters worse, inflation will erode the value of the partially indexed family allowance as well, which will drop from $786 in 1986 to $616 in 1997 – a 22 per cent cut. Even if this and future governments carry through on the Finance Minister's promise that the threshold will be 'reviewed periodically and adjusted as appropriate', without question it will decline with time and will surely not maintain what most Canadian families would consider an 'appropriate' value (Wilson, 1989a, pp. 9–12).

The Minister of Finance claims that the clawback will affect only 14 per cent of all families in receipt of the family allowance – an estimated 167,000 families will still retain some benefits after paying the clawback and another 368,000 will repay all of their family allowances at income tax time (Wilson, 1989a, pp. 9–11). However, eight years after the clawback is put in place, it will reach another 530,000 middle-income families with incomes in the $40,000 – $50,000 range; the average income for a family of four in 1989 is an estimated $50,800. By the turn of the century, more than 1 million families or 29 per cent of the 3.8 million total will be hit by the clawback and so will end up with less – and in many cases no – family allowance benefits (NCW, 1989a, p. 10).

The brave new world of child benefits

The Conservatives' numerous changes to Canada's child benefits system over the past five years have failed to correct the problems inherited from the Liberals. In some ways, they have made the system worse.

On the positive side, replacing the children's tax exemption with a non-refundable credit and substantially increasing the refundable child tax credit are progressive steps. On the negative side, doubling the regressive child care expense deduction wastes even more scarce public funds on upper-income families and offsets the progressive changes. Doubling the non-refundable child tax credit for the third and subsequent children discriminates against smaller families; increasing the refundable child tax credit and doubling the child care expense deduction for children under 7 introduces yet another categorical distinction into the system. The clawback on family allowances will reduce child benefits to higher-income families, but the partially-indexed threshold will hit more and more middle-income parents as time goes by, and the clawback also will discriminate against one-earner families.

The Conservatives have not come to terms any more successfully than the Liberals with the competing purposes of Canada's child benefits system – an incompatibility that is exacerbated by the mounting fiscal pressure to constrain social spending. While the Mulroney Government claims to want to 'target' child benefits on lower-income families and has taken some actions to achieve this anti-poverty objective, at the same time it has enriched the child care expense deduction which serves the parental recognition function for higher-income families. Consistency does not appear to be a Tory virtue: upper-income families will enjoy twice the tax break from the child care expense deduction, but will lose part or all of their family allowance to the clawback.

Partial de-indexation inexorably will sap the value of child benefits over time and soon rob low-income families of any gains they may have made from increases in the refundable child tax credit. And the Tories have managed to turn an already complex system of child benefits into an incomprehensible labyrinth.

Figure 11.1 compares the child benefit system as it was in 1948 to what it will look like in 1991, after the Tory changes. We look at two-earner couples, since families with both spouses in the paid labour force are now the norm in Canada.[8] Two striking patterns emerge. First, the new system is not progressive overall and is at best less regressive than the old; families with incomes over $80,000 receive larger child benefits than middle-income families earning $45,000 (which, in fact, get the least of all the income groups), although at least now the poorest families receive the biggest child benefit. Secondly, the poorest ($10,000 and under) couples will be only marginally better off in 1991 than they were in 1984, while all other families – including those with incomes as low as $15,000 – will receive less child benefits in 1991.

The clawback on old age pensions

The clawback mechanism will operate the same way for Old Age Security payments. However, the 'old age pension', as it is popularly known, poses some noteworthy differences from family allowances.

First, the Old Age Security is a much larger benefit than family allowances – $3,950 per senior or ten times the $393 per child family allowance – and so is a more important component of the incomes of elderly Canadians, who tend to cluster on the lower rungs of the income ladder. The clawback will initially affect a relatively small percentage of the elderly population - an estimated 128,000 or 4.3 per cent – and the income level above which the old age pension is completely taxed back will be much higher than in the case of the family allowance – $76,332 as opposed to $55,240. Many Canadians would see nothing wrong about taxing back more or all of the old age pension of the few elderly persons with such high incomes.

However, as with the family allowance, the falling threshold of the clawback will affect increasing numbers of pensioners at lower income levels as time passes. Even with periodic adjustments of the threshold (i.e. above the annual partial indexing), the clawback will extend its reach.

The National Council of Welfare's analysis looked at the future old age pension prospects for three representative middle-income 35 year-old workers, earning $40,000, $45,000 and $50,000 in 1989; the average male full-time worker earns about $39,000 (NCW, 1989a). The study considered four scenarios – one (the most pessimistic) in which the clawback threshold is only partially indexed and is not periodically adjusted, so that it loses 3 per cent in value each year; a scenario in which the threshold is periodically adjusted enough that it falls only 2 per cent on average each year; a third in which it is adjusted so that it falls 1 per cent each year; and, finally (and unrealistically), a scenario in which it is fully indexed so that it retains its original $50,000 value. (All figures are expressed in constant 1989 dollars.)

When the $40,000 worker turns 65 and begins to collect his $3,950 Old Age Security cheque, under the first scenario he would be hit harshly by the clawback – to the tune of $2,273 – and would end up with net benefits (i.e. after income taxes and clawback) of only $1,001 or 25 per cent of his gross payments. Under the next-to-worse scenario, he would pay $1,189 to the clawback and end up with a net old age pension of $1,648 or 42 per cent of gross payments. Under the third and fourth scenarios, the clawback is adjusted enough that the employee is not affected by it and pays only normal income taxes on his benefits, thus keeping $2,358 or 60 per cent of gross old age pension payments.

The prospects are bleaker for the workers with higher incomes. The $45,000 employee would end up with only 15 per cent of his gross old age pension under the first scenario, 32 per cent under the second and 54 per cent under the third; he would escape the clawback only if the threshold were fully indexed, which will not happen under the Government's plan. The $50,000 worker would end up with only 5 per cent of his Old Age

Security payments under the worst scenario, 22 per cent under the second and 44 per cent under the third, avoiding the clawback only if it were fully indexed. Clearly, the clawback's value to future governments in terms of constraining spending on old age pensions to the ever-increasing elderly population will hinge critically on how often and how much the threshold is adjusted.

The politics of universality

The Prime Minister has plunged himself into hot water more than once over the universality issue. During both election campaigns, in 1984 and 1988, he insisted that old age pensions are a 'sacred trust' and that his Government is firmly committed to the principle of universality. Yet his Finance Minister than proceeded to take a rather more secular attitude toward social programmes. His 1985 budget failed to partially de-index the Old Age Security programme, as noted earlier, but did succeed in partially de-indexing child benefits. The 1989 budget aims to meld two techniques – a clawback with a partially indexed threshold – in a bid to recoup increasing millions from more and more parents and seniors as time goes by; the clawback will save about half a billion dollars a year – a welcome contribution to the Government's anti-deficit crusade.

Armed with criticisms from the National Council of Welfare and the Canadian Council on Social Development, seniors' organizations such as One Voice and the National Pensioners and Senior Citizens Federation are trying to repeat their successful 1985 campaign against partial indexation of the old age pension and make the Mulroney Government back down on the clawback. In addition to political lobbying and garnering media attention, they are planning a legal challenge under the Canadian Charter of Rights and Freedoms on the grounds that the clawback discriminates on the basis of age. The seniors' lobby condemns the clawback as an abrogation of their entitlement to benefits which they were promised as part of their retirement income and which they helped pay for through their taxes and, from 1952 to 1971, a special tax on income ear-marked for the Old Age Security programme. The clawback sticks all the harder in their throats because it is being advocated by the same government that, in its 1985 *Child and Elderly Benefits Consultation Paper*, repudiated the very notion on the grounds that it 'would seriously disrupt our retirement income system, both for current pensioners and those now planning for retirement, and would unduly penalize those most affected by reason of retirement income resulting from private savings in earlier years' (Minister of National Health and Welfare, 1985).

Parents, on the other hand, are not well organized, and family rights groups and other women's and social policy organizations have had no success so far in fighting cuts to child benefit programmes. Nor have the media shown the same interest in child benefits as they have with seniors who, for some reason, make for better newspaper copy and television in Canada. The poll-mesmerized Mulroney Government may feel more confident in imposing a clawback on family allowances, since both public and private surveys find less support for universal child benefits than for universal old age pensions and universal public health insurance. Indeed, social policy advocates may have overestimated the Canadian public's commitment to universality, especially at a time when many voters appear susceptible to the Government's well-publicized campaign (at public expense) for belt-tightening and deficit-reduction.

Another factor that could work in the Government's favour is the Goods and Services Tax. Witness after witness has trooped before the Commons Finance Committee to lambast the Finance Minister's sales tax proposals. Business as well as labour and groups representing consumers, women, seniors and the poor have criticized the Goods and Services Tax; the opposition parties launched a frontal assault; Tory backbenchers are feeling the heat from worried and suspicious constituents; and the media are giving the controversy extensive play. Conceivably the furore over the new sales tax could draw attention away from the clawback and allow the Government to slide the income tax changes required to implement the scheme through Parliament with relatively little trouble.

Incredibly, Prime Minister Mulroney continues to wrap himself in the cloak of universality, of all things, a stance which serves only to revive memories of his past troubles with the issue of elderly benefits. He dismissed the critique of the clawback published by his Welfare Minister's advisory body, the National Council of Welfare – most of whose members are card-carrying Conservatives and in some cases prominent party workers – responding to reporters: 'We don't accept that view at all....In fact, that view has been contradicted by both the facts and by other experts who have analyzed it very carefully' (*Toronto Star*, 1989). Presumably these 'other experts' are the same bureaucrats who designed the clawback. Both the Prime Minister and his Finance Minister insist that the principle of universality is not in jeopardy because the Government will continue to mail out cheques to all parents and pensioners. That assurance will come as small comfort to family allowance and old age pension recipients who have to pay back all their benefits at tax time.

Social policy groups and seniors' advocates did not even have to point out that the Emperor and his Treasurer are scandalously naked in their bizarrely original interpretation of universality: Don Blenkarn, the outspoken chairman of the Commons finance committee, said it for them. In a letter responding to a complaint from an Alberta pensioner, Mr Blenkarn admitted that his Government has 'decided to eliminate universality and we do that in a sense by the clawback in both family allowance and the old age pension...While the clawback may be unfair and sneaky, it is there' (*Ottawa Citizen*, 1989).

If the clawback on old age pensions and family allowances goes ahead as planned, with its partially indexed threshold, the Conservative Government will have succeeded in effecting a significant structural change in Canada's tax and transfer system. Along with the partial de-indexation of the personal income tax system, of federal transfers to the provinces for health and post-secondary education, of child benefits and of the sales tax credit, the clawback will form part of a potent mechanism of hidden tax hikes and social programme cuts that will automatically generate billions of dollars each year in additional tax revenue and programme savings – all without the knowledge and consent of the Canadian public. Will future finance ministers, even if they hail from the other two political parties, choose to dismantle so powerful and smooth-running a revenue engine?

Notes

1. For other analyses see Gray (1990), Canadian Centre for Policy Alternatives (1988), Prince (1988) and Graham (1989).
2. NCW (1989a) Table F. The basic data are taken from the 1989 federal budget (Department of Finance Canada, 1989), then recalculated by the National Council of Welfare to constant 1989 dollars in order to gauge real changes over time.
3. For a detailed critique of Phase 1 of the Conservatives' tax reform (i.e., changes to the personal and corporate income tax systems) see Battle (1988) and Maslove (1988).
4. Family income is made up chiefly of spouses' employment earnings, though the middle- and upper-income families have a modest amount of income from interest ($600 for the middle-income family, $1,400 for the upper-income family). The middle- and upper-income families claim the child care expense deduction for one child under age 6; the other child is assumed to be older and not in care.
5. The Goods and Services Tax proposals are presented in Wilson (1989b). For an analysis of its impact on lower-income Canadians, see the National Council of Welfare's brief to the Commons finance committee (NCW, 1989b).
6. The poverty lines are the 'low income cut-offs' established by Statistics Canada. For an explanation, see NCW (1989c).
7. The Social Policy Reform Group, a coalition of six major national women's and social policy organizations (the Canadian Advisory Council on the Status of Women, Canadian Council on Social Development, National Action Committee on the Status of Women, Canadian Association of Social Workers, National Anti-Poverty Organization and National Council of

Welfare), presented a response to the Consultation Paper to the Commons Standing Committee on Health, Welfare and Social Affairs; see its brief *Child Benefits* (Social Policy Reform Group, 1985). For a more detailed analysis, see NCW (1985).

8. The picture differs somewhat for one-earner couples. Because they are not eligible for the child care expense deduction, then the overall distribution of child benefits (from the family allowance, refundable child tax credit and non-refundable child tax credit) is progressive after the Tory changes. However, all but the poorest families lose benefits over time because of partial indexation.

References

Battle, K. (1988) 'The 1987 White Paper on tax reform: a commentary and critique', *Journal of Law and Social Policy* 3 Winter, 66–103.

Canadian Centre for Policy Alternatives (1988) *Canada Under the Tory Government*, Ottawa: The Centre.

Department of Finance Canada (1989) *The Fiscal Plan: controlling the Public Debt*, Ottawa: Department of Finance.

Graham, K (ed.) (1989) *How Ottawa Spends, 1988–89: The Conservatives heading into the stretch*, Ottawa: School of Public Administration, Carleton University.

Gray, G. (1990) 'Social Policy by Stealth', *Policy Options* **11**, (2), 17–29, March.

Laurendeau, M. and E. Overstreet (1985) *The Importance of Family Allowances to Mothers*, Ottawa: Health and Welfare Canada.

Maslove, A. (1988) *Distributional Impacts of Personal Income Tax Reform*, Ottawa: The Institute for Research on Public Policy.

Minister of National Health and Welfare (1985) *Child and Elderly Benefits Consultation Paper*, Ottawa: Government of Canada.

NCW (National Council of Welfare) (1985) *Opportunity for Reform*, Ottawa: NCW.

NCW (National Council of Welfare) (1989a) *The 1989 Budget and Social Policy*, Ottawa: NCW.

NCW (National Council of Welfare) (1989b) *Help Wanted: Tax relief for Canada's poor*, Ottawa: NCW.

NCW (National Council of Welfare) (1989c) *1989 Poverty Lines*, Ottawa: NCW.

NCW (National Council of Welfare) (1989d) *The 1989 Budget and Social Policy*, p.10, Ottawa: NCW.

Ottawa Citizen (1989) 'MP contradicts PM over "sacred trust": Universality is history, says Blenkam', 23 September.

Prince, M. (ed.) (1987) *How Ottawa Spends, 1986–87: Tracking the Tories*, Toronto: Methuen.

Prince, M. (ed.) (1988) *How Ottawa Spends, 1987–88: Restraining the State*, Toronto: Methuen.

Social Policy Reform Group (1985) *Child Benefits*, Ottawa: Social Policy Reform Group.

Toronto Star (1989) 'Tory budget kills universal social benefits, council warns', 14 September.

Wilson, Hon. M. (1985) *Securing Economic Renewal: Budget Papers*, pp. 42-3, Ottawa: Department of Finance Canada.

Wilson, Hon. M. (1987) *The White Paper on Tax Reform, 1987*, p. 29–31, Ottawa: Department of Finance Canada.

Wilson, Hon. M. (1989a) *Budget Papers*, Ottawa: Department of Finance Canada, 27 April.

Wilson, Hon. M. (1989b) *Goods and Services Tax Technical Paper*, Ottawa: Department of Finance Canada.

PART 4
United States of America

12

Heavy with human tears

Free market policy, inequality and social provision in the United States

Elliott Currie

Center for the Study of Law and Society, University of California, Berkeley, United States

> Some treasures are heavy with human tears, as an ill-stored harvest
> with untimely rain... That which seems to be wealth may in verity be
> only the gilded index of far-reaching ruin.
>
> (John Ruskin, *Unto this Last*)

How has 'free market' policy affected social life in the United States? The question is important not only for those of us in North America who must confront the consequences of the continuing Reagan–Bush experiment in our daily lives, but for those in other countries whose leaders look hopefully or wistfully to the United States as a kind of beacon lighting the way out of economic stagnation and unemployment; for in most respects the United States does remain the quintessential free market nation. We were already, before Ronald Reagan, historically the most market-dominated of industrial societies, with the greatest resistance to collective provision, the lowest level of labour organization and the least potent social-democratic political and cultural tradition. There is no country outside the developing world where economic and social policy, as well as moral culture and political discourse, have been so pervasively shaped by the imperatives of private profit-seeking; where the 'forces of the market' are so permeating, extreme and unchallenged. Eight years of a radically conservative administration have surely intensified that imbalance: Ronald Reagan came into office vowing to roll back such collective provision as we had managed haltingly to achieve since the New Deal, and left office comforted by the thought that he had accomplished much of what he set out to do.

To be sure, the post-Reagan reality – what the Swedish writer Goran Therborn (1988, p. 30) calls 'actually existing Reaganomics' – is a more

299

complex animal than either its avid proponents or some of its critics suppose. *The Economist* (1989, p. 74) goes so far as to say that though 'future historians are sure to find the notion of a Reagan revolution irresistible', the truth is that 'Reaganomics stands for an idea about the role of government that in the end was never really put to the test'. The American critic Emma Rothschild, surveying patterns of government expenditure in the Reagan years, goes even farther: the 'real' Reagan economy, she writes, is 'virtually the opposite' of the conservative 'idyll' his administration proposed to create (Rothschild, 1988, p. 46).

There is an important truth in these comments, but it shouldn't be exaggerated. It is true that, as *The Economist* continues, 'two terms of Reaganomics failed to shift the boundaries of government'. Federal Government spending was roughly the same proportion of the US gross national product – about 22 per cent – in the last year of the Carter administration as in the last year of Reagan's. But within those 'boundaries', the *terrain* of government changed considerably, and it changed in ways entirely consistent with the Reagan mandate. Thus the vast military build-up kept the boundaries of government from any noticeable shrinkage overall, and tied government yet more intricately into the upper levels of the private corporate economy. And there was a simultaneous expansion of government spending to underpin what Rothschild calls the 'semi private welfare state' – the vast network of benefits and services that increasingly accompany high-level, stable employment in the United States (Rothschild, 1988, p. 46). At the same time, at the other end of the social scale, the Reagan administration carried out, in the name of freeing the private market, a systematic and often quite successful assault on those forms of government spending mainly or wholly designed to benefit lower-income Americans. Many of the administration's key victories on that terrain came in the early 1980s, and some were countered and even partly reversed by an awakening Congress in the later years of the Reagan era. But the overall impact has been considerable, and has ranged across a broad spectrum of social institutions. As a result, the already rudimentary system of public provision for the more vulnerable in America has been substantially, and in some realms drastically, diminished.

These effects have been compounded by the impact of the Reagan administration's *de facto* employment policy, which, though largely unarticulated, has likewise adhered consistently to the logic of the private market. The administration drastically slashed public employment, training and job-creation efforts, while simultaneously encouraging the growth of low-wage employment, in part by holding down the real value of the minimum wage and (as we shall see) chopping away at income support benefits to protect those out of work. This has helped give the post-Reagan 'market' economy in America its peculiar and distinctive shape – characterized by spreading deprivation amidst rising employment and moderate economic 'growth', by a superficial 'prosperity' that is also 'heavy with human tears'.

The 'unleashing' of the market in the Reagan years has, in short, been both very real – and very selective; filtered through the complex web of protections that serve to insulate many groups in the modern US economy from the market's most extreme and immediate impacts. For those protected (at least for the present) by stable, high-level employment and the consequent benefits of the 'semi-private welfare state', the effects of the market's unleashing have mainly been felt indirectly and typically at some social distance; in the discomfort and disturbance of public life caused by escalating homelessness, drug abuse and violence; in the deterioration of environmental quality; and in a certain sense of accelerating risk and insecurity that has come to pervade life in post-Reagan America. In most other respects – at least in the short run and as measured by the conventional indices of material well-being – the living conditions of those protected groups have improved in the 1980s. At the other end of the scale, for those least protected by private affluence or semi private provision, the unleashing of market forces in the past decade has been a massive disaster. It has thrown millions of working Americans into poverty; substantially reduced the supports that could cushion them against economic deprivation and dislocation; and radically diminished their access to habitable housing, basic medical care and the preventive and reparative social services that might offset the personal and familial impacts of growing poverty and economic stress.

At the very bottom of the social ladder, the withdrawal of both public and private services has reached the point where, in the most stricken communities, the most basic human needs are now routinely unmet and social life has descended to a level rarely seen outside the Third World. A little higher up the scale, the selective imposition of free market policies has brought wrenching changes in the lives of a broad segment of American working people. Especially if they are younger adults trying to raise a family, many of these 'ordinary' Americans have been put at great and unprecedented risk of impoverishment, of homelessness or 'house poverty', and of the deprivation of basic medical care.

Thus the selective or 'filtered' free market of the 1980s has brought an increasingly desperate social emergency to America. But it is not an emergency for everyone. It has therefore substantially widened the already abysmal inequalities of living conditions in the United States – all the more so because of the compounding effect of growing income inequality combined with widening gaps in the provision of housing, health care and social services. Most of these shifts were already underway, if at a lesser pace, during the Carter years. But the Reagan administration distinctly accelerated them, and America is a different country as a result; poorer, less equitable, less secure, sicker and more dangerous.

In the following pages I will chart some of the most important of these changes. I will argue that, measured along these human dimensions, the 'free market' has been a massive and tragic failure. But, again, it has not necessarily been so for everyone. That selective impact is crucial to the American experience today. It both imparts a certain schizoid quality to social life in the United States, and represents a powerful obstacle to the development of a coherent and effective political movement for an alternative.

Deepening poverty

The most immediate consequence of the 'filtered' free market policies of the 1980s has been both an increase and a deepening and 'hardening' of poverty in the United States. Between 1979 and 1987 – both years of economic 'recovery' – about 8 million more people were added to the ranks of the officially poor, 3 million of them children (CBPP, 1988a, p. v). Not only were their numbers vastly increased, however, but the poor were also, on average, sunk more deeply below the poverty line; and it had become considerably harder for them to get out. In 1987 roughly two out of five poor people in the United States had incomes below *one-half* the official poverty line, the highest proportion in a decade (in 1987, the poverty line was just over $9,000 for a family of three) (US Congress, 1988a, p. 12). And, according to research from the University of Michigan's Panel Study of Income Dynamics, their so-called 'exit probabilities' – the chances that someone poor in a given year would have escaped poverty in the following year – after rising during the 1960s and early 1970s, fell sharply through the early 1980s. It is sometimes said that this mainly reflects the growing proportion of single women heading families among the poor. But the Michigan research shows that, while this demograhic change does help explain the deepening poverty of the 1980s, it cannot account for the bulk of it. Indeed, taken as a whole, the demographic shifts affecting the poor in these years, other things being equal, should have *increased* the chances of escaping from poverty; for though more poor families were headed by single women, whose 'exit probabilities' are lower, fewer families were large or headed by someone with less than a high-school education – both shifts that should have increased the probabilities of escape. But the more powerful factor was that 'greater economic inequality has made poverty so deep that exit has become more elusive' (Adams *et al.*, 1988, pp. 93–5).

It has also become the conventional wisdom to attribute the recent rise in poverty to the cultural or behavioural problems of a specifically black urban 'underclass'. But in fact the fastest rise in poverty during the 1980s was among whites and Hispanics. The child poverty rate among blacks rose about 6 per cent between 1979 and 1985; for whites, it rose by a startling 37 per cent and for Hispanic children by 43 per cent (Sandejur, 1988, p. 50). The idea that only a small, marginal and behaviourally troubled underclass is failing to benefit from the prosperity of the post-Reagan years has served to deflect attention from the larger structural crisis that is the harsh downside of that prosperity; but the bare poverty figures, even by themselves, reveal a far grimmer reality. It is not simply that a troubled few have failed to 'make it' into the American 'mainstream': the mainstream itself is increasingly eroding.

Perhaps more precisely, the mainstream is *bifurcating* – with great numbers of working Americans seeing their economic well-being plummet significantly, while others, better placed strategically, have seen their incomes rise substantially. The process is quite linear; those in the bottom fifth of the income distribution have lost the most, those in the top fifth have gained the most, with those in between spread out along a predictable continuum. According to data compiled by the House Committee on Ways and Means, real personal income fell almost 10 per cent, on average, among the lowest fifth of the American income distribution between the two 'recovery' years 1970 and 1987. It also fell slightly among the second-lowest quintile. But among the wealthiest fifth, personal income rose by close to 16 per cent, and by 9 per cent among the second-wealthiest quintile (*New York Times*, 1989).

Not only for the urban 'underclass', then, but for the lower 40 per cent of the population – and especially for those in the lower third of the scale – income has declined significantly over a few short years of the 'prosperous' 1980s, simultaneously with an increase, often substantial, at the other end of the scale. And these aggregate figures greatly mask the seriousness of the decline for some groups within the lower 40 per cent – most notably the young. As Emma Rothschild has pointed out (1988, p. 49), the average real incomes of people over 65 actually increased across *every* income fifth in the Reagan years – chiefly because of the indexing of social security benefits to inflation. Virtually the entire burden of the rising income inequality of the 1980s, in short – in a pattern we will see repeated across other realms of social policy – has fallen on younger people, especially those now under 35. So it was that the median income of American families with children headed by someone under 25 dropped by an astonishing 43 per cent from 1970 to 1986 (US Congress, 1988a, p. 2). Again, part of this trend – but only a part – results from a rising proportion of young families headed by a single woman. But much more is going on as well.

What else accounts for these shifts? Two things, primarily; the declining value and coverage of income support benefits, coming as it did simultaneously with a downward shift in the structure of jobs. Both trends began before the Reagan administration, but gathered momentum in the 1980s.

Even pre-Reagan, the United States' notoriously stingy system of income support helped give us the highest rates of family and child poverty in the advanced industrial world. In 1979, according to data from the recent Luxemburg Income Study – before the Reagan administration systematically unleashed the free market on the poor – the United States shared with Australia the distinction of having the highest proportion of families with children in poverty among eight countries studied, as well as the highest proportion of 'severely poor' families – defined as those with incomes below 75 per cent of the poverty line. That was partly due to a longstanding pattern of lower earnings and higher unemployment, giving the United States a higher rate of so-called 'pretransfer' poverty than most other industrial countries. But it was also because, as the economist Timothy Smeeding notes, 'we spend less in transfers per poor family with children than does any other country studied'. After government transfers were counted, the rate of family poverty at the beginning of the 1980s was about 4 per cent in Sweden and Switzerland, 6–7 per cent in West Germany and Norway, 8 per cent in Canada and the United Kingdom – and 14 per cent in the United States. What Smeeding calls the 'poverty population reduction rate' – the percentage of families poor before transfers who were brought above the poverty line by government benefits – ranged from a startling 58 per cent in Sweden and 47 per cent in Norway to just 17 per cent in the United States (and 15 per cent in Australia). The proportion of American children who remained 'severely poor' after transfers was four to five times higher than that in Sweden or West Germany. This was not simply a reflection of demographic differences among these countries – such as a higher proportion of single-parent families in the United States. Indeed, the United States had, pre-Reagan, about the same proportion of children in single-parent families as did Norway and Sweden; but while Sweden's poverty rate among those families was around 9 per cent and Norway's 22 per cent, the American rate was 51 per cent. The American rate of poverty in 'intact' families was actually higher than the Swedish rates for *single-parent* families (Smeeding, 1988, pp. 82–96.[1]

The relative failure of the income support system to lift American families out of poverty historically reflected both a low level of benefits and low rates of coverage. Both problems worsened considerably in the Reagan years – especially in the early 1980s, when rapid cuts in benefits at the federal level came on top of several years of inflation that had already reduced their real value. The average AFDC benefit (Aid to Families with Dependent Children, the main income support programme for the poor in the United States) dropped about 20 per cent in real terms from 1979 to 1986, while the proportion of poor children receiving those benefits dropped from 72 to 60 per cent. Thirty-five US states, and the District of Columbia, now pay average welfare benefits that amount to less than one-half the poverty level (US Congress, 1988a, p. 44; Caputo, 1989, p. 89). Meanwhile, the proportion of the unemployed covered by the weakened unemployment insurance system fell to less than one-third – only about two-thirds what it had been in the late 1970s (Levinson, 1987, p. 206). As a result, government cash benefits now lift a far smaller proportion of the poor from poverty than they did pre-Reagan. The Center on Budget and Policy Priorities calculates that about one in five poor families in 1979 were brought above the poverty line by some combination of AFDC, unemployment insurance and social security payments; just one in nine by 1986. About one-third of the overall increase in family poverty in those years, the CBPP estimates, resulted from these benefit reductions; about half a million fewer families would have been poor in 1986 had the 'antipoverty impact' of government cash benefits been the same as it was in 1979 (CBPP, 1988b). Nor were these decreases in the effectiveness of cash benefits offset by increases in the so-called 'in kind' benefits for low-income people – including Food Stamps and (as we'll see in a moment) subsidized housing and health care. Indeed the value of those benefits generally fell even faster than cash transfers in the early 1980s; the combined value of average AFDC and Food Stamp benefits fell by 22 per cent between 1971 and 1983 (US Congress, 1987a, p. 2).[2]

What makes the shrinking of the income support system much more damaging than these figures alone indicate is that it has occurred simultaneously with a downward shift in the labour market that has strongly increased the risks of 'pretransfer' poverty for people who work. It is the compounded effect of these two trends that has pushed so many Americans below the poverty line in the Reagan years. Recent research for the Senate Budget Committee has shed new light on this trend, illustrating how the specific pattern of job decline has helped shape the new contours of poverty and inequality in America in the 1980s. 'The dominant trend in American job creation in the 1980s', their report notes, 'has been for low-paying jobs to replace those which provided a middle-class standard of living'. As with income, there has been a simultaneous increase of both very low-paying jobs and of high-paying ones; but the share of jobs paying less than poverty-level wages has grown more than twice as fast as that of jobs this study defines as 'high-wage' – those paying wages more than four times the poverty level.

But the impact of this shift has not been uniform – it has varied sharply by age, sex, race and region. Most strikingly, the job decline has been mainly an affliction of the young. For workers under 35, there was a net loss of roughly 1.6 million 'middle-wage' jobs from 1979 to 1987; for workers over 35 things indeed improved slightly – there was no change in their share of low-wage jobs and a slight shift upwards from middle- to high-paying ones. The downwards trend in the job market has also struck with particular severity at men. Male workers, the Budget Committee observes, 'fared extremely poorly in this decade, experiencing extreme downward wage polarization'. Despite an increase of several million in the male labour force, there was a net *loss* of nearly a quarter of a million jobs that paid men middle-level wages in these years; while 'fully 82% of the gain in male employment in this decade has been in jobs paying below poverty-level wages'. Women, of course, are still far more likely than men to be stuck in poor jobs; in 1987, according to this study, 43 per cent of women, and 27 per cent of men, held low-wage jobs. But the *change* since the end of the 1970s has hit men hardest: for women, the share of low-wage jobs declined slightly in this decade. Finally, the impact of the downwards job shift has varied by region; in some Northeast and Mid-Atlantic states, the general trend has been toward what the study calls 'wage enrichment', with more of an increase in high-wage than in low-wage jobs. At the other extreme is the sheer 'wage impoverishment' that has struck some states in the South Central and Mountain regions – especially those dependent on the energy economy; in those states, the *only* increase in job shares in the 1980s was in those paying wages below the poverty level. Across the United States as a whole, the more common trend was 'downwards wage polarization' – an increase in jobs at both ends of the scale, but much faster at the bottom (US Congress, 1988b, pp. vii–3).[3]

On close inspection, then, the most often-touted success of the Reagan economic recovery – the 'boom' in employment that distinguishes the United States from a number of European countries in this period – turns out to have been a blessing only for some. For millions of others, it has been a direct ticket into poverty; and has helped to define and enforce the new inequality of the post-Reagan era. But jobs and income are only part of the story. To appreciate how deeply the Reagan version of free market policy has driven the wedge of inequality in American society, we need to look simultaneously at its effects on housing, medical care and human services.

The scramble for shelter

The fate of shelter under Reaganite policy follows a similar pattern. A recent report from Harvard's Joint Center for Housing Studies (1988, p. 232) puts the general trend bluntly: 'America is increasingly becoming a nation of housing haves and have-nots'. At the top is a world of second homes, designer room additions and huge appreciation in equity values resulting from the wild and unregulated stampede of the upscale real estate market. At the bottom, the stark reduction of the federal effort – already historically anaemic – to provide affordable housing for low-income people has not only intensified the problem of homelessness, but also created a vast population of the 'near' homeless, those at high risk in the housing market; people for whom the escalating cost of housing coupled with declining income has meant a dramatic change in the quality of life.

In the 1980s there was considerable new housing construction in the United States; indeed, the boom in new housing (along with the construction of hotels and shopping malls) helped fuel the job growth so hailed by the conservative administration as a key achievement of Reagan policies. But this was overwhelmingly housing for the affluent, especially those who already owned homes. 'More and more', according to the House Select Committee on Children, Youth and Families, 'the housing market – even for older homes – is dominated not by families looking for first homes, but by families who already own their own homes' (US Congress, 1988a, p. 6). For those who do not, it's by now well-known that the effect of the unfettered free market has been to price even modest first homes beyond their reach.

But, as with jobs and income, the aggregate statistics on housing greatly understate the severity of the problem among some groups, masking the fragmenting of opportunities that characterizes the 'filtered' free market of the 1980s. It is often pointed out that in the 1980s, for the first time, the percentage of American families owning their own homes fell from about 66 to 63 per cent. What's less often noted is that the chance of owning a home did not fall for everyone. It fell sharply for younger people, while *rising* slightly for older people; and it fell for lower-income families, while rising slightly for the affluent.

In the 1980s, homeownership rates for young married-couple families dropped from about 39 to about 29 per cent; for young single-parent families, from about 14 to about 6 per cent. In general, the rates for young adults were very stable during the 1970s, and in some cases increased; they dropped significantly in the 1980s while those for people over 55 rose. Between 1973 and 1980 the homeownership rate for people aged 30 to 34 was consistently around 60 per cent; by 1987 it had fallen to 53 per cent. For those aged 55 to 64, meanwhile, it rose from 75 to 81 per cent, and for those over 65 from 71 to 78 per cent, between 1973 and 1987. Thus if you are 30-years-old in America today you are considerably less likely to own a home than your counterpart in 1973; if you are 60, your chances have risen, steadily if not spectacularly (Joint Center for Housing Studies, 1988, p. 12). The difference appears, unsurprisingly, across lines of class as well. People with incomes below $17,500 (in 1986 dollars) were much less likely to own homes in 1987 than in 1974, those making over $35,000 *more* likely (Joint Center for Housing Studies, 1988, p. 7). And these numbers, of course, obscure the sacrifices many younger and less affluent people who do own homes are making in order to buy and maintain them.

But rates of homeownership are just the tip of the iceberg. The far worse damage has been done further down the scale – to those low-income renters dependent on America's traditionally rudimentary system of public housing and housing subsidies. Here the decline has been nothing short of catastrophic; and as the Harvard report points out, this is especially remarkable because it has 'occurred during one of the most sustained and vigorous housing recoveries on record' (Joint Center for Housing Studies, 1988, p. 13). The housing industry, in brief, has been doing just fine. But – more than at any time in recent history – it is building houses for some people and not for others. In the 1980s, as the National Low-Income Housing Coalition (1987) comments, 'The federal government has all but abandoned its historic commitment to "a decent home and a suitable living environment for every American family" as low income housing programs have been slashed more deeply than any other federal activity'. Housing, moreover, has been the area in which federal cutbacks have been least compensated by increased state and local spending.

Under Reagan, the Federal Government set out both to dismantle and to discredit the US public housing effort. In the years from 1976 to 1982, federal subsidies and tax incentives helped support the construction of about 200,000 units of affordable housing a year for low-income people; by the late 1980s the number had fallen to about 25,000 – much of it targeted specifically to the elderly and disabled (Connell, 1988, p. 6). Simultaneous cuts in funds to maintain and improve existing public housing helped to solidify public housing's reputation as shoddy, decrepit and intrinsically inferior to privately marketed housing. Sharp reductions in federal subsidies for affordable housing for ordinary working people meant that public housing did indeed often become housing of last resort – too often inhabitated mainly by the poorest and most demoralized of the urban poor. The resulting concentration of social pathology – drug dealing, violence, gang warfare, family disruption – in public housing was (and is) routinely offered, with convenient if curious logic, as yet another piece of evidence for the superiority of market approaches to social provision.

The slashing of funds for public housing (and the conversion of many formerly subsidized units into market-rent private ones) has forced many more low-income people into the private housing market. But that market itself changed dramatically in the Reagan years. Rents rose sharply; between 1974 and 1983 alone, the number of units renting for less than $300 (in 1986 dollars) fell by nearly 1 million (Joint Center for Housing Studies, 1988, p. 6). The shortfall in low-income rental units – the gap between the number of families needing them and the number available – has shot up by 120 per cent since 1980 (US Congress, 1988a, p. 26).

The most spectacular result has been the dramatic increase in homelessness across both urban and rural areas. But that is only the most dramatic aspect of a more general crisis in access to shelter. Even more widespread is the sharply rising burden of paying for shelter among the bottom 40 per cent of the income distribution – a burden vastly compounded by the simultaneous decline in real incomes. Once again, the impact has been most heavily felt by the relatively young. Among the bottom fifth of American families generally, the median rent burden (rent as a proportion of income) went up by about a third from 1974 to 1987: for young households with children it rose by 50 per cent; and for young single-parent families, it rose from an already painful 35 per cent of income to a crippling 58 per cent over these years (Joint Center for Housing Studies, 1988, p. 14). Those proportions are, of course, *far* higher in areas with especially high housing costs – where what these dry figures mean in practice is that it is virtually impossible for a low-income family to put even a rudimentary roof over their heads without having more than one low-wage job. That's difficult enough for 'intact' families; for single parents, it poses a brutal choice between the threat of homelessness and the enormous stresses of working at two (or more) low-wage jobs in order to pay for shelter.

The retreat of public health care

A similar pattern appears in the provision of health care. The 'filtered' unleashing of the market in the Reagan years deepened the already well-established inequalities in access to care – although here, in contrast to housing, Congressional resistance managed to keep the most serious cuts confined to the early Reagan years and achieved some limited but significant victories against 'free market' policies after the mid-1980s.

Before the 1980s the United States already stood out as the only major industrial society without some form of comprehensive health care system accessible to all. That default led to a curious and distinctive tripartite system of health care: at the top, those covered by private health insurance, usually through employment; at the bottom, those without such protection but not poor enough to qualify for means-tested 'poverty medicine'; in the middle, somewhat oddly, those of the truly poor who could meet the stringent eligibility requirements for subsidized care. Under Reagan, many more Americans – about 9 million since the late 1970s – joined the ranks of the uninsured, mainly from the legions of workers in the low-wage, non-union jobs which, as we've seen, dominated the 'job boom' of the Reagan era. (The overwhelming majority – about nine in ten – of medically uninsured children live in families with one or more workers, over half in families with at least one full-time, year-round worker.) Meanwhile, severe cuts in public health provision – especially in preventive care – and the accelerated closing of public hospitals and clinics has meant that, even for the 40 per cent of the poor officially covered by Medicaid, decent care – sometimes *any* care – is increasingly difficult to come by (US Congress, 1988c, p. 21).

What has made the shrinking of public provision of health care so devastating in the 1980s is that it has occurred in the face of both sharply rising numbers of the poor and a growing incidence of some health problems, notably those associated with poverty and with the spread of hard drugs – and with the often-related epidemic of AIDS in the cities. There are more poor people, and they tend to be sicker, just as both the public and the private health care available to the poor is shrinking. So it was that in the years from 1978 to 1984, Medicaid spending per child dropped, in constant dollars, by 13 per cent, and Federal spending on three key sources of health care for the poor – maternal and child health services, community health centres and migrant health centres – dropped by a stunning 32 per cent. The Medicaid cuts have been held at the early 1980s level since then, but the slashing of direct community health services, especially maternal and child health care and community health centres, means that even many of the poor who are officially covered by Medicaid are unable to find affordable health care (US Congress, 1987b, p. 43).

In California, for example, about one in four pregnant women gets care, in theory, through MediCal (California's version of Medicaid); but close to a third of those women live in counties where there are so few MediCal providers that 'care virtually does not exist'. In many California counties, clinics routinely turn away thousands of pregnant women seeking prenatal care each year; in Los Angeles County in 1987, women waited an average of sixteen weeks for a prenatal appointment. At

Martin Luther King General Hospital in South-Central Los Angeles, about 30 per cent of mothers delivering babies in 1988 had received no prenatal care at all – which may help to explain why the infant mortality rate at Martin Luther King is the same as that on the island of Jamaica (US Congress, 1988d).[4] The combination of declining public health provision and rising numbers of poor women and children, as a report from the Congressional Office of Technology Assessment suggests, is strongly implicated in the rising incidence of low birth weight and the slowing – and sometimes reversing – of progress against infant mortality in the mid- to late-1980s (US Congress, 1987b, p. 43).[5]

The consequences of diminished care for the poor have become still more ominous because of the massive influx of hard drugs into low-income communities in the past several years. The crack cocaine epidemic in particular has struck with special ferocity at younger adult women; and in the absence of adequate prenatal care, increasing numbers of them are carrying their addiction into the delivery room. The number of babies born in a state of drug withdrawal at Martin Luther King hospital increased eightfold from 1981 to 1987; about 80 per cent of mothers of babies found to have suffered prenatal drug exposure there had received *no* prenatal care (US Congress, 1988d, pp. 45–9).

Thus the most troubling aspect of the shrinking of public health care in the name of the market is the particularly adverse impact on the kinds of preventive care for low-income people that might forestall worse problems down the road; and we will surely continue to suffer (and pay for) the consequences many years hence. But the 'free market' has also struck hard at even the most urgent, reactive forms of care, leaving the uninsured and the inadequately insured without the certainty of care even in severe emergencies. 'Overwhelmed by patients suffering from AIDS, drug abuse and a poverty-related deterioration in health', observes the *New York Times* (1988),

> New York City's emergency rooms are increasingly unable to provide acute care . . . the root of the problem is that the city's patient population is becoming sicker and sicker, a consequence of a rapidly growing poor population and the twin epidemics of AIDS and crack.

In the face of increased needs and simultaneous cost-cutting pressures, many hospitals now routinely practise what's often called 'wallet diagnosis'; it is the patient's insurance status, rather than medical condition, that determines what kind of care they will receive or indeed whether they will receive care at all. The process is dramatically illustrated by the sharp rise in 'patient dumping' in the 1980s. A recent study defines patient dumping as 'the denial of or limitation in the provision of medical services to a patient for economic reasons and the referral of that patient elsewhere' (Ansell and Schiff, 1987). The number of patients thus 'dumped' increased in Chicago, for example, from about 1,300 in 1980 to over 5,600 in 1984; among patients 'transferred' to the city's one remaining public hospital emergency room from other hospitals, 89 per cent were black or Hispanic, 81 per cent were unemployed and 87 per cent were transferred because they lacked health insurance. It's estimated that roughly a quarter of a million patients are transferred for economic reasons annually in the United States today; the accumulating evidence already points to adverse consequences for health. In Chicago, transferred patients incur an average delay in treatment of about five hours, in some cases as much as eighteen hours; a third of those transferred in an Oakland, California study had their health threatened by the resulting delay (Himmelstein *et al.*, 1984). As with housing, what makes this especially troubling is the paradox that meanwhile the upper levels of the health care system are doing very well in market terms. The sharp increase in patient dumping, according to David Ansell and Robert Schiff (1987), 'comes at a time when the profit margin of the private hospital sector in the United States is at its highest level in 20 years'.

But if the most troubling picture from the world of free market medicine in the America of the 1980s is that of poor patients marooned in ambulances because no emergency room will accept them, the more pervasive reality is a more mundane withdrawal of access to care – one which is now reversing the progress made before the 1980s in lowering the barriers to decent care for all. According to survey research by Howard E. Freeman and his associates, the percentage of Americans without a regular source of health care increased from 11 to 18 per cent from 1982 to 1986; the percentage who had not seen a doctor in the past year nearly doubled, from 19 to 33 per cent. And again, the overall figures mask the growing effect of income and race on access to care. Physician visits by people who reported their health to be only fair or poor – those needing to see a doctor – dropped by about 8 per cent in those years for people with incomes below 150 per cent of the poverty line, while they *rose* 42 per cent for those above that level. In 1982, blacks rating their health as poor were about 12 per cent less likely than whites to see a doctor; in 1986, they were *33 per cent* less likely (Freeman *et al.*, 1987).

Rising needs, shrinking services

As with health care, so with a wide range of other social services. It's well-known that many services – from mental health care through child protective services to remedial education for delinquent youth – have been severely reduced at the Federal level in the 1980s. But the full impact of those reductions can only be appreciated against the backdrop of rising *needs* for services resulting from the economic and social dislocations of the Reagan years. Economic insecurity and stress, overwork in poor jobs, spreading impoverishment and excess mobility in search of jobs and affordable housing have taken a deep toll, especially on younger families with children – putting intense pressure on an already strained and minimalist social service apparatus.

Consider child protective services. At the federal level, most funds for intervention with abused and neglected children come through the Title XX Social Services Block Grant, which was cut by almost a third between 1981 and 1988 (CBPP, 1988a, p. 37). Meanwhile, child abuse and neglect reports have risen startlingly – by 365 per cent in California, for example, between 1982 and 1986. Faced with this 'crunch', the response to abuse and neglect has become increasingly reactive, with any efforts at preventive intervention largely abandoned. By the mid-1980s, only about 5 per cent of spending on child protection in Los Angeles County, for example, went for early intervention and prevention; the vast bulk of funds went towards after-the-fact services, mainly the most costly, the removal of the child from the home. There, as elsewhere across the United States, great numbers of children are now routinely placed in group care, foster care or the juvenile justice system because there are no longer any alternative, intermediary services for them; no drug treatment, no family support, mental health care or preventive medical assistance (US Congress, 1988d, p. 5). As with public medical care, that pattern of the substitution of largely reactive – and almost invariably more costly – interventions in place of preventive strategies has appeared as a paradoxical consequence of the 'free market' approach to social services across the board – in mental health care, juvenile justice and care for the elderly and disabled. The bare figures on social service spending, therefore, do not adequately capture the reality of a society increasingly and helplessly inundated with the untended casualties of neglectful social policies.

Conclusion: two futures

Six years into the Reagan–Bush economic recovery, then, the United States is a riven country, wracked by the highest levels of poverty and income inequality in twenty years. And the evidence on income and poverty, bad as it is, only begins to describe the depth of the deprivation that 'market' policies have brought to the bottom third of the social scale. The widening gaps in income and job quality have been matched and compounded by accelerating disparities in the prospects for habitable shelter, basic social services and medical care. The withdrawal of services from poorer communities, moreover, comes just when the adverse economic and social changes have sharply intensified the need for them. At the bottom, conditions in America's poorer communities, both urban and rural, now increasingly resemble those of the middle-income countries of the developing world; the Reagan years have brought us considerably closer to the scenario that Goran Therborn calls the 'Brazilianization of advanced capitalism' (Therborn, 1988, p. 32).

Moreover, because the unleashing of the market – in the selective or 'filtered' form it has taken in America in the 1980s – has struck hardest at many of those aspects of common life and social provision that most affect the nurturance and socialization of the young, its full social and personal consequences will not be felt until many years down the road: as the children of the Reagan legacy grow into adolescence and young adulthood bearing the wounds of public neglect.

But the 'unleashing' of the market has been selective in its imposition and uneven in its outcome. Different groups have been affected in widely varying ways by the social policies of the Reagan era; and as a result the social landscape has changed in complex ways. Some have benefited – at least in the short run and as measured by the conventional indicators. There are many more poor people in America than there were a decade ago; but there are also more truly affluent people; more people with insecure and poorly paying jobs, but also more people with good and well-paying ones; more people without homes, but also more people with second homes. In the selective and 'filtered' unleashing of the market in the 1980s, the young have been hit far worse than the old, the lower 40 per cent of the income distribution far more than the upper 40 per cent, the working poor even more than the dependent poor.

How will these divisions affect the prospects for a coherent political movement to return some semblance of balance between private gain and public need to American life? Two alternative scenarios present themselves.

In the first, the deepening social and economic divisions wrought by the market policies and broad economic shifts of the past decade and a half might translate directly into political divisions between the market's 'winners' and 'losers' that would effectively stymie any serious progressive movement for social change. This would pit a smug, if anxious, upper 40 per cent against a desperate and often demoralized lower third in the political arena – an inherently unequal contest made more so because of the increasing influence of dollars on the American electoral process.[6] In its more humane versions, such a scenario would surely include some at least minimal governmental efforts to soften the edges of the market's impact on the poor, especially on children and families. For the dangers to social stability posed by that impact have not been lost on the corporate community in the United States: by the close of the 1980s, there are signs of the emergence – at least on the level of political rhetoric – of what the economic columnist Robert Samuelson calls a 'crude consensus' that 'government should do more'.[7] But, without a direct challenge to the continued domination of economic life by the private market, even that minimal 'consensus' will almost certainly be rendered nearly meaningless in practical terms by the continuing impoverishment of the public sector. We may see spreading agreement, outside the ranks of hard-core free market conservatives, on the need for early intervention with disadvantaged children, preventive health care for poor women, drug treatment for the urban poor; but there will be no money to pay for them.

But a second and more encouraging scenario is also possible. Opinion surveys routinely reveal that Americans are much more willing to take serious steps to redress the imbalance between public and private life than their political leaders typically imagine. Substantial majorities believe that government should provide good jobs at good wages to lift people out of poverty; that adequate health care should be accessible to all as a matter of right; that providing the preventive and nurturing social services that will enable the children of the 1980s to become contributive citizens in the 21st century is more important than further inflating an already swollen military. Those attitudes reach upwards to many of those who have in the short term reaped some material benefits from the policies of the 1980s. It is entirely possible that, as the longer-range consequences of social imbalance and neglect become increasingly apparent, those beliefs may be translated into common political action.

Neither outcome, of course, is fated. As always, the shape of the future depends crucially on how assiduously we work to build an intelligent and compelling political alternative to the market's long domination of American life.

Notes

1. In addition to the United States, the countries in this study include Australia, Canada, West Germany, Norway, Sweden, Switzerland and the United Kingdom.
2. As this report indicates, the impact of Federal benefit reductions on the availability of food for the poor has been compounded by the withdrawal – also prompted by market considerations – of the *private* food sector. In South Central Los Angeles, for example, the number of supermarkets fell from fifty-five in 1965 to thirty in 1988, with a loss of eleven stores since 1983 alone. This trend, as the *Los Angeles Times* (1989) notes, 'has begun to severely limit access to food for some of the region's poorest residents – a problem that could eventually prove as intractable as finding housing for the homeless'.

3. This research extends the findings of several other recent studies, notably those of Barry Bluestone, Bennett Harrison and Chris Tilly; cf. Bluestone and Harrison in *New York Times* (1987).
4. Hospital infant mortality figure from *Los Angeles Times* (1987); Jamaica figure from World Bank 1988, p. 266.
5. In 1986, the overall death rate for non-white infants failed to improve, for the second year in a row. The post-neonatal death rate – deaths of infants between 28 days and 1 year – increased by over 3 per cent for blacks. Fifteen states, including the District of Columbia, suffered rising overall infant mortality rates, for all races, in 1986 (Children's Defense Fund, pp. 3–4).
6. On this trend, see Edsall (1985).
7. Robert Samuelson, in *Newsweek* (1988). See also *Business Week's* cover story on 'Human Capital', 19 September 1988, which warns that 'the US may now be entering an era when neglect of the bottom half of society begins to threaten the welfare of the entire nation' (p. 103).

References

Adams, T. K., G. J. Duncan and W. C. Rodgers (1988) 'The persistence of urban poverty' in F. M. Harris and R. W. Wilkins (eds.) *Quiet Riots: Race and poverty in the United States*, New York: Pantheon.

Ansell, D. A. and R. L. Schiff (1987) 'Patient dumping: status, implication, and policy recommendations', *Journal of the American Medical Association*, 20 March, 1500–2.

Caputo, R. K. (1989) 'The limits of welfare reform', *Social Casework*, February, **70** (20), 89.

CBPP (Center on Budget and Policy Priorities) (1988a) *Still Far From the Dream: Recent developments in black income, employment and poverty*, Washington, DC: CBPP.

CBPP (Center on Budget and Policy Priorities) (1988b) *Impact of Government Benefit Programs Declines, Adds to Number of Poor Families*, Washington, DC: CBPP.

Children's Defense Fund (1989) *CDF Reports*, February – March, Washington, DC: Children's Defense Fund.

Connell, K. M. (1988) 'Opening statement' in US Congress, Senate, Committee on Banking, Housing and Urban Affairs *National Policy Conference and Public Hearing*, Washington, DC: US Government Printing Office.

Edsall, T. B. (1985) *The New Politics of Inequality*, New York: Norton.

Freeman, H. E., R. J. Blendon, L. H. Aiken, S. Sudman, C. F. Mullinix and C. Corey (1987) 'Americans report on their access to health care', *Health Affairs* Spring, 8–17.

Himmelstein, D. *et al.* (1984) 'Patient transfers: medical practice as social triage', *American Journal of Public Health*, **74**, (5), 495.

Joint Center for Housing Studies (1988) *The State of the Nation's Housing, 1988*, Harvard, Cambridge: JCHS.

Levinson, M. (1987) 'Statement' in US Congress, House Committee on Ways and Means, Hearing, *Reform of the Unemployment Compensation Program*, Washington, DC: US Government Printing Office.

Los Angeles Times (1987) 9 November, p. 3.

Los Angeles Times (1989) 'Poor penalised as food chains flee inner city', 2 January.
National Low Income Housing Coalition (1987) *Low Income Housing Policy Statement*, Washington, DC: National Low Income Housing Coalition.
Newsweek (1988) 14 November, p. 559.
New York Times (1987) 'The grim truth about the job miracle', 1 February.
New York Times (1988) 'Emergency rooms swamped as New York's poor get sicker', 19 December.
New York Times (1989) 23 March.
Rothschild, E. (1988) 'The real Reagan economy', *New York Review of Books*, 30 June.
Sandejur, G. D. (1988) 'Blacks, Hispanics, American Indians and poverty – and what worked' in F.M. Harris and R.W. Wilkins (eds.) *Quiet Riots: Race and poverty in the United States*, New York: Pantheon.
Smeeding, T. M. (1988) 'The children of poverty: the evidence on poverty and comparative income support policies in eight countries' in US Congress, House Select Committee on Children, Youth, and Families, Hearing. *Children and Families in Poverty: The Struggle to Survive*, Washington, DC: US Government Printing Office.
The Economist (1989) 'Assessing Reaganomics: The trouble with theories', *The Economist* 21 January.
Therborn, G. (1988) *Why Some Peoples are More Unemployed than Others*, London: Verso.
US Congress (1987a) *Obtaining Food: Shopping Constraints on the Poor*, House Select Committee on Hunger, Washington, DC: US Government Printing Office.
US Congress (1987b) *Healthy Children: Investing in the Future*, Office of Technology Assessment, Washington, DC: US Government Printing Office.
US Congress (1988a) *Children and Families: Key trends in the 1980s*, House Select Committee on Children, Youth and Families, Washington, DC: US Government Printing Office.
US Congress (1988b) *Wages of American Workers in the 1980s*, Senate, Budget Committee, Washington, DC: US Government Printing Office.
US Congress (1988c) *An Assault on Medicare and Medicaid in the 1980s; The legacy of an administration*, House Select Committee on Aging, Washington, DC: US Government Printing Office.
US Congress (1988d) *Young Children in Crisis*, House Select Committee on Children, Youth and Families, Hearing, Washington, DC: US Government Printing Office.
World Bank (1988) *World Development Report, 1988*, Washington, DC: World Bank.

13

Something for nothing
The informal economy outcomes of free market policies

Stuart Henry
Department of Sociology, Anthropology and Criminology,
East Michigan University, Ypsilanti, Michigan, United States
Jeffrey Brown
Department of Sociology, Anthropology and Criminology,
East Michigan University, Ypsilanti, Michigan, United States

This chapter examines the ways in which changes in the macro-economic structure of American capitalism during the 1980s affected informal economic activity and crime among the underclass.[1] In particular, we shall be concerned with influences on the patterns of work and non-work that stem from the combined effects of a shift away from Keynesian economics toward the Reagan administration's 'free market' economic policy, and the restructuring of employment from manufacturing to service industries. We argue that for members of the underclass these changes during the Reagan era dramatically altered the opportunities for work and welfare.[2] Increased unemployment and reduced income levels combined with less federal and state support for welfare and social programmes to expand the size of the underclass. Depleted of skills, resources and the fabric of social support at a time of increased local competition for employment, members of the underclass found that even the informal economy excluded them. Their choice was between poverty and crime.

In this chapter we attempt to outline the broad national macro-structural context of the Reagan era changes and then examine the economic, political and social impact of Reaganomics on one severely affected state. We go on to consider the impact of these changes on the informal economy. We describe the social process whereby these broad structural changes shape, though do not determine, the opportunities for particular individuals to be enticed into criminal activities. We show how this process, in turn, fuels increases in expenditure on the control apparatus, further spiralling costs which further reduces the protective programmes that would prevent future escalations.

The shift to Reaganomics

The 'free market' economic programme labelled 'Reaganomics' has had a dramatic impact on US economic and social conditions in the 1980s. Put simply, free market economics refers to a national economic system in which the activities of production, distribution and exchange are understood as the outcome of private transactions. Under this system, supply and demand fix prices and government intervention is at a minimum and preferably non-existent. In contrast to the belief that the free market is the ultimate regulator, Keynesian economics, which had been the prevalent post-Second World War policy of western governments, states that variations in aggregate spending and income have an effect on economic performance and can be manipulated to that end by governments. In particular, Keynes (1936) held that the market could not guarantee full employment and that unemployment might last indefinitely unless government took steps to remedy it. In practice these measures took the form of increased expenditure on public service employment to absorb the unemployed. Since Keynesian economics increased the demand for labour, and thereby for consumption, it was also called demand-side economics.

According to Reagan, Keynesian policies were responsible for the rising inflation and unemployment that had taken hold during the 1970s. His administration argued that artificially stimulating demand, by providing income and employment, actually sent too much money chasing too few goods. This demand-led inflation fuelled whatever inflationary pressures were already underway and ultimately further reduced 'real jobs'. The concurrent rise in inflation and unemployment, argued Reagan, justified the end of demand-side Keynesian economics.

To replace this approach Reagan offered a policy of supply–side economics, central to which were dramatic cuts in personal tax rates. Under the Carter presidency the wealthiest Americans paid personal income taxes at a rate of up to 70 per cent of their earnings. Reagan aimed to reduce their top rate to 50 per cent and succeeded in reducing it significantly further. The marginal tax rate for those earning over $75,000, which in 1970 stood at 56 per cent, by 1985 stood at 42 per cent. As a result of the 1986 Tax Reform Act, the top rate of tax in 1988 for those families with incomes of over $61,651 was 33 per cent. For those families with incomes in excess of $123,791 the top rate was 28 per cent.

These tax cuts aimed to stimulate investment, employment and production but it was clear how, in the short term, they would also further increase inflation. This is because they made more money available for consumption, without simultaneously increasing production. It follows too, that the wealthy were prime beneficiaries under Reagan. Their taxes were cut so they had the opportunity to participate in investment, a form of 'welfare', indeed, for the wealthy.[3] In addition to the tax cuts, Reagan also strove to cut government spending on certain areas of the budget.

The Reagan budget initiatives rested on his belief that government had assumed an excessive, intrusive, domineering position in society. For him, social welfare exemplified this overbearing role. Unlike liberal welfare theorists, Reagan saw welfare in a particularly narrow sense, as something draining society and the economy. Liberal theorists had, throughout the earlier post-Second World War period, seen taxation and welfare as part of a redistributive system serving the wider interests of society. The famous British social policy scholar, Richard Titmuss (1969, p. 42), for example, saw welfare in terms of the totality of social, fiscal and occupational public assistance. He defined it as all those 'collective interventions to meet certain needs of the individual and/or to serve the wider interest of society'.

In contrast, Reagan could only see welfare as a support to those below the poverty threshold and saw welfare payments, in general, as locking people into a dependency relationship with the state from which they could not easily escape. Welfare to low-income recipients consists of federal cash assistance, and a variety of in-kind benefits, including subsidized housing, medical care, free surplus food, job training and referral services. Reagan believed that this battery of support had reached a level where it had become a disincentive to work. As George Gilder, writing at the start of the Reagan era in the *Wall Street Journal* said:

> These redistribution schemes, by eroding the incentive to work, save, or support families, have created in our inner cities a tragic wreckage of demoralization, rage, unemployment and crime... In this heartbreaking harvest of liberal 'compassion,' all the necessary disciplines of upward mobility and small business activity have given way to the vandalism and chaos of gangs and drugs, illegitimacy and prostitution. Thus poverty has been intensified and perpetuated by income redistribution.[4]

Similarly, Tom Bethell, another opponent of the pre-Reagan welfare system, stated in 1980, 'when welfare benefits are comparable to take-home pay, there is a danger of creating permanent dependency'. He declared that if you want to work your way up the ladder of achievement in America, it is first necessary to get on the ladder: 'But those left behind are people denied access to the bottom rungs by the "poverty wall" of high welfare tax rates on work' (Bethell, 1980, p. 149). He claimed there are only two ways to reduce the poverty wall: one is to reduce welfare payments and the other is to allow people to work and simultaneously remain eligible for welfare for a period. Bethell cites David Stockman, the then Republican Congressional Representative from Michigan who went on to become the first Budget Director in the Reagan administration, for the answer. Stockman saw removal of work disincentives from welfare as the analytical key to the problem:

> The only real solution to the problems of means-tested welfare for the working or work-eligible population is simply to do away with it. 'Welfare' as we know it should be abolished for all but the non-working – the aged, blind, and disabled – whose eligibility can be ascertained by reference to physical characteristics. (Bethell, 1980, p. 149)

For Bethell, Stockman and others who shaped the welfare policies of Reaganomics, the expansion of the welfare state encouraged welfare dependency and created a painless existence where welfare 'scroungers' could live off the state:

> A society probably does itself incalculable harm when it weakens or eliminates the push of poverty, by putting the poor on welfare, giving them more money than they can earn at the bottom of the ladder... people below the poverty line are given money, told that they are disadvantaged, and so, in fact, are threatened with permanent disadvantage. If the U.S. economy is now stagnant, as we are told that it is, the demoralizing, enervating effects of welfare on the poor should be considered one of the causes. (Bethell, 1980, p. 150)

Armed with evidence claiming that increases in social welfare expenditure result in an increase in the percentage of those in poverty, the Reagan administration found it easier to justify policies that would cause millions more to lose their jobs. By misrepresenting the issue as one of simply eliminating welfare 'scroungers' in order to stem creeping inflation, Reagan was able to gain popular support for the implementation of his policies.

The Reagan plan to reverse the alleged welfare dependency process had three basic components. First, it required a shift of power and decision-making responsibilities from central government to state and local government. Second, it placed renewed emphasis on private sector response, rather than public welfare intervention, in addressing social needs. Third, it put restrictions on the eligibility requirements and on the total allocations for welfare programmes.

Although the administration pledged that it would protect the 'truly needy' by not making dramatic cuts in the income security programmes which formed the social safety net, administrative action violated that promise. Those who had come to rely on Food Stamps, Aid for Families with Dependent Children (AFDC), Medicaid, CETA jobs and Housing Assistance had at best a tattered net between themselves and certain poverty. Drastic slashing of programme funding prompted the elimination of some entitlement programmes and substantial cut-backs in others. For programmes that escaped the administration's cuts, eligibility requirements became stricter. Only those with little or no income could claim benefit. Millions of poor who before had been able to piece together a living wage by combining their earnings from formal economy work with federal cash assistance and in-kind government provision, now had fewer resources to deal with their economic woes.

Moreover, as research by Richard Coe showed, although a small subset of all welfare recipients, consisting essentially of those with extremely unfavourable job prospects, is indeed dependent upon the welfare system for an extended period, many recipients of welfare used it as a fall-back insurance system against unforeseen adverse circumstances. Analyzing data for the pre-Reagan decade of 1969–1978, Coe showed that for a representative sample of the US population, one-quarter (25.2 per cent) were in a household receiving welfare at some time in the ten year period. He says:

> The conclusion to be drawn from this simple fact is that the welfare experience is not limited to a stable, relatively small percent of the population. On the contrary, a surprisingly large segment of the population (one out of every four) received some support from the welfare system at some time over the ten year period. (Coe, 1982, p. 153)

It is important to note that this study describes a time of relatively high employment before the economic restructuring of the 1980s. The latest data available covering the thirty-two months from fall 1983 to summer 1986 are from the 1989 US Census Bureau's national study of the use of programmes including AFDC, Supplementary Security Income, Medicaid, Federal Food Stamps, Federal–State Rent Assistance and General Assistance. Confirming the pattern of Coe's earlier work, the survey showed that while only 7 per cent of people were on the welfare rolls for the entire thirty-two months of the survey, 18.3 per cent or 40.6 million collected benefit for at least one month. The most likely recipients were the young, the old, minorities, single-parent families and working adults with incomes below the poverty threshold.[5] Echoing Coe, Bob Greenstein, director of the Center on Budget and Policy Priorities, said, 'There are people who stay on the rolls indefinitely, but they are a small fraction... The large majority of people who ever receive aid are people going through hardships that they recover from' (*Ann Arbor News*, 1989). With Reagan's cuts in welfare coming at a time when economic recession was beginning to bite, one can only speculate at the number that would have taken some comfort from the system during this period had it remained intact.[6]

Recent growth in total and chronic unemployed in the United States

It is unnecessary for this analysis to determine the causes of capitalist unemployment. We will not be concerned, here, in some abstract sense with whether unemployment is an outcome of externally driven recession, an inherent feature of the capitalist business cycle, the product of government policy, or is caused by changes in the level of wages, the character of labour markets or the mobility of labour (Blinder, 1988). What is important for us is to focus on the pattern that developed under the period of consideration, the Reagan era decade of 1979–89. As we have seen, the political context was one of an ideological shift away from collective provision toward individual self-help, under the guise of 'free market economics' and concomitant cuts in government support to those in need. But it is crucial to understand the economic context within which this policy began to develop and gain popularity in influential quarters.

In the United States, total unemployment began to rise in the 1970s to reach a post-Second World War peak of 9.7 per cent in 1982. The rise was not continuous, but characterized by a series of peaks and troughs. In a thorough examination of these patterns, Fieser (1989) shows that the period since 1968 has not only been characterized by three peaks and three troughs but that the problem of chronic unemployment has been even more accentuated.[7] Using 1948 as a base year, he shows that in 1983 chronic unemployment had increased to 22 times the 1948 level (see Figure 13.1). Moreover, Fieser demonstrates that states with traditionally high rates of durable goods manufacturing and those in the industrial manufacturing belt of the Mid-West such as Michigan, Illinois and Ohio suffered the worst levels of chronic unemployment. In these states during the worst period the proportion of chronic unemployed rose to between 24 per cent and 38 per cent of total unemployment. In addition, persons of colour bore a disproportionate share of the unemployment and chronic unemployment as a result of discrimination, low seniority, low educational attainment, etc.[8]

It is important to realize that official unemployment figures fail to show the true numbers who were affected and so do not acknowledge the overall social and psychological consequences that unemployment has on the well-being of individuals and their surrounding communities, dependants and other interrelated social groups. The official statistics list only those persons who have actively sought work in the previous thirty days. This method excludes people who have become frustrated with their inability to find work and have given up the search.[9] It also excludes the millions who suffer underemployment. Regardless of the wage earned, if employed at all, even for just one hour a week, a person is listed as

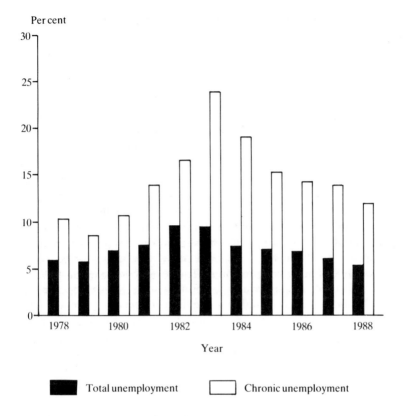

Per cent

Figure 13.1 Total and chronic (twenty-seven weeks or more) unemployment in the United States 1978–88 (Source: US Bureau of Labor Statistics, *Employment and Earnings Monthly*)

employed in the official statistics. In addition, national unemployment statistics yield a figure of unemployment at only one point in time. If, for example, 11 million people are registered as unemployed, twice this number will be likely to experience unemployment during the year. Thus, looking at the unemployment statistics gives only a partial account of the true picture.

Not only were 10.7 million people officially unemployed at the height of the recession in 1982, but many of those remaining in work took cuts in pay or reduced their working hours to avoid being laid off. Others joined the increasing proportion of underemployed. Those who lost their jobs and those with jobs generating poverty-level earnings bore the burden of the Reagan revolution, while suffering the relative deprivation of seeing the rich get richer.

Moreover, although research on unemployment has repeatedly claimed a link between joblessness and physical, social and psychological ill-health (Brenner, 1976; US Congress, 1977, p. 29; Ferman and Gordus, 1979), the issue here is not whether unemployment is a cause or consequence of ill-effects of being without formal employment. Such crude empiricist logic has been shown to be particularly unhelpful since it masks the process whereby unemployment clusters with other 'measures' of deprivation to produce destructive human consequences for individuals, families and communities.[10] Thus, when the difficulties of unemployment are compounded by other factors such as a weakened support network, the polarization of youth and parent cultures, cumulative effects of occupational hazard, then the devastation of unemployment is exacerbated. Indeed, the public and private expenditures required over time to redress the perceived consequences of increased unemployment and the associated social, mental and physical dysfunctions may eventually outweigh the capitalist accumulation that Reaganomics proudly claims to have restored. The social constructionist insight that the effects of the powerful's perceptions of reality on policy might actually be more consequential than the direct effects of the reality itself should not be lost in the rush to formulate elegant causal chains of 'explanation'.

Whether directly, or indirectly, these policy and structural changes taken on a national scale had a major impact upon the lives of most Americans. The new jobs created through Reagan's restructuring were neither in the traditional manufacturing area, nor in the reduced public sector, but in the expanding private service sector. As we shall see in more detail below, this restructuring brought lower wages which, in turn, reduced tax revenues, and added to the federal and state fiscal crisis. Despite the ability to maintain or even introduce compensatory increases in welfare and social support programmes, the Reagan administration retained their commitment to programmes such as defence. The consequence was that at the very time those facing hardship needed support, government was ideologically and fiscally committed to reducing it.

The national picture, however, masks the severity of the changes in some of the hardest hit regions. In order to document the impact of the Reagan era economic changes we have chosen to look at one of the severely depressed midwestern manufacturing states.

Economic restructuring in the state of Michigan.

The rate of total unemployment in the state of Michigan successively rose and fell in the late 1960s through the late 1970s before rising to a

Unemployment rate (per cent)

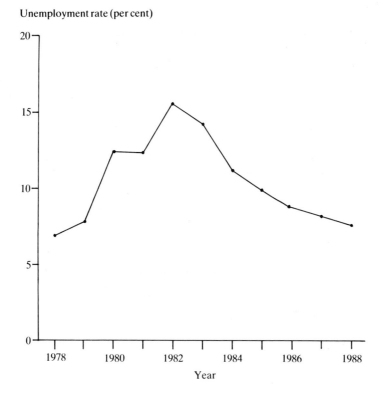

Figure 13.2   Unemployment in Michigan 1978–88 (Source: US Department of Labor, Bureau of Labor Statistics)

post-second World War peak of 15.5 per cent in 1982 (see Figure 13.2)[11,12] Importantly, the measure of chronic unemployment shows that by 1983 Michigan was at the heart of the most severely affected Mid-West region (see figure 13.3).

Reflecting nationwide developments, Michigan underwent a trend toward a service-oriented economy. The waning fortunes of the automobile industry in the face of international competition served only to amplify this shift. Total manufacturing employment in Michigan declined 20.8 per cent, from 1.2 million in 1978 to 934,000, in 1988. During the 1979–82 recession alone, Michigan lost 431,000 jobs, 292,000 of which were in manufacturing (Fulton *et al.*, 1988, p. 8). As a proportion of all jobs, manufacturing plummeted from 30.2 per cent of total employment in 1978 to 22.2 per cent in 1988, a decline of 26.4 per cent. In contrast,

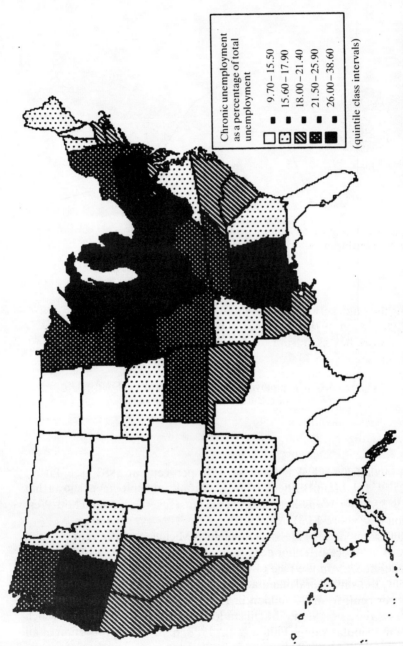

Fig 13.3   Chronic US unemployment, annual average for 1983; US average is 23.9 per cent (Source: US Bureau of Labor Statistics (collected by Census CPS), from: Fieser, 1989, p. 4)

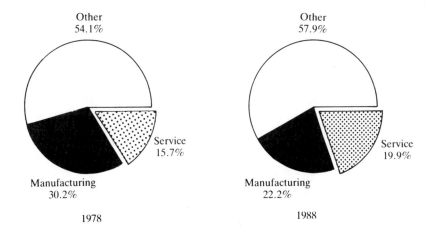

Other
54.1%

Service
15.7%

Manufacturing
30.2%

1978

Other
57.9%

Service
19.9%

Manufacturing
22.2%

1988

Figure 13.4   Employment patterns in manufacturing and service industries in
the state of Michigan (Source: Gregory, 1989a, p. 14)

during the same period service employment increased 36.2 per cent, from
614,000 jobs in 1978 to 836,000 in 1988. As a proportion of all jobs,
service work has risen from 15.7 per cent to 19.9 per cent, a rise of 26.6
per cent (see Figure 13.4; Gregory, 1989a).

This change in the pattern of formal employment has significantly
affected Michigan's fiscal situation. In 1987 the average income for a
manufacturing job was $32,525, compared with $19,111 for a service job.
Service sector income amounted to only 58.8 per cent of manufacturing
income (Gregory, 1989a, p. 13). Expressed another way, from 1979 to
1986, Michigan experienced a net loss of 126,300 jobs paying $34,300 and
over, and made a net gain of 33,700 jobs paying between $17,200–
$34,300, and 121,600 jobs paying $17,200 or less, of which half paid
$11,400 or less (Abbey and Schwartz, 1989, p. 3). As Gregory says,
'manufacturing jobs pay substantially more and when such jobs are lost,
the state receives less revenues to support the state budget' (1989a, p. 13).
This change towards non-manufacturing resulted in an approximate
annual loss of $300 million in state revenues through reductions in state
income, sales and other taxes.

At the same time as restructuring occurred at the state level,
fundamental changes in investment priorities were taking place at the
national level. Fuelled by high inflation, the energy crisis, and the
ideological shift from collective to individual provision, federal grants to
states were also cut. In Michigan, federal disinvestment resulted in

cumulative reductions of $7.6 billion in the period since 1980 (Gregory, 1988, p. 19). Between 1982 and 1988, federal aid to Michigan was cut for various programmes: 64 per cent for Job Training; 18 per cent for educationally deprived children; 20 per cent for employment services; 7.3 per cent for Medicare; 47 per cent for General Revenue Sharing. The cuts in this last category, culminating in the 1987 elimination of the programme, were the most devastating, since General Revenue Sharing had previously totalled 25.5 per cent of all federal aid to local governments in Michigan (Gregory, 1988; Abbey and Schwartz, 1989, pp. 5–6). As can be seen, the change in the revenue and budget system has operated in conjunction with the decrease in federal revenue, at a time when Michigan's income was already declining from economic restructuring, to produce a significant reduction in the level of support for welfare. These forces have moved to 'seriously damage the state's human services network' (Abbey and Schwartz, 1989, p. 28), and they have exacerbated inequality, particularly in respect of the overall distribution of human misery.

The Reagan administration's funding priorities also served to intensify the problems created by economic restructuring itself. As restructuring began to grasp the nation, there was a corresponding increase in demands on state services. One type of demand came from the increased use of support services; another came in response to the accompanying social problems, notably the perception and fear of increased levels of crime. The first 'demand' – reflecting the rising unemployment trends – took the form of a massive increase in welfare case loads (see Figure 13.5). By 1984 Aid for Families with Dependent Children had risen 44.1 per cent higher than 1973 levels, while General Assistance's 1984 level jumped to 246 per cent higher than it was in 1973. By 1983, 15.7 per cent of the state's population was receiving some form of public assistance (Abbey and Schwartz, 1989, p. 3).

Second, the growing rate of unemployment, correlated with a growing rate of crime, particularly violent crime and drug use, fuelled a demand for greater use of police resources and manpower. National unemployment and crime statistics are too general to show correlations since these measures tend to average out any patterns of significance. Moreover, as with unemployment and health correlations discussed earlier, such connections impede rather than enhance our understanding of the social process. However, as Box and Hale (1986) point out, while unemployment cannot be directly and causally linked to increases in crime, the belief that recessionary features such as unemployment cause crime is enough to affect government and judicial practice. They argue that during a prolonged period of economic crisis, when the 'problem' population of unemployed is growing, the State cannot maintain living

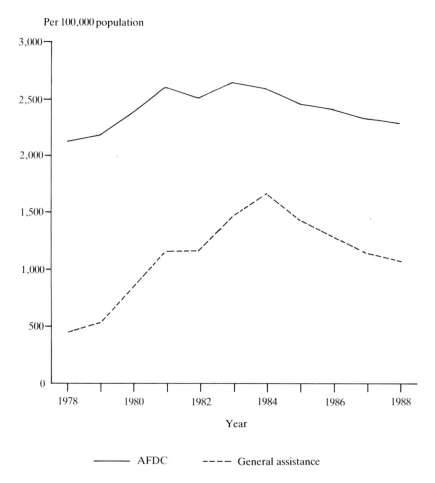

Per 100,000 population

Figure 13.5 Michigan's welfare case loads (Source: Michigan Department of Social Services, Data Reporting Section)

standards and welfare services, without adversely affecting the interests of capital. As the economic crisis deepens the judiciary become increasingly anxious about the possible threat to social order posed by unemployed young males, particularly black males, and 'it responds to this perception by increasing the use of custodial sentences, particularly against property offenders, in the belief that such a response will deter, incapacitate, and thus diffuse the threat' (Box and Hale, 1986, p. 86). The result of Box and Hale's statistical analysis broadly supports the view that sentences to immediate imprisonment positively co-vary with annual

Rate per 100,000 population

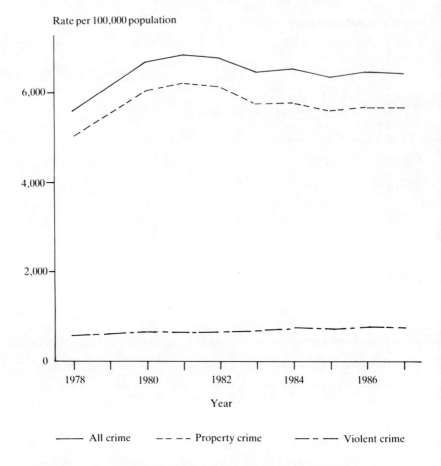

——— All crime   – – – – Property crime   — – — Violent crime

Figure 13.6   Crime index, US rate per 100,000 (Source: FBI Uniform Crime Reports)

unemployment levels. Moreover, they argue that the reason nothing is done to solve the prison overcrowding problem is because overcrowding is a useful ideological device to legitimate an anxious state's real policy of expanding prison capacity where 'social order is threatened by the current economic crisis undermining consent amongst those suffering the worst ravages' (Box and Hale, 1986, p. 94).[13]

In the state of Michigan there is evidence for both a shift in philosophy from rehabilitation to punishment and a tendency to give longer sentences and use community alternatives less frequently. The national crime index for the period 1978–87, based on official crimes known to the

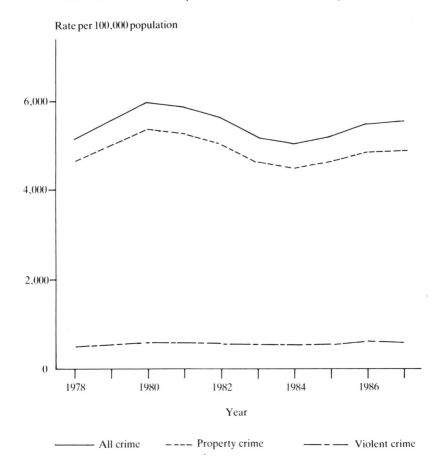

Figure 13.7   Crime index, Michigan rate per 100,000 (Source: FBI Uniform Crime Reports)

police (the FBI's Uniform Crime Reports), shows an initial rising trend to 1980, followed by a decline until 1984 when the rate again began to rise (see Figure 13.6).[14] Similarly, the Uniform Crime Reports for Michigan shows that following an initial rise to a peak in 1981, crimes known to the police have remained relatively stable (see Figure 13.7). This pattern is similar to the national victimization data on crime which, although peaking in 1979, has shown a steadily declining trend since then (see Figure 13.8). However, in spite of these relatively stable rates, and even declining crime rates, there is a considerable difference between different geographical areas. It would seem that the intensity of crime in certain

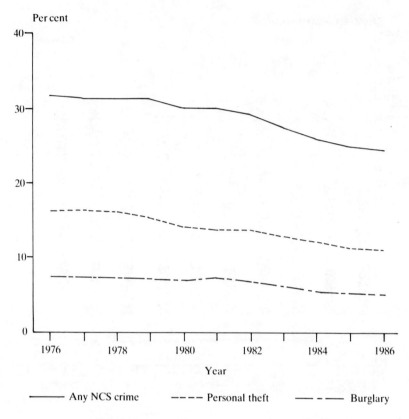

Figure 13.8   Victimization: households touched by crime each year (1976–86) in the United States (Source: US Department of Justice, Bureau of Justice Statistics, 1987. Based on National Crime Survey data)

areas, and the general sense that crime has risen, is at least partly responsible for the increase in punitive action by the criminal justice system. In a recent report to the Michigan House Representatives, Gregory (1989b) shows that the period has seen prison commitment rates rise from 45.5 per 100,000 of the population in 1973 to 119.3 per 100,000 of the population in 1988. This, among other factors, has created a 'crisis in corrections'. According to Gregory, the crisis results from the dramatic increase in prison population coupled with soaring prison construction and operation costs that are destabilizing state budgets. Gregory shows that from 1980 the average annual Michigan prison population has more than doubled, going from 13,899 in 1980 to an estimated 32,500 for 1991 (see Figure 13.9; Gregory, 1989b, p. 2). In addition, data from Michigan

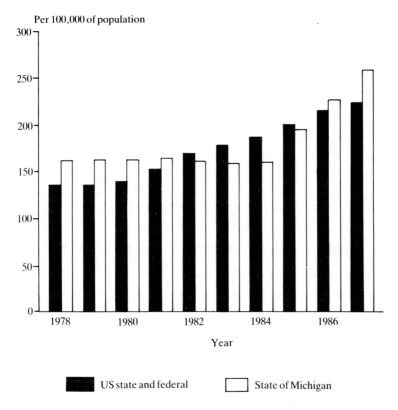

Per 100,000 of population

Figure 13.9 Prisoners: US and Michigan inmates per 100,000 population (Source: US Department of Justice, Bureau of Justice Statistics, 1988, and Michigan House Fiscal Agency, 1989)

Department of Corrections show that since 1973 the average length of sentence for prison commitments climbed from 3.3 years to a 1988 level of 4.5 years. At the same time, parole activity represented by the percentage of prisoners paroled on their minimum date fell from 43.2 per cent in 1977 to 15.2 per cent in 1987. Another way of expressing the stricter parole policy is to consider the total percentage of prisoners paroled, which has fallen from 69 per cent in 1977 to 46.3 per cent in 1987 (Gregory, 1989b, p. 4). Clearly, the fewer paroles there are, the more time offenders will spend in prison. The result of this combination of events has been to produce a situation of gross overcrowding in the state prisons.

In response, Michigan's policy makers initiated a six year programme in 1985 to build an additional twenty-six prisons. Not surprisingly, during the period 1979 to 1990 the rise in corrections-spending has far out-paced spending in all other budget areas. In particular, corrections-spending on prison operations increased 357.4 per cent compared with an average increase in all other areas of 78.2 per cent. The corrections budget has increased from 2.8 per cent of the total budget in 1979 to 7.2 per cent of the budget in 1990, a 156.7 per cent rise. Capital outlay expenditure, consisting primarily of outlays for the new prison construction, increased by 482.8 per cent over the same period. These rises have been paid for by expenditure on education. As Gregory says:

> To gain this share necessarily means that the budget share is lost elsewhere. In this case it came most from Education. In Fiscal Year 1979, Education's share of the state budget equaled 36.6 per cent. By Fiscal Year 1990, it will drop to 30.1 per cent. (Gregory, 1989a, p. 27)

As the damage from the recession intensified, demands on diminished state resources grew as people and industry required increased assistance. Reductions in Federal and state human services have affected the quality of Michigan's human services for those most in need. Many social service agencies were forced to take on increased case loads at the very time they were confronting decreased resources. In a plea to end the destruction of human services, Abbey and Schwartz proclaim:

> Michigan's human services network has not withstood the buffeting of the last decade. The loss of federal revenues and a decade of lean budgets has damaged the state's human services infrastructure. Human service programs are largely operating with fewer fiscal and human resources than they had prior to 1980. . . . If human services agencies are forced to sustain additional budget cuts, these lifeboats for Michigan's most vulnerble citizens will in all likelihood, sink. (1989, pp. 17, 29)

As we have shown, the economic restructuring and policy initiatives of the Reagan era changed the formal opportunities for income, employment and social support for many in the state of Michigan, which is illustrative of the broader national picture. Returning to the national level, we can generalize that two sectors of the population were dramatically affected by Reaganomics. The first group, the wealthy, experience changes which significantly lowered their tax rates, thereby vastly increasing their incomes. The other group includes all those who have been economically harmed by the Reagan initiatives, those who have been removed from the welfare payroll, those laid off or made unemployed, and the millions who can find no escape from their poverty. As we shall see, the changes in economic opportunity and social support for this second group altered their opportunities for participation in informal economic activity and crime.

Capitalism, informal economies and crime

The informal economy refers to all economic transactions for which governments ordinarily seek to account but which escape its detection because of the manner in which they occur. Essentially, the informal economy includes any activity that could legally be conducted in the formal economy but for a variety of reasons is not. Even though governments do not tax, measure or prohibit a vast proportion of the work in the informal economy, these transactions are nonetheless included because the same activities would generate tax revenue if they were conducted in the regular or formal economy. At its broadest level, the definition includes activities that range from self-provisioning, through the provisioning of goods and services for others, whether or not this involves monetary payment or no more than a reciprocity of favours. Examples include homemaking, do-it-yourself repairs, barter and social exchange, and working off-the-books.

What these diverse informal activities have in common is certainly difficult to describe without first specifying the total societal context. For advanced western capitalist societies, activities comprising the informal economy seem to share the following characteristics:[15]

1. Concealed from the state accounting system and are largely unregistered by its economic and criminal measurement techniques.
2. Small scale.
3. Labour intensive, requiring little capital.
4. Locally based, with trading taking place through face-to-face relationships among friends, relatives or acquaintances in a limited geographical area.

Beyond this, characteristics such as whether altruistic or avaricious, autonomous or parasitic, legal or illegal, whether using cash or kind as a medium of exchange, are criteria used by commentators to distinguish different constituent sub-economies.[16] An important consideration is whether informal activities exist as an economy, as sub-economies, or whether the activity is part of a continuum ranging from formal to informal and from economic to non-economic.[17]

It is important here to contrast the criminal and informal economies since we shall argue later that the shared structural position of these, relative to the regular or formal economy, is a significant part of the reason why free market economic policies are particularly harm-producing (Henry, forthcoming). The criminal economy includes those activities which are not subject to tax but are liable for criminal prosecution if conducted in the formal economy. Transactions in the criminal economy include illegal drug trading, prostitution, many forms of gambling, dealing in stolen merchandise and any other exchanges that are forbidden by criminal law. The extent to which criminal and informal economies overlap depends in part on definition, but, importantly, it also depends on their actual operation, for as we shall see, work and trading in one exchange network can give rise to work and trading in the other (Mattera, 1985; Simon and Witte, 1982, Henry, 1978). By understanding the factors that influence participation in these economies we shall expose the ways in which the free market policies of the Reagan era shaped people's choices such that they were more likely to engage in these activities.

People participate in the informal and criminal economies for a variety of reasons. A primary reason is to obtain income, goods and services denied to them by the formal economy. Conservatives argue that taxation and redistribution systems generally, and legislation designed to protect certain sections of the population from discrimination and work-place injury, in particular, create a disincentive for people to trade in the formal economy (Gutmann, 1977; Bawly, 1982).[18] Liberals and radicals, in contrast, argue that it is the capitalist system itself that creates informal economies by encouraging inequalities in the distribution of wealth, based on class, ethnic and cultural segregation, and economic specialization. They argue that, in response, protectionist trade unions and professional associations coalesce to protect their own members and, as a consequence, some goods and services are not widely available or are too expensive for those with low or non-existent incomes and who are not members of a protective association. The direct result is that a market is created outside the formal regular economy for cheap goods and services and

> once regular patterns are established they provide training and opportunity for those members of the community who choose to earn their livelihood this way and are supported by a population that has few viable alternatives for the purchase of goods and services. (Ferman and Ferman, 1973, p. 17)

Commentators also claim that the informal economy, and particularly the social economy, provides a network of social support and mutual aid to enable people to survive in times of hardship (Dow, 1977; Lowenthal, 1975; Stack, 1974).

Of course the tacit Mertonian assumption behind all of these arguments is that social structures exclude some people from the commonly shared goals of material wealth. Those excluded will reject their exclusion and seek to increase their share of wealth through alternative, illegitimate means, most notably by establishing a series of trading relationships outside the formal economy.[19]

In situations where financial pressures are manifest, participation in the irregular economy for monetary reasons is likely to be significantly enhanced. Faced with financial burdens, people consider the options available to eliminate or mediate their distress. In so far as the formal economy is perceived as the source of their hardship, it is seen as incapable, at least in the short term, of providing the solution. Economically troubled persons must then examine other ameliorative options. One such option that seems attractive is the informal economy.

Implications of restructuring and the reduction of state welfare and benefit services on informal economic activity

What then are the consequences of being forced out of the regular economy? At a personal level, as many studies have shown, it is associated with a psychological syndrome of denial followed by dejection. For a few with skills, however, the informal and irregular economy offers an apparent escape. It offers various opportunities for goods and services, and for doing useful work. However, contrary to popular opinion, the informal economy often excludes the very people who are most desperate to reap its rewards. Many of those drawn to the informal economy to get by are unable to meet their needs through its operation. This is because success in the informal economy depends upon many of the same factors required in the formal economy, such as skills, resources and materials. Recent studies by Ray Pahl and others in England show that simultaneously increasing unemployment and cutting social programmes produces an uneven polarizing effect on social class structure (Pahl, 1984; also Alden, 1981; Henry, 1982; Morris 1987). Instead of the mutual aid and self-help characteristic of the 1970s poverty studies, Pahl found major divisions of labour among the lower-class populations. He reveals there is a polarization in forms of informal work between men and women, and between 'work-rich households with multiple earners engaging in all forms of work and work-poor households typically headed by elderly people, single parents, or unemployed people'.

His evidence suggests that those with the most resources and a structurally sound economic position are the ones most likely to succeed at informal work, to the exclusion of those with less means. Those who have a car, who have tools, who know how to fix a roof, repair plumbing, take down an engine or be adept with a paint brush are likely to be most active in the informal economy (Pahl, 1987). This is because much informal work requires particular skills, finances and motivation which are possessed by the very same people who already have occupations in the formal economy. As a result, those who are already in formal work are the ones found to be most able to benefit from the informal economy, and who will, if given longer holidays or shorter hours, take extra overtime, double jobs and so on. For an unemployed urban manufacturing worker with few skills and less than a high-school education, the path to informal work will be as restrictive as the path to formal employment, and considerably less profitable. Depleted of skills, resources and social support at a time of increased local competition, many of the young, retired, poor and unemployed have become part of a growing population of truly impoverished.

In the American context we can be reasonably assured that those excluded from both formal and informal work are most likely to be poor urban minorities, many of whom are persons of colour, particularly Afro-American.[20] However, this section of the population, which William Julius Wilson (1980) has termed the underclass, has also undergone another kind of restructuring. There has been a out-migration of those with skills and resources from the urban ghetto. Those minorities who have made use of governmental equal employment legislation and the authorization of affirmative action programmes have been the talented and educated.[21] This has accentuated the economic problems for the 'black underclass who have been effectively screened out of the corporate and government industries' (Wilson, 1980, p. 19). Literature on the sociology of the black underclass shows that this is increasingly made up of a concentration of those with few skills or abilities who have little prospect of re-entering the formal labour force, other than into lower-class jobs (Wilson, 1980, 1988). Moreover, the implications of this structural change in the underclass are that neighbourhood networks have been seriously damaged by upward migration. In Warren's terms such neighbourhoods have been transformed from the 'parochial and stepping stone' into the 'anomic' (Warren, 1981). In short, the result is that for those people who really need it, the combined effects of economic restructuring, Reaganomics and protective legislation for various groups has meant that even the informal economy has been destroyed.

In order to be clear about precisely who is affected we need to identify those who make up the category of impoverished that are called the underclass. The underclass comprises five groups:

1. The unemployed who are heavily dependent on welfare and use this as their sole source of income.
2. The unemployed, receiving welfare but who are increasingly dysfunctional and are in and out of various mental health and drug treatment facilities.
3. The unemployed who do not receive welfare or other forms of assistance.

4. Those underemployed and receiving inadequate welfare assistance.
5. The underemployed not receiving welfare.

It is difficult to be precise about the size of the underclass since this is considerably affected by how it is defined. What is certain is that once snared in its clutches it is relatively difficult to escape.

Many in the last three categories above live by participation in a variety of forms of work and non-work. This participation includes informal economic activity but it also includes crime. The process whereby participation in informal work also becomes participation in crime is not well understood at present. What leads some members of the underclass to engage in crime while others do not requires an appreciation, not only of theories of crime causation, but also theories of bonding to conventionality and knowledge of protective factors. Clearly simplistic assumptions that the pressures or frustrations of underclass hardships causes informal economy and crime are highly speculative and not particularly productive. At the same time, it would be foolish to ignore the observation that whatever the specific forces shaping some persons' proclivity to crime, their motivational context can be made more conducive to such behaviour by virtue of a series of relationships and activities that, without their underclass situation, might have been less likely. Put simply, membership of the underclass can narrow the opportunity for lawful income-generating activity and, in some cases, simultaneously open up the opportunity for unlawful activity.

As we have seen earlier, informal economic activity requires skills that many of those in the underclass do not possess. This is also true for participation in crime. Nonetheless, it is possible to trace a pathway of narrowing opportunity from informal or irregular work to participation in crime, drug addiction, and to an intensification of income-generating criminal activity. Indeed, some have argued that this is precisely how young people can become involved in and addicted to narcotics. The conventional view is that narcotics can cause some crimes, such as robbery, larceny, burglary and cheque-forging, by generating the need for income to support a drug habit. The logic of such a position is that to cut addiction will cut crime. Auld, *et al.* (1986) however, writing of Margaret Thatcher's Britain, argue that the low level of welfare payments are inadequate for the purchase of basic needs such as housing, clothing, heating and food. In order to meet these needs people engage in irregular work in the informal economy, and it is through their involvement in this partially illegal irregular economy that they encounter and come to buy and sell narcotics such as cocaine and heroin. Such trading is more lucrative than other irregular work that they may encounter and requires more in the way of street survival skills than employment skills.

Thus in some instances, crime, in the form of illegal trading in goods and services, can promote heroin use. Indeed, recent research on the link between crime and drug use in the United States shows that for many, not only does a person's first crime precede their first drug use, but that those who have engaged in crime before becoming addicted dramatically increase their criminal activity after addiction. In a review of studies on male addiction to narcotics, Speckart and Anglin (1985) conclude that addiction to narcotics does not so much cause crime as *amplify* income-generating criminal activities. Even more striking is that for female addicts the typical pattern was: first criminal involvement, first juvenile arrest, first drug use, first narcotic addiction and first adult arrest (James, 1976; James *et al.*, 1979). Commenting on the evidence from such research, Anglin and Hser (1987, p. 365) say, 'For most female addicts, crime precedes the onset of first use while drug use maintains and increases later criminal behaviours'. Put simply, rather than cause initial involvement in crime 'narcotics addiction is an amplifier of income-generating criminal activities' (p. 393).

Thus excluded from formal employment, provided with inadequate welfare, and denied access to the informal economy, the underclass are confronted with the question of whether crime is a viable option for survival. Many reject this option on moral grounds. Others do not wish to confront the inherent risk of physical harm and arrest that accompanies such participation. Such persons are forced into abject poverty and its accompanying social dysfunctions. Some, however, seeing successful neighbourhood role models, and perhaps seeking the glamour of instant material solutions to their problems, are tempted to engage in crime. As John Conyers, a member of the Congressional Black Caucus and a Michigan representative, has said:

> When survival is at stake, it should not be surprising that criminal activity begins to resemble an opportunity rather than a cost, work rather than deviance, and a possibly profitable undertaking that is superior to a coerced existence directed by welfare bureaucrats. (Harris, 1981, p. 126)

Criminological literature on control theory (Hirschi, 1969) suggests that a lack of conventional bonding or a weakening of bonds to convention allows people to be free to commit crime. Whether they do so depends, in considerable part, on the extent to which they learn appropriate behaviours and skills from peers (Matsueda, 1982; Matsueda and Heimer, 1987). While all will be affected, the urban underclass welfare male suffering from a recent job loss will be particularly vulnerable. Having withdrawn sentiment from the formal system that has rejected him, and having formed alliances with a subculture of fellow chronically unemployed males in neighbourhood hangouts, he will be under considerable pressure from family and peers. Not least will be the pressure to provide for himself and his family and to provide an input to the neighbourhood network of support. Such a person may find it very difficult to refuse the profits of street crime or drug trading to restore his economic and social fortitude. This will be a particularly viable option if other members of his unemployed subculture are themselves available to teach him key skills and rationalizations and for those having both the necessary skills and courage to risk short-term harm or arrest. Once in crime they encounter drugs, and if they become addicted they will increase their income-generating criminal activities to sustain their addiction. Sadly, unless they happen to possess particular crime and survival skills, these are the very people who are also most likely to be caught and arrested within months of their first crime.

Conclusion

In this chapter we have shown that the harmful effects of macro-societal changes in economic structure can be intensified by political ideology, and that these combined forces have different impacts on certain regions and social classes. In particular, citing Michigan as an example, we have shown how these forces shape state revenue, human support services and local opportunity structures. We have considered the ways these same macro-forces shape informal exchange networks. For some sections of the population, particularly the underclass, the pincer effect of the lack of both formal and informal income opportunities, coupled with reductions in state welfare services and reduced informal economy activities, throws criminal opportunities into sharp relief. In this context, an individual's choice of whether to commit crime has little competition.

Importantly too, we have shown how individuals influence the wider socio-political structure. In generating their alternative forms of income, some of which might involve crime, the underclass challenges governmental control. This, as we have seen, is translated into increased expenditure on crime control budgets. The result is a further depletion of funding available for welfare support, which, at a time of restructuring and declining formal employment, is precisely the opposite of the kind of response that a socially responsible government might be expected to provide. Only governments are in a position to take the initiative on major macro-interventions. Although it is now established that they cannot fully protect populations from the impact of market forces in a global context, they can and should stop fuelling the underclass–crime nexus. Instead of leaving free market policies to purge the bowels of the class structure, governments have a responsibility to protect society's least fortunate members from external hardships.

Notes

1. Wilson has defined the underclass as those at the very bottom of the economic hierarchy that 'not only includes those lower class-workers whose income falls below the poverty level but also the more or less permanent welfare recipients, the long-term unemployed, and those who have dropped out of the labour market' (Wilson, 1980, p. 156).
2. Ronald Reagan was inaugurated 20 January 1981 and succeeded Democrat Jimmy Carter who had held office since 20 January 1977. Reagan's second term of office ended on 20 January 1989.
3. While welfare derives much of its funding from taxation, the tax system is, itself, another type of welfare. People who are relieved of a disproportionate share of their social contribution are receiving a relative benefit.
4. Quoted by R. Coe (1982).
5. The poverty threshold for a family of four was $10,989 in 1985 and $12,091 in 1988.
6. The proportion of persons classified as being in poverty in 1975 was 12.3 per cent. By 1983 this figure had reached a level of 15.2 per cent.
7. Fieser defines chronic unemployment as 'unemployment of 27 weeks or longer' (Fieser, 1989, p. 1).
8. Fieser's work claims that this is less conclusive than had previously been thought. However, in a paper presented at the 1990 Annual Meeting of the AAG in Toronto entitled 'Black Long-Duration Unemployment in the U.S., 1981–1988,' Fieser finds that the already disproportionately high percentages of blacks among the unemployed and among the long-duration unemployed during the 1982–83 recession became even higher as the two all-race unemployment rates decreased during the subsequent economic recovery. Thus, blacks have at least recently conformed to a common conceptual BLS definition of structural or chronic unemployment: 'workers who bear substantial unemployment in high employment periods'.
9. This category, according to the Bureau of Labor Statistics, included an additional 1.1 million people for 1986. The actual number of discouraged workers may be three times the levels reported by the Bureau of Labor Statistics.
10. For a critique of the Brenner thesis see especially Stern (1982), and Taylor and Jamieson (1983).
11. In 1987, according to the US Bureau of the Census, Michigan's population was 9,200,000 and it was the eighth most populous state; Detroit City had a population of 1.2 million according to the 1980 census, but the wider Detroit Metropolitan Area had a population in excess of 4 million and ranks as the nation's fifth largest urban conglomeration. For a detailed analysis of development in the area see Sinclair and Thompson (1975).
12. The actual high reached in 1982 was 17 per cent (see Governor's Blue Ribbon Commission, n.d., p. 16).
13. For more detailed discussion on this general relationship see Box (1986).
14. Unfortunately the crime index is notoriously unreliable as a measure of actual crime committed since it accounts for only those crimes known to police and omits the 70 per cent of crimes unreported. As a result small changes in reporting rates can result in large changes in the crime index, without there being any actual increase or decrease in actual crimes

committed. For this reason the victimization data in Figure 13.8 is more accurate.

15. For a review of the Third World informal sector see Bromley and Gerry (1979) and Portes *et al.* (1989).

16. Classification schemes abound in the literature. A typical distinction is to call self-provisioning or provisioning for other family members, the household or domestic economy; provisioning of goods and services for others on a reciprocal basis but without payment, the social or communal economy; and working to provide goods, labour or other services for payment, the irregular, cash or underground economy. The terms underground or hidden economy are also used but tend to refer to activities which, not only evade national tax and accounting systems, but also involve stolen property, although these shade off into illicit trading in vice and drugs, itself part of the criminal economy. For recent literature reviews on definitions and typologies see Ferman *et al.* (1987) and Henry (1988).

17. Those taking the view that no separate informal economy exists nevertheless recognize that the activity described above is an important and integral part of modern capitalist society and, as such, is worthy of consideration. See, for example, Harding and Jenkins (1989). For a similar critique of the informal sector concept in the Third World literature see Connolly (1985).

18. For more recent argument on the way the State creates and sustains informal economies see Weiss (1987).

19. Although there is considerable evidence that informal economies provide non-monetary rewards such as peer prestige, fun, excitement and social bonding, it is the monetary rather than social opportunities that concern us here. However, see Henry (forthcoming), Ferman and Berndt (1981), Gaughan and Ferman (1987), also Mars (1982).

20. In 1970 33.5 per cent of blacks were living below the poverty line compared to 9.9 per cent of whites. In 1986 31.1 per cent of blacks were below the $11,200 annual income for a family of four, compared with 11 per cent whites. It is important to note however, that underclass does not equal black. Nor can it be restricted to persons of colour since it also includes poor southern whites, small farmers suffering foreclosure.

21. This is reflected in the slight decline in the proportion of blacks below the poverty line and the slight increase of whites in that category.

References

Abbey, J. M. and I. M. Schwartz (1989) *Plotting and Course for Michigan's Children*, Ann Arbor, MI: University of Michigan, Center for the Study of Youth Policy.

Alden, J. (1981) 'Holding two jobs: an examination of moonlighting' in S. Henry (ed.) *Informal Institutions*, New York: St. Martin's Press.

Anglin, M. D. and Y. Hser (1987) 'Addicted women and crime', *Criminology* **25**, 359–97.

Ann Arbor News (1989), 'Welfare not dead end for most, survey finds', 28 April, p. 1.

Auld, J., N. Dorn and N. South (1986) 'Irregular work, irregular pleasures: heroin in the 1980's' in R. Matthews and J. Young (eds.) *Confronting Crime*, pp. 166–87, Beverly Hills: Sage.

Bawly, D. (1982) *The Subterranean Economy*, New York: McGraw-Hill.

Bethell, T. (1980) 'Treating poverty', *Harper's Magazine*, February; reprinted in P. J. Baker and L. E. Anderson (eds.) *Social Problems: A critical thinking approach*, pp. 145–50, Belmont, CA: Wadsworth (1987).

Blinder, A. S. (1988) *The Challenge of High Unemployment*, Cambridge: National Bureau of Economic Research.

Box, S. (1986) *Recession, Crime and Punishment*, London: Macmillan.

Box, S. and C. Hale (1986) 'Unemployment, crime and imprisonment and the enduring problem of prison overcrowding' in R. Matthews and J. Young (eds.) *Confronting Crime*, pp. 72–96, London: Sage.

Brenner, M. H. (1976) *Estimating the Social Costs of National Economic Policy*, US Congress Joint Economic Committee, Washington DC: US Government Printing Office.

Bromley, R and C. Gerry (eds.) (1979) *Casual Work and Poverty in Third World Cities*, London: Wiley.

Coe, R. (1982) 'Welfare dependency: fact or myth', *Challenge* September–October; reprinted in P.J. Baker and L. E. Anderson (eds.) *Social Problems: A critical thinking approach*, Belmont, CA: Wadsworth (1987).

Connolly, P. (1985) 'The politics of the informal sector: a critique' in N. Redclift and E. Mingione (eds.) *Beyond Employment: Household, gender and subsistence*, pp. 55–91, Oxford: Basil Blackwell.

Dollars and Sense (1987) *Real World Macro: A macro economics reader from 'Dollars and Sense'*, Somerville, Mass.

Dow, L. M. (1977) 'High weeds in Detroit', *Urban Anthropology* **6**, 111–28.

Ferman, K. A. and L. E. Berndt (1981) 'The irregular economy' in S. Henry (ed.) *Informal Institutions*, New York: St. Martin's Press.

Ferman, P. R. and L. A. Ferman (1973) 'The structural underpinning of the irregular economy', *Poverty and Human Resources Abstracts* **8**, 17.

Ferman, L. A. and J. P. Gordus (eds.) (1979) *Mental Health and the Economy*, Kalamazoo, MI: W. E. Upjohn Institute for Employment Research.

Ferman, L. A., S. Henry and M. Hoyman (eds.) (1987) 'The informal economy', *Annals of the American Academy of Social and Political Science* **493**.

Fieser, J. B. (1989) 'Causes and characteristics of long-duration unemployment in the U.S. 1976–1987', paper presented at the 1989 Annual Meeting of the Association of American Geographers, Baltimore, Maryland, 20 March.

Fulton, G. A. (1988) *The Michigan Economy in 1989*, Ann Arbor, MI: Research Seminar in Quantitative Economics, 18 November.

Gaughan, J. P. and L. A. Ferman (1987) 'Towards an understanding of the informal economy', *Annals of the American Academy of Political and Social Science* **493**, 15–25.

Governor's Blue Ribbon Commission (n.d.) *Reducing Dependency in a Changing Economy*, Final Report of the Governor's Blue Ribbon Commission on Welfare Reform, Lansing, MI: Office of the Governor.

Gregory, W. C. (1988) *The Federal Budget Deficit: Impacts of the Reagan era budgets on the state of Michigan*, Lansing, MI: Michigan House of Representatives, 15 August.

Gregory, W. C. (1989a) *The House Fiscal Agency Economic and Fiscal Outlook for Michigan in 1989 and 1990*, Lansing, MI: House Fiscal Agency.

Gregory, W. C. (1989b) *The Crisis in Michigan's Criminal Justice System*, Lansing, MI: House Fiscal Agency.

Gutman, P. M. (1977) 'The subterranean economy', *Financial Analysts Journal* **34**, 26–7.

Harding, P. and R. Jenkins (1989) *The Myth of the Hidden Economy: Towards a new understanding of informal economic Activity*, Milton Keynes: Open University Press.

Harris, M. (1981) *America Now: The anthropology of a changing culture*, New York: Simon & Schuster.

Henry, S. (1978) *The Hidden Economy*, Oxford: Martin Robertson; also republished in Port Townsend, WA: Loompanics Unlimited (1988).

Henry, S. (1982) 'The working unemployed: perspectives on the informal economy and unemployment', *Sociological Review* **30**, 460–77.

Henry, S. (1988) 'Can the informal economy be revolutionary? Toward a dialectical analysis of the relations between formal and informal economies', *Social Justice* **15**, 29–60.

Henry, S. (forthcoming) 'The informal economy: a crime of omission by the state?' in G. Barak (ed.) *Crimes by the State*, Albany: SUNY Albany Press.

Hirschi, T. (1969) *The Causes of Delinquency*, Berkeley: University of California Press.

James, J. (1976) 'Prostitution and addiction: an interdisciplinary approach', *Addictive Diseases and International Journal* **2**, 601–18.

James, J. C. Gosho and R. Watson Wohl (1979) 'The relationship between female criminality and drug use', *International Journal of the Addictions*, **14**, 215–29.

Keynes, J.M. (1936) *The General Theory of Employment, Interest, and Money*, New York: Harcourt Brace.

Lowenthal, M. (1975) 'The social economy of urban working class communities' in G. Gappert and H. Ross (eds.) *The Social Economy of Cities*, Newbury Park: Sage.

Mars, G. (1982) *Cheats at Work*, London: Allen & Unwin.

Matsueda, R. L. (1982) 'Testing control theory and differential association: a casual modeling approach', *American Sociological Review* **47**, 489–504.

Matsueda, R. L. and K. Heimer (1987) 'Race, family structure and delinquency: a test of differential association and social control theories', *American Sociological Review* **52**, 826–40.

Mattera, P. (1985) *Off the Books: The rise of the underground economy*, London: Pluto Press.

Morris, L. D. (1987) 'Local social polarization: a case study of Hartlepool', *International Journal of Urban and Regional Research* **11**, 331–50.

Pahl, R. E. (1984) *Divisions of Labour*, Oxford: Basil Blackwell.

Pahl, R. E. (1987) 'Does jobless mean workless?: unemployment and informal work', *Annals of the American Academy of Political and Social Science* **493**, 36.

Portes, A., M. Castellis and L. A. Benton (eds.) (1989) *The Informal Economy: Studies in advanced and less developed countries*, Baltimore: John Hopkins University Press.

Simon, C. P. and A. D. Witte (1982) *Beating the System: The underground economy*, New York, Auburn.

Sinclair, R. and B. Thompson (1975) *Metropolitan Detroit: An anatomy of social change*, Cambridge, MA: Ballinger.

Speckart, G. and M.D. Anglin (1985) 'Narcotics use and crime: an analysis of existing evidence for a causal relationship', *Behavioural Sciences and the Law* **3**, 259–83.

Stack, C. B. (1974) *All Our Kin: Strategies for survival in a black community*, New York: Harper & Row.

Stern, J. (1982) 'Does unemployment really kill?', *New Society* 10 June, 421–2.

Taylor, I. and R. Jamieson (1983) 'Young people's responses to the job crisis in Canada: a framework for theoretical work and empirical research', mimeo Ottawa: Unpublished report prepared for Statistics Canada (available only via authors).

Titmuss, R. (1969) *Essays on the Welfare State*, Boston: Beacon Press.

Warren, D. (1981) *Helping Networks: How people cope with the problems in the urban community*, Notre Dame, Ind: University of Notre Dame Press.

Weiss, L. (1987) 'Explaining the underground economy: state and social structure', *British Journal of Sociology* **38**, 216–34.

Wilson, W. J. (1980) *The Declining Significance of Race: Blacks and changing American institutions*, Chicago: The University of Chicago Press.

Wilson, W. J. (1988) 'The ghetto underclass: social science perspectives', *Annals of the American Academy of Political and Social Science*, **501**.

US Congress (1977) M. Harvey Brenner's testimony to US Congress, *House Hearings, Unemployment and Crime*, Washington, DC: US Government Printing Office.

PART 5
New Zealand

14

New Zealand
The advance of the New Right

Ian Shirley
*Department of Social Policy and Social Work,
Massey University, New Zealand*

Introduction

In July 1984, the Conservative National Party led by Robert Muldoon, was replaced as the Government of New Zealand by the Labour Party under the leadership of David Lange. The transfer of power was expected to produce a traditional Labour Government committed to the economic defence of wage- and salary-earners and the reinstatement of full employment. Since the advent of the first Labour Government in the 1930s the Labour Party had been associated with a broad philosophical commitment to the welfare state and to individual and social security, but in 1984 these traditions were set aside as the fourth Labour Government sponsored a free market 'revolution' which has redrawn the political landscape of New Zealand.[1]

At the change of government the New Zealand currency was devalued by 20 per cent and by early 1985 the dollar was floated and the regulatory structure that was in place when the Labour Government took office was almost completely dismantled. Interest rate controls were removed and restrictions were lifted on the flow of money in and out of New Zealand. The economy was opened up to competition from imports, and foreign companies were given greater access to the New Zealand market. Agricultural subsidies were terminated and the protective shield was removed from manufacturing. State departments were reorganized along commercial lines as a preliminary step in the sale of public assets and the privatization of the newly formed state corporations. Whereas the goals of this social and economic strategy were defined in terms of efficiency, consumer choice and user-pays, the means actually adopted have centred around a restrictive monetary policy, financial deregulation, and the dismantling of state social services. The reform programme, referred to as economic liberalization, and popularized in New Zealand as 'Rogernomics', is a misleading abbreviation for the advance of the New Right and the restructuring of economic and social relations.[2]

Post-war reconstruction

In order to understand the historical 'achievements' of the New Right, it is necessary to examine the forces and conditions out of which economic liberalization emerged. As in other western nations, the New Right surfaced in the 1970s, towards the end of what some historians have referred to as the post-war consensus (Armstrong *et al.*, 1984). It was a period in which western states, such as New Zealand, developed a concern with distribution as well as production, and with social well-being as well as material progress. Both National and Labour administrations generally accepted the notion of a mixed economy – that is, a market system of production and distribution with the State accepting responsibility for fiscal and monetary policy and the enhancement of social well-being. Trade unions secured employment as a component of the social wage, and employers accepted arbitration and conciliation in return for a profitable and stable political environment. Political consensus was based on widespread public confidence and this in turn helped maintain accumulation. Accumulation generated jobs, regular increases in living standards, and resources for social services as well as profits. These factors in turn reproduced the post-Second World War consensus.

Although the notion of 'consensus' is a misleading interpretation of post-war reconstruction, the achievements of the industrialized world were considerable. In a period of twenty-three years (1950–73) output in the advanced industrialized societies increased by 180 per cent.[3] More was produced in that period than in the previous seventy-five years. Real wages rose in line with productivity and reserves of unemployed labour were progressively exhausted. Civil spending on goods and services, such as health and education, increased by 50 per cent more than total output, and transfer payments in the form of social security also accelerated.

The main factors behind this rising productivity can be identified as a substantial increase in both the quantity and quality of the means of production. Productive output per worker more than doubled in this period, an achievement that can be attributed to technological advances in new machinery accompanied by changes in work practices.[4] Old and poorly productive equipment was replaced by a new generation of machines, and work practices were altered to accommodate the new technology. These changes were introduced without undermining the decision-making authority of private capital and thus the essential relationship between capital and labour was maintained. Despite the tenuous nature of his relationship, the productive achievements of the time generated enough wealth to convince social theorists such as Daniel Bell (1960, 1973) that political and economic conflict had been transcended forever.

The illusion of consensus was most pronounced within New Zealand where it was interpreted as an extension of the colonial dream:

> a specially favoured place . . . where race did not matter in any harmful way, where class divisions did not exist as barriers, where the old and the young were equally looked after, and where the family and woman as its cornernstone were kept secure and protected. (Oliver, 1978, pp. 51–2)

The evidence to support the illusion was impressive. For almost thirty years New Zealand experienced full employment (Shirley *et al.*, 1990). On 31 March 1956 only five unemployment benefits were being paid, and thus there was some substance to the claims of politicians that they knew the unemployed by name. By international standards the country was socially and politically stable and the increasing affluence of the citizenry was reflected in New Zealand's consistent rating among the top five of the world's wealthiest nations.[5]

The policies which produced these three decades of stability were established in the wake of the 1930s depression, and they were substantially aided by the circumstances and requirements of war (Baker, 1965; Martin, 1981). In contrast to the Coalition Government, which responded to the depression by a retraction in public expenditure, the first Labour Government developed a social and economic programme which gave the State a strong interventionist role in the process of reconstruction. Labour created a regulated and protected economy by means of exchange and import controls, protective tariffs and the provision of subsidies for New Zealand's primary producers. Guaranteed prices for primary products were established and the State became actively involved in marketing these products overseas. Whereas its external policies effectively insulated the New Zealand economy from undue overseas influence, the Labour Government's internal programme concentrated on maintaining the viability of small-scale farming and manufacturing. Internal regulations included price stabilization, the linking of wages to prevailing economic conditions by means of Arbitration Court rulings, and the use of quasi State agencies as instruments of government policy. These instruments included an expanded role for the Reserve Bank in areas such as agriculture and housing, the promotion of scientific and advisory services which were designed to facilitate productive growth. While Labour's economic policy was concerned primarily with the interests of small urban and rural capital, its welfare innovations concentrated on the redistribution of wealth and the development of a social wage.

The concept of a social wage was at the centre of the 1938 Social Security Act which emphasized the maintenance of a healthy community.[6] Health was not limited to the treatment of the sick, but rather the creation of a social and economic environment in which individuals might live healthy and productive lives. The social philosophy of the first Labour Government embraced free education, a community-based preventive health scheme, a salaried medical service, a free public hospital system, adequate standards of housing, improved physical working conditions, a basic minimum wage and full employment. Although this philosophy was severely compromised in order to accommodate powerful sector groups such as the Medical Association, the expansionist programme based on Keynesian economic policies did produce full employment, and along with full employment came increasing social and economic security.

The stable environment of the post-war period was reflected in the labour market which was characterized by occupational mobility and which in turn contributed to the public perception of a classless society. Employees were confident that even if a new job proved unsatisfactory, there would be little difficulty in securing an alternative position and employers contributed to an expanding labour market by means of private investment. The business community was willing to invest because government policies assured the private sector that even if an investment proved to be temporarily unprofitable, the total market would eventually expand to 'ratify' the investment decision and workers were protected by the re-introduction of compulsory arbitration, compulsory unionism and the establishment of a forty-hour week. These latter measures strengthened the trade unions, whose cooperation was an essential component of the Government's stabilization policy.[7]

A significant factor in the success of the State's stabilization programme was the secure and prosperous trading relationship which had been established with Britain in the nineteenth century. It was a colonial relationship which provided a guaranteed market for staple products such as meat, wool and dairy produce. Such guarantees were important because of the narrow productive base of the New Zealand economy, and one of the main beneficiaries of this colonial relationship was the highly efficient family farm. Wage-earners also benefited, although the trade unions in New Zealand were relatively weak when compared with their counterparts in Europe and Scandinavia (Roth, 1973). This weakness stemmed from the size of productive units in New Zealand and the dispersed nature of both capital and labour interests within the rural and industrial sectors. These two factors, namely the dependent nature of the colonial economy in the international market-place, and the dispersed nature of capital and labour interests within, produced a class structure which was radically different from that found in industrial societies such as Britain.[8] As a 'new' society, New Zealand had no established aristocracy or landless peasantry, and because of the diffused character of the class formation, small capital interests predominated. Even by the 1950s, nearly two-thirds of the total number of factories in New Zealand employed ten or fewer workers, and thus the scale of production has been an important factor in ensuring that the development of policy would continue to be characterized by minimal organizational capacities. It also explains why New Zealanders view the State as a mediating agency arbitrating between widely disparate factions and interest groups but with an overriding responsibility for ensuring economic security and social well-being.[9]

For over thirty years the welfare state effectively met the diverse interests of capital and labour and, in return, the various sector groups modified their political aspirations. Wage- and salary-earners gained full employment and a modicum of security, and in return, the socialist tendencies of the working class were modified. The business community benefited from an extended period of prosperity and stability, but they surrendered a certain amount of commercial freedom in the process. The farming sector was protected by guaranteed prices of dairy products and by supplementary minimum prices, but escalating land and servicing costs meant that it became increasingly difficult for young farmers to obtain blocks of their own and thus continue the tradition of the family farm. Even the Maori community which had been suppressed by military and legal action in the nineteenth century appeared to accept the post-war emphasis on cultural as well as social assimilation.[10]

Overseas observers have interpreted this historical compromise as a form of pragmatic socialism without the doctrinal and theoretical underpinnings of socialism in Europe, but these observations ignore the structural conditions which produced a labour movement highly dependent on the State for its continuing viability.[11] The working class sought tangible benefits from the State in the form of wage and employment security rather than the more comprehensive forms of welfare which emerged in Scandinavia. Although the doctrines of Marx, Owen, Lasselle and Fourier were widely understood even in the nineteenth century, the pragmatism of the working class produced a union movement, which concentrated on securing a living wage within the framework of a highly regulated market economy. Until the 1970s, the strategy appeared to be relatively successful (Easton, 1986).

The same could be said of the interests of small farmers, manufacturers and employers. Although the writings of Henry Lloyd, John Stuart Mill, Herbert Spencer and Adam Smith were influential in the development of a liberal tradition, employers were equally pragmatic in their relations with the trade unions and the State. Small business interests relied on the State for economic security which took the form of protection from overseas competition, and regular adjustments to the labour market by means of controlled immigration. Policies such as the foreign exchange controls which were introduced in conjunction with the import licensing system in 1938, played an important role in maintaining economic stability during the recurring exchange crises of the 1950s and 1960s. At the same time, the business sector supported state-sponsorship of education, health and social welfare as an investment in human capital, which produced a stable work-force at a limited cost to employers. While the record of state-sponsorship following the defeat of the first Labour Government in 1949 was both more reluctant and erratic. National and Labour administrations continued to support the broad objectives of the welfare state which were established during the period of post-war reconstruction.[12]

Towards economic liberalization

If the post-Second World War period can be described as a watershed in terms of social and economic policy, the intervening years (late 1960s to 1984) were marked by cycles of expansion and depression. These fluctuations in the country's economic performance stemmed in the first instance from New Zealand's vulnerability as a trading nation. New Zealand exports were dominated by agricultural products for a predominantly British market, but it became an increasingly restricted market as Britain forged closer economic relations with Europe. Despite policies aimed at diversifying New Zealand's export base, the value of foreign trade declined (see Figure 14.1). The increasing gap between export receipts and import prices was influenced by external factors, such as the oil crisis of 1973, and the actions of overseas governments who sought to protect their productive sectors. At the same time overseas markets set new requirements for primary industries such as dairying and meat, which imposed additional costs on the processing of these commodities. Synthetic substitutes for wool and butter and alternative red meat products directly affected New Zealand trade, as did changes to the transportation industry, such as containerization which might have been economically advantageous to Europe and North America, but was of doubtful economic benefit to New Zealand (Birks and Chatterjee, 1988).

   In response to this changing international environment, the economy

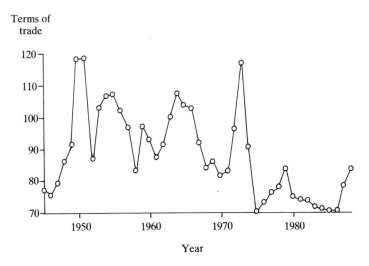

Figure 14.1   Terms of trade 1945–88 (Source: Department of
Statistics, Wellington)

was slowly opened up to overseas competition by the dismantling of some
import controls and by means of incentives which were designed to
strengthen the export potential of both the agricultural and manufacturing sectors (Bollard and Buckle, 1987). Although the State created an
environment for economic restructuring, the reform programme was led
by the private sector.

Industry was reorganized through mergers, take-overs and amalgama-
tions thus increasing the size of plants and in some instances changing
the basis of ownership from individuals to one of interlocking company
ownership and control.[13] A significant component in the changing
ownership pattern was the role played by financial institutions such as
insurance companies, many of which were overseas owned or subsidiaries
of overseas-based companies. During the 1960s there was a fourfold
increase in the level of overseas ownership in New Zealand and this
changing pattern of ownership was reflected in the control of small
businesses demonstrating their inability to affect major decisions. The
small grocer became in effect a salesperson for Unilever and Watties as
retailers became increasingly dependent upon the patronage of large
companies. National economic decisions were dominated by fewer
companies, thus reinforcing centralized control, and at the same time
industry became concentrated in certain regions of the country in order to
meet the transportation, labour and cost requirements of the private
sector.[14]

The role of the State was important in facilitating the programme of economic restructuring. In the 1960s a form of indicative planning was promoted which produced growth targets for the various sectors of the economy in consultation with employers and unions. This form of assistance, which was backed by export incentives, encouraged industrial diversification and promoted industries such as horticulture, timber and tourism. It not only widened the base of the New Zealand economy but it expanded the labour market during a period in which jobs were being replaced by new technology, industrial restructuring and resource depletion. As new jobs were created, especially in the service sector, redundancies occurred in traditional areas of manufacturing, such as textiles, which lost 11 per cent of its labour force between 1973 and 1978. Agricultural processing was also affected with the closure of older, smaller plants in both the dairy and freezing industries. The changes had a detrimental impact upon the services of small towns in rural communities.

As the global economic crisis deepened in the 1970s the State embarked on a programme of substituting domestic energy for imported oil and increasing exports of energy-related commodities. This capital intensive programme was based around industries such as petro-chemical production, electricity generation, aluminium smelting, the manufacturing of steel and the processing of forestry products. It was prompted by the significant hike in world energy prices in 1973, the growing electricity surplus in New Zealand and a stagnant domestic economy. The programme was ill-conceived, however, in that the partnership between private companies and the State resulted in the companies being relatively immune from risk while the New Zealand taxpayer was forced to bear a disproportionately large share of any subsequent deficit.[15] The full import of this risk factor can be gauged from New Zealand's growing external deficit. By 1974, after thirty-five years of full employment, the external debt was less than 500 million dollars, but with the steady reduction of import controls, and the consequential growth of import surpluses, New Zealand's international indebtedness (public and private) by 1984 was 16 billion dollars. With the abolition of exchange controls and the further dismantling of import controls and tariffs after 1984, this debt rose to over 40 billion dollars by 1989. Whereas the fourth Labour Government blamed this increasing indebtedness on the energy-related programmes of the previous National administration, recent evidence (Shirley *et al.*, 1990) suggests that the projects did generate employment, both in the construction and operation of the projects themselves and in providing scarce foreign exchange through export and import substitution. Furthermore, the dramatic turnround in the balance of payments between the early 1980s and the late 1980s can be attributed in part to the state-sponsored programme. These empirical facts have been largely ignored because the 'Think Big' programme became a convenient scapegoat for those who viewed the State as an impediment to economic liberalization.

The reforming zeal of the State in the economic realm was not matched in traditional areas of social policy, which were characterized by incrementalism as successive governments were forced to meet the consquences of a rapidly increasing post-war population. Throughout the 1970s as the State continued to meet its substantial commitments in health care, education, employment and housing, tension emerged between the rhetoric and the realities of material life. The rising costs of living coupled with demographic changes (such as early marriage and smaller families) encouraged increasing numbers of women to enter paid work. Paid employment offered women some degree of financial security and independence. It also offered companionship and an alternative to domesticity but increasing participation rates did not lead to social and economic equality. Women continued to be engaged in a narrow range of occupations at lower rates of pay and with limited opportunities for advancement. Even the advent of equal pay legislation did not bring equal opportunity (Hyman, 1978; Report of the Select Committee, 1975).

As far as households were concerned, disparities were most evident between one- and two-income families and thus, despite the achievements of the welfare state over forty years, relative poverty was rediscovered in New Zealand. In 1975 it was estimated than 18 per cent of the population could be classified as relatively poor and, within that classification, families with dependent children and those on age benefits were identified as being most vulnerable (Easton, 1983). Although inflation throughout the post-war period was more or less in line with that experienced by New Zealand's trading partners, rising prices for land and property meant householders faced increasing pressure on income.

The New Zealand Maori was particularly disadvantaged.[16] At the time of the 1971 Census the average Maori male income was $1,109 compared to an average male income of $2,067. Even if there were an adjustment for the difference in age distribution the Maori average income was only 72.3 per cent of the national average. In education, 74 per cent of young Maori men and 36 per cent of young Maori women left the school systems without any national academic qualifications and after leaving school 25.9 per cent of all Maori workers went into unskilled occupations compared with 6.5 per cent of the non-Maori population. Similar disparities were evident in housing and health. In response to these growing disparities, the State encouraged assimilationist policies, best exemplified by the 'pepper-potting' policies of the Department of Maori Affairs which dispersed its dwellings throughout the urban communities. However most Maori could not afford to live outside areas of cheap housing, and thus state housing areas on the periphery of the large urban centres became symbols of class and racial disadvantage (Thorns, 1977).

There were other symbols too, such as the emergence of a dual system of health which came under increasing criticism for producing inequalities of access and treatment (Davis, 1981; Ward and Asher, 1984). Under the dual system of health, the private sector expanded its hospital and insurance provisions throughout the 1960s and 1970s, fostered by compliant governments and a medical profession which supported the general ethos of market forces. In education, as in health, the ideal of equality receded. As these disparities increased, various sector groups became more strident, each demanding policy initiatives to counter the perceived decline in social and economic conditions. Unions sought compensation for the escalation in price increases and the relative decline of the social wage and employers agitated for greater profitability and an end to over-full employment. These demands brought the State directly into wage determination as it attempted to control prices and wages (Boston, 1984). However, this task proved to be extremely difficult because production slowed considerably. Although the economy grew between 1978 and 1984 at the same rate as the rest of the OECD countries (see Figure 14.2), New Zealand faced major difficulties because of falling relative prices for its pastoral exports and stagnant demand for other tradeable commodities.

After decades of political and economic stability, the veneer of consensus was fractured. The visibility and strength of a Maori renaissance (Metge, 1976; Walker, 1982); the changing parameters of the labour market as women sought paid employment as an alternative to domesticity; the rediscovery of poverty despite the achievements of the welfare state; and overt political conflict between different interest groups demanding action on a range of social and moral issues; these cultural and social divisions revealed a society which was no longer able to insulate itself from the rest of the world, or disguise its internal contradictions.

In political terms, the years 1967 to 1984 represented a period of transition.[17] It was a period in which the ideas of free market liberalism surfaced in the finance sector, the economics profession and on the periphery of the National Party. These ideas challenged the historical compromise between capital and labour, and in particular they focused on the role and performance of the State. It was a period in which the affluent middle class articulated a highly individualistic liberal philosophy, which was concerned with individual as opposed to social well-being. These values were influential in the protest politics of the

Percentage of
OECD average

Year

Figure 14.2   New Zealand *per capita* GDP as a proportion of OECD
per capita GDP since 1950 (Source: Shirley *et al.*, 1990)

1960s and 1970s which emanated out of moral dissent and which found
expression in the peace and anti-apartheid movements. In contrast to
previous working-class movements which concentrated on issues of
political economy, the liberal politics of the 1960s and 1970s centred
around foreign policy issues, such as the Vietnam War, and moral issues,
such as apartheid and abortion. The politics of classical liberalism
celebrated diversity, self-determination and individual responsibility. It
simultaneously undermined the notion of a universal moral code, and it
inevitably challenged the social conservatism and traditional moral
attitudes which were associated with the post-war consensus.

Classical liberalism embraced factions of both the Left and the Right.[18]
It enveloped the liberals of political and moral protest, and the young
careerists of the Labour Party who entered politics during the 1960s and
1970s somewhat ambivalent about links between the Labour Party and
the trade union movement. It also included feminists who were opposed
to patriarchy and authoritarianism with the State being viewed as an
instrument of male authority and control. These forces came together in
the early 1980s, galvanized by the rigid authoritarianism of Prime
Minister Muldoon and by a South African Rugby tour which divided the
country but united the various liberal factions living in the large urban
centres. It was not a coherent or structured movement, but rather the
merging of different interest groups committed to individual rather than
class-based politics.

The libertarian Right also surfaced during this period despite the fact that *laissez-faire* economics had been discredited during the 1930s Depression. The doctrine of economic individualism was never totally abandoned, for as Gamble (1986, p. 29) observes 'the ideological ascendancy of Keynesianism and collectivist welfare policies was always much greater than their domination in practice'. This was certainly true of New Zealand which did produce a comprehensive set of welfare provisions in response to the mass unemployment and hardship of the great depression, but provisions, nevertheless which fell well short of the country's 'reputation' as a leading welfare state. The conditions and circumstances of the 1970s cast doubts on the ability of traditional Keynesian policies to manage the twin problems of stagnant economic growth and rising inflation and when the major international currencies moved to a regime of floating exchange rates, it strengthened the appeal of monetarism. At a time of floating exchange rates and world recession, national states were obliged to adopt tight monetary policies in order to reduce inflation and stabilize currency fluctuations. These changing global pressures elevated monetarism from a technical option advocated by a small group of right-wing economists to a revitalized model of political economy in tune with the increasing liberalization of world trade and the internationalization of production (Jessop, 1987; Lipietz, 1987).[19] These ideas were transported to New Zealand by financial interests within the business community encouraging the development of an enterprise culture and a reduction in public expenditure and taxation. It was an aggressive, individualistic ethos which contrasted sharply with the traditional and rather old-fashioned business milieu of post-war New Zealand which was based on producing established products for secure overseas markets in 'cooperation' with the trade union movement. The libertarian Right advocated a return to voluntary unionism and a reassertion of those market principles which had been undermined by the welfare state, and when the finance sector was partially deregulated during the early stages of economic restructuring, these ideas became more appealing. This does not mean to say that monetarism became a fashionable or popular theory. Rather the structure of social relations out of which the New Right emerged produced a range of individuals and sector groups who were critical of the *ad hoc* assortment of controls which dominated the New Zealand economy under the traditional conservatism of Muldoon. By the 1980s even conventional Keynesian economists opposed the Draconian policies of the New Zealand State, and thus it was difficult to differentiate between those who were opposed to the excesses of state interventionism and those who sought a market economy in the tradition of the libertarian Right.

The New Right gains the ascendancy[20]

The forces and conditions which produced the New Right in New Zealand were similar in many respects to the circumstances which produced Thatcherism and Reaganomics, but whereas the affirmation of market forces in Britain and North America was led by traditional Conservative governments, the New Zealand experiment was implemented by a social-democratic party which had been responsible for establishing the welfare state. The changing international environment created the conditions for economic liberalization, but domestic factors were important in the advance of the New Right. Opposition to the autocratic rule of Sir Robert Muldoon emerged from within his own Cabinet and when the snap election was called in 1984, the Prime Minister maintained that he could no longer count on all members of his Government to support crucial legislation.[21] Similar conflicts were evident within the Labour Party, which spent most of the post-war period after 1949 in opposition. Between 1981 and 1984 a crucial debate took place within the Labour Party over the issue of participation.[22] A liberal group within the party was committed to the fostering of a broad national consensus on economic policy and they promoted negotiations between the State, employers and unions as a way of democratizing society and thereby re-establishing a variant of the post-war consensus. An alternative group with strong links to the New Zealand Treasury maintained that the institutions and practices of representative democracy were a threat to the proper conduct of economic policy and, in the tradition of Hayek, they argued that politics should be removed from the economic realm by transferring decision making to the market-place.[23] Whereas the expression of popular demand during the Keynesian era was treated as a positive and beneficial influence on economic policy, an aid to the continuing expansion of the economy, Labour's libertarian Right believed that fiscal and monetary policies were only subverted by social goals and political values. Social and economic policies were perceived as being contradictory and mutually exclusive.

The outcome of this debate represented a policy struggle which was spread over several years. It involved the conversion of Labour's finance spokesman to an anti-interventionist position, a concerted campaign by the libertarian Right to remove Sir Robert Muldoon and associate his government with state interventionism, and the emergence of a right-wing cabal uniting top businessmen with Treasury, the Reserve Bank and the free marketeers of the new Labour Cabinet.[24] The most significant aspect of his New Right coalition centred around the way in which the programme of economic liberalization was introduced. While there was widespread agreement that the restructuring programme which began in the 1970s needed further expansion, the Labour Party was divided over economic policy and during the election campaign it studiously avoided any in-depth scrutiny of its economic agenda. Even after the campaign was over and Labour was installed as the Government of New Zealand, debate over economic priorities continued.

Whereas Labour's economic policy was confused, the reform agenda promoted by the Government's economic advisers was clear. This agenda was developed during the early 1980s by a small group of public servants within the New Zealand Treasury.[25] The group known as Economics II was strongly influenced by the Chicago School of Economics which was in the ascendancy in the 1970s, when several members of Economics II spent varying periods of time at North American universities. These officials became converts to the theories of Hayek and Friedman, and in turn they became vehicles for intellectual colonialism. Keynesian views within Treasury were marginalized as the market evangelists advanced economic liberalization as the only feasible alternative to the fiscal crisis of the State.[26]

The transformation which took place in Treasury during the early 1980s became apparent in August 1984 when Treasury published its 352-page document prepared as a brief for the incoming Government (New Zealand Treasury, 1984). This document, which has since become the blueprint for the economic policies of the New Right was not a dispassionate analysis of various options open to the new Labour administration, but rather a set of ideological statements based on the libertarian ideas of the Chicago School. While the policies advocated in *Economic Management* were in tune with a deeper historical transformation taking place in New Zealand's political economy, Treasury was in the vanguard of this movement and its coherent and systematic ideological position contrasted strongly with the confused policies of the incoming Government.

Treasury argued that the most efficient economy was one in which market forces were allowed to operate free of state intervention, and thus they recommended policy reforms such as deregulation, the abolition of controls on interest rates, user-pays and the phasing-out of industrial and agricultural subsidies. Criticisms of the welfare state levelled by unions, racial minorities and working-class interests during the 1970s were used to demonstrate that the interventionist policies of the State had produced distortions in the market economy. In order to operate efficiently Treasury maintained that any barriers and controls should be removed, thus creating a 'policy configuration which enables markets to clearly signal and respond to changes in relative prices and which does not unduly increase the uncertainty faced by market agents' (New Zealand

Treasury, 1984, p. 238). The philosophy in practice meant a 'market determined' exchange rate, the 'freeing up' of interest rates, fiscal restraint and monetary control.

Although Treasury papers concentrated on 'the economy', its underlying philosophy was aimed at attacking the assumptions as well as the mechanisms on which the post-war consensus had been built. Social factors were separated out from economic policy with the State reduced to a residual role, facilitating the process of restructuring and 'targeting' assistance to individuals in 'exceptional' circumstances. Unemployment was treated as an adjustment problem with one of the major impediments to employment being identified as the lack of labour market flexibility. Inefficiencies in the State sector were blamed on conflicting social and economic objectives and this confusion in turn was said to create political imperatives such as the need to provide uneconomic social services to sustain employment levels or to hold prices below the cost of supply. As a counter to these 'inefficiencies' within the state sector, Treasury proposed a separation of 'market' and 'non-market' activities and this distinction laid the foundation for the establishment of state corporations and the subsequent programme of privatization.

The reform agenda articulated by Treasury had no precedent in New Zealand's political history. Despite a long-standing tradition which provides state departments with the opportunity to brief the incoming government, Treasury went well beyond normal constitutional boundaries in presenting a set of briefing papers advocating free market policies which were not of the Government's own creation. However the conversion of Finance Minister Roger Douglas to the policies of the New Right ensured Treasury a receptive audience in cabinet, while the Labour Party itself had no realistic strategy of its own. It was not only the persuasiveness of Treasury's free market agenda which created the climate for economic liberalization, but the circumstances and events surrounding the 1984 election campaign. During the campaign in which Labour maintained an ascendancy throughout, it became apparent to the financial sector that the New Zealand currency would be devalued after the election. Douglas, the Finance Minister elect, had already indicated that he favoured devaluation and this course of action was strongly advanced by the New Right in Treasury and the Reserve Bank. As a consequence, 'the business community took the obvious – if unpatriotic – course and speculated against the New Zealand dollar' (Jesson, 1989, p. 63). When business interests converted their New Zealand funds into other currencies, a foreign exchange crisis was precipitated. The Reserve Bank ran out of overseas funds and the foreign exchange markets were closed immediately after the election. Treasury and Reserve Bank officials recommended to the new Labour administration that they initiate a 20 per cent devaluation of the New Zealand currency, and when this was approved the business sector converted their overseas currency into New Zealand dollars making a substantial profit in the process.

The most significant aspect of the devaluation decision emanated from the fact that it was made before the Labour cabinet was confirmed in office. Devaluation was not Labour Party policy – it was advocated by the New Right in Treasury and the Reserve Bank, and thus a small group of state entrepreneurs assumed inordinate power. This power was inevitably enhanced by the administrative structure of the government in New Zealand – which lacks the constitutional safeguards of other western democracies. As a consequence there was no effective restraint on the state executive. The right-wing coalition established by Treasury, the Reserve Bank and Finance Ministers within the Labour Cabinet was able to initiate a series of radical free market reforms to which there was little effective opposition. On those occasions when opposition was mounted, Treasury officers became active political agents both in promoting their favoured option and in subverting alternative prescriptions. As it assumed greater power under a revamped cabinet committee system, Treasury infringed on the territory of other departments, commenting on policy proposals where they lacked both knowledge and expertise and even resorting to subterfuge in pursuit of ideological purity.[27] There is mounting evidence to demonstrate that Treasury was directly involved in sanitizing committees and commissions which were in conflict with its economic programme, thus belying the assertions of the Minister of Finance, that Treasury merely provides the Government with 'independent, economic and financial analysis free of party political positions and ideology' (Douglas and Callen, 1987, p. 129).

In the early years (1984–7) of this reform programme, the Government received widespread support from large business corporations in the form of the Business Round Table, right-wing think-tanks such as the Centre for Independent Studies, the finance sector and middle-class liberals advocating a greater role for the market in economic and social policy. Any criticisms of financial deregulation were muted and even the centre left of the Labour Party was consoled by the Government's anti-nuclear stance and its humanitarian foreign policy. The introduction of a consumer-based tax in the form of Goods and Services Tax (GST) shifted the emphasis from direct to indirect taxation and although working-class interests were concerned about the inevitable inequities of an across-the-board tax on basic necessities, such as food, shelter and clothing, the affluent middle class strongly supported the change in emphasis.[28] Similarly, the removal of agricultural subsidies produced a strong reaction from the farming community despite the fact that Federated Farmers had long advocated a move toward economic liberalization, but the rural sector concentrated its criticisms on anomalies in the State's financial reforms, with their major energies directed at encouraging the Government to go further by deregulating the labour market and removing all protective subsidies and legislation from New Zealand industry. In the urban centres, the advent of financial deregulation was greeted by commercial interests as a new liberating force capable of elevating New Zealand to the international status of a leading financial centre and the media became obsessed with the stock market which was treated as an alternative form of Lotto, as investors large and small were swept along in the euphoria of share speculation.

The confidence of the New Right grew as the Labour Government was re-elected to office, promising that the second term of Government would concentrate on delivering the benefits of a revitalized economy in the traditional social policy domains of health, education and social welfare. A Royal Commission on Social Policy was established during Labour's first term and it was scheduled to report back to Government in 1988. For those ideologically opposed to the programme of economic liberalization, considerable faith was placed in the Commission to provide an alternative strategy to the free market policies of the New Right. There was some disjuncture, however, between the social policy agenda which motivated those making submissions to the Royal Commission and that which was articulated by the New Zealand Treasury in a second set of briefing papers presented to the Government after their re-election in 1987. In a two-volume report, which went even further than their 1984 document, Treasury not only advanced the need for substantial reforms in government management, but it provided a philosophical justification for the pursuit of a minimal state. Based on the writings of Locke, Mill, Rawls and Nozick, Treasury portrayed society as a collection of individuals without any social or cultural identity:

> Families and tribes are not organic entities with morality, rationality and senses, they cannot feel pleasure and pain . . .if social entities derive their value from the fact that people as individuals derive value from them, then it would seem that the individual person is the logical basis for analysis. (New Zealand Treasury, 1987, Vol. 1, p. 410)

Human groups, institutions and collectivities of one sort or another were reduced to a world of rational individual beings seeking to maximize their productive capacities. Even concepts such as justice and fairness were proscribed by individual rights and responsibilities and as a consequence the State was limited to a residual role, reminiscent of the reluctant liberal state which operated towards the end of the nineteenth century. When Treasury turned its attention to the management structure of government it based its arguments on the egalitarian critique of the British Welfare State contained in the writings of Le Grand and the 'rent-seeking' ambitions of special interest groups which have dominated the writings of public choice theorists such as Buchanan and Tullock.[29] Le Grand's position in favour of monetary redistribution, rather than the provision of state social services, coincided with Treasury's desire to seek a reduction in the role of State while the 'rent-seeking' ambitions of Buchanan's special interest groups were reproduced in *Government Management* with Treasury arguing that the State was susceptible to both external and internal 'capture'. Middle-class capture became a convenient yet unsubstantiated 'explanation' for the failure of the welfare state to achieve equity and justice for all, and thus Treasury argued for a state system which reflected the goals, management structure and ethos of the private sector. A distinction was drawn between the 'commercial' and 'social service' functions of the State, and on the basis of this artificial division. State owned enterprises (SOEs) were established with a direction from Government to operate at a profit. The obligatory reference to the social responsibilities of state owned enterprises was described by Treasury as 'motherhood clauses' and this definition proved to be an accurate prediction of the SOE legislation in practice. The Public Service structure of strategic state corporations was converted to a commercial management system controlled by boards of directors, dominated by members of the Business Round Table and disciples of the New Right. The 'permanent' heads of these State corporations were replaced by chief executives, so imbued with the enterprise culture that they proved to be 'less socially responsible than their private enterprise counterparts'.[30] Post Offices were closed, soil erosion programmes were stopped, government charges were put on to a user-pays basis and 'surplus labour' was paid off with redundancy agreements.

As far as traditional 'welfare' departments of the State are concerned, Treasury advocated 'similar principles of organization' although the techniques aimed at establishing efficiency and management accountability were different. Social service departments such as Health, Education and Social Welfare were subjected to task force reviews with working parties being dominated by private sector entrepreneurs and ideologues of the New Right.[31] The outcome of these reviews emphasized a reduced role for the State by the contracting out of central services and the introduction of commercial criteria into those areas of the State that remained. Although there was little objective research or evaluation of current services, the simplistic faith of the New Right in market forces as a means of increasing efficiency and accountability was prescribed as an antidote to the fiscal crisis of the State. In areas such as education and health this meant devolving departmental responsibilities to the 'consumers' of these services and Treasury provided the legitimation for this transformation by using the language of devolution, empowerment and decentralization: 'Government intervention produces its own internal dynamics and hence problems . . . In attempting to redress the situation. . . the key element . . . is empowering, through choice and through maximising information flows, the family, parent or individual as the customer' (New Zealand Treasury, 1987, 41–2).

The New Right was now firmly in control of the policy agenda. Although opposition to the social implications of economic liberalization was mounting, largely because of the New Right's systematic attack on the welfare state, the devolution of social services to local control reinforced a long-standing commitment of traditional Labour Party supporters who were philosophically in favour of community participation.[32] The concept of local control coincided with the interests of voluntary social service groups seeking a greater role in the administration and direction of the welfare state. Devolution also met the management and resource demands of the Maori Sovereignty Movement, which was based on tribal development, rather than national or centralized control.

Despite these endorsements and continuing electoral support for Labour's programme of economic liberalization, the hegemony of the New Right proved to be as fragile as the historical compromise which had dominated the consciousness of the post-war consensus. While desenchantment was gradual, two events were largely responsible for shattering the New Right's illusion of 'success'. The first was the share market crash in October 1987 which struck a highly vulnerable economy and which graphically demonstrated the fallibility of private sector efficiency. New Zealand companies collapsed in the aftermath of the crash, and large as well as small investors lost their life savings.[33] Investors who had speculated on the 'casino economy' watched their favoured companies go to the wall, and as the implications of the crash became apparent, high-flying entrepreneurs, some with their own assets intact, fled the country leaving angry shareholders to lament at the inadequate safeguards of the share market and the quiescence of a government which seemed incapable of administering justice.[34] Members of the public who had previously invested in the New Zealand share market transferred their funds overseas and confidence in the New Zealand economy was substantially undermined.

The second event which mobilized opposition to the New Right centred around the 'December 17 statement' by seven government ministers outlining another series of reforms to be pursued by the Labour administration during its second parliamentary term.[35] These reforms were proposed by Finance Minister Douglas who advocated supply-side theories in the form of a flat tax regime, the abolition of the family benefit, a user-pays element in public health and substantial reductions in state expenditure. The policies advocated by Douglas and the New Right cut across the deliberations of the Royal Commission on Social Policy and mobilized opposition to a government which had promised to deliver on social policy during its second term in Parliament. The Labour Government's programme came under increasing attack and conflicts over the free market policies of the New Right emerged within the Cabinet itself. Prime Minister Lange called for a slow down in the pace of change and a reaffirmation of traditional Labour Party priorities in social policy, and he broke with traditional conventions by cancelling the flat tax proposals, which had previously been approved by a Cabinet majority.[36] This open conflict marked the end of the superficial unity of purpose which appeared to dominate the first parliamentary term of the Labour administration.

Within twelve months of their public debate with the Prime Minister, Douglas and Prebble, the right-wing dogmatists of the Labour Government, were removed from Cabinet. Nine months later when Douglas was re-elected to Cabinet by his caucus colleagues, Prime Minister Lange resigned. The Labour Party was marked by conflict and division. Some trade union affiliates dissociated themselves from the party and Anderton, one of the Government's most consistent internal critics, broke ranks to establish a New Labour Party, taking many disaffected groups with him. As the Labour Party became increasingly fractured, so the Government moved to temper the hard-line policies of the New Right.[37] This more balanced approach to market liberalization was designed to counter Labour's declining electoral chances and, at the same time, ameliorate the social effects of a development strategy which has produced an increasingly fragmented and divided society.

The social effects of free market policies in New Zealand

Despite the fluctuating fortunes of the Labour Government in terms of electoral support, the 1990 election is unlikely to produce an alternative economic programme or a different set of priorities from those advanced by the New Right. Both Labour and National are committed to continuing economic liberalization while the New Labour Party has been depicted as a coalition of disenfranchised individuals and interest groups, disenchanted with the policies of the New Right, but without a popular counter-programme necessary for short-term electoral success.

The continuing viability of the social market economy is not only conditioned by the absence of any credible alternative, but also by the constellation of forces which continue to influence public opinion.

Although the advent of economic liberalization predates the arrival of the fourth Labour Government, the policies of the former National administration have been characterized as state interventionism, and as a consequence there are few New Zealanders who would choose to return to the autocratic regime of Sir Robert Muldoon. There have also been a number of beneficiaries as a consequence of the economic reforms implemented by the Labour Government, such as middle- and high-income earners who have increased their consumer power as a direct consequence of substantial reductions in taxation.[38] These advantages have been reinforced by sections of the news media which have historically supported conservative business interests, and by a series of economic commentators endorsing the notion that widespread deregulation will inevitably unleash the forces of capital investment needed to create a healthy economy. Recent reports from the OECD contain 'optimistic' comments about the New Zealand economy based on forecasts of private investment and consumption over the next eighteen months, while the New Zealand Planning Council notes that very substantial progress has been made towards the achievement of low inflation, fiscal control and external balance. The Planning Council concludes that any 'transitional' costs such as unemployment will inevitably produce a superior long-term growth path (OECD, 1988–9; New Zealand Planning Council, 1989b).

Not only do these economic interpretations of the State's free market strategy fail to understand the transformation in social and political relations which has occurred over recent years, but the evidence on which they base their assertions is suspect. The Planning Council document provides a good illustration of this phenomenon. Despite the assumption by the Council's economic monitoring group that New Zealand's economic performance deteriorated between 1978 and 1986, a recent report on unemployment in New Zealand (Shirley *et al.*, 1990) demonstrates that throughout these years, the relative decline in New Zealand's productive growth was stabilized, and this was then followed by a dramatic down-swing in the wake of market deregulation. The Council provides no evidence of any long-term recovery, thus basing its conclusions on faith rather than empirical data, and yet the 'favourable outlook' forecast by both the OECD and the Planning Council continues to be used in demonstrating that the economic programme is on course to produce a 'more efficient economy and a more just society'.[39] Given these conclusions, let us consider the evidence.

The devaluation of the New Zealand dollar in 1984 and the expectation that there might be further depreciation once it was floated was intended to compensate exporters for the removal of incentives and subsidies, and at the same time maintain growth in the traded goods sector. However, the combined effect of sustained fiscal deficits and tight monetary policy forced up domestic interest rates.[40] High interest rates emerged because the Government decided to finance its budget deficits primarily from the domestic money market and in turn the higher rates of interest within New Zealand attracted considerable injections of foreign capital. Pressures generated by foreign investors seeking New Zealand dollars forced up the exchange rate so that by July 1985 it rose sharply to levels which were above those recorded prior to the July 1984 devaluation. The higher exchange rate meant that it was more profitable to import rather than export, a situation which was reinforced by the removal of subsidies to the export sector, and the scaling-down of protective subsidies to manufacturing. The volatility of exchange and interest rates around historically high levels directed spending flows away from productive and into speculative investment. As it became more difficult to compete in the international market-place, firms reduced production and employment, and the economy moved into deep recession.

The monetary and fiscal policies initiated by the State were inadequate to deal with the powerful inflationary pressures (devaluation, strong business growth, end of wage/price freeze) which existed in 1984 and which were substantially increased as a result of financial deregulation and the removal controls.[41] These conditions led to a sharp acceleration in consumer, share and commercial property prices based on unsustainable and highly speculative developments. Speculative booms have been a common feature of market economies for at least three centuries with their inherent logic based on the value of paper assets which must continually increase beyond levels that can be sustained either by the cash-flow or the paper profits associated with capital assets. Once the upswing falters, and with the fundamentals out of line, the complicated debt leverage which underpins the boom unwinds. This was the case in New Zealand from 1985 to 1987 as the paper wealth generated by the world share market boom, and augmented by debt leverage within, conveyed an impression of prosperity and wealth. Investors spent some of their paper gains on housing, property and luxury goods and young urban dwellers, in particular, became infatuated with conspicuous consumption. The business sector was able to avoid corporate tax while bad securities legislation facilitated widespread share manipulation and speculation. High rates of inflation and acute inflationary expectations precipitated a major tightening of monetary policy in the second half of 1985. Interest rates and the exchange rate rose appreciably, the latter causing a major run-down in farm industry reserves which were necessary to sustain farm incomes. In addition, high domestic interest rates encourage a major switch to cheaper overseas funds.

The lifting of restrictions on prices and wages saw real disposable wages fall by 10 per cent between the June quarter of 1984 and the September quarter of 1985 (Department of Statistics, 1984 and 1985). In order to offset the unexpectedly large consumer price increases during this same period, the union movement applied pressure for a significant wage increase and although this increase measured 20 per cent for the year ending 1986, real disposable wages by December 1987 were at the same level as in September 1984. There was also a substantial increase in public debt interest payments arising from the high interest rate policies, and this proved to be a major barrier to deficit reduction. The cumulative impact of these policies over a period of more than two and a half years resulted in severe damage to the tradeable sector. Profits, employment and investment were all affected, and at the same time export growth sharply diminished.

The impact of these policies on the farming sector has been dramatic (*NZ Listener*, 1989; *Dominion*, 1989a). Subsidies were withdrawn and land values dropped between 50 and 70 per cent of government valuation. The withdrawal of agricultural subsidies coincided with the New Zealand dollar rising to nearly 60 cents US thus eliminating any return for the producer. The price for New Zealand lamb fell from $24 in 1984–5 to $12 in 1985–6. Production levels went down, confidence declined and many farmers who had borrowed unwisely for expansion during the years of government subsidies and high land values found themselves operating uneconomic units. The personal costs borne by individual farmers were inevitably reflected in the national economy. Although two out of every three dollars earned overseas comes from agriculture, farm investment in 1987 dropped to less than half what it was in 1985. The high interest and exchange rate policies meant that farmers could not maintain the fertility of the soil, a trend which will take some years to reverse. Production has already been affected. Lost sheep production in 1988 and 1989 will cost the country $425 million, and lost beef production an extra $100 million in the 1989 season alone. The export lamb kill is also down more than 12 million from its 1984–5 high of 30 million and it is predicted to fall another three to four million in 1990. Bone and beef production in 1990 is expected to fall 15 per cent or 67,000 tonnes because of a 10 per cent decline in the kill and lower carcass weights. Wool production has fallen 45,600 tonnes since its 1980–1 peak of 380,000 tonnes, including more than 11,000 tonnes this year. The Meat and Wool Board's economic service predicts that this decline will continue.

There has also been a substantial change in New Zealand's industrial pattern (Figure 14.3) with labour-intensive industries, such as clothing and furniture, suffering large falls in exports, while imports have been allowed into a depressed domestic market (Bollard, 1987). Factory closures in these industries have produced a significant increase in

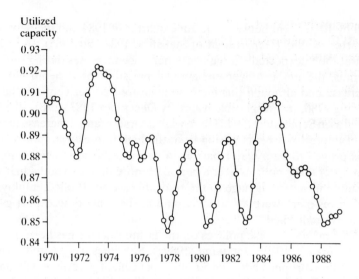

Figure 14.3   Median utilized capacity of manufacturers (Source: *Quarterly Survey of Business Opinion*)

unemployment. Whereas manufacturing accounts for 23 per cent of gross domestic product, about 30 per cent of merchandise exports and almost 20 per cent of the work-force, investment in New Zealand manufacturing has halved in real terms since 1985 and 50,000 jobs have been lost. Manufacturing investment in 1987 was 1.76 billion compared with 2.14 billion in 1985. If those figures are adjusted for inflation, they correspond to 3.93 billion investment in 1985 and 1.97 billion in 1987, which is almost a 50 per cent decline in real terms.

It is in the sphere of unemployment that the social effects of economic restructuring are most obvious (Shirley *et al.*, 1990). In the twelve months to March 1989, unemployment in New Zealand increased by 50 per cent. One out every nine in the labour force is currently unemployed (March 1990), and in some areas of the country, such as Whangarei, the figure is one in five. Employment in manufacturing industries is down 18 per cent to 20 per cent on what it was in 1984. Other sectors, notably retailing, hotel, and social services started to restructure in late 1987 and over the past twelve months 40,000 jobs have been lost. In the public sector more than 10,000 jobs have been eliminated since 1984. At the end of June 1984, 62,361 people worked in government departments. By 31 October 1988, the number had dropped 16 per cent to 52,278. In the forestry industry 8,000 jobs have disappeared since 1985 and more than 70 sawmills have been closed. Some regions of the country have been particularly affected. In Tokomaru Bay, a small rural settlement on the East Coast of the North Island, 50 per cent of the district work-force has been without a job for up to six months, while 30 per cent of those unemployed in the Gisborne/East Coast region of the country have been without work for more than six months. After decades of full employment, New Zealand has emerged as the country with the worst employment outlook of all the OECD nations (Figure 14.4).

From being a 'low unemployment' nation in 1978, with a rate of registered unemployment of only 1 per cent, New Zealand has become, by world standards, a nation of high unemployment, with 13.7 per cent registered as unemployed or on special training and work programmes by December 1988. Although unemployment statistics seriously underestimate the level of surplus labour, they nevertheless reveal a social problem of some magnitude. In the case of long-term unemployment, for example, the figures show a disturbing rise from 15 per cent of total unemployment in June 1986, to 26 per cent in January 1988, and by June 1989, 46.8 per cent of men and 39.9 per cent of women who were registered as unemployed had been out of work for six months or more. Until 1985 the absolute levels of unemployment in both the rural and urban centres were on a par. After 1985, however, registered unemployment rose sharply in the regions, doubling and trebling in a matter of years, whereas unemployment in the main centres continued to fall through 1986 only to begin a sharp rise in 1988 (Figure 14.5).

This process of bifurcation has had serious implications for rural communities in the deterioration of both services and income. The regions most affected by redundancies are areas where there is a high Maori population. These communities have been badly affected by restructuring in industries such as forestry and coal-mining and, given that the Maori population of working age is increasing numerically, the contraction in employment has serious long-term implications. The proportion of the Maori working age population in paid employment between March 1987 and March 1989 dropped from 74 to 57 per cent for Maori men and from 47 to 38 per cent for Maori women (Department of Statistics, 1987–9; Robinson, 1989). This contraction represents a shedding of one-fifth of the actively employed Maori work-force in just two years. The reduction in the non-Maori workforce was 5 per cent women and 7 per cent for men. Similar disparities are evident in unemployment rates between young workers aged 15 to 19. The household labour force survey in December 1987 revealed that 8 per cent of European youth were unemployed: the rate of Maori youth was 30 per cent. Given that Maori workers on average have the lowest incomes when employed, they are less likely to have accumulated savings to withstand periods of unemployment. Thus the deteriorating employment situation

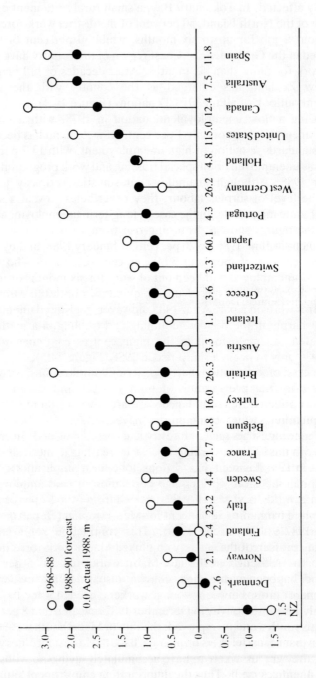

Figure 14.4 Average annual employment change (Source: *The Economist*, 22–28 July 1989, p. 91)

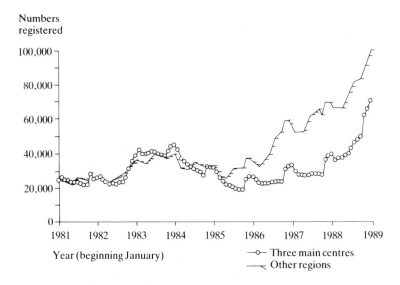

Figure 14.5   Registered unemployment (since 1981) in the three main centres and other regions (Source: Department of Labour)

has seriously disadvantaged the Maori at a time when the State is withdrawing its social programmes.

The deterioration of unemployment after decades of stability and full employment reflects wider structural changes occurring in New Zealand's political economy. The move toward economic liberalization which commenced in the 1970s and which was accelerated by the advance of the New Right in 1984 has seen an apparent increase in social disorganization as capital sheds labour and moves away from older patterns of production towards new forms which emphasize market individualism and work-place bargaining (Thorns, 1988). In this new enterprise culture, labour market flexibility is celebrated as the answer to unemployment, thus creating pressure for change which focuses almost exclusively on the role of labour. Although each phase of New Zealand's economic and social history has been marked by a certain interdependence between the State and major groups in the private sector, in the 1980s these interests were openly fused. A convulsion occurred in the corporate sector with mergers, take-overs and an increasing domination of the New Zealand economy by a small cartel of international and national corporations. The old firms gave way to aggressive and acquisitive individuals who built commercial edifices on borrowed capital, and in this process they also secured a degree of political power. Not only has a small group of right-wing businessmen been able to dominate the commercial sector under the patronage of the State, but they have been appointed to key political positions to both initiate and supervise the restructuring of New Zealand society.[42] Rather than restrict the power of the corporate sector, the State has actively promoted it and in this process it has established a free economy and a strong state (Gamble, 1979). Although Gamble first referred to this phenomenon in the context of Thatcherism, it is perhaps even more appropriate when applied to New Zealand. In contrast to Britain, New Zealand does not have a second legislative chamber and thus the State executive in this country wields enormous power. Once a party is elected to power in a first past the post system, Cabinet becomes the State Executive without the constitutional checks and balances which characterize other western democracies. The establishment of a free economy in New Zealand required a State Executive which was committed to economic liberalization, and although leading members of this cabinet are now seeking to distance themselves from the theology of the New Right, the free market policies are in place. In the course of this liberalization programme the power of the State has been enhanced. Although the State may be conceived as a relatively autonomous site for the development of policy and its implementation, the capacities of the New Right to control this process have been immeasurably advanced.[43] While the interests of factions opposed to economic liberalization have directed their attention at what the State should control, the New Right have concentrated their capacities on controlling the State, and in the process they have effected a fundamental shift in economic and social relations.

The most obvious transformation has occurred in the labour market where production has become increasingly internationalized as a consequence of economic liberalization. Whereas the mass production mode of the 1950s and 1960s was based on the growing importance of the semi-skilled worker and a levelling of income standards, the flexible production schedule of the 1970s and 1980s centres around a skill-flexible core and a marginal, less skilled, more part-time 'sometimes in work, sometimes out of work' periphery (Jessop, 1987; Jessop *et al.*, 1987). This new division of labour is characterized by a fragmented labour market which encourages workers to identify with their company as part of the new enterprise culture. As a consequence, wage bargaining takes place on a plant by plant basis, thereby undermining national awards and placing the trade unions under increasing attack. The move toward greater labour market flexibility has further undermined the organizational capacities of the trade union movement and, at the same time, the power of capital has substantially increased.[44]

The reorganization of the state sector has been a significant factor in this transformation. State departments were corporatized during the first term of the Labour administration and this reorganization along commercial lines required them to trade at a profit and pay taxes to the State. Changes to the management structure of the state corporations promoted increasing flexibility in work practices and this was reinforced by the appointment of senior management with experience and interests in the private sector. Chief executives now replace departmental heads and five year contracts replace tenure. In this process, the traditional security and stability of the public service have been undermined. Although the reorganization of the state sector has partially satisfied popular demands for the devolution of social services and community participation – themes which have a long history in Labour Party rhetoric – the devolution of control has been selectively managed. Whereas 'commercial' departments such as Electricity, NZ Post, Transport and Telecom have become entities in the centrally controlled corporate sector, and thus further removed from public scrutiny and control, social service departments such as Health, Education, Social Welfare and Maori Affairs have been decentralized under the management of the State. These apparently contradictory policies have strengthened the power of the corporate sector and limited public involvement in 'the economy'. At the same time, the State has encouraged public participation in the restructuring of social services.

The restructuring of social services is an interesting phenomenon because it has enabled the New Right to deal with what Habermas (1975) has referred to as the legitimation crisis. It enables the functions of state departments to be concentrated around essential activities such as the formation and management of policy as well as the ability to exercise fiscal control, and it simultaneously serves to deal with popular pressure on the State by lowering public expectations of the State's capacity to satisfy insatiable demands. The State manages this dichotomy between stronger state control and increasing public participation by relinquishing control in areas over which there is considerable conflict (such as discretionary expenditure) while at the same time consolidating its control in areas which concern the management of the system.

In this way the New Zealand State has attempted to deal with two problems, both of which lie at the heart of the legitimation crisis. On the one hand it has supported capital accumulation by advancing economic liberalization, and on the other hand it has attempted to placate public expectations by encouraging a selected form of community participation. Not only has this been effective in legitimating the State's role in the process of recommodification[45], but it has also relieved the State Executive of certain political problems by transporting the social effects of economic restructuring out into a community which has become increasingly divided and fractured.

As New Zealand society has become increasingly fragmented so it has reflected growing inequalities of income and lifestyle[46] as well as escalating rates of crime[47] and disorder.[48] While these trends predate the advent of the fourth Labour Government, the advance of the New Right has effectively undermined any coherent response to social dislocation by creating an environment which encourages individual rather than collective action. Individuals and groups within local communities have been set one against the other as they compete for resources in education, housing, employment and health, and in this process lawyers have become both beneficiaries and defenders of the public interest.[49]

When we therefore consider the 'benefits' of increasing plant efficiency (yet to be empirically established) and stand to applaud[50] the profitability of state corporations, these 'advantages' need to be set alongside the closure of community facilities such as Post Offices and hospitals, and the reappearance of long-term unemployment. These negative indices of economic liberalization reflect a society which is becoming both spatially and socially divided: the 1989 budget declaration of a 'more efficient economy and a more just society' is decidedly suspect. Indeed the relative stability and security of post-war reconstruction in New Zealand now impresses as an interlude between two periods of relative chaos as the old battles over freedom, justice and equality are once more engaged.

Notes

1. The most comprehensive political interpretations of this free market 'revolution' are contained in two publications by Bruce Jesson (1987, 1989), a political reader by Boston and Holland (1987), and an MA thesis in sociology by Hugh Oliver (1987). The most comprehensive economic interpretation is contained in Bollard and Buckle (1987).
2. 'Rogernomics' derives its name from the Minister of Finance in the fourth Labour Government, Roger Douglas. See Collins (1987) and Easton (1989b).
3. The tables on which these calculations are based are contained in Maddison (1982, p. 91).
4. Productivity between 1952 and 1973 increased at a rate of 3.3 per cent a year.
5. In 1953 New Zealand had the third highest income *per capita* in the world. European New Zealanders at birth were among those with the highest life expectancy rates, and social disorders such as crime, suicide and admissions to psychiatric hospital were all at historically low levels.
6. An excellent account of the philosophy and politics of the 1938 Social Security Act is contained in Hanson (1980).
7. The history of the post-war period is comprehensively covered by Oliver and Williams (1981). See especially the chapters by G. Hawke and Graeme Dunstall.

8. Early New Zealand history is covered in Sinclair (1959) and Oliver and Williams (1981). See also W. B. Sutch (1966). A recent book which addresses the distinctive character of the Welfare State in New Zealand and Australia is Francis Castles (1985).

9. In 1921 Lord Bryce wrote that New Zealanders viewed the State as 'an instrument ready to hand to be employed for diffusing among themselves and their neighbours comfort and prosperity' (1921, p. 355).

10. The 'apparent' acceptance of cultural assimilation by the Maori was conditioned by the stable environment which existed in the post-war period, especially the achievement of full employment. As the Maori migration from rural to urban centres accelerated in the 1960s, cultural conflict became more evident and thus the notion of assimilation was advanced by Pakeha (European) rather than Maori interests. The Maori community consistently returns to the Treaty of Waitangi as the constitutional base on which the notion of biculturalism is established. See Orange (1987). Also Kawharus. (1989).

11. New Zealand has frequently been described as 'a laboratory of social experiment', a term first attributed to Lord Asquith in the 1880s. Others who investigated this antipodean phenomenon include the Fabians, Sidney and Beatrice Webb, the American 'progressive' Henry Lloyd and two French scholars, André Siegfried and Albert Métin. The Frenchmen in particular were struck by the absence of socialist doctrine which they had been led to expect in view of New Zealand's radical legislation (Métin 1977; Sinclair 1961).

12. In an analysis of welfare expenditure in the post-war period Martin concludes that the 'rate of expansion has been only consistent with, or perhaps below, the rate of economic growth'. He identifies a series of discontinuous steps until the 1970s with National placing emphasis on slow and gradual improvement in education and health services, letting social security provisions fall away in real terms, whereas Labour's emphasis centred around remedying social security (Martin, 1981, pp. 68–9).

13. Pearson and Thorns (1983), especially the section on 'Corporate New Zealand and foreign ownership', pp. 54–63.

14. The trend toward industrial concentration in New Zealand is comprehensively addressed by Kirk (1984).

15. The conflict between public and private interests in the operation of New Zealand's energy programme is canvassed in Shirley (1982). For an economic analysis of aluminium smelting see van Moeseke (1980).

16. Comparisons drawn from tables in the Population Census, Department of Statistics (1971).

17. Graeme Dunstall (1981) provides a comprehensive overview of the 'social pattern'.

18. Bruce Jesson (1989) describes the development of classical liberalism.

19. An excellent account of the rise of monetarism is contained in Clarke (1987).

20. In this chapter I have emphasized the New Zealand origins and composition of the New Right despite the fact that there are obvious similarities between the theology and policies of this movement in the Pacific and in the Northern Hemisphere. See Jessop *et al.* (1984), Levitas (1986) and King (1987).

21. Prime Minister Muldoon's rationale for calling the snap election of 1984 was prompted by two outspoken National Members of Parliament, Marilyn Waring and Michael Minogue.

22. Conflicts within the New Zealand Labour Party over the emerging policies of the New Right are discussed in Oliver (1987).

23. In 1983 a treasury official who had become a convert to free market orthodoxy during a period at the World Bank became the liaison person between Treasury and the Labour Party opposition. This official organized a group of economists to meet with finance spokesman Roger Douglas, and it was a faction of this group which eventually produced the Labour Party's economic policy for the 1984 election.

24. The right-wing cabal which emerged in the 1980s represented Treasury officials (Scott, Secretary of Treasury, and Kerr, later to be appointed the Executive Officer of the Business Round Table), Reserve Bank Deputy Governor Roderick Dean (later to become Chairman of the State Services Commission and the person responsible for initiating and implementing state restructuring), Business Round Table members Gibbs (later appointed to chair the Hospital Services Review and now the chairman of Forestcorp) and Trotter (Chairman of New Zealand's largest private company and now Chairman of Telecom) and Douglas, Minister of Finance in the fourth Labour Government from 1984–8.

25. Economics II was responsible to Scott (then Deputy Secretary, now Secretary, of Treasury), a close acquaintance of Kerr, the Director of Economics II later to become Executive Officer of the Business Round Table. Two other members of the group (Wilkinson and Cameron) spent time on Fellowships at Harvard University. This group was largely responsible for writing the Treasury Briefing paper for the Labour Government entitled *Economic Management*.

26. New Right politicians and economists in New Zealand frequently referred to the 'TINA' option (there is no alternative), when describing why Government had 'no choice' but to implement the deflationary strategy which has been at the centre of the New Right's economic programme. Similar claims were made by Margaret Thatcher in Britain. See Clarke (1987 p. 404).

27. This section on the activities of Treasury officials draws on the work of Bruce Jesson (1987, 1989), and Easton (1987). Evidence was also provided by a leaked audit of Treasury communications which was carried out by Simon Walker of Communicor Consultants 26 June 1987 and followed up in a series of critical articles in the *Dominion*. See for example, the *Dominion* (1988).

28. Major opposition to a consumer-based tax came from working-class interests within the Labour Party and these concerns were articulated at Regional Labour Party seminars during 1985.

29. As used here the sense of 'rent-seeking ambitions' is that taken directly from Buchanan and Tullock, who believe that government intervention is inherently unproductive: 'rent-seeking is designed to describe behaviour in institutional settings where individual's efforts to maximise value generate social waste rather than social surplus' (Buchanan, Tollison and Tullock, 1980, p. 4). The examples they go on to give include bribes taken by officials in charge of import licensing in India and Turkey and royal grants of lucrative monopolies to political favourites in the high age of monarchy in post-Renaissance Europe, thus implying that any government activity which generates rewards for particular individuals is *ipso facto* rent-seeking and wasteful. Treasury made extensive use of Le Grand's (1984) material, Part 2, Chapter 12 Section 5(d). Treasury's argument goes considerably further

than Le Grand, however, in drawing strong conclusions from evidence which is in fact inconclusive. For an excellent critique see Bertram (1988).

30. The detrimental social implications of the state corporatization programme are canvassed in two articles by Alastair Morrison in the *Dominion* (1989b, 1989c).

31. New Right ideologues include Gibbs of the Business Round Table and Chairman of the right-wing think-tank, the Centre of Independent Studies – Gibbs, a close friend of Finance Minister Douglas, was appointed as Chairman of the Hospital Services Review. Picot, Chairman of Philips and Pacific Venture and a Director of a food chain, Progressive Enterprises, was appointed Chairman of a Review Committee on Education – Quigley, a former National Party Minister and a free marketeer who left politics after crossing swords with Sir Robert Muldoon, established his own consultancy business and has subsequently conducted reviews on Defence and the Department of Justice.

32. The first Labour Party Conference following Labour's re-election in 1987 was devoted to a debate on social policy. It was organized by the hierarchy of Labour's administration in an attempt to prevent 'Rogernomics' from taking control of traditional social service areas such as health, education and social welfare. A full account of the Labour Party's debate on social policy and the growing apprehension of party members with liberalization is contained in an MSW thesis by Kathleen Livingston, Massey University (in progress).

33. The full impact of the share market crash on the New Zealand economy is still being assessed but it affected personal investors, pension funds, finance and development companies and large banks such as the Bank of New Zealand, which had to be 'bailed out' by the State. The bankruptcy rate to June 1988 was up 60 per cent on the previous June quarter and compulsory liquidations for the same comparative period increased by 86 per cent. Insolvency figures are compiled by the Department of Justice.

34. In the wake of the share market crash the head of the Justice Department's Corporate Fraud Unit admitted publicly that the Department had neither the manpower nor the resources to investigate corporate fraud. The *Dominion* newspaper called for a full judicial inquiry and produced evidence of declared bankrupts setting up in business once again and negotiating deals worth millions of dollars. Others absconded overseas and throughout the Justice Department seemed incapable of taking judicial action (*Dominion Sunday Times* 1988a, 1988b; *Dominion*, 1988b, 1988c, 1988d, 1988e).

35. In the wake of the 1987 election and the October 1987 share market crash Finance Minister Douglas proposed a series of radical reforms to restore 'confidence in the economy'. These reforms included a flat income tax rate of 23 per cent, a guaranteed minimum family income designed to ensure a margin of $70 between 'workers' and 'beneficiaries', income-tested health care payments, the devolution of housing assistance to local authorities, deregulation of the labour market and enterprise bargaining. Although the reforms were in line with Treasury's programme as outlined in *Government Management* (New Zealand Treasury, 1987), Douglas argued that the main purpose of this reform programme was to assist families on low incomes. The package was eventually modified and presented to the public on 17 December. Prime Minister Lange later claimed that cabinet had not fully

understood the implications of the proposed reforms and when a working party of officials reported on the fiscal implications of these proposals Lange made it clear to the public that Treasury (and Douglas) had based their conclusions on faulty arithmetic. The private debates which took place between the Prime Minister and his Minister of Finance were made public in a series of letters published in the *New Zealand Herald* (1989a, 1989b, 1989c) and realised by Douglas as his private campaign against the Prime Minister gathered momentum in 1989.

36. On the 28 January 1988 Prime Minister Lange took his concerns over the flat tax proposal directly to the public and repudiated central components of the December 17 statement. Although a compromise agreement was eventually reached with the highest marginal tax rate being reduced to 33 rather than 23 per cent the main thrust of the New Right policies continued. Lange did not have the numbers in Cabinet and he and his supporters did not have an alternative strategy.

37. The 1989 Budget released by new Finance Minister Caygill continued the programme of economic liberalization but tempered these reforms by emphasizing the social policy components of the Budget (Caygill, 1989).

38. Families on benefits or with incomes near the benefit level have faced accumulated inflation about 15 per cent higher than average households since 1984. Whereas personal tax cuts in 1988 benefited income-earners on $39,000 or above, low income-earners have been hit more severely by a consumer-based tax on all basic commodities. Work currently underway at the Social Policy Research Centre indicates that disparities between different socio-economic groups have substantially increased over the past four years and these income disparities have been exacerbated by consumer-based taxation, and the Government's programme of user-pays.

39. The term 'a more efficient economy and a more just society' was advanced by Douglas in his 1984 budget and these words were echoed by Finance Minister Caygill in 1989.

40. In January 1988, when the annual inflation rate was 9.6 per cent, the average first mortgage interest rate was 19.33 per cent. However these average rates do not reflect the full impact of high interest rates on personal and corporate indebtedness. The Consumers Institute reveals that in 1988 many families were borrowing to pay overdue rent and power bills and in the Wellington area alone an estimated 3000 people were paying rates of 64 per cent (*Dominion*, 1988a).

41. The inflation rate at June 1984 was 4.7 per cent. By June 1985 it had risen to 16.6 per cent. Although OECD reports and conservative interests such as the *Financial Times* (1989) adopt the rhetoric of the New Right by claiming 'success' for the disinflationary policies of the Labour administration in getting inflation down, they fail to explain why the rate of inflation in 1985 rose 11.9 per cent when the New Zealand Treasury predicted an increase of 2.8 per cent. While the lifting of the wage/price freeze was an important factor the policy measures of the incoming Government were crucial in that they pushed up costs. These costs included higher government charges, higher indirect taxes, and a devaluation of the exchange rate which led to higher import costs.

42. This small group of businessmen (including Sir Ron Trotter, Alan Gibbs and Roderick Dean) has been the driving force behind the Business Round Table and the right-wing Centre for Independent Studies.

43. The notion of relative autonomy is advanced by Poulantzas (1975) who rejects the instrumental determinism of those Marxist writings which view the capitalist state as an instrument of the economically dominant classes.

44. The top ten listed companies nearly doubled their dominance of the New Zealand share market between 1987 and 1989. The market capitalization of these ten companies increased from 44 per cent of the total market to 72.5 per cent. If publicly listed subsidiaries of these companies are included, the figure rises to 78 per cent.

45. Recommodification is a concept used to indicate the movement from the production and distribution of goods in order to meet the social needs of society, to the production and distribution of goods and services for individual needs. Recommodification involves the return of commodities, such as public health, from the State to the private sector, a process which is somewhat different from recapitalization, which refers to the return of capital to the private sector, as in the case of reduced state mortage money and an increase in the size of the private mortgage market.

46. In a background paper for the Royal Commission on Social Policy, Allan Levatt (1988, p. 1) points to increasing inequalities between

> the successful and the unsuccessful, the well and the poorly educated and housed, and between those who get the best out of health care provisions and those who do not. As the gap has increased so has the incidence of social distress.

47. Escalating rates of crime (as measured according to crimes reported to the police) have accompanied the period of economic liberalization. In 1972 crimes reported to the police stood at 200,937 – by 1988 the figure had increased to 439,093. The recorded offences of violence between 1972 and 1986 increased by 135 per cent and in this same period sexual attacks by males on women and children increased by 611 per cent. As Pratt (1987) has illustrated, 'the general increases in crime levels have coincided with major economic change and concomitant social and cultural dislocation'. See also annual reports to Parliament from the Police Department, Wellington, 1972–1986.

48. Other indicators of distress include an increase in the custodial sentences imposed by juvenile courts (Justice Statistics, Department of Statistics) increasing rates of admission to psychiatric hospitals, especially for Maori of all ages (mental health data, Department of Health) and increasing rates of suicide (mortality and demographic data, Department of Health).

49. Ian Taylor (1987) draws attention to the significance of lawyers in the writings of Friedrich Hayek, one of the New Right theologians from the Austrian School of Economics:

> The Law is central to the theory of the social market economy in at least two senses. First, and quite unremarkably to any student of the law in capitalist society, the law must provide a general framework to underwrite contracts between individual entrepreneurs, and also give predictability and certainty to the rules governing social behaviour in general (the conditions of existence of a capitalist market place). But second, the

extension of laws allows for the minimisation of intrusion by bureaucrats and sectional interest in the market place – an intrusion which has resulted both in inefficiency (since the market cannot truly be planned and coordinated) and loss of individual liberty. Freedom and liberty are to be defended and extended, in the Hayekian vision, by lawyers and entrepreneurs, at the expense of the pretenders to democratic will, the politicians and bureaucrats.

50. Habermas (1975, p. 37) refers to this phenomenon in advanced capitalism as citizen depoliticization – citizens 'enjoy the status of passive (subjects) with only the right to withhold acclamation'.

Bibliography and references

Armstrong, P., A. Glyn and J. Harrison (1984) *Capitalism Since World War II*, London: Fontana.

Baker, J. V. (1965) *The New Zealand People at War: War economy,* Wellington: Department of Internal Affairs/Whitcombe & Tombs.

Bell, D. (1960) *The End of Ideology*, New York: The Free Press.

Bell, D. (1973) *The Coming of Post-industrial Society*, New York: Basic Books.

Bertram, G. (1988) 'Middle-class capture: a brief survey', a background paper for the Royal Commission on Social Policy, Victoria University, Wellington.

Birks, S. and S. Chatterjee (eds.) (1988) *The New Zealand Economy*, Palmerston North: Dunmore Press.

Bollard, A. (1987) 'More market: the deregulation of industry' in A. Bollard and R. Buckle (eds.) *Economic Liberalisation in New Zealand*, pp. 25–45, Wellington: Allen & Unwin.

Bollard, A. and R. Buckle (eds.) (1987) *Economic Liberalisation in New Zealand*, Wellington: Allen & Unwin.

Boston, J. (1984) *Incomes Policy in New Zealand: 1968–1984*, Wellington: Victoria University.

Boston, J. and M. Holland (eds.) (1987) *The Fourth Labour Government: Radical politics in New Zealand*, Auckland: Oxford University Press.

Bryce, J. (1921) *Modern Democracies*, Vol. II, London: Macmillan.

Buchanan, J. M. and G. Tullock (1962) *The Calculus of Consent: Logical foundations of constitutional democracy*, Ann Arbor: University of Michigan Press.

Buchanan, J. M., R. D. Tollison and G. Tullock (eds.) (1980) *Towards a Theory of the Rent-seeking Society*, Texas: Texas A & M University Press.

Burdon, R. M. (1985) *The New Dominion: A social and political history of New Zealand, 1918–1939*, Wellington: A. H. & A. W. Reed.

Business Round Table (1987) 'Fiscal strategy: the next stages', a background paper.

Castles, F. (1985) *The Working Class and Welfare: Reflections on the political development of the welfare state in Australia and New Zealand 1890–1980*, Wellington: Allen & Unwin.

Caygill, Hon. D. (1989) *Securing Economic Recovery*, Budget Speech, Economic Strategy, Summary of Social Policy Announcements, 27 July, Wellington: Government Printer.

Chapman, R. (ed.) (1961) *Ends and Means in New Zealand Politics*, Bulletin No. 60, History Series No. 7, Auckland: University of Auckland.

Clarke, S. (1987) 'Capitalist crisis and the rise of monetarism' in R. Miliband, L. Panitch and J. Seville (eds.) *The Socialist Register 1987*, pp. 393–427, London: Merlin Press.

Collins, S. (1987) *Rogernomics*, Wellington: Pitman.

Davis, P. (1981) *Health and Health Care in New Zealand*, Auckland: Longman Paul.

Department of Statistics (1971) *Population Census*, Wellington: Government Printer.

Department of Statistics (1984) *Monthly Abstract of Statistics*, Wellington: Government Printer.

Department of Statistics (1985) *Quarterly Household Labour Force Survey*, Wellington: Government Printer.

Dominion (1988a) 'Desperate borrowers pay 64 pc interest', 29 February.

Dominion (1988b) 'Crash brings out the dirty washing', 16 May.

Dominion (1988c) '10,000 left in dark by RSL's closure', 17 July.

Dominion (1988d) 'Call for an enquiry', 1 August.

Dominion (1988e) 'Minister of Justice: RSL call unwarranted – the editor replies', 8 August.

Dominion (1988f) 'Treasury power', 3 November.

Dominion (1989a) 'Shadow of disaster looms over farming', 3 April.

Dominion (1989b) 'Putting profit before service', 10 May.

Dominion (1989c) 'Betrayal of the social contract', 11 May.

Dominion Sunday Times (1988a) 'Corporate fraud too big to handle', 17 January.

Dominion Sunday Times (1988b) 'Bankrupts in big money deals', 15 May.

Douglas, R. and L. Callen (1987) *Toward Prosperity: People and politics in the 1980's*, Auckland: David Batement.

Dunstall, G. (1981) 'The social pattern' in W. H. Oliver and B. R. Williams (eds.) *The Oxford History of New Zealand*, pp. 396–429, Wellington: Oxford University Press.

Easton, B. (1986) *Wages and the Poor*, Wellington: Allen & Unwin.

Easton, B. (1987) 'Labour's economic strategy' in J. Boston and M. Holland (eds.) *The Fourth Labour Government: Radical politics in New Zealand*, pp. 134–50, Auckland: Oxford University Press.

Easton, B. (1983) 'Poverty in New Zealand: estimates and reflections' in *Income Distribution in New Zealand*, pp. 264–79, Wellington: New Zealand Institute of Economic Research.

Easton, B. (1989a) 'Structural change and market liberalisation: the New Zealand experience', paper presented to the Economic Society of Australia, Adelaide.

Easton, B. (ed.) (1989b) *The Making of Rogernomics*, Auckland: Auckland University Press.

Financial Times (1989) 'Applause of New Zealand economic reform', 2 May.

Friedman, M. (1962) *Capitalism and Freedom*, Chicago: University of Chicago Press.

Gamble, A. (1979) 'The free economy and the strong state' in R. Miliband, L. Panitch and J. Saville (eds.) *The Socialist Register 1987*, pp. 1–25, London: Merlin Press.

Gamble, A. (1986) 'The political economy of freedom' in R. Levitas (ed.) *The Ideology of the New Right*, pp. 25–54, Cambridge: Polity Press.

Habermas, J. (1975) *Legitimation Crisis*, translated by Thomas McCarthy, London: Heinemann.

Hanson, E. (1980) *The Politics of Social Security*, Auckland: Oxford University Press.

Hawke, G. (1981) 'The growth of the economy' in W. H. Oliver and B. R. Williams (eds.) *The Oxford History of New Zealand*, Wellington: Oxford University Press.

Holt, J. (1976) 'The political origins of compulsory arbitration in New Zealand. A comparison with Great Britain' *New Zealand Journal of History* **10** (2) 99–111.

Hyman, P. (1978) 'Women in the New Zealand labour force' in R. Seymour (ed.) *Research Papers '78: Women's studies*, pp. 24–36, Hamilton: Women's Studies Association.

Jesson, B. (1987) *Behind the Mirror Glass: The growth of wealth and power in New Zealand in the eighties*, Auckland: Penguin.

Jesson, B. (1989) *Fragments of Labour: The story behind the Labour Government*, Auckland: Penguin.

Jessop, B. (1987) 'The political economy of Thatcherism', a seminar presented at Massey University, September.

Jessop, B., K. Bonnett, S. Bromley and T. Ling (1984) 'Authoritarian populism, two nations, and Thatcherism', *New Left Review* **147**, 32–60.

Jessop, B., K. Bonnett, S. Bromley and T. Ling (1987) 'Popular capitalism, flexible accumulation and left strategy', *New Left Review* **165**, 104–22.

Kawharu, I. H. (ed.) (1989) *Waitangi: Maori and Pakeha perspectives on the Treaty of Waitangi*, Auckland: Oxford University Press.

King, D. (1987) *The New Right: Politics, markets and citizenship*, London: Macmillan.

Kirk, A. (1984) 'Work in the private sector' in C. Wilkes and I. Shirley (eds.) *In the Public Interest: Health, work and housing in New Zealand*, pp. 152–67, Auckland: Benton/Ross.

Lee, J. A. (1938) *Socialism in New Zealand*, London: T. Werner Laurie.

Le Grand, J. (1982) *The Strategy of Equality*, London: Allen & Unwin.

Le Grand, J. (1984) 'The Future of the Welfare State' *New Society*, **68**, 385–6.

Levatt, A. (1988) *Social Change and the Welfare State*, a background paper for the Royal Commission on Social Policy, unpublished.

Levitas, R. (ed.) (1986) *The Ideology of the New Right*, Cambridge: Polity Press.

Lipietz, A. (1987) *Mirages and Miracles: The crises of global Fordism*, London: Verso.

Lloyd-Prichard, M. F. (1970) *An Economic History of New Zealand to 1939*, Auckland: Collins.

Maddison, A. (1964) *Economic Growth in the West*, London: Twentieth Century Fund.

Maddison, A. (1982) *Phases of Capitalist Development*, Oxford: Oxford University Press.

Martin, J. (1981) *State Papers*, Department of Sociology, Massey University, Palmerston North.

Metge, J. (1976) *The Maoris of New Zealand*, 2nd edn, London: Routledge & Kegan Paul.

Métin, A. (1977) *Socialism Without Doctrine*, Chippendale, Australia: The Alternative Publishing Cooperative.

Miliband, R., L. Panitch and J. Saville (eds.) (1987) *The Socialist Register 1987*, London: Merlin Press.

New Zealand Herald (1988a) 'The Douglas dossier', 3 January.
New Zealand Herald (1988b) 'The Douglas dossier', 4 January.
New Zealand Herald (1988c) 'The Douglas dossier', 5 January.
New Zealand Planning Council (1989a) *Prospects: Economic and sectoral trends to 1997*, Wellington: New Zealand Planning Council.
New Zealand Planning Council (1989b) *The Economy in Transition: Restructuring to 1989*, a report by the Economic Monitoring Group, Wellington: New Zealand Planning Council.
New Zealand Treasury (1984) *Economic Management*, Wellington: Government Printing Office.
New Zealand Treasury (1987) *Government Management: Brief to the incoming government*, Wellington: Government Printing Office.
NZ Listener (1989) 'Farming: out of the cold, a special report', 15–21 July, Wellington.
O'Connor, J. (1973) *The Fiscal Crisis of the State*, New York: St Martin's Press.
OECD (1988–9) 'New Zealand'. in *Economic Surveys*, Paris: Organization for Economic Cooperation and Development.
Oliver, H. (1987) 'The New Zealand Labour Party and the rise of Rogernomics 1981–84', MA Thesis, Massey University.
Oliver, W. H. (1978) 'An uneasy retrospect' in I. Wards (ed.) *Thirteen Facets*, pp. 39-65, Wellington: Government Printer.
Oliver, W. H. and B. R. Williams (eds.) (1981) *The Oxford History of New Zealand*, Wellington: Oxford University Press.
Orange, C. (1987) *The Treaty of Waitangi*, Wellington: Allen & Unwin.
Pearson, C. and D. Thorns (1983) *Eclipse of Equality*, Sydney: Allen & Unwin.
Poulantzas, N. (1969) 'The problem of the capitalist state', *New Left Review* **58**, 67–98.
Poulantzas, N. (1973) *Political Power and Social Classes*, London: New Left Books.
Poulantzas, N. (1975) *Classes in Contemporary Capitalism*, London: New Left Books.
Pratt, J. (1987) 'Law and order politics in New Zealand 1986: a comparison with the United Kingdom 1974–9', Massey University.
Report of the Select Committee (1975) *The Role of Women in New Zealand Society*, Appendices to the Journals of the House of Representatives (AJHR), **1**, 13.
Robinson, J. (1989) 'Employment and unemployment into 1989', unpublished.
Roth, H. (1973) *Trade Unions in New Zealand: Past and present*, Wellington: A. H. & A. W. Reed.
Rowling, Rt Hon. Sir W. (1988) 'New Zealand: The sacrificial lamb on the altar of economic purity', Walding Memorial Lecture, Massey University, Palmerston North.
Shirley, I. F. (ed.) (1982) *Development Tracks*, Palmerston North: Dunmore Press.
Shirley, I. F. (1988) 'State policy and employment' in D. Corson (ed.) *Education for Work*, pp. 146–63, Palmerston North: Dunmore Press.
Shirley, I., B. Easton, C. Briar and S. Chatterjee (1990) *Unemployment in New Zealand*, Palmerston North: Dunmore Press.
Sinclair, K. (1959) *A History of New Zealand*, Harmondworth: Pelican.
Sinclair, K. (1961) 'The Liberal Party's legislation' in R. Chapman (ed.) *Ends and Means in New Zealand Politics*, University of Auckland, Bulletin **60**, History Series 7, 11–17.

Spoonley, P., D. Pearson and I. Shirley (eds.) (1982) *New Zealand: Sociological perspectives*, Palmerston North: Dunmore Press.

Sutch, W. B. (1966) *The Quest for Security in New Zealand, 1840 to 1966*, Wellington: Oxford University Press.

Sutch, W. B. (1969) *Poverty and Progress in New Zealand*, Wellington: A. H. and A. W. Reed.

Taylor, I. (1987) 'Law and order, moral order: the changing rhetorics of the Thatcher Government' in R. Miliband, L. Panitch and J. Saville (eds.) *The Socialist Register 1987*, pp. 297–331, London: Merlin Press.

Thorns, D. (1977) 'Urbanisation, suburbanisation and social class in New Zealand' in D. Pitt (ed.) *Social Class in New Zealand*, pp. 56–77, Auckland: Longman.

Thorns, D. (1988) 'Regional and urban change: the restructuring of New Zealand's traditional social base', paper presented at the Social Sciences Research Fund Committee (SSRFC) Seminar, Massey University, November.

Van Moeseke (1980) 'Aluminium smelting in New Zealand: an economic approach', No. 8008, University of Otago.

Walker, R. (1982) 'Development from below: institutional transformation in a plural society' in I. F. Shirley (ed.) *Development Tracks*, pp. 69–89, Palmerston North: Dunmore Press.

Ward, R. (1977) *Métin: Socialism without doctrine*, Chippendale, Australia: Alternative Publishing Cooperative.

Ward, J. and B. Asher (1984) 'Organisation and financing of health care in New Zealand' in C. Wilkes and I. Shirley (eds.) *In the Public Interest: Health, work and housing in New Zealand*, pp. 90–101, Auckland: Benton/Ross.

Wilkes, C. and I. Shirley (eds.) (1984) *In the Public Interest: Health, work and housing in New Zealand*, Auckland: Benton/Ross.

Author index

391

Subject index